images of SOCIETY

Readings That Inspire and Inform Sociology

SECOND EDITION

D1307299

images of SOCIETY

Readings That Inspire and Inform Sociology

SECOND EDITION

Michael Carroll
University of Western Ontario

Jerry P. White
University of Western Ontario

NELSON / EDUCATION

NELSON / **EDUCATION**

Images of Society: Readings That Inspire and Inform Sociology, Second Edition
by Michael Carroll and Jerry P. White

**Associate Vice President,
Editorial Director:**
Evelyn Veitch

**Editor-in-Chief,
Higher Education:**
Anne Williams

Executive Editor:
Laura Macleod

**Executive Marketing
Manager:**
David Tonen

Developmental Editor:
Liisa Kelly

Permissions Coordinator:
Natalie Barrington

**Senior Content Production
Manager:**
Anne Nellis

Production Service:
Macmillan Publishing Solutions

Copy Editor:
Michael Kelly

Proofreader:
Laura Lawrie

Indexer:
Patti Schiendelman

Production Coordinator:
Ferial Suleman

Design Director:
Ken Phipps

Managing Designer:
Franca Amore

Interior Design Modifications:
Jennifer Leung

Cover Design:
Johanna Liburd

Cover Image:
Masterfile

Compositor:
Macmillan Publishing Solutions

Printer:
R.R. Donnelley

**Library and Archives Canada
Cataloguing in Publication**

Images of society : readings that
inspire and inform sociology /
edited by Michael Carroll and
Jerry P. White.

Includes index.
ISBN 978-0-17-650123-5

1. Sociology—Textbooks. I. Carroll,
Michael P., 1944– II. White, Jerry P.
(Jerry Patrick), 1951–

HM586.I46 2009   301
C2008-907405-X

ISBN-13: 978-0-17-650123-5
ISBN-10: 0-17-650123-1

Contents

Preface

When we first began this project, we set ourselves several goals. Because we have each taught Introductory Sociology for many years (and so have read or reviewed a great many readers), our first goal was to avoid what we saw to be some of the weaknesses associated with readers while preserving the strengths. This led to our first critical decision: to produce a reader that was relatively inexpensive. This meant restricting the number of readings while still offering choice, and editing out material that could safely be deleted without damaging the core argument in that particular reading. Unlike many readers, then, which contain far more readings than can be used in a term, this book has been designed on the assumption that instructors will use a majority of the selections. Students will find that the readings are to the point, and that they avoid redundant discussions, repetition, and overlap between chapters.

Another critical decision we made concerned the selection of the particular readings to be included. This is not as simple a process as it might appear. It is our view that editors too often select readings based primarily on how appealing those readings are going to be with instructors. While this is not surprising given that instructors are the ones who decide if a text is adopted, it often leads (in our view) to the inclusion of readings that students cannot relate to or that belong more in an advanced course than an introductory course. We wanted to include selections that, in our experience, students taking Introductory Sociology would find interesting and accessible. We sought readings that students would want to read. As a result, although this book contains a number of "classic" articles that are routinely encountered in sociology readers, it also contains, we believe, many other articles that you will find both interesting and unique to this book.

Finally, we had a third goal that was paramount: to convey to you the passion to understand the world, in all its complexity, that fuels the sociological enterprise. We want to open up the distinctive ways of thinking that sociologists bring to bear on what they study. This meant looking for articles that (for the most part) went beyond simple description in order to generate insight into the world in which we all live. Paraphrasing Peter Berger (in one of the included readings): You can't be a sociologist and not want to open every door in front of you to see what's behind it. We want to engender in you that same feeling and to equip you with what C. Wright Mills calls the "sociological imagination" so that when you go through those doors you can understand what you encounter.

The focus groups of students that we have conducted, and the interviews with tutorials, teaching assistants, and lecturers, have confirmed that this reader does achieve these goals.

CHANGES TO THIS EDITION

This edition has some important changes. Based on feedback from students and professors, we have dropped several chapters that were either too difficult or less relevant for sociology students today. This has allowed the book to take on several new subjects that are of great interest and importance. Overall, the book offers the same wide variety as the first edition but with some timely additions. For example, the debate concerning how well universities are doing at educating is discussed in a new selection by Anton Allahar (co-author of the popular book, *Ivory Tower Blues: A University System in Crisis*). Recently, controversies have arisen over whether there is addiction to pornography and if so what problems can arise from it. We have included a hard-hitting piece by Annie Ruth Sabangan called "The Signs of Cybersex Addiction." The book also looks at the impact of the popular television series *CSI* (and its spinoffs) and other related forensic crime shows. Is there a CSI effect concerning law and justice in the United States and Canada today? As well, Aboriginal peoples' issues and the research concerning Aboriginal well-being is of great importance, and a new addition to the book examines this issue, pointing out the problems that Canada faces if these problems are not dealt with.

THE ORGANIZATION OF THE BOOK

The readings are grouped together into sections that map the way most sociology texts are arranged. This organization should facilitate coordinating these readings with whatever textbook you will be using. Please note that the articles are written in the original language, just as their authors presented them. In the case of some selections, then, especially those published several decades ago, this means that you may find some words that are archaic, even disrespectful. For example, you will occasionally find African-Americans referred to as "Negro." In some articles the only pronoun used is "he," which reflects the gender bias of the time in which they were written. Although we still believe that the core argument being made in such articles is insightful, we do not suggest that these problematic elements should be overlooked.

Each article has a brief prologue that gives you an idea of the main points contained in the work, as well as some pointers on what you might think about as you read it. The articles can be used to broaden your understanding, or they may be used to promote class and tutorial discussion. Finally, we also feel they are very easily used by graduate teaching assistants to make points and engage students in discussion.

ACKNOWLEDGMENTS

We want to thank all those who have contributed so much to this project, including the team at Nelson Education Ltd.: Laura Macleod (Executive Editor), Liisa Kelly (Developmental Editor), and Anne Nellis (Senior Content Production Manager). And thanks also to the many students and professors who have given us the feedback we needed to make this an effective teaching tool.

Enjoy.

MICHAEL P. CARROLL
JERRY P. WHITE
The University of Western Ontario

PART 1
The Sociological Imagination

Chapter 1

Invitation to Sociology: A Humanistic Perspective

PETER L. BERGER

In this classic article, Peter Berger tries to explain two things at once: what makes sociological thinking different from other ways of thinking about things, and what drives most sociologists to do what they do. Although much of the language used (especially the constant reference to "men" when talking of men and women generally) is dated, the central points are as valid today as they were in the past. Indeed, some of his insights—such as those relating to the ethical issues of employing sociologists in government—are likely more valid today than ever before. Pay special attention to what Berger sees to be those features of sociological thinking that distinguish it from "common sense" (e.g., the fact that sociologists seek to explain not only the exotic but also those aspects of social life that most of us take for granted).

Sociology has, from its beginnings, understood itself as a science. There has been much controversy about the precise meaning of this self-definition. For instance, German sociologists have emphasized the difference between the social and the natural sciences much more strongly than their French or American colleagues. But the allegiance of sociologists to the scientific ethos has meant everywhere a willingness to be bound by certain scientific canons of procedure. If the sociologist remains faithful to his calling, his statements must be arrived at through the observation of certain rules of evidence that allow others to check on or to repeat or to develop his findings further. It is this scientific discipline that often supplies the motive for reading a sociological work as against, say, a novel on the same topic that might describe matters in much more impressive and convincing language. As sociologists tried to develop their scientific rules of evidence, they were compelled to reflect upon methodological problems. This is why methodology is a necessary and valid part of the sociological enterprise.

At the same time it is quite true that some sociologists, especially in America, have become so preoccupied with methodological questions that they have ceased to be interested in society at all. As a result, they have found out nothing of significance about any aspect of social life, since in science as in love a concentration on technique is quite likely to lead to impotence. Much of this fixation on methodology can be explained in terms of the urge of a relatively new discipline to find acceptance on the academic scene. Since science is an almost sacred entity among Americans in general and American academicians in particular, the desire to emulate the procedures of the older natural sciences is very strong among the newcomers in the marketplace of erudition. Giving in to this desire, the experimental psychologists, for instance, have succeeded to such an extent that their studies have commonly nothing more to do with anything that human beings are or do. The irony of this process lies in the fact that natural scientists themselves have been giving up the very positivistic dogmatism that their emulators are still straining to adopt. But this is not our concern here. Suffice it to say that sociologists have succeeded in avoiding some of the more grotesque exaggerations of this "methodism," as compared with some fields close by. As they become more secure in their academic status, it may be expected we would look at an image of the sociologist not so much in his professional role as in his being, supposedly, a certain kind of person. This is the image of the sociologist as a detached, sardonic observer, and a cold manipulator of men. Where this image prevails, it may represent an ironic triumph of the sociologist's own efforts to be accepted as a genuine scientist. The sociologist here becomes the self-appointed superior man, standing off from the warm vitality of common existence, finding his satisfactions not in living but in coolly appraising the lives of others, filing them away in little categories, and thus presumably missing the real significance of what he is observing. Further, there is the notion that, when he involves himself in social processes at all, the sociologist does so as an uncommitted technician, putting his manipulative skills at the disposal of the powers that be.

This last image is probably not very widely held. It is mainly held by people concerned for political reasons with actual or possible misuses of sociology in modern societies. The problem of the political role of the social scientist is, nevertheless, a very genuine one. For instance, the employment of sociologists by certain branches of industry and government raises moral questions that ought to be faced more widely than they have been so far. These are, however, more questions that concern all men in positions of responsibility in modern society.

How then are we to conceive of the sociologist? In discussing the various images of him that abound in the popular mind we have already brought out certain elements that would have to go into our conception. We can now put them together. In doing so, we shall construct what sociologists themselves call an "ideal type." This means that what we delineate will not be found in reality in its pure form. Instead, one will find approximations to it and deviations from it, in varying degrees. Nor is it to be understood as an empirical average. We would not even claim that all individuals who now call themselves sociologists will recognize themselves without reservations in our conception, nor would we dispute the right of those who do not so recognize themselves to use the appellate. Our business is not excommunication. We would, however, contend that our "ideal type" corresponds to the self-conception of most sociologists in the mainstream of the discipline, both historically (at least in this century) and today.

The sociologist, then, is someone concerned with understanding society in a disciplined way. The nature of this discipline is scientific. This means that what the sociologist finds and says about the social phenomena he studies occurs within a certain rather strictly defined frame of reference. One of the main characteristics of this scientific frame of reference is that operations are bound by certain rules of evidence. As a scientist, the sociologist tries to be objective, to control his personal preferences and prejudices, to perceive clearly rather than to judge normatively. This restraint, of course, does not embrace the totality of the sociologist's existence as a human being, but is limited to his operations *qua* sociologist. Nor does the sociologist claim that his frame of reference is the only one within which society can be looked at. For that matter, very few scientists in any field would claim today that one should look at the world only scientifically. The botanist looking at a daffodil has no reason to dispute the right of the poet to look at the same object in a very different manner. There are many ways of playing. The point is not that one denies other people's games but that one is clear about the rules of one's own. The game of the sociologist, then, uses scientific rules. As a result, the sociologist must be clear in his own mind as to the meaning of these rules. That is, he must concern himself with methodological questions. Methodology does not constitute his goal. The latter, let us recall once more, is the attempt to understand society. Methodology helps in reaching this goal. In order to understand society, or that segment of it that he is studying at the moment, the sociologist will use a variety of means. Among these are statistical techniques. Statistics can be very useful in answering certain sociological questions. But statistics does not constitute sociology. As a scientist, the sociologist will have to be concerned with the exact significance of the terms he is using. That is, he will have to be careful about terminology. This does not have to mean that he must invent a new language of his own, but it does mean that he cannot naively use the language of everyday discourse. Finally, the interest of the sociologist is primarily theoretical. That is, he is interested in understanding for its own sake. He may be aware of or even concerned with the practical applicability and consequences of his findings, but at that point he leaves the sociological frame of reference as such and moves into realms of values, beliefs and ideas that he shares with other men who are not sociologists.

We daresay that this conception of the sociologist would meet with very wide consensus within the discipline today. But we would like to go a little bit further here and ask a somewhat more personal (and therefore, no doubt, more controversial) question. We would like to ask not only what it is that the sociologist is doing but also what it is that drives him to it. Or, to use the phrase Max Weber used in a similar connection, we want to inquire a little into the nature of the sociologist's demon. In doing so, we shall evoke an image that is not so much ideal-typical in the above sense but more confessional in the sense of personal commitment. Again, we are not interested in excommunicating anyone. The game of sociology goes on in a spacious playground. We are just describing a little more closely those we would like to tempt to join our game.

We would say then that the sociologist (that is, the one we would really like to invite to our game) is a person intensively, endlessly, shamelessly interested in the doings of men. His natural habitat is all the human gathering places of the world, wherever men come together. The sociologist may be interested in many other things. But his consuming interest remains in the world of men, their institutions, their history, their passions. And since he is interested in men, nothing that men do can be altogether tedious for him. He will naturally be interested in the events that engage men's ultimate beliefs, their moments of tragedy and grandeur and ecstasy. But he will also be fascinated by the commonplace, the everyday. He will know reverence, but this reverence will not prevent him from wanting to see and to understand. He may sometimes feel revulsion or contempt. But this also will not deter him from wanting to have his questions answered. The sociologist, in his quest for understanding, moves through the world of men without respect for the usual lines of demarcation. Nobility and degradation, power and obscurity, intelligence and folly—these are equally *interesting* to him, however unequal they may be in his personal values or tastes. Thus his questions may lead him to all possible levels of society, the best and the least known places, the most respected and the most despised. And, if he is a good sociologist, he will find himself in all these places because his own questions have so taken possession of him that he has little choice but to seek for answers.

It would be possible to say the same things in a lower key. We could say that the sociologist, but for the grace of his academic title, is the man who must listen to gossip despite himself, who is tempted to look through keyholes, to read other people's mail, to open closed cabinets. Before some otherwise unoccupied psychologist sets out now to construct an aptitude test for sociologists on the basis of sublimated voyeurism, let us quickly say that we are speaking merely by way of analogy. Perhaps some little boys consumed with curiosity to watch their maiden aunts in the bathroom later become inveterate sociologists. This is quite uninteresting. What interests us is the curiosity that grips any sociologist in front of a closed door behind which there are human voices. If he is a good sociologist, he will want to open that door, to understand these voices. Behind each closed door he will anticipate some new facet of human life not yet perceived and understood.

The sociologist will occupy himself with matters that others regard as too sacred or as too distasteful for dispassionate investigation. He will find rewarding the company of priests or of prostitutes, depending not on his personal preferences but on the questions he happens to be asking at the moment. He will also concern himself with matters that others may find much too boring. He will be interested in the human interaction that goes with warfare or with great intellectual discoveries, but also in the relations between people employed in a restaurant or between a group of little girls playing with their dolls. His main focus of attention is not the ultimate significance of what men do, but the action in itself, as another example of the infinite richness of human conduct. So much for the image of our playmate.

In these journeys through the world of men the sociologist will inevitably encounter other professional Peeping Toms. Sometimes these will resent his presence, feeling that he is poaching on their preserves. In some places the sociologist will meet up with the economist, in others with the political scientist, in yet others with the psychologist or the ethnologist. Yet chances are that the questions that have brought him to these same places are different from the ones that propelled his fellow-trespassers. The sociologist's questions always remain essentially the same: "What are people doing with each other here?" "What are their relationships to each other?" "How are these relationships organized in institutions?" "What are the collective ideas that move men and institutions?" In trying to answer these questions in specific instances, the sociologist will, of course, have to deal with economic or political matters, but he will do so in a way rather different from that of the economist or the political scientist. The scene that he contemplates is the same human scene that these other scientists concern themselves with. But the sociologist's angle of vision is different. When this is understood, it becomes clear that it makes little sense to try to stake out a special enclave within which the sociologist will carry on business in his own right. Like Wesley the sociologist will have to confess that his parish is the world. But unlike some latter-day Wesleyans he will gladly share this parish with others. There is, however, one traveler whose path the sociologist will cross more often than anyone else's on his journeys. This is the historian. Indeed, as soon as the sociologist turns from the present to the past, his preoccupations are very hard indeed to distinguish from those of the historian. However, we shall leave this relationship to a later part of our considerations. Suffice it to say here that the sociological journey will be much impoverished unless it is punctuated frequently by conservation with that other particular traveler.

Any intellectual activity derives excitement from the moment it becomes a trail of discovery. In some fields of learning this is the discovery of worlds previously unthought and unthinkable. This is the excitement of the astronomer or of the nuclear physicist on the antipodal boundaries of the realities that man is capable of conceiving. But it can also be the excitement of bacteriology or geology. In a different way it can be the excitement of the linguist discovering new realms of human expression or of the anthropologist exploring human customs in faraway countries. In such discovery, when undertaken with passion, a widening of awareness, sometimes a veritable transformation of consciousness, occurs. The universe turns out to be much more wonder-full than one had ever dreamed. The excitement of sociology is usually of a different sort. Sometimes, it is true, the sociologist penetrates into worlds that had previously been quite unknown to him—for instance, the world of crime, or the world of some bizarre religious sect, or the world fashioned by the exclusive concerns of some group such as medical specialists or military leaders or advertising executives. However, much of the time the sociologist moves in sectors of experience that are familiar to him and to most people in his society. He investigates communities, institutions and activities that one can read about every day in the newspapers. Yet there is another excitement of discovery beckoning in his investigations. It is not the excitement of coming upon the totally unfamiliar, but rather the excitement of finding the familiar becoming transformed in its meaning. The fascination of sociology lies in the fact that its perspective makes us see in a new light the very world in which we have lived all our lives. This also constitutes a transformation of consciousness. Moreover, this transformation is more relevant existentially than that of many other intellectual disciplines, because it is more difficult to segregate in some special compartment of the mind. The astronomer does not live in the remote galaxies, and the nuclear physicist can, outside his laboratory, eat and laugh and marry and vote without thinking about the insides of the atom. The geologist looks at rocks only at appropriate times, and the linguist speaks English with his wife. The sociologist lives in society, on the job and off it. His own life, inevitably, is part of his subject matter. Men being what they are, sociologists too manage to segregate their professional insights from their everyday affairs. But it is a rather difficult feat to perform in good faith.

The sociologist moves in the common world of men, close to what most of them would call real. The categories he employs in his analyses are only refinements of the categories by which other men live—power, class, status, race, ethnicity. As a result, there is a deceptive simplicity and obviousness about some sociological investigations. One reads them, nods at the familiar scene, remarks that one has heard all this before and don't people have better things to do than to waste their time on truisms—until one is suddenly brought up against an insight that radically questions everything one had previously assumed about this familiar scene. This is the point at which one begins to sense the excitement of sociology.

People who like to avoid shocking discoveries, who prefer to believe that society is just what they were taught in Sunday School, who like the safety of the rules and the maxims of what Alfred Schuetz has called the "world-taken-for-granted," should stay away from sociology. People who feel no temptation before closed doors, who have no curiosity about human beings, who are content to admire scenery without wondering about the people who live in those houses on the other side of that river, should probably also stay away from sociology. They will find it unpleasant or, at any rate, un-rewarding. People who are interested in human beings only if they can change, convert or reform them should also be warned, for they will find sociology much less useful than they hoped. And people whose interest is mainly in their own conceptual constructions will do just as well to turn to the study of little white mice. Sociology will be satisfying, in the long run, only to those who can think of nothing more entrancing than to watch men and to understand things human.

Chapter 2

The Sociological Imagination

C. WRIGHT MILLS

In one sense, Mills's goal in this article, another classic in sociology, is much the same as Berger's: to convey a sense of what is distinctive about the way sociologists think and to train their students to think. On the other hand, in pursuing this goal, Mills focuses a little more clearly than Berger on two things. First, he calls attention to the fact that the "sociological imagination" must take into account not only how society operates at a given point in time but also how societies have been affected by the massive changes that have taken place over the past century or so. Second, Mills makes a clear distinction between two sorts of explanation, each valid in itself: explanations that focus on the local interactions between individuals to explain something, and explanations that look to the organization of society and societal structure to explain the same thing. Thus, to use one of his own examples, divorce can certainly result from tensions within a marriage, but soaring divorce rates can also be traced to a number of societal changes that transcend any particular couple. Mills is making what is still the common distinction between micro-sociology and macro-sociology.

THE PROMISE

Nowadays men often feel that their private lives are a series of traps. They sense that within their everyday worlds, they cannot overcome their troubles, and in this feeling, they are often quite correct: What ordinary men are directly aware of and what they try to do are bounded by the private orbits in which they live; their visions and their powers are limited to the close-up scenes of job, family, neighborhood; in other milieux, they move vicariously and remain spectators. And the more aware they become, however vaguely, of ambitions and of threats which transcend their immediate locales, the more trapped they seem to feel.

Underlying this sense of being trapped are seemingly impersonal changes in the very structure of continent-wide societies. The facts of contemporary history are also facts about the success and the failure of individual men and women. When a society is industrialized, a peasant becomes a worker; a feudal lord is liquidated or becomes a businessman. When classes rise or fall, a man is employed or unemployed; when the rate of investment goes up or down, a man takes new heart or goes broke. Neither the life of an individual nor the history of a society can be understood without understanding both.

Yet men do not usually define the troubles they endure in terms of historical change and institutional contradiction. Seldom aware of the intricate connection between the patterns of their own lives and the course of world history, ordinary men do not usually know what this connection means for the kinds of men they are becoming and for the kinds of history-making in which they might take part. They do not possess the quality of mind essential to grasp the interplay of man and society, of biography and history, of self and world.

Surely it is no wonder. In what period have so many men been so totally exposed at so fast a pace to such earthquakes of change? That Americans have not known such catastrophic changes as have the men and women of other societies is due to historical facts that are now quickly becoming 'merely history.' The history that now affects every man is world history. Within this scene and this period, in the course of a single generation, one sixth of mankind is transformed from all that is feudal and backward into all that is modern, advanced, and fearful. Political colonies are freed; new and less visible forms of imperialism installed. Revolutions occur; men feel the intimate grip of new kinds of authority. Totalitarian societies rise, and are smashed to bits—or succeed fabulously. Everywhere in the underdeveloped world, ancient ways of life are broken up and vague expectations become urgent demands. Everywhere in the overdeveloped world, the means of authority and of violence become total in scope and bureaucratic in form.

The very shaping of history now outpaces the ability of men to orient themselves in accordance with cherished values. And which values? Even when they do not panic, men often sense that older ways of feeling and thinking have collapsed and that newer beginnings are ambiguous to the point of moral stasis. Is it any wonder that ordinary men feel they cannot cope with the larger worlds with which they are so suddenly confronted? That they cannot understand the meaning of their epoch for their own lives? That—in defense of selfhood—they become morally insensible, trying to remain altogether private men? Is it any wonder that they come to be possessed by a sense of the trap?

It is not only information that they need—in this Age of Fact, information often dominates their attention and overwhelms their capacities to assimilate it. It is not only the skills of reason that they need—although their struggles to acquire these often exhaust their limited moral energy.

What they need, and what they feel they need, is a quality of mind that will help them to use information and to develop reason in order to achieve lucid summations of what is going on in the world and of what may be happening within themselves. It is this quality, I am going to contend, that journalists and scholars, artists and publics, scientists and editors are coming to expect of what may be called the sociological imagination.

1

The sociological imagination enables its possessor to understand the larger historical scene in terms of its meaning for the inner life and the external career of a variety of individuals. It enables him to take into account how individuals, in the welter of their daily experience, often become falsely conscious of their social positions. Within that welter, the framework of modern society is sought, and within that framework the psychologies of a variety of men and women are formulated. By such means the personal uneasiness of individuals is focused upon explicit troubles and the indifference of publics is transformed into involvement with public issues.

The first fruit of this imagination—and the first lesson of the social science that embodies it—is the idea that the individual can understand his own experience and gauge his own fate only by locating himself within his period, that he can know his own chances in life only by becoming aware of those of all individuals in his circumstances. In many ways it is a terrible lesson; in many ways a magnificent one. We do not know the limits of man's capacities for supreme effort or willing degradation, for agony or glee, for pleasurable brutality or the sweetness of reason. But in our time we have come to know that the limits of 'human nature' are frighteningly broad.

We have come to know that every individual lives, from one generation to the next, in some society; that he lives out a biography, and that he lives it out within some historical sequence. By the fact of his living he contributes, however minutely, to the shaping of this society and to the course of its history, even as he is made by society and by its historical push and shove.

The sociological imagination enables us to grasp history and biography and the relations between the two within society. That is its task and its promise. To recognize this task and this promise is the mark of the classic social analyst. It is characteristic of Herbert Spencer—turgid, polysyllabic, comprehensive; of E. A. Ross—graceful, muckraking, upright; of Auguste Comte and Emile Durkheim; of the intricate and subtle Karl Mannheim. It is the quality of all that is intellectually excellent in Karl Marx; it is the clue to Thorstein Veblen's brilliant and ironic insight, to Joseph Schumpeter's many-sided constructions of reality; it is the basis of the psychological sweep of W. E. H. Lecky no less than of the profundity and clarity of Max Weber. And it is the signal of what is best in contemporary studies of man and society.

No social study that does not come back to the problems of biography, of history and of their intersections within a society has completed its intellectual journey. Whatever the specific problems of the classic social analysts, however limited or however broad the features of social reality they have examined, those who have been imaginatively aware of the promise of their work have consistently asked three sorts of questions:

1. What is the structure of this particular society as a whole? What are its essential components, and how are they related to one another? How does it differ from other varieties of social order? Within it, what is the meaning of any particular feature for its continuance and for its change?
2. Where does this society stand in human history? What are the mechanics by which it is changing? What is its place within and its meaning for the development of humanity as a whole? How does any particular feature we are examining affect, and how is it affected by, the historical period in which it moves? And this period—what are its essential features? How does it differ from other periods? What are its characteristic ways of history-making?
3. What varieties of men and women now prevail in this society and in this period? And what varieties are coming to prevail? In what ways are they selected and formed, liberated and repressed, made sensitive and blunted? What kinds of 'human nature' are revealed in the conduct and character we observe in this society in this period? And what is the meaning for 'human nature' of each and every feature of the society we are examining?

Whether the point of interest is a great power state or a minor literary mood, a family, a prison, a creed—these are the kinds of questions the best social analysts have asked. They are the intellectual pivots of classic studies of man in society—and they are the questions inevitably raised by any mind possessing the sociological imagination. For that imagination is the capacity to shift from one perspective to another—from the political to the psychological; from examination of a single family to comparative assessment of the national budgets of the world; from the theological school to the military establishment; from considerations of an oil industry to studies of contemporary poetry. It is the capacity to range from the most impersonal and remote transformations to the most intimate features of the human self—and to see the relations between the two. Back of its use there is always the urge to know the social and historical meaning of the individual in the society and in the period in which he has his quality and his being.

That, in brief, is why it is by means of the sociological imagination that men now hope to grasp what is going on in the world, and to understand what is happening in themselves as minute points of the intersections of biography and history within society. In large part, contemporary man's self-conscious view of himself as at least an out-sider, if not a permanent stranger, rests upon an absorbed realization of social relativity and of the transformative power of history. The sociological imagination is the most fruitful form of this self-consciousness. By its use men whose mentalities have swept only a series of limited orbits often come to feel as if suddenly awakened in a house with which they had only supposed themselves to be familiar. Correctly or incorrectly, they often come to feel that they can now provide them-selves with adequate summations, cohesive assessments, comprehensive orientations. Older decisions that once appeared sound now seem to them products of a mind unaccountably dense. Their capacity for astonishment is made lively again. They acquire a new way of thinking, they experience a transvaluation of values: in a word, by their reflection and by their sensibility, they realize the cultural meaning of the social sciences.

2

Perhaps the most fruitful distinction with which the sociological imagination works is between 'the personal troubles of milieu' and 'the public issues of social structure.' This distinction is an essential tool of the sociological imagination and a feature of all classic work in social science.

Troubles occur within the character of the individual and within the range of his immediate relations with others; they have to do with his self and with those limited areas of social life of which he is directly and personally aware. Accordingly, the statement and the resolution of troubles properly lie within the individual as a biographical entity and within the scope of his immediate milieu—the social setting that is directly open to his personal experience and to some extent his willful activity. A trouble is a pri-vate matter: values cherished by an individual are felt by him to be threatened.

Issues have to do with matters that transcend these local environments of the individual and the range of his inner life. They have to do with

the organization of many such milieux into the institutions of an historical society as a whole, with the ways in which various milieux overlap and interpenetrate to form the larger structure of social and historical life. An issue is a public matter: some value cherished by publics is felt to be threatened. Often there is a debate about what that value really is and about what it is that really threatens it. This debate is often without focus if only because it is the very nature of an issue, unlike even widespread trouble, that it cannot very well be defined in terms of the immediate and everyday environments of ordi-nary men. An issue, in fact, often involves a crisis in institutional arrangements, and often too it involves what Marxists call 'contradictions' or 'antagonisms.'

In these terms, consider unemployment. When, in a city of 100,000, only one man is unem-ployed, that is his personal trouble, and for its relief we properly look to the character of the man, his skills, and his immediate opportunities. But when in a nation of 50 million employees, 15 million men are unemployed, that is an issue, and we may not hope to find its solution within the range of opportunities open to any one indi-vidual. The very structure of opportunities has collapsed. Both the correct statement of the problem and the range of possible solutions require us to consider the economic and political institutions of the society, and not merely the personal situation and character of a scatter of individuals.

Consider war. The personal problem of war, when it occurs, may be how to survive it or how to die in it with honor; how to make money out of it; how to climb into the higher safety of the military apparatus; or how to contribute to the war's termination. In short, according to one's values, to find a set of milieux and within it to survive the war or make one's death in it mean-ingful. But the structural issues of war have to do with its causes; with what types of men it throws up into command; with its effects upon economic and political, family and religious institutions, with the unorganized irresponsibility of a world of nation-states.

Consider marriage. Inside a marriage a man and a woman may experience personal troubles, but when the divorce rate during the first four years of marriage is 250 out of every 1,000 attempts, this is an indication of a structural issue having to do with the institutions of marriage and the family and other institutions that bear upon them.

Or consider the metropolis—the horrible, beautiful, ugly, magnificent sprawl of the great city. For many upper-class people, the personal solution to 'the problem of the city' is to have an apartment with private garage under it in the heart of the city, and forty miles out, a house on a hundred acres of private land. In these two controlled environments—with a small staff at each end and a private helicopter connection—most people could solve many of the problems of personal milieux caused by the facts of the city. But all this, however splendid, does not solve the public issues that the structural fact of the city poses. What should be done with this wonderful monstrosity? Break it all up into scattered units, combining residence and work? Refurbish it as it stands? Or, after evacuation, dynamite it and build new cities according to new plans in new places?

In so far as an economy is so arranged that slumps occur, the problem of unemployment becomes incapable of personal solution. In so far as war is inherent in the nation-state system and in the uneven industrialization of the world, the ordinary individual in his restricted milieu will be powerless—with or without psychiatric aid—to solve the troubles this system or lack of system imposes upon him. In so far as the family as an institution turns women into darling little slaves and men into their chief providers and unweaned dependents, the problem of a satisfactory marriage remains incapable of purely private solution. In so far as the overdeveloped megalopolis and the overdeveloped automobile are built-in features of the overdeveloped society, the issues of urban living will not be solved by personal ingenuity and private wealth.

What we experience in various and specific milieux, I have noted, is often caused by structural changes. Accordingly, to understand the changes of many personal milieux we are required to look beyond them. And the number and variety of such structural changes increase as the institutions within which we live become more embracing and more intricately connected with one another. To be aware of the idea of social structure and to use it with sensibility is to be capable of tracing such linkages among a great variety of milieux. To be able to do that is to possess the sociological imagination.

PART 2

Sociological Inquiry: Methods

Chapter 3

The Nature of Attitude Surveys (from "The American Soldier—An Expository Review")

PAUL F. LAZARSFELD

Sociologists, as you will soon come to discover, use a wide variety of methodologies to satisfy what Peter Berger (in his earlier reading) called "the curiosity that grips any sociologist in front of a closed door behind which there are human voices." On the other hand, it seems fair to say that since the end of the Second World War, an increasing number of sociologists have come to rely on the "attitude survey" to gather data about the societies in which they live. In this brief selection, Paul Lazarsfeld first identifies the limitations of the "attitude survey" but then discusses some of the ways in which attitude surveys can provide us with quite unexpected insights.

The limitations of survey methods are obvious. They do not use experimental techniques; they rely primarily on what people say, and rarely include objective observations; they deal with aggregates of individuals rather than with integrated communities; they are restricted to contemporary problems—history can be studied only by the use of documents remaining from earlier periods.

In spite of these limitations survey methods provide one of the foundations upon which social science is being built. The finding of regularities is the beginning of any science, and surveys can make an important contribution in this respect. For it is necessary that we know what people usually do under many and different circumstances if we are to develop theories explaining their behavior. Furthermore, before we can devise an experiment we must know what problems are worthwhile; which should be investigated in greater detail. Here again surveys can be of service.

Finding regularities and determining criteria of significance are concerns the social sciences have in common with the natural sciences. But there are crucial differences between the two fields of inquiry. The world of social events is much less "visible" than the realm of nature. That bodies fall to the ground, that things are hot or cold, that iron becomes rusty, are all immediately obvious. It is much more difficult to realize that ideas of right and wrong vary in different cultures; that customs may serve a different function from the one which the people practising them believe they are serving; that the same person may show marked contrasts in his behavior as a member of a family and as a member of an occupational group. The mere description of human behavior, of its variation from group to group and of its changes in different situations, is a vast and difficult undertaking. It is this task of describing, sifting and ferreting out interrelationships which surveys perform for us. And yet this very function often leads to serious misunderstandings. For it is hard

Source: P. F. Lazarsfeld, "The American Soldier—An Expository Review," in *Public Opinion Quarterly*, 13(3) (1949):378–380, by permission of Oxford University Press.

to find a form of human behavior that has not already been observed somewhere. Consequently, if a study reports a prevailing regularity, many readers respond to it by thinking "of course that is the way things are." Thus, from time to time, the argument is advanced that surveys only put into complicated form observations which are already obvious to everyone.

Understanding the origin of this point of view is of importance far beyond the limits of the present discussion. The reader may be helped in recognizing this attitude if he looks over a few statements which are typical of many survey findings and carefully observes his own reaction. A short list of these, with brief interpretive comments, will be given here in order to bring into sharper focus probable reactions of many readers.

1. Better educated men showed more psychoneurotic symptoms than those with less education. (The mental instability of the intellectual as compared to the more impassive psychology of the-man-in-the-street has often been commented on.)
2. Men from rural backgrounds were usually in better spirits during their Army life than soldiers from city backgrounds. (After all, they are more accustomed to hardships.)
3. Southern soldiers were better able to stand the climate in the hot South Sea Islands than Northern soldiers (of course, Southerners are more accustomed to hot weather).
4. White privates were more eager to become non-coms than Negroes. (The lack of ambition among Negroes is almost proverbial.)

5. Southern Negroes preferred Southern to Northern white officers. (Isn't it well known that Southern whites have a more fatherly attitude toward their "darkies"?)
6. As long as the fighting continued, men were more eager to be returned to the States than they were after the German surrender. (You cannot blame people for not wanting to be killed.)

We have in these examples a sample list of the simplest type of interrelationships which provide the "bricks" from which our empirical social science is being built. But why, since they are so obvious, is so much money and energy given to establish such findings? Would it not be wiser to take them for granted and proceed directly to a more sophisticated type of analysis? This might be so except for one interesting point about the list. *Every one of these statements is the direct opposite of what actually was found.* Poorly educated soldiers were more neurotic than those with high education; Southerners showed no greater ability than Northerners to adjust to a tropical climate; Negroes were more eager for promotion than whites; and so on.

If we had mentioned the actual results of the investigation first, the reader would have labelled these "obvious" also. Obviously something is wrong with the entire argument of "obviousness." It should really be turned on its head. Since every kind of human reaction is conceivable, it is of great importance to know which reactions actually occur most frequently and under what conditions; only then will a more advanced social science develop.

Chapter 4

The Study Design for a Survey of American Sexual Behavior

EDWARD O. LAUMANN, JOHN H. GAGNON,
ROBERT T. MICHAEL, AND STUART MICHAELS

Sexual intercourse in our society is generally thought to be something that is private and intimate. On the face of it, then, you might expect that it would be difficult to get people to participate in a study designed to investigate their sexual behaviour and beliefs. It turns out, however, that this is not the case. As sociologists, we know that there are ways of designing surveys (in general) that elicit trust and cooperation on the part of respondents—and if these things are built into a survey of sexual habits, as this selection demonstrates, people will cooperate here as well. This selection, then, is valuable most of all because it provides a clear and concise overview of how to go about designing a *good survey,* no matter what it is that you are investigating.

Most people with whom we talked when we first broached the idea of a national survey of sexual behavior were skeptical that it could be done. Scientists and laypeople alike had similar reactions: "Nobody will agree to participate in such a study." "Nobody will answer questions like these, and, even if they do, they won't tell the truth." "People don't know enough about sexual practices as they relate to disease transmission or even to pleasure or physical and emotional satisfaction to be able to answer questions accurately." It would be dishonest to say that we did not share these and other concerns. But our experiences over the past seven years, rooted in extensive pilot work, focus-group discussions, and the fielding of the survey itself, resolved these doubts, fully vindicating our growing conviction that a national survey could be conducted according to high standards of scientific rigor and replicability. . . .

When we began working on the design of the survey in 1988, the only comprehensive American study of sexuality based on a large cross section of the population was the famous two-volume Kinsey Report published almost forty years before; but Kinsey's sampling design, essentially volunteer and purposive in character, failed to meet even the most elementary requirements for drawing a truly representative sample of the population at large.

The society in which we live treats sex and everything related to sex in a most ambiguous and ambivalent fashion. Sex is at once highly fascinating, attractive, and, for many at certain stages in their lives, preoccupying, but it can also be frightening, disturbing, or guilt inducing. For many, sex is considered to be an extremely private matter, to be discussed only with one's closest friends or intimates, if at all.

Source: From *The Social Organization of Sexuality,* by Edward O. Laumann et al., The University of Chicago Press, 1994. Copyright © 1994 by Edward O. Laumann, Robert T. Michael, CSG Enterprises, Inc., and Stuart Michaels.

And, certainly for most if not all of us, there are elements of our sexual lives never acknowledged to others, reserved for our own personal fantasies and self-contemplation. It is thus surprising that the proposal to study sex scientifically, or any other way for that matter, elicits confounding and confusing reactions.

The fact remains that, until quite recently, scientific research on sexuality has been taboo and therefore to be avoided or at best marginalized. While there is a visible tradition of (in)famous sex research, what is, in fact, most striking is how little prior research exists on sexuality in the general population. "Normal sex" was somehow off limits, perhaps because it was considered too ordinary, trivial, and self-evident to deserve attention. To be fair, then, we cannot blame the public and the politicians entirely for the lack of sustained work on sexuality at large— it also reflects the prejudices and understandings of researchers about what are "interesting" scientific questions. There has simply been a dearth of mainstream scientific thinking and speculation about sexual issues.

While we entered relatively uncharted waters in choosing the sexual content to be included in our survey, we found that we faced many of the same problems that any major survey research enterprise confronts. We discovered that the techniques that work in other domains work just as well when studying sexuality. For example, most of the problems involved in securing the participation of respondents in a survey are the same whether one is conducting a general purpose survey of political opinions, a study of labor force participation, or one of sexual behavior. Respondents must be convinced that the research has a legitimate purpose, that it is not some attempt to trick them into buying something, that their confidentiality will be protected, etc.

In order to understand the results of our survey, the National Health and Social Life Survey (NHSLS), one must understand how these results were generated. To construct a questionnaire and field a large-scale survey, many research design decisions must be made.

To understand the decisions made, one needs to understand the multiple purposes that underlie this research project. Research design is never just a theoretical exercise. It is a set of practical solutions to a multitude of problems and considerations that are chosen under the constraints of limited resources of money, time, and prior knowledge.

SAMPLE DESIGN

The sample design for the NHSLS is the most straightforward element of our methodology because nothing about probability sampling is specific to or changes in a survey of sexual behavior.

Probability sampling, that is, sampling where every member of a clearly specified population has a known probability of selection—what lay commentators often somewhat inaccurately call random sampling—is the sine qua non of modern survey research. There is no other scientifically acceptable way to construct a representative sample and thereby to be able to generalize from the actual sample on which data are collected to the population that that sample is designed to represent. Probability sampling as practiced in survey research is a highly developed practical application of statistical theory to the problem of selecting a sample. Not only does this type of sampling avoid the problems of bias introduced by the researcher or by subject self-selection bias that come from more casual techniques, but it also allows one to quantify the variability in the estimates derived from the sample. . . .

SAMPLE SIZE

How large should the sample be? There is real confusion about the importance of sample size. In general, for the case of a probability sample, the bigger the sample, the higher the precision of its estimates. This precision is usually measured in terms of the amount of sampling error accruing to the statistics calculated from the sample. The most common version of this is the statement that estimated proportions (e.g., the proportion of likely voters planning to vote for a particular candidate) in national political polls are estimated as being within $\pm$ 2 or 3 percent of the overall population figure. The amount of this discrepancy is inversely related to the size of the sample: the larger the sample, the smaller the likely error in the estimates. This is not, however, a simple linear relation. Instead, in general, as the sample size increases, the precision of the estimates derived from the sample increases by the square root of the sample size. For example, if we quadruple the sample size, we improve the estimate only by a factor of two. That is, if the original sample has a sampling error of $\pm$ 10 percent, then the quadrupled sample size will have an error of $\pm$ 5 percent.

In order to determine how large a sample size for a given study should be, one must first decide how precise the estimates to be derived need to be. To illustrate this reasoning process, let us take one of the simplest and most commonly used statistics in survey research, the proportion. Many of the most important results reported in this book are proportions. For example, what proportion of the population had more than five sex partners in the last year? What proportion engaged in anal intercourse? With condoms? Estimates based on our sample will differ from the true proportion in the population because of sampling error (i.e., the random fluctuations in our estimates that are due to the fact that they are based on samples rather than on complete enumerations or censuses). If one drew repeated samples using the same methodology, each would produce a slightly different estimate. If one looks at the distribution of these *estimates*, it turns out that they will be normally distributed (i.e., will follow the famous bell-shaped curve known as the Gaussian or normal distribution) and centered around the true proportion in the population. The larger the sample size, the tighter the distribution of estimates will be.

We began with an area probability sample, which is a sample of households, that is, of addresses, not names. Rather than approach a household by knocking on the door without advance warning, we followed standard practice of sending an advance letter, hand addressed by the interviewer, about a week before the interviewer expected to visit the address. In this case, the letter was signed by the principal investigator, Robert Michael, who was identified as the dean of the Irving B. Harris Graduate School of Public Policy Studies of the University of Chicago. The letter briefly explained the purpose of the survey as helping "doctors, teachers, and counselors better understand and prevent the spread of diseases like AIDS and better understand the nature and extent of harmful and of healthy sexual behavior in our country." The intent was to convince the potential respondent that this was a legitimate scientific study addressing personal and potentially sensitive topics for a socially useful purpose.

Gaining respondents' cooperation requires mastery of a broad spectrum of techniques that successful interviewers develop with experience, guidance from the research team, and careful field supervision. This project required extensive training before entering the field. While interviewers are generally trained to be neutral toward topics covered in the interview, this was especially important when discussing sex, a topic that seems particularly likely to elicit emotionally freighted sensitivities both in the respondents and in the interviewers. Interviewers needed to be fully persuaded about the legitimacy and importance of the research. Toward this end, almost a full day of training was devoted to presentations and discussions with the principal investigators in addition to the extensive advance study materials to read and comprehend. Sample answers to frequently asked questions by skeptical respondents and brainstorming about strategies to convert reluctant respondents were part of the training exercises.

MODE OF ADMINISTRATION: FACE-TO-FACE, TELEPHONE, OR SELF-ADMINISTERED

Perhaps the most fundamental design decision, one that distinguishes this study from many others, concerned how the interview itself was to be conducted. In survey research, this is usually called the *mode* of interviewing or of questionnaire administration. We chose face-to-face interviewing, the most costly mode, as the primary vehicle for data collection in the NHSLS.

We decided to use face-to-face interviewing as our primary mode of administration of the NHSLS for two principal reasons: it was most likely to yield a substantially higher response rate for a more inclusive cross section of the population at large, and it would permit more complex and detailed questions to be asked.

Recruiting and Training Interviewers

We firmly believed that it was very important to recruit and train interviewers for this study very carefully. In particular, we worried that interviewers who were in any way uncomfortable with the topic of sexuality would not do a good job and would adversely affect the quality of the interview. We thus took special steps in recruiting interviewers to make it clear what the survey was about, even showing them especially sensitive sample questions.

The Questionnaire

The questionnaire itself is probably the most important element of the study design. It determines the content and quality of the information gathered for analysis. Unlike issues related to sample design, the construction of a questionnaire is driven less by technical precepts and more by the concepts and ideas motivating the research.

The problem that we faced in writing the questionnaire was figuring out how best to ask people about their sex lives. There are two issues here that should be highlighted. One is conceptual, having to do with how to define sex, and the second has to do with the level or kind of language to be used in the interview.

There are a number of activities that commonly serve as markers for sex and the status of sex partner, especially intercourse and orgasm. While we certainly wanted to include these events and their extent in given relationships and events, we also felt that using them to define and ask about sexual activity might exclude transactions or partners that should be included. Since the common meaning and uses of the term *intercourse* involve the idea of the intromission of a penis, intercourse in that sense as a defining act would at the very least exclude a sexual relationship between two women. There are also many events that we would call sexual that may not involve orgasm on the part of either or both partners.

For these reasons, in the key section of the questionnaire where we ask respondents to enumerate their sex partners in the past twelve months, we use the following definition of sex: "Here, by 'sex' or 'sexual activity,' we mean any mutually voluntary activity with another person that involves genital contact and sexual excitement or arousal, that is, feeling really turned on, even if intercourse or orgasm did not occur." This definition serves to elicit a broader list of partners and events than some more common definitions. In the description of the sexual relationship, the specific content in terms of sexual techniques and outcomes such as orgasm are collected. This definition also excluded forced sex. This was dealt with separately in a later section of the questionnaire. This was done to protect respondents from emotional upset earlier in the questionnaire and also because forced sex seems to define a partially separate domain.

Another major issue is what sort of language is appropriate in asking questions about sex. It seemed obvious that one should avoid highly technical language because it is unlikely to be understood by many people. One tempting alternative is to use colloquial language and even slang since that is the only language that some people ever use in discussing sexual matters. Slang and other forms of colloquial speech, however, are likely to be problematic in several ways. First, the use of slang can produce a tone in the interview that is counterproductive because it downplays the distinctiveness of the interviewing situation itself. An essential goal in survey interviewing, especially on sensitive topics like sex, is to create a neutral, nonjudgmental, and confiding atmosphere and to maintain a certain professional distance.

The second major shortcoming of slang is that it is highly variable across class and education levels, ages, regions, and other social groupings. It changes meanings rapidly and is often imprecise.

Masturbation was generally felt to be the most sensitive topic of any we discussed, making both respondents and interviewers the most uncomfortable. We thus adopted a form to be filled out by the respondents themselves in an effort to increase the accuracy of the report of the practice. The forms were administered in such a way that the interviewer did not see the answers. On completion, the form was put immediately into an envelope, which was then sealed before it was returned to the interviewer.

Issues of respondent confidentiality are at the very heart of survey research. The willingness of respondents to report their view and experiences fully and honestly depends on the rationale offered for why the study is important and on the assurance that the information provided will be treated as confidential. We offered respondents a strong rationale for the study, our interviewers made great efforts to conduct the interview in a manner that protected respondents' privacy, and we went to great lengths to honor the assurances that the information would be treated confidentially.

Chapter 5

The Sociologist as Rubbernecker

MORTEN G. ENDER, CAROL A. HAGEN,
CLIFFORD O. HAGEN, JR., CORINA A. MORANO-ENDER,
AND KATHLEEN A. TIEMANN

It seems obvious that there are times when the sudden appearance of a sociologist can be downright annoying. If you and your neighbours had just lost your home to a flood, as happened in the case described in this selection, would you really want to be confronted by a team of busybody sociologists who look upon your tragedy as something to be studied? Possibly not. And yet, not to study how ordinary people respond to extraordinary events would be to close our eyes to some important social processes. This selection tries to address some of these issues. As a practical matter, it describes some of the strategies that these researchers used to defuse the quite legitimate resentment that people in extreme situations can have toward sociologists. More importantly, though, the authors suggest that such resentment can also be defused if people come to understand that a sociologist wants to make sense of human responses to tragedy in ways that go way beyond, say, what is found in journalistic accounts of these same tragedies.

CURIOSITY KNOCKS

For the average American, seeing is believing. We are a visually oriented society, fascinated by spectacle. Extraordinary public events are routinely captured visually and become emblazoned in our collective memories. The images come to us primarily via mass media—through newspapers, magazines, radio, and television—as people, close enough to bear witness, share their stories and pictures with others. The term *rubberneck* can be used to describe people who bear witness to a spectacle. This term is also applicable to those who walked and drove through the devastated neighborhoods of Grand Forks, North Dakota, and East Grand Forks, North Dakota, and East Grand Forks, Minnesota, after the Red River Valley Flood of 1997. *Webster's New World Dictionary* defines a rubberneck as "a person who stretches his [sic] head to gaze about in curiosity . . ." (Neufeldt, 1988: 1172). The key word in this definition is curiosity, especially as it relates to interest about an atypical event.

For those unable to bear witness, the journalist becomes a conduit between the interested public and an event. The journalist finds the story, provides facts about the event, and relates it verbally and visually to us, the public. Indeed, the visual evidence of "being there" is not only saved for posterity through journalistic efforts, but it allows us to participate in the historical event with others. But we are sociologists, not

Source: Excerpted from "The Sociologist as Rubbernecker: Photographing the Aftermath of the Red River Valley Flood of 1997," by Morten G. Ender et al., *North Dakota Quarterly,* Vol. 65, No. 4, 1998. Reprinted with permission.

journalists. Therefore, our curiosity motivated us to go beyond bearing witness, to the spectacle of the flood, to analyze it systematically.

SOCIOLOGICAL CURIOSITY

Unlike the layperson or the journalist, a sociologist is a rubbernecker with a plan. Sociologists are concerned with more than witnessing an event of historical or cultural significance and perhaps documenting it via amateur video or in still photographs. We do not simply provide some human-interest feature for others to functionally gauge their own experience on some subjective or objective level. We analyze, interpret, put into perspective, and focus on the interrelationships among the phenomena. For example, Laud Humphreys taught us a great deal about deviance by becoming an observer of the sexual encounters that occurred between men in public restrooms during the 1960s (Humphreys 1989). He took voyeurism to a higher level and connected his findings to deviance in general. The result was the eradication of many stereotypes about the kinds of men who engaged in sexual encounters in public restrooms. Some social situations, such as those described by Humphreys, do not allow us to use the traditional "scientific" methods where we test theoretically driven hypotheses in a fairly controlled environment.

Sometimes, sociologists must simply jump into the fray. A classic example serves as illustration. In his award-winning book, *Everything in Its Path: Destruction of Community Following the Buffalo Creek Flood*, uncovering prolonged trauma that followed a flash flood in West Virginia, sociologist Kai Erikson notes that some situations are too pressing to allow for objective social science, at least early on in a project. As he put it, ". . . traditional methods of sociology do not really equip one to study discrete moments in the flow of human experience" (1976: 13).

So too is our experience. We sought to put into sociological perspective the events that unfolded after the flood of the Red River Valley during the spring and summer of 1997. The immediacy of the flood, our personal experiences and losses from the flood, our professional training, and our penchant for inquisitiveness brought us together in an attempt to understand how the flood affected residents of Grand Forks and East Grand Forks. Our curiosity got the best of us. We moved beyond the sensation of the river which flowed over our community and pursued our interests and the serendipitous set of patterns that emerged: a flood, rural America, and graffiti formed an unprecedented dalliance.

THE RED RIVER AND SPRAY PAINT

The residents of the Red River Valley aren't the first to experience people craning their necks for a view of their disaster. Smith and Belgrave (1995), in their study of people's accounts following Hurricane Andrew in Florida, document rubbernecking:

> The enormity and extent of the hurricane damage was an irresistible draw. The appearance in devastated areas of empty-handed voyeurs added indignity to the pain of those living there, creating resentment. As Rachel [an interviewee] observed, "I felt really invaded. I was angry at these assholes out there, knowing that if they are out there looking at us, they didn't lose anything." Individuals and families in their automobiles gawking at the misery of others for their own entertainment and the continual helicopters . . . were also a part of the problem. (255)

Because we are aware of how people felt about rubberneckers, this essay is our attempt to let the "Rachels" and other Greater Grand Forks community members know that we were not all empty-handed gawkers. Ours was not idle curiosity about a spectacle; we had a plan. Therefore, we want to return, in a small part, some of the words and sentiments of those who survived the flood. We did not steal away your experience with our cameras; we tried to make some sense of it for others and for ourselves.

THE ART AND SCIENCE OF RUBBERNECKING

We combed the streets of Greater Grand Forks on foot, by bicycle, and by car for a number of months after the flood, and we took photographs of murals, of the debris on berms and houses, and of graffiti. We canvassed neighborhoods at various times of the day and night. At times, we felt obtrusive and tried to document the results of the flood unobtrusively to avoid causing additional pain to those who had already suffered losses. To diffuse situations and manage impressions, one of the authors and his one-year-old son rode their bicycle into some neighborhoods and took pictures figuring that people would be less likely to get angry at a parent on a bicycle with a child in tow who was taking photographs than at people locked inside their cars who cruised by slowly, snapping pictures. After a short while, we became more comfortable as we took photographs. Sometimes people invited us to photograph their personal tragedy and even posed next to the debris that had previously been part of their lives.

We took over 150 slides and collected 290 instances of graffiti from neighborhoods in Grand Forks and East Grand Forks. We found graffiti on homes, garages, and household items such as washers, dryers, refrigerators, freezers, ranges, couches, chairs, hot water heaters, pieces of insulation, buckets, a stove top, and signboards. Graffiti was written mostly with spray paint, but sometimes with mud.

Because we are interested in making sense of the flood and the graffiti that appeared after the flood, we read what other researchers had to say about graffiti. This research helped us develop a procedure to study disaster graffiti as a new and singular form of public graffiti. Because they were most helpful in categorizing what we found, we relied heavily upon previously published studies that examined graffiti in public restrooms. We began with 19 subcategories of graffiti and collapsed them into five categories that better organized the data. The final categories included different types of humor, various forms of social and political commentary, statements of frustration, crude drawings, and other miscellaneous forms of graffiti. We hope that our efforts may help readers understand how sociological rubbernecking can help make sense of the artifacts that remain after a devastating event like a flood. Additionally, we hope our efforts have piqued your curiosity about new ways to took at the world.

WORKS CITED

Erikson, Kai T. Everything in Its Path: Destruction of Community at Buffalo Creek. New York: Simon & Schuster, 1976.

Hagen, Carol, Morten G. Ender, Kathleen A. Tiemann, and Clifford O. Hagen, Jr. "Graffiti on the Great Plains: A Social Reaction to the Red River Valley Flood of 1997." Paper presented at the Annual Meetings of the American Sociological Association, San Francisco, CA, August 1998.

Humphreys, Laud. "The Sociologist as Voyeur." In Carolyn D. Smith and William Kornblum, eds. Field: Readings on the Field Research Experience. New York: Praeger, 1989. 126–33.

Neufeldt, Victoria, ed. Webster's New World Dictionary of English. New York: Simon & Schuster, 1988.

Smith, Kenneth J., and Linda Liska Belgrave. "The Reconstruction of Everyday Life: Experiencing Hurricane Andrew." Journal of Contemporary Ethnography, 1995 24(3), 244–69.

PART 3
Ethics in Research

Chapter 6
The Tuskegee Syphilis Experiment

It's useful to begin thinking about the "Tuskegee Syphilis Experiment," the study described here, by taking note of something mentioned at the end of this article: A substantial number of black Americans believe that the U.S. government created AIDS in order to exterminate blacks. Why would so many people believe something so seemingly preposterous? The answer lies in recognizing that something like the Tuskegee Syphilis Experiment could happen. Here was a U.S. government–sponsored study that sought to determine the effects of syphilis by following poor black men infected with syphilis over several decades and by ensuring that these men did not receive treatments that were available. How are we to explain how something like this came to be? Racist attitudes are certainly part of the answer, although—as the author makes clear—something else needs to be added if we're to explain why black professionals and black institutions contributed to the study's "success."

"The United States government did something that was wrong—deeply, profoundly, morally wrong. It was an outrage to our commitment to integrity and equality for all our citizens . . . clearly racist."

—President Clinton's apology for the Tuskegee Syphilis Experiment to the eight remaining survivors, May 16, 1997

For forty years between 1932 and 1972, the U.S. Public Health Service (PHS) conducted an experiment on 399 black men in the late stages of syphilis. These men, for the most part illiterate sharecroppers from one of the poorest counties in Alabama, were never told what disease they were suffering from or of its seriousness. Informed that they were being treated for "bad blood,"[1] their doctors had no intention of curing them of syphilis at all. The data for the experiment was to be collected from autopsies of the men, and they were thus deliberately left to degenerate under the ravages of tertiary syphilis—which can include tumors, heart disease, paralysis, blindness, insanity, and death. "As I see it," one of the doctors involved explained, "we have no further interest in these patients until they die."

USING HUMAN BEINGS AS LABORATORY ANIMALS

The true nature of the experiment had to be kept from the subjects to ensure their cooperation. The sharecroppers' grossly disadvantaged lot in life made them easy to manipulate. Pleased at the prospect of free medical care—almost none of them had ever seen a doctor before—these unsophisticated and trusting men became the pawns in what James Jones, author of the excellent history on the subject, *Bad Blood*, identified as "the longest nontherapeutic experiment on human beings in medical history."

The study was meant to discover how syphilis affected blacks as opposed to whites—the theory being that whites experienced more neurological complications from syphilis whereas blacks were more susceptible to cardiovascular damage. How this knowledge would have changed clinical treatment of syphilis is uncertain. Although the PHS touted the study as one of great scientific merit, from the outset its actual benefits were hazy. It took almost forty years before someone involved in the study took a hard and honest look at the end results, reporting that "nothing learned will prevent, find, or cure a single case of infectious syphilis or bring us closer to our basic mission of controlling venereal disease in the United States." When the experiment was brought to the attention of the media in 1972, news anchor Harry Reasoner described it as an experiment that "used human beings as laboratory animals in a long and inefficient study of how long it takes syphilis to kill someone."

A HEAVY PRICE IN THE NAME OF BAD SCIENCE

By the end of the experiment, 28 of the men had died directly of syphilis, 100 were dead of related complications, 40 of their wives had been infected, and 19 of their children had been born with congenital syphilis. How had these men been induced to endure a fatal disease in the name of science? To persuade the community to support the experiment, one of the original doctors admitted it "was necessary to carry on this study under the guise of a demonstration and provide treatment." At first, the men were prescribed the syphilis remedies of the day—bismuth, neoarsphenamine, and mercury—but in such small amounts that only 3 percent showed any improvement. These token doses of medicine were good public relations and did not interfere with the true aims of the study. Eventually, all syphilis treatment was replaced with "pink medicine"—aspirin. To ensure that the men

would show up for a painful and potentially dangerous spinal tap, the PHS doctors misled them with a letter full of promotional hype: "Last Chance for Special Free Treatment." The fact that autopsies would eventually be required was also concealed. As a doctor explained, "If the colored population becomes aware that accepting free hospital care means a post-mortem, every darky will leave Macon County . . ." Even the Surgeon General of the United States participated in enticing the men to remain in the experiment, sending them certificates of appreciation after 25 years in the study.

FOLLOWING DOCTORS' ORDERS

It takes little imagination to ascribe racist attitudes to the white government officials who ran the experiment, but what can one make of the numerous African Americans who collaborated with them? The experiment's name comes from the Tuskegee Institute, the black university founded by Booker T. Washington. Its affiliated hospital lent the PHS its medical facilities for the study, and other predominantly black institutions as well as local black doctors also participated. A black nurse, Eunice Rivers, was a central figure in the experiment for most of its forty years. The promise of recognition by a prestigious government agency may have obscured the troubling aspects of the study for some. A Tuskegee doctor, for example, praised "the educational advantages offered our interns and nurses as well as the added standing it will give the hospital." Nurse Rivers explained her role as one of passive obedience: "we were taught that we never diagnosed, we never prescribed; we followed the doctor's instructions!" It is clear that the men in the experiment trusted her and that she sincerely cared about their well-being, but her unquestioning submission to authority eclipsed her moral judgment. Even after the experiment was exposed to public scrutiny, she genuinely felt nothing ethical had been amiss.

One of the most chilling aspects of the experiment was how zealously the PHS kept these men from receiving treatment. When several nationwide campaigns to eradicate venereal disease came to Macon County, the men were prevented from participating. Even when penicillin was discovered in the 1940s—the first real cure for syphilis—the Tuskegee men were deliberately denied the medication. During World War II, 250 of the men registered for the draft and were consequently ordered to get treatment for syphilis, only to have the PHS exempt them. Pleased at their success, the PHS representative announced: "So far, we are keeping the known positive patients from getting treatment." The experiment continued in spite of the Henderson Act (1943), a public health law requiring testing and treatment for venereal disease, and in spite of the World Health Organization's Declaration of Helsinki (1964), which specified that "informed consent" was needed for experiment [*sic*] involving human beings.

BLOWING THE WHISTLE

The story finally broke in the *Washington Star* on July 25, 1972, in an article by Jean Heller of the Associated Press. Her source was Peter Buxtun, a former PHS venereal disease interviewer and one of the few whistle blowers over the years. The PHS, however, remained unrepentant, claiming the men had been "volunteers" and "were always happy to see the doctors," and an Alabama state health officer who had been involved claimed "somebody is trying to make a mountain out of a molehill."

Under the glare of publicity, the government ended their experiment, and for the first time provided the men with effective medical treatment for syphilis. Fred Gray, a lawyer who had previously defended Rosa Parks and Martin Luther King, filed a class action suit that provided a $10 million out-of-court settlement for the men and their families. Gray, however, named only whites and white organizations in the suit, portraying Tuskegee as a black and white case when it was in fact more complex than that—black doctors and institutions had been involved from beginning to end.

The PHS did not accept the media's comparison of Tuskegee with the appalling experiments performed by Nazi doctors on their Jewish victims during World War II. Yet in addition to the medical and racist parallels, the PHS offered the same morally bankrupt defense offered at the Nuremberg trials: they claimed they were just carrying out orders, mere cogs in the wheel of the PHS bureaucracy, exempt from personal responsibility.

The study's other justification—for the greater good of science—is equally spurious. Scientific protocol had been shoddy from the start. Since the men had in fact received some medication for syphilis in the beginning of the study, however inadequate, it thereby corrupted the outcome of a study of "untreated syphilis."

In 1990, a survey found that 10 percent of African Americans believed that the U.S. government created AIDS as a plot to exterminate blacks, and another 20 percent could not rule out the possibility that this might be true. As preposterous and paranoid as this may sound, at one time the Tuskegee experiment must have seemed equally farfetched. Who could imagine the government, all the way up to the Surgeon General of the United States, deliberately allowing a group of its citizens to die from a terrible disease for the sake of an ill-conceived experiment? In light of this and many other shameful episodes in our history, African Americans' widespread mistrust of the government and white society in general should not be a surprise to anyone. — *BB*

NOTE

1. All quotations in the article are from *Bad Blood: The Tuskegee Syphilis Experiment,* James H. Jones, expanded edition (New York: Free Press, 1993).

Chapter 7

An Ethical Market in Human Organs

CHARLES A. ERIN AND JOHN HARRIS

Read this article and the next one, by J. Savulescu, carefully, and then think about each in relation to the Tuskegee Syphilis Experiment. Erin and Harris lay out their argument in a seemingly straightforward and no-nonsense manner. Thus, the number of organs needed for transplants far exceeds the number available from cadavers. One obvious solution is to solicit some organs (like kidneys) from living donors; this would of course require safeguards to ensure that organ donors are not exploited and that they and their families receive some benefit in exchange for their organ donation. The article by Savulescu makes many of the same points, but adds one new element: If we allow people to risk their lives in other areas (as we do), why shouldn't we similarly allow them to risk their lives by selling an organ if they want to? Taken together, these two articles seem to be making a reasonable argument. And yet, do you believe that the envisioned safeguards would really work? That the poor would be tempted to sign away their organs with the same likelihood as the rich? That people driven to sell their organs by economic necessity are making an "informed" choice? That the medical system would function to ensure that both rich and poor had equal access to the organs that come on the market? There is of course no way to provide certain answers to these questions in advance of setting up such a system, but should we take the risk, given that if anyone suffers it will be (as in the Tuskegee experiment) the poorest and least educated segment of the population, those least able to mount an effective protest?

While people's lives continue to be put at risk by the dearth of organs available for transplantation, we must give urgent consideration to any option that may make up the shortfall. A market in organs from living donors is one such option. The market should be ethically supportable, and have built into it, for example, safeguards against wrongful exploitation. This can be accomplished by establishing a single purchaser system within a confined marketplace.

Statistics can be dehumanising. The following numbers, however, have more impact than most: as of 24th November, during 2002 in the United Kingdom, 667 people have donated organs, 2055 people have received transplants, and *5615 people are still awaiting transplants*.[1] It is difficult to estimate how many people die prematurely for want of donor organs. "In the world as a whole there are an estimated 700 000 patients on dialysis . . . . In India alone 100 000 new patients present with kidney failure each year" (few if any of whom are on dialysis and only 3000 of whom will receive transplants). Almost "three million Americans suffer from congestive heart

Source: "An Ethical Market in Human Organs," by Charles A. Erin and John Harris, *Journal of Medical Ethics* 2003; 29: 137–138. Reprinted with permission from the BMJ Publishing Group.

failure . . . deaths related to this condition are estimated at 250 000 each year . . . 27 000 patients die annually from liver disease . . . . In Western Europe as a whole 40 000 patients await a kidney but only . . . 10 000 kidneys"[2] become available. Nobody knows how many people fail to make it onto the waiting lists and so disappear from the statistics. It is clear that loss of life, due in large measure to shortage of donor organs, is a major crisis, and a major scandal.

At its annual meeting in 1999, the British Medical Association voted overwhelmingly in favour of the UK moving to a system of presumed consent for organ donation,[3] a proposed change in policy that the UK government immediately rejected.[4] What else might we do to increase the supply of donor organs? At its annual meeting in 2002, the American Medical Association voted to encourage studies to determine whether financial incentives could increase the supply of organs from cadavers.[5] In 1998, the International Forum for Transplant Ethics concluded that trade in organs should be regulated rather than banned.[6] In 1994, we made a proposal in which we outlined possibly the only circumstances in which a market in donor organs could be achieved ethically, in a way that minimises the dangers normally envisaged for such a scheme.[7] Now may be an appropriate time to revisit the idea of a market in donor organs.[8] Our focus then, as now, is organs obtained from the living since creating a market in cadaver organs is uneconomic and is more likely to reduce supply than increase it and the chief reason for considering sale of organs is to improve availability.

To meet legitimate ethical and regulatory concerns, any commercial scheme must have built into it safeguards against wrongful exploitation and show concern for the vulnerable, as well as taking into account considerations of justice and equity.

There is a lot of hypocrisy about the ethics of buying and selling organs and indeed other body products and services—for example, surrogacy and gametes. What it usually means is that everyone is paid but the donor. The surgeons and medical team are paid, the transplant coordinator does not go unremunerated, and the recipient receives an important benefit in kind. Only the unfortunate and heroic donor is supposed to put up with the insult of no reward, to add to the injury of the operation.

We would therefore propose a strictly regulated and highly ethical market in live donor organs and tissue. We should note that the risks of live donation are relatively low: "The approximate risks to the donor . . . are a short term morbidity of 20% and mortality, of 0.03% . . . . The long term risks of developing renal failure are less well documented but appear to be no greater than for the normal population."[9] And recent evidence suggests that living donor organ transplantation has an excellent prognosis, better than cadaver organ transplantation.[10] Intuitively, the advantage also seems clear: the donor is very fit and healthy, while cadaver donors may well have been unfit and unhealthy, although this will not be true of many accident victims.

The bare bones of an ethical market would look like this: the market would be confined to a self governing geopolitical area such as a nation state or indeed the European Union. Only citizens resident within the union or state could sell into the system and they and their families would be equally eligible to receive organs. Thus organ vendors would know they were contributing to a system which would benefit them and their families and friends since their chances of receiving an organ in case of need would be increased by the existence of the market. (If this were not the case the main justification for the market would be defeated.) There would be only one purchaser, an agency like the National Health Service (NHS), which would buy all organs and distribute according to some fair conception of medical priority. There would be no direct sales or purchases, no exploitation of low income countries and their populations (no buying in Turkey or India to sell in Harley Street). The organs would be tested for HIV, etc, their provenance known, and there would be strict controls and penalties to prevent abuse.

Prices would have to be high enough to attract people into the marketplace but dialysis, and other alternative care, does not come cheap. Sellers of organs would know they had saved a life and would be reasonably compensated for their risk, time, and altruism, which would be undiminished by sale. We do not after all regard medicine as any the less a caring profession because doctors are paid. So long as thousands continue to die for want of donor organs we must urgently consider and implement ways of increasing the supply. A market of the sort outlined above is surely one method worthy of active and urgent consideration.

REFERENCES

1. UK Transplant. http://www.uktransplant.org.uk/

2. Cooper DKC, Lanza RP. *Xeno—the promise of transplanting animal organs into humans.* New York: Oxford University Press, 2000: 7–17.

3. Beecham L. BMA wants presumed consent for organ donors. *BMJ* 1999; 319: 141.

4. Anon. Organ donor reform rejected. BBC News Online. 16 July 1999. http://news.bbc.co.uk/1/hi/health/396430.stm

5. Josefson D. AMA considers whether to pay for donation of organs. *BMJ* 2002; 324: 1541.

6. Radcliffe-Richards J, Daar AS, Guttman RD, *et al.* The case for allowing kidney sales. *Lancet* 1998; 351: 1950–2.[CrossRef][Medline]

7. Erin CA, Harris J. A monopsonistic market—or how to buy and sell human organs, tissues and cells ethically. In: Robinson I, ed. *Life and death under high technology medicine.* Manchester: Manchester University Press in association with the Fulbright Commission, London, 1994: 134–53. See also Harris J, Erin CA. An ethically defensible market in organs. *BMJ* 2002; 325: 114–15.

8. Tuffs A. Debate fuels controversy over paid-for live organ donation. *BMJ* 2002; 325: 66; Hopkins Tanne J. International group reiterates stance against human organ trafficking. *BMJ* 2002; 325: 514.

9. Allen RDM, Lynch SV, Strong RW. The living organ donor. In: Chapman JR, Deierhoi M, Wight C, eds. *Organ and tissue donation for transplantation.* London: Arnold, 1997: 165 (original references omitted). See also—for example, Bay WH, Herbert LA. The living donor in kidney transplantation. *Ann Intern Med* 1987; 106: 719–27; Spital A. Life insurance for kidney donors—an update. *Transplantation* 1988; 45: 819–20. In this last study it was reported that in a sample of American life insurance companies, all would insure a transplant donor who was otherwise healthy and only 6% of companies would load the premium. We are indebted to Søren Holm for pointing us to these latter two sources.

10. Hariharan S, Johnson CP, Bresnahan BA, *et al.* Improved graft survival after renal transplantation in the United States, 1988 to 1996. *N Engl J Med* 2000; 342: 605–12. See also Gjertson DW, Cecka, MJ. Living unrelated kidney transplantation. *Kidney International* 2000; 58: 491–9; Terasaki PI, Cecka JM, Gjertson DW, *et al.* High survival rates of kidney transplants from spousal and living unrelated donors. *N Engl J Med* 1995; 333: 333–6. We are indebted to Aaron Spital for pointing us to these sources. *J Med Ethics* 2003; 29: 138–139.

Chapter 8

Is the Sale of Body Parts Wrong?

J. SAVULESCU

In late August 2002, a general practitioner (GP) in London, Dr. Bhagat Singh Makkar, 62, was struck off the medical register after he was discovered to have bragged to an undercover journalist about being able to obtain a kidney from a live donor in exchange for a fee. He told the journalist, who posed as the son of a patient with renal failure: "No problem, I can fix that for you. Do you want it done here, do you want it done in Germany or do you want it done in India?" The price he quoted included payment to the donor and "my administration costs." Dr. Makkar said he regretted giving "stupid answers" to the journalist. He had been "tired, confused, and upset after a long day dealing with emotional patients."[1]

Deliberation about ethics is often muddied by the personalities involved in a particular issue. Many people are uninspired by Richard Seed or Jack Kevorkian. This contaminates their view about the much broader and important issues such as cloning or euthanasia that Seed and Kevorkian, whom some people might describe as mavericks, have shoved their finger in.

Discussion of the sale of organs is overshadowed by cases of exploitation, murder, and corruption. But there is also a serious ethical issue about whether people should be allowed to sell parts of the body. It applies not only to organs, such as the kidney or parts of the liver, but also to tissues, such as bone marrow, gametes (eggs and sperm) and even genetic material. The usual argument in favour of allowing the sale of organs is that we need to increase supply. In the US, as few as 15% of people who need kidney transplants ever get a kidney. Cadaveric organs will never satisfy the growing demand for organs. Worldwide, hundreds of thousands, if not millions, die while waiting for a transplant.

Those opposed to a market in organs argue that markets reduce altruistic donation and may also threaten the quality of organ supply. They also claim it will exploit those who are forced by poverty to enter such a market.

Charles Erin and John Harris have proposed an "ethical market" in organs (p. 37). The market would be confined to a self governing geopolitical area—for example, the UK or Australia. Vendors could sell into the system, from which their family members would stand a chance of benefiting. Only citizens from that area could sell and receive organs. There would be only one purchaser, an agency like the National Health Service (NHS) or Medicare, which would buy all organs and distribute according to some fair conception of medical priority. There would be no direct sales or purchases, no exploitation of low income countries and their populations.[2]

But there seems to me to be a much stronger argument in favour of sale of body parts. People have a right to make a decision to sell a body part.

Source: "Is the Sale of Body Parts Wrong?" by J. Savulescu, *Journal of Medical Ethics*, 2003; 29: 138–139. Reprinted with permission from the BMJ Publishing Group.

If we should be allowed to sell our labour, why not sell the means to that labour? If we should be allowed to risk damaging our body for pleasure (by smoking or skiing), why not for money which we will use to realise other goods in life? To ban a market in organs is, paradoxically, to constrain what people can do with their own lives.

Think about a couple with two young children who are contemplating buying a house. They find one for $150 000, but in a heavily polluted and unsafe area. They could spend another $50 000 and live in a cleaner, safer area. But they decide to save the money and expose their children to a greater risk in order to pay for private education.

Or consider the diver. He takes on a job as a deep sea diver which pays him an extra $30 000 than he could otherwise earn. This loading is paid because the job has higher risks to his life and health. He takes the job because he likes holidays in expensive exotic locations.[3]

In both these cases, people take risks for money. They judge that the benefits for their own lives or their family's outweigh the risks. To prevent them making these decisions is to judge that they are unable to make a decision about what is best for their own lives. It is paternalism in its worst form.

There are two crucial issues. Firstly, we need to ensure that the risk involved is reasonable compared with the benefits it will offer to the person undertaking the risk and society. Secondly, people need to be fully informed and to give their consent freely. By "freely", I mean that they are not in a situation which is itself wrong or unacceptable. Poverty which is acceptable to a society should not be a circumstance which prevents a person taking on a risk or harm to escape that poverty. It is double injustice to say to a poor person: "You can't have what most other people have and we are not going to let you do what you want to have those things".

When people go to war voluntarily, risking their lives for their country, they are heralded as heroes. If we allow people to die for their country, it seems to me we should allow them to risk death or injury for the chance to improve the quality of their lives or their children's lives or for anything else they value. Money for these people is just a means to realise what they value in life. Whether or not a private market in organs will increase supply or improve its quality, it seems that people have a right to sell them.

REFERENCES

1. GP struck off for organ trading. *The Guardian,* accessed at http://society.guardian.co.uk/nhsperformance/story/0,8150,783399,00.html on 25/9/02.
2. Erin CA, Harris J. An ethical market in organs *J Med Ethics* 2003; 29: 137–8. [Free Full Text]
3. Savulescu J. Taking the plunge. *New Scientist* 2001; 169: 50. *J Med Ethics* 2003; 29: 139–140. [Medline]

PART 4
Culture

Chapter 9

Body Ritual among the Nacirema

HORACE MINER

This particular selection is widely reprinted in sociology readers, but it is one for which a prologue would only spoil the fun. Let us say only that one of the things Miner wanted to do was to demonstrate that much of what strikes us as "exotic" in anthropological accounts of other cultures might appear quite differently to the people involved.

The anthropologist has become so familiar with the diversity of ways in which different people behave in similar situations that he is not apt to be surprised by even the most exotic customs. In fact, if all of the logically possible combinations of behavior have not been found somewhere in the world, he is apt to suspect that they must be present in some yet undescribed tribe. In this light, the magical beliefs and practices of the Nacirema present such unusual aspects that it seems desirable to describe them as an example of the extremes to which human behavior can go.

The Nacirema are a North American group living in the territory between the Canadian Cree, the Yaqui and Tarahumare of Mexico, and the Carib and Arawak of the Antilles. Little is known of their origin, although tradition states that they came from the east. According to Nacirema mythology, their nation was originated by a culture hero, Notgnihsaw, who is otherwise known for two great feats of strength—the throwing of a piece of wampum across the river Pa-To-Mac and chopping down of a cherry tree in which the Spirit of Truth resided.

While much of the people's time is devoted to economic pursuits, a large part of the fruits of these labors and a considerable portion of the day are spent in ritual activity. The focus of this activity is the human body, the appearance and health of which loom as a dominant concern in the ethos of the people. While such a concern is certainly not unusual, its ceremonial aspects and associated philosophy are unique.

The fundamental belief underlying the whole system appears to be that the human body is ugly and that its natural tendency is to debility and disease. Incarcerated in such a body, man's only hope is to avert these characteristics through the use of ritual and ceremony. Every household has one or more shrines devoted to this purpose. The more powerful individuals in the society have several shrines in their houses and, in fact, the opulence of a house is often referred to in terms of the number of such ritual centers it possesses. Most houses are of wattle and daub construction, but the shrine rooms of the more wealthy are walled with stone. Poorer families imitate the rich by applying pottery plaques to their shrine walls.

While each family has at least one such shrine, the rituals associated with it are not family ceremonies but are private and secret. The rites are normally only discussed with children, and then only during the period when they are being initiated into these mysteries. I was able, however, to establish sufficient rapport with the natives to examine these shrines and to have the rituals described to me.

The focal point of the shrine is a box or chest which is built into the wall. In this chest are kept the many charms and magical potions without which no native believes he could live. These preparations are secured from a variety of specialized practitioners. The most powerful of these are the medicine men, whose assistance must be rewarded with substantial gifts. However, the medicine men do not provide the curative potions for their clients, but decide what the ingredients should be and then write them down in an ancient and secret language. This writing is understood only by the medicine men and by the herbalists who, for another gift, provide the required charm.

The charm is not disposed of after it has served its purpose, but is placed in the charm-box of the household shrine. As these magical materials are specific for certain ills, and the real or imagined maladies of the people are many, the charm-box is usually full to overflowing. The magical packets are so numerous that people forget what their purposes were and fear to use them again. While the natives are very vague on this point, we can only assume that the idea in retaining all the old magical materials is that their presence in the charm-box, before which the body rituals are conducted, will in some way protect the worshiper.

Beneath the charm-box is a small font. Each day every member of the family, in succession, enters the shrine room, bows his head before the charm-box, mingles different sorts of holy water in the font, and proceeds with a brief rite of ablution. The holy waters are secured from the Water Temple of the community, where the priests conduct elaborate ceremonies to make the liquid ritually pure.

In the hierarchy of magical practitioners, and below the medicine men in prestige, are specialists whose designation is best translated as "holy-mouth-men." The Nacirema have an almost pathological horror of and fascination with the mouth, the condition of which is believed to have a supernatural influence on all social relationships. Were it not for the rituals of the mouth, they believe that their teeth would fall out, their gums bleed, their jaws shrink, their friends desert them, and their lovers reject them. They also believe that a strong relationship exists between oral and moral characteristics. For example, there is a ritual ablution of the mouth for children which is supposed to improve their moral fiber.

The daily body ritual performed by everyone includes a mouth-rite. Despite the fact that these people are so punctilious about care of the mouth, this rite involves a practice which strikes the uninitiated stranger as revolting. It was reported to me that the ritual consists of inserting a small bundle of hog hairs into the mouth, along with certain magical powders, and then moving the bundle in a highly formalized series of gestures.

In addition to the private mouth-rite, the people seek out a holy-mouth-man once or twice a year. These practitioners have an impressive set of paraphernalia, consisting of a variety of augers, awls, probes, and prods. The use of these items in the exorcism of the evils of the mouth involves almost unbelievable ritual torture of the client. The holy-mouth-man opens the client's mouth and, using the above mentioned tools, enlarges any holes which decay may have created in the teeth. Magical materials are put into these holes. If there are no naturally occurring holes in the teeth, large sections of one or more teeth are gouged out so that the supernatural substance can be applied. In the client's view, the purpose of these ministrations is to arrest decay and to draw friends. The extremely sacred and traditional character of the rite is evident in the fact that the natives return to the holy-mouth-men year after year, despite the fact that their teeth continue to decay.

It is to be hoped that, when a thorough study of the Nacirema is made, there will be careful inquiry into the personality structure of these people. One has but to watch the gleam in the eye of a holy-mouth-man, as he jabs an awl into an exposed nerve, to suspect that a certain amount of sadism is involved. If this can be established, a very interesting pattern emerges, for most of the population shows definite masochistic tendencies. It was to these that Professor Linton referred in discussing a distinctive part of the daily body ritual which is performed only by men. This part of the rite includes scraping and lacerating the surface of the face with a sharp instrument. Special women's rites are performed only four times during each lunar month, but what they lack in frequency is made up in barbarity. As part of this ceremony, women bake their heads in small ovens for about an hour. The theoretically interesting point is that what seems to be a preponderantly masochistic people have developed sadistic specialists.

The medicine men have an imposing temple, or *latipso*, in every community of any size. The more elaborate ceremonies required to treat very sick patients can only be performed at this temple. These ceremonies involve not only the thaumaturge but a permanent group of vestal maidens who move sedately about the temple chambers in distinctive costume and headdress.

The *latipso* ceremonies are so harsh that it is phenomenal that a fair proportion of the really sick natives who enter the temple ever recover. Small children whose indoctrination is still incomplete have been known to resist attempts to take them to the temple because "that is where you go to die." Despite this fact, sick adults are not only willing but eager to undergo the protracted ritual purification, if they can afford to do so. No matter how ill the supplicant or how grave the emergency, the guardians of many temples will not admit a client if he cannot give a rich gift to the custodian. Even after one has gained and survived the ceremonies, the guardians will not permit the neophyte to leave until he makes still another gift.

The supplicant entering the temple is first stripped of all his or her clothes. In everyday life the Nacirema avoids exposure of his body and its natural functions. Bathing and excretory acts are performed only in the secrecy of the household shrine, where they are ritualized as part of the body-rites. Psychological shock results from the fact that body secrecy is suddenly lost upon entry into the *latipso*. A man, whose own wife has never seen him in an excretory act, suddenly finds himself naked and assisted by a vestal maiden while he performs his natural functions into a sacred vessel. This sort of ceremonial treatment is necessitated by the fact that the excreta are used by a diviner to ascertain the course and nature of the client's sickness. Female clients, on the other hand, find their naked bodies are subjected to the scrutiny, manipulation and prodding of the medicine men.

Few supplicants in the temple are well enough to do anything but lie on their hard beds. The daily ceremonies, like the rites of the holy-mouth-men, involve discomfort and torture. With ritual precision, the vestals awaken their miserable charges each dawn and roll them about on their beds of pain while performing ablutions, in the formal movements of which the maidens are highly trained. At other times they insert magic wands in the supplicant's mouth or force him to eat substances which are supposed to be healing. From time to time the medicine men come to their clients and jab magically treated needles into their flesh. The fact that these temple ceremonies may not cure, and may even kill the neophyte, in no way decreases the people's faith in the medicine men.

There remains one other kind of practitioner, known as a "listener." This witchdoctor has the power to exorcise the devils that lodge in the heads of people who have been bewitched. The Nacirema believe that parents bewitch their own children. Mothers are particularly suspected of putting a curse on children while teaching them the secret body rituals. The counter-magic of the witchdoctor is unusual in its lack of ritual. The patient simply tells the "listener" all his troubles and fears, beginning with the earliest difficulties he can remember. The memory displayed by the Nacirema in these exorcism sessions is truly remarkable. It is not uncommon for the patient to bemoan the rejection he felt upon being weaned as a babe, and a few individuals even see their troubles going back to the traumatic effects of their own birth.

In conclusion, mention must be made of certain practices which have their base in native esthetics but which depend upon the pervasive aversion to the natural body and its functions. There are ritual fasts to make fat people thin and ceremonial feasts to make thin people fat. Still other rites are used to make women's breasts larger if they are small, and smaller if they are large. General dissatisfaction with breast shape is symbolized in the fact that the ideal form is virtually outside the range of human variation. A few women afflicted with almost inhuman hyper-mammary development are so idolized that they make a handsome living by simply going from village to village and permitting the natives to stare at them for a fee.

Our review of the ritual life of the Nacirema has certainly shown them to be a magic-ridden people. It is hard to understand how they have managed to exist so long under the burdens which they have imposed upon themselves. But even such exotic customs as these take on real meaning when they are viewed with the insight provided by Malinowski when he wrote (1948:70):

> Looking from far and above, from our high places of safety in the developed civilization, it is easy to see all the crudity and irrelevance of magic. But without its power and guidance early man could not have mastered his practical difficulties as he has done, nor could man have advanced to the higher stages of civilization.

REFERENCES CITED

Linton, Ralph. 1936. *The Study of Man.* New York, D. Appleton-Century Co.

Malinowski, Bronislaw. 1948. *Magic, Science, and Religion.* Glencoe, The Free Press.

Chapter 10
Mother Cow

MARVIN HARRIS

It is common for Westerners to think of themselves as rational and progressive in contrast to people living in non-Western cultures, who are often seen as clinging to traditions (religious traditions in particular) that promote irrationality and lack of progress. Marvin Harris (1927–2001) was an anthropologist who made a career of demonstrating that cultural practices that often strike Westerners as irrational are in fact very reasonable adaptations to the material conditions of life in which many non-Western populations find themselves. In this selection, he demonstrates just that in connection with the emphasis on "cow love" found in the Hindu tradition in India.

Whenever I get into discussions about the influence of practical and mundane factors on lifestyles, someone is sure to say, "But what about all those cows the hungry peasants in India refuse to eat?" The picture of a ragged farmer starving to death alongside a big fat cow conveys a reassuring sense of mystery to Western observers. In countless learned and popular allusions, it confirms our deepest conviction about how people with inscrutable Oriental minds ought to act. It is comforting to know—somewhat like "there will always be an England"—that in India spiritual values are more precious than life itself. And at the same time it makes us feel sad. How can we ever hope to understand people so different from ourselves? Westerners find the idea that there might be a practical explanation for Hindu love of cow more upsetting than Hindus do. The sacred cow—how else can I say it?—is one of our favorite sacred cows.

Hindus venerate cows because cows are the symbol of everything that is alive. As Mary is to Christians the mother of God, the cow to Hindus is the mother of life. So there is no greater sacrilege for a Hindu than killing a cow. Even the taking of human life lacks the symbolic meaning, the unutterable defilement, that is evoked by cow slaughter.

According to many experts, cow worship is the number one cause of India's hunger and poverty. Some Western-trained agronomists say that the taboo against cow slaughter is keeping one hundred million "useless" animals alive. They claim that cow worship lowers the efficiency of agriculture because the useless animals contribute neither milk nor meat while competing for croplands and foodstuff with useful animals and hungry human beings. A study sponsored by the Ford Foundation in 1959 concluded that possibly half of India's cattle could be regarded as surplus in relation to feed supply. And an economist from the University of Pennsylvania stated in 1971 that India has thirty million unproductive cows.

It does seem that there are enormous numbers of surplus, useless, and uneconomic animals, and that this situation is a direct result of irrational Hindu doctrines. Tourists on their way through Delhi, Calcutta, Madras, Bombay, and other Indian cities are astonished at the liberties enjoyed by stray cattle. The animals wander through the streets, browse off the stalls in the market place, break into private gardens, defecate all over the sidewalks, and snarl traffic by pausing to chew their cuds in the middle of busy intersections. In the countryside, the cattle congregate on the shoulders of every highway and spend much of their time taking leisurely walks down the railroad tracks.

Love of cow affects life in many ways. Government agencies maintain old age homes for cows at which owners may board their dry and decrepit animals free of charge. In Madras, the police round up stray cattle that have fallen ill and nurse them back to health by letting them graze on small fields adjacent to the station house. Farmers regard their cows as members of the family, adorn them with garlands and tassels, pray for them when they get sick, and call in their neighbors and a priest to celebrate the birth of a new calf. Throughout India, Hindus hang on their walls calendars that portray beautiful, bejeweled young women who have the bodies of big fat white cows. Milk is shown jetting out of each teat of these half-woman, half-zebu goddesses.

Aside from the beautiful human face, cow pinups bear little resemblance to the typical cow one sees in the flesh. For most of the year their bones are their most prominant feature. Far from having milk gushing from every teat, the gaunt beasts barely manage to nurse a single calf to maturity. The average yield of whole milk from the typical humpbacked breed of zebu cow in India amounts to less than 500 pounds a year. Ordinary American dairy cattle produce over 5,000 pounds, while for champion milkers, 20,000 pounds is not unusual. But this comparison doesn't tell the whole story. In any given year about half of India's zebu cows give no milk at all—not a drop.

To Western observers familiar with modern industrial techniques of agriculture and stock raising, cow love seems senseless, even suicidal. The efficiency expert yearns to get his hands on all those useless animals and ship them off to a proper fate. And yet one finds certain inconsistencies in the condemnation of cow love. When I began to wonder if there might be a practical explanation for the sacred cow, I came across an intriguing government report. It said that India had too many cows but too few oxen. With so many cows around, how could there be a shortage of oxen? Oxen and male water buffalo are the principal source of traction for plowing India's fields. For each farm of ten acres or less, one pair of oxen or water buffalo is considered adequate. A little arithmetic shows that as far as plowing is concerned, there is indeed a shortage rather than a surplus of animals. India has 60 million farms, but only 80 million traction animals. If each farm had its quota of two oxen or two water buffalo, there ought to be 120 million traction animals—that is, 40 million more than are actually available.

The shortage of draft animals is a terrible threat that hangs over most of India's peasant families. When an ox falls sick a poor farmer is in danger of losing his farm. If he has no replacement for it, he will have to borrow money at usurious rates. Millions of rural households have in fact lost all or part of their holdings and have gone into share-cropping or day labor as a result of such debts. Every year hundreds of thousands of destitute farmers end up migrating to the cities, which already teem with unemployed and homeless persons.

The Indian farmer who can't replace his sick or deceased ox is in much the same situation as an American farmer who can neither replace nor repair his broken tractor. But there is an important difference: tractors are made by factories, but oxen are made by cows. A farmer who owns a cow owns a factory for making oxen. With or without cow love, this is a good reason for him not to be too anxious to sell his cow to the slaughterhouse. One also begins to see why Indian farmers might be willing to tolerate cows that give only 500 pounds of milk per year. If the main economic function of the zebu cow is to breed male traction animals, then there's no point in comparing her with specialized American dairy animals, whose main function is to produce milk. Still, the milk produced by zebu cows plays an important role in meeting the nutritional needs of many poor families. Even small amounts of milk products can improve the health of people who are forced to subsist on the edge of starvation.

When Indian farmers want an animal primarily for milking purposes they turn to the female water buffalo, which has longer lactation periods and higher butterfat yields than zebu cattle. Male water buffalo are also superior animals for plowing in flooded rice paddies. But oxen are more versatile and are preferred for dry-field farming and road transport. Above all, zebu breeds are remarkably rugged, and can survive the long droughts that periodically afflict different parts of India.

Agriculture is part of a vast system of human and natural relationships. To judge isolated portions of this "ecosystem" in terms that are relevant to the conduct of American agribusiness leads to some very strange impressions. Cattle figure in the Indian ecosystem in ways that are easily overlooked or demeaned by observers from industrialized, high-energy societies. In the United States, chemicals have almost completely replaced animal manure as the principal source of farm fertilizer. American farmers stopped using manure when they began to plow with tractors rather than mules or horses. Since tractors excrete poisons rather than fertilizers, a commitment to large-scale machine farming is almost of necessity a commitment to the use of chemical fertilizers. And around the world today there has in fact grown up a vast integrated petrochemical-tractor-truck industrial complex that produces farm machinery, motorized transport, oil and gasoline, and chemical fertilizers and pesticides upon which new high-yield production techniques depend.

For better or worse, most of India's farmers cannot participate in this complex, not because they worship their cows, but because they can't afford to buy tractors. Like other underdeveloped nations, India can't build factories that are competitive with the facilities of the industrialized nations nor pay for large quantities of imported industrial products. To convert from animals and manure to tractors and petrochemicals would require the investment of incredible amounts of capital. Moreover, the inevitable effect of substituting costly machines for cheap animals is to reduce the number of people who can earn their living from agriculture and to force a corresponding increase in the size of the average farm. We know that the development of large-scale agribusiness in the United States has meant the virtual destruction of the small family farm. Less than 5 percent of U.S. families now live on farms, as compared with 60 percent about a hundred years ago. If agribusiness were to develop along similar lines in India, jobs and housing would soon have to be found for a quarter of a billion displaced peasants.

Since the suffering caused by unemployment and homelessness in India's cities is already intolerable, an additional massive build-up of the urban population can only lead to unprecedented upheavals and catastrophes.

With this alternative in view, it becomes easier to understand low-energy, small-scale, animal-based systems. As I have already pointed out, cows and oxen provide low-energy substitutes for tractors and tractor factories. They also should be credited with carrying out the functions of a petrochemical industry. India's cattle annually excrete about 700 million tons of recoverable manure. Approximately half of this total is used as fertilizer, while most of the remainder is burned to provide heat for cooking. The annual quantity of heat liberated by this dung, the Indian housewife's main cooking fuel, is the thermal equivalent of 27 million tons of kerosene, 35 million tons of coal, or 68 million tons of wood. Since India has only small reserves of oil and coal and is already the victim of extensive deforestation, none of these fuels can be considered practical substitutes for cow dung. The thought of dung in the kitchen may not appeal to the average American, but Indian women regard it as a superior cooking fuel because it is finely adjusted to their domestic routines. Most Indian dishes are prepared with clarified butter known as *ghee*, for which cow dung is the preferred source of heat since it burns with a clean, slow, long-lasting flame that doesn't scorch the food. This enables the Indian housewife to start cooking her meals and to leave them unattended for several hours while she takes care of the children, helps out in the fields, or performs other chores. American housewives achieve a similar effect through a complex set of electronic controls that come as expensive options on late-model stoves.

Cow dung has at least one other major function. Mixed with water and made into a paste, it is used as a household flooring material. Smeared over a dirt floor and left to harden into a smooth surface, it keeps the dust down and can be swept clean with a broom.

Because cattle droppings have so many useful properties, every bit of dung is carefully collected. Village small fry are given the task of following the family cow around and of bringing home its daily petrochemical output. In the cities, sweeper castes enjoy a monopoly on the dung deposited by strays and earn their living by selling it to housewives.

From an agribusiness point of view, a dry and barren cow is an economic abomination. But from the viewpoint of the peasant farmer, the same dry and barren cow may be a last desperate defense against the moneylenders. There is always the chance that a favorable monsoon may restore the vigor of even the most decrepit specimen and that she will fatten up, calve, and start giving milk again. This is what the farmer prays for; sometimes his prayers are answered. In the meantime, dung-making goes on. And so one gradually begins to understand why a skinny old hag of a cow still looks beautiful in the eyes of her owner.

But sooner or later there must come a time when all hope of an animal's recovery is lost and even dung-making ceases. And still the Hindu farmer refuses to kill it for food or sell it to the slaughterhouse. Isn't this incontrovertible evidence of a harmful economic practice that has no explanation apart from the religious taboos on cow slaughter and beef consumption?

No one can deny that cow love mobilizes people to resist cow slaughter and beef eating. But I don't agree that the anti-slaughter and beef-eating taboos necessarily have an adverse effect on human survival and well-being. By slaughtering or selling his aged and decrepit animals, a farmer might earn a few more rupees or temporarily improve his family's diet. But in the long run, his refusal to sell to the slaughterhouse or kill for his own table may have beneficial consequences. An established principle of ecological analysis states that communities of organisms are adapted not to average but to extreme conditions. The relevant situation in India is the recurrent failure of the monsoon rains. To evaluate the economic significance of the anti-slaughter and anti-beef-eating taboos, we have to consider what these taboos mean in the context of periodic droughts and famine.

The taboo on slaughter and beef eating may be as much a product of natural selection as the small bodies and fantastic recuperative powers of the zebu breeds. During droughts and famines, farmers are severely tempted to kill or sell their livestock. Those who succumb to this temptation seal their doom, even if they survive the drought, for when the rains come, they will be unable to plow their fields. I want to be even more emphatic: Massive slaughter of cattle under the duress of famine constitutes a much greater threat to aggregate welfare than any likely miscalculation by particular farmers concerning the usefulness of their animals during normal times. It seems probable that the sense of unutterable profanity elicited by cow slaughter has its roots in the excruciating contradiction between immediate needs and long-run conditions of survival. Cow love with its sacred symbols and holy doctrines protects the farmer against calculations that are "rational" only in the short term. To Western experts it looks as if "the Indian farmer would rather starve to death than eat his cow." The same kinds of experts like to talk about the "inscrutable Oriental mind" and think that "life is not so dear to the Asian masses." They don't realize that the farmer would rather eat his cow than starve, but that he will starve if he does eat it.

The survival into old age of a certain number of absolutely useless animals during good times is part of the price that must be paid for protecting useful animals against slaughter during bad times.

Chapter 11

Modern Magic: The Case of Examinations

DANIEL ALBAS AND CHERYL ALBAS

Around the time of the First World War, anthropologist Bronislaw Malinowski studied the use of magic among the Trobriand Islanders in the South Pacific. He argued that they practised magic to relieve the anxiety caused by the danger and uncertainty associated with ocean fishing. A belief in magic, in other words, gave them the illusion of control in a dangerous and uncertain situation they could not avoid. Final exams are not dangerous, but they do produce anxiety and cannot be avoided. It is hardly surprising then, as this selection reports, that students at a large Canadian university often turned to magic. Does that mean that there is no difference between Trobriand Islanders and you? Not quite. The fact that modern culture is less homogeneous than Trobriand culture affects (these authors argue) the sort of magic that modern students practise. This study was conducted in the 1980s; do Canadian university students still practise magic? Discuss among yourselves (preferably before the final exam!).

MAGIC AND SUCCESS: THE CASE OF EXAMINATIONS

Magic seems inevitably to be associated with anxiety-causing events, whether its function is to allay the anxiety, as Malinowski suggests, or to generate anxiety where it does not exist and for societal reasons should, as Radcliffe-Brown suggests (Homans 1941). Examinations are highly tense and anxiety-causing events, and the practices described in the article as magic are essentially anxiety-coping mechanisms.

The examination arena is one in which students, no matter how well prepared, encounter a number of uncertainties. These include, for example, whether they have interpreted the questions correctly; whether the professors will interpret their answers as they intend them; and not least, whether they themselves are "up" for the contest in terms of the sharpness of their memories, organizational abilities, and ability to complete the task on time. Accordingly, it is not surprising to find surrounding the examination a number of practices by students that are clearly intended as uncertainty-coping mechanisms and which could be called magic, if magic is defined as *an action directed toward the achievement of a particular outcome with no logical relationships between the action and the outcome or, indeed, any empirical evidence that the one produces the other.* In effect, this is nonrational behavior in a setting where one might expect maximum rationality. Clearly we are not dealing with the magic of the sleight-of-hand professional magicians intend for entertainment, nor with that of preliterate shamans or urban gypsies (i.e., cultic magic). Such behavior is directed toward achieving an outcome, involves many everyday and

Source: © 1989 by JAI Press. Reprinted from The Sociological Quarterly, Vol. 30, No. 4, Issue: Winter 1989, pp. 603–613, by permission of the publisher, Blackwell Publishing, a company of John Wiley & Sons, Inc.

commonplace acts, yet does seem to rely for the achievement of the outcome on some mystical element.

In this article we attempt to depict and analyze magical practices students use to allay anxiety and so increase their chances for success.

METHOD

We gathered the data over the last thirteen years from over 300 students in our own and others' classes in the province's largest university (now enrolling 24,000 students). The sample represents a complete spectrum of student background as to age, sex, marital status, and social class. We observed and interacted with students as they studied in libraries, took study breaks, and made last-minute preparations before making their way to their respective exam sites. We continued our tracking as students gathered outside the exam centers, entered, chose their seats, and wrote their exams. Finally, we monitored students as they again congregated outside the exam sites and even as they gathered in pubs and local restaurants for the traditional "post-mortems." As a result we were able to record the increased frequency of magical practices as they neared culmination on the day of the exam and dropped dramatically (though not entirely) immediately upon completion of the exam.

The methodological process involved triangulation: data of different kinds were collected from a variety of sources in such a way that the weaknesses of one data-collecting technique were compensated for by the strengths of another, thus better ensuring reliability and validity. The four sources employed were: (1) exam logs, (2) surveys, (3) observation and probing for meaning, and (4) student accounts to explain failures.

GENERAL CHARACTERISTICS OF STUDENT MAGIC

We found that from one-fifth to one-third of our students used magic, predominantly of the kind intended to bring good luck rather than to ward off bad luck. In Fraser's (1958) terms, it was largely "contagious" magic rather than "imitative" (no more than half a dozen cases of the latter), and there was only a handful of cases in which "omens" were given credence. The descriptions of magical behaviors and material items employed by students fall into the two major categories of Material Items (Figure 11.1) and Behavior (Figure 11.2). In turn, these categories are further divided into Prescribed for

FIGURE 11.1 AREAS OF MAGIC: MATERIAL ITEMS

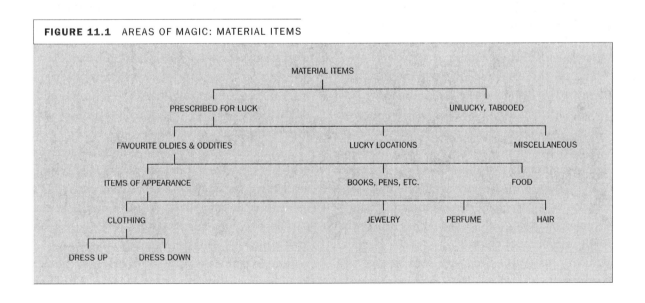

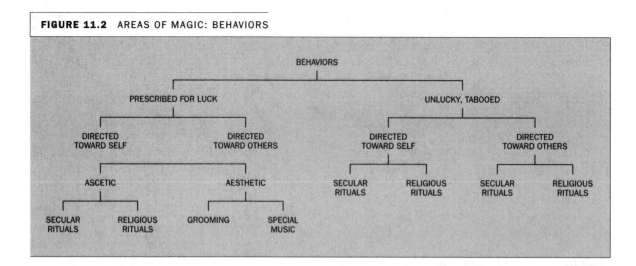

FIGURE 11.2 AREAS OF MAGIC: BEHAVIORS

Luck, on the one hand, and Unlucky or Tabooed, on the other. Focusing first on Material Items Prescribed for Luck, these can be sub-classified as Favorite Oldies and Oddities, Lucky Locations, and Miscellaneous. Favorite Oldies and Oddities are represented by Items of Appearance, Books and Pens, and Food. Items of Appearance include not only Clothing but also Jewelry, Perfume, and Modes of Wearing the Hair. Thus, Items Prescribed for Luck exhibit a variety of at least seven different classes of items. If one distinguishes between Dressing Up and Dressing Down, the number of different classes of Items Prescribed for Luck increases to eight. It did not seem feasible to classify Unlucky Items. Accordingly, the total variety of classes into which magical Material Items fall is nine—eight Prescribed for Luck and an unclassified miscellany of Unlucky Items.

Within the other major category, Behavior, there are five distinct classes prescribed for Luck: Secular Rituals, Religious Rituals, Grooming, Special Music, and a Miscellany of Behavior Directed Toward Others. Under Tabooed Behavior, in regard to both Behavior Directed Toward Self and Behavior Directed Toward Others, is the twofold classification of Secular Rituals and Religious Rituals. This brings the total number of distinct classes of magical Behavior to nine. We now turn to specific descriptions of bottom-line Items and Behavior

(those that appear on the bottom line of each of the two figures are not further subclassified).

MAGICAL ITEMS

Items Prescribed for Luck

In regard to Clothing, most students at exam time dress down (i.e., untidily, sloppily), though there are a few who dress up. Among the notable down dressers were: a young woman who always wore to exams her boyfriend's sweatshirt "which was in a deplorable condition with holes everywhere, stretched out of shape and much too big for me"; a science student who always wore an ancient scarf that he insisted "carries parts of my brain in it"; and an engineering student who wore a pink sweatshirt with purported magical qualities. An example of dressing up is the case of a student who always wore a three-piece suit that he had found particularly efficacious when he wore it on one occasion to a job interview.

Notable items of Jewelry listed by students as bringing them luck were mother's wedding ring, mother's R.N. pin, and father's class ring. In all of these cases, the students mentioned that the parent was particularly bright and successful, thus implying a faith in magic by contagion.

Under the heading of Perfume, which includes one case of burning incense, all of the accounts suggest a conviction on the part of the students that association with success has the magical power to produce success. One woman wears the perfume that she wore when she met her boyfriend (a lucky event)—"I feel it brings me good luck, as it was luck that brought us together."

Hair is felt by our sample population to possess magical qualities both by its presence and by its absence. One student always has his hair cut short before an exam to permit, as he says, "knowledge to flow freely around my head." Another student, like Sampson, always allows his hair to grow long before exams "in order to keep the knowledge in."

The general impression is that certain favorite items provide a "security blanket" even if students can only see them (e.g., at the front of the room on the floor) and not actually handle them during the examination. Some "special pens" have written previous successful examinations and, without them, students would have less confidence in their ability to do well. Books and notes, although strictly prohibited from use during the exam, are often placed in heaps at the front and along the walls of the room, where students can see them. Many students claim that, in merely looking at the books, "summaries come up through the covers" to them. One student said that on the infrequent occasions she is allowed to take her books with her to her seat, she puts them on the floor and then puts her feet on them. She swears that the knowledge comes up to her through her legs. She adds the disclaimer that she is not crazy and that "it is true."

The magical properties of certain foods or food eaten in a special way at a special time or bought from some particular vendor—all have been claimed to bring good luck. One student insists that the purchase of a *carrot muffin* (no other kind) at the "*patty wagon*" (no other vendor) on the way to the examination room is most potent. Failure to secure the right muffin at the right place is an ill omen for her. Another student insists that on examination days she has to have the following breakfast in the following manner: one sausage placed vertically on the left of the plate and beside it two eggs sunny side up to make the configuration "100" (percent).

Examples of Lucky Locations are specific zones of the examination room and may include the back, sides, front, or middle. Students arrive early to secure these Lucky Locations because to sit anywhere else is to court confusion and disaster. Some students insist on a specific seat number that has proved lucky in the past.

Miscellaneous Items include the usual rabbit's feet, dice, coins, as well as tiny teddy bears, kangaroos, and other cuddly toys. One young medical student, very much a positivist in other areas of her life, must, like Christopher Robin, have "Roo" along when she writes her examinations. A young male student is reluctant to write an exam unless he has "found" a coin, which he takes as a sign of "luck." He searches for a coin on the day of the exam, often using up precious study time by "scrounging around bus stops" until he is successful, even at the risk of being late. Another student carries around a lock of his ex-girlfriend's hair in the hope that her extraordinary brightness will illuminate his own efforts.

Unlucky, Tabooed Items

Unlucky Items, interestingly enough, often turn out to be Oldies and Oddities once thought to be lucky but which have failed the owner and so become Tabooed Items. For example, a pink shirt (not the same one mentioned earlier) that had been a lucky talisman was found to be unlucky and thus shunned ever after. What is more, any other student at the same exam who wore a pink shirt was also to be shunned. Another example is the student who reported that in high school he once "crammed" for an exam at home the same day he was to write it and, when he was hungry, heated up a frozen TV dinner. He did unusually well on that exam, so he repeated the pattern of "cramming" at home the day of the exam and eating frozen waffles for breakfast and a TV dinner for lunch. However, when this student arrived at the university he found that studying only on the day of the exam was woefully inadequate and his performance was dreadful. Instead of changing his study habits he changed his "faith" in his lucky food: "It was to the point that even if I ate a whole freezer full of frozen food I would still do poorly on the exam. . . . I not only stopped eating frozen TV dinners before exams, I now make a point of always avoiding them."

MAGICAL BEHAVIORS

Turning now to Magical Behaviors, by far the most prevalent practices—whether directed toward self or others, whether lucky or unlucky—are those which could be termed rituals. In turn, these rituals can be subclassified as secular or religious.

Behaviors Directed Toward Self Prescribed for Luck

Examples of Secular Rituals Directed Toward Self include: knocking on the exam room door three times before entering the room (cf. knocking on wood); stepping over the threshold of the exam room with the right foot first (right in both senses); and making a circuit of the exam building, whatever the weather. However, [B]ehaviors Directed Toward Self Prescribed For Luck consist almost entirely of prayer, even in cases where students by their own admission are not particularly religious. Such students nevertheless express a dread of offending God, particularly around examination time, and become compulsively scrupulous in their prayer life and penitent if they forget this duty. There is also, at exam time, an emphasis on virtuous behavior, particularly toward members of the immediate family, but often also even toward people met on the street.

Another example of Behavior Directed Toward Self Prescribed for Luck involves students who report that being well groomed contributes to good performance. This in itself may not be magical even by our broad definition. However, when one student states that she puts special care into the manicuring of the three

fingers that hold her pen, this begins to seem like magic, certainly the *imitative magic* described by Frazer (i.e., polished fingernails produce polished answers).

Behaviors Directed Toward Others Prescribed for Luck

The category, Behaviors Prescribed For Luck Directed Toward Others, might better be described as behavior required of others by the student. Examples of this are students who insist that before leaving for an examination they be wished good luck by various members of their families according to a formula of specific wording and at a high volume. Quite often it is not sufficient for the formula of the wishes to be secular; they must be invoked by prayer. "At the moment before I walk out of the door I make sure that my parents wish me good luck and especially add 'God Bless You.' The good luck part I could probably do without, but not hearing 'God Bless You' leaves me feeling I'm not getting all the help I could for an exam." In some cases the others who are expected to tender good luck wishes are non-human others. For one student, it was essential for her dog to sit upon his haunches, offer a paw, and "woof" her good luck.

Tabooed Behaviors Directed Toward Others

Secular examples of this include refraining from sexual intercourse even, in some cases, by married partners; refraining from discussing the exam, particularly joking about it; and, above all, in this context, avoiding well-wishing. This is particularly interesting since it seems to contradict the notion of imitative magic that we saw in the case of the student with the manicured pen fingers. Some students avoid others, even lovers and spouses, who are liable to wish them luck. One student who followed this taboo emphatically avowed that he did not believe in luck. He was nevertheless very upset if someone wished him good luck, and he therefore went out of his way to avoid being so wished.

TOWARD A THEORY

On the basis of our information it appears that student magic can be thought of as being at one end of a continuum that began with preliterate magic and emerged through other forms such as those practiced by soldiers in warfare, miners, and sports competitors. At the preliterate-magic end of the continuum, magic is a communal, cooperative enterprise in which the participants have shared meanings in regard to the practices and are motivated by a strong collectivity orientation. Among the soldiers, miners, and athletes, magic is still practiced in a community in which there are, to some extent, shared meanings and also, to some extent but considerably less than among preliterate peoples, a collectivity orientation. When we come to students writing exams, we have reached the near end of the continuum of magical practices. Here we find magic practiced individually and in isolation, without shared meaning (even, to some extent, with contradictory meanings), and completely self-oriented in its motivation. In an attempt to understand these differences along the continuum, it might be suggested that for preliterate peoples living in a less complex and completely homogeneous society, one would expect shared meanings in a way that is not to be expected among heterogeneous, largely anonymous groups of students in contemporary urban society. However, even in contemporary society it is reasonable to expect that, within a group of soldiers who have been trained together to act in unison and whose very lives depend upon the actions of every other one in the group, there would tend to be more of a collectivity orientation than among university students writing exams (although perhaps not as much as within more homogeneous, preliterate groupings). The phenomenon of shared meanings would also be expected to be in an intermediate position, since even though soldiers, miners, and athletes are the products of a heterogeneous socialization compared to preliterate peoples, they nevertheless work together and constitute communities to a greater degree than do exam-writing students. As such, this "middle category" has developed many well-known agreed-upon magical rituals such as "break a leg," "three on a match," not referring to a "winning streak," and "the fatal last shift." In effect then, the particular aspects of student magic that we described earlier, which may seem atypical of magic in the past and in some ways inexplicable, may be partially explained in terms of increasing societal complexity and heterogeneity as well as shifts in cultural values.

In sum, as society moves from preliterate to contemporary, increasing in complexity as well as scientific sophistication, we might expect magic to be transformed from: (1) being publicly performed to being privately and individually performed; (2) being culturally transmitted to being spontaneously generated; (3) being completely shared by the whole community to being utilized privately by individuals; and (4) being unvaryingly uniform and consistent in its rituals to being highly variable and even contradictory. Clearly, with an ideal-type polar construct of this kind, no actual case of magic (including student magic) will in all respects conform to the characteristics of either pole. The burden of this article, however, is that students' magic falls rather toward the latter end of each of these four continua.

ACKNOWLEDGMENT

This article is a revised version of a paper presented at the Qualitative Research Conference/ Ethnographic Research. We thank D. Rennie and R. Clifton for their comments on an earlier draft of this article.

REFERENCES

Albas, D., and C. Albas. 1984. *Student Life and Exams: Stresses and Coping Strategies.* Dubuque, IA: Kendall/Hunt.

Frazer, J. 1958. The Golden Bough: *A Study in Magic and Religion.* New York: Macmillan.

Gmelch, G. 1971. "Baseball Magic." *Society* 8(8): 39–41.

Henslin, J. 1967. "Craps and Magic." *The American Journal of Sociology* 73: 316–330.

Homans, G. 1941. "Anxiety and Ritual: The Theories of Malinowski and Radcliffe-Brown." *American Anthropologist* 43: 164–172.

Jahoda, G. 1969. *The Psychology of Superstition.* London: The Penguin Press.

Stouffer, S., A. Lumsdaine, M. Lumsdaine, R. Williams, Jr., M. Smith, I. Janis, and L. Cottrell, Jr. 1949. *Studies in Social Psychology in World War II: The American Soldier, Combat and Its Aftermath.* Princeton, NJ: Princeton University Press.

Wilson, W. 1942. "Miners' Superstitions." *Life and Letters Today* 32: 86–93.

PART 5
Socialization

Chapter 12

The Civilizing of Genie

MAYA PINES

Cases of children who were deprived of social interaction while they were young have long fascinated sociologists. Some investigators believe that by examining how such children develop in later life, one can assess the relative importance of "nurture" versus "nature" in making us human. Others want to determine if there is some "critical period" in child development during which, say, language must be learned if it is to be learned effectively. Both themes are apparent in this selection. This case, however, raises other issues as well. Research on "Genie" was brought to a halt by a lawsuit (filed by Genie's mother), which alleged that investigators had made Genie endure "unreasonable and outrageous testing" for purposes other than treatment. As you read through this selection, determine for yourself if the researchers seem more interested in helping Genie "get better" or in using Genie as "data."

Only a few cases are recorded of human beings who have grown up without any real contact with other humans. So rare is the phenomenon that when a 12-year-old "wild boy" was found in the forest of Aveyron in 18th-century France, the government ordered him brought to Paris to be examined by doctors in an institution for deaf-mutes. There he came under the care of the physician Jean Itard, who also acted as the boy's tutor. Itard left detailed records of his experience, which was later dramatized in the 1970 movie *The Wild Child*. Although the boy was not deaf, and despite Itard's work, the child never learned to speak.

In 1970, a wild child was found in California: a girl of 13 who had been isolated in a small room and had not been spoken to by her parents since infancy. "Genie," as she was later dubbed to protect her privacy by the psycholinguists who tested her, could not stand erect. At the time, she was unable to speak; she could only whimper.

The case came to light when Genie's 50-year-old mother ran away from her 70-year-old husband after a violent quarrel and took the child along. The mother was partially blind and applied for public assistance. The social worker in the welfare office took one look at Genie and called her supervisor, who called the police. Genie was sent to the Los Angeles Children's Hospital for tests. Charges of willful abuse were filed against both her parents, according to the *Lost Angeles Times*. On the day he was due to appear in court, however, Genie's father shot himself to death. He left a note in which he wrote, "The world will never understand."

The discovery of Genie aroused intense curiosity among psychologists, linguists, neurologists, and others who study brain development. They were eager to know what Genie's mental level was at the time she was found and whether she would be capable of developing her faculties. "It's a terribly important case," says Harlan Lane, a psycholinguist at Northeastern

Source: "The Civilizing of Genie," by Maya Pines, *Psychology Today,* September 1981. Reprinted by permission of the author.

University who wrote *The Wild Boy of Aveyron*. "Since our morality doesn't allow us to conduct deprivation experiments with human beings, these unfortunate people are all we have to go on."

Genie is now 24 years old. Through years of rehabilitation and special training, she has been observed and repeatedly tested. Hundreds of videotapes record her progress. She has been the subject of several journal articles and a book. Since the book was published in 1977, additional studies have brought into focus some of the issues raised by Genie's case. Far from settling any scientific controversies, she has provided fresh ammunition for arguments on both sides of a major issue: is there a "critical period" in a child's development during which, if language acquisition is not stimulated or encouraged, it may be impaired later on or not emerge at all? She has inspired a California researcher who worked with her, Susan Curtiss, to develop a controversial hypothesis about how language learning affects the two hemispheres of the brain. Genie has also stirred up debate about the relationship between language and other mental abilities. As a result, new research is now in progress on the surprising language ability of some mentally retarded children.

As described in Curtiss's book, *Genie: A Psycholinguistic Study of a Modern-Day "Wild Child"* (Academic Press), Genie is living proof of human resilience. It is surprising that she survived at all. Her father apparently hated children and tried to strangle Genie's mother while she was pregnant with her first child. According to Curtiss's book, when an earlier baby girl was born, he put the child in the garage because he couldn't stand her crying; the baby died of pneumonia at two-and-a-half months. A second child, a boy, died two days after birth, allegedly from choking on his own mucus. A third child was rescued and cared for by his grandmother when he was three years old and is still alive. Genie, the fourth child, was denied such help, however, because shortly after she was born, her grandmother was hit by a truck and killed.

From the age of 20 months, when her family moved into her grandmother's house, until she was 13 and a half, Genie lived in nearly total isolation. Curtiss's book, and newspaper reports, describe Genie's life at the time: naked and restrained by a harness that her father had fashioned, she was left to sit on her potty seat day after day. She could move only her hands and feet. She had nothing to do. At night, when she was not forgotten, she was put into a sort of straitjacket and caged in a crib that had wire-mesh sides and an overhead cover. She was often hungry.

If she made any noise, her father beat her. "He never spoke to her," wrote Curtiss. "He made barking sounds [and] he growled at her. . . . Her mother was terrified of him—and besides, she was too blind to take much care of Genie. The task fell largely on Genie's brother, who, following his father's instructions, did not speak to Genie either. He fed her hurriedly and in silence, mostly milk and baby foods. There was little for Genie to listen to. Her mother and brother spoke in low voices for fear of her father.

When Genie arrived in Children's Hospital in November 1970, she was a pitiful, malformed, incontinent, unsocialized, and severely malnourished creature. Although she was beginning to show signs of pubescence, she weighed only 59 pounds. She could not straighten her arms or legs. She did not know how to chew. She salivated a great deal and spent much of her time spitting. And she was eerily silent.

Various physicians, psychologists, and therapists were brought in to examine her during those first months. Shortly after Genie was admitted as a patient, she was given the Vineland Social Maturity Scale and the Pre-school Attainment Record, on which she scored as low as normal one-year-olds. At first, she seemed to recognize only her own name and the word *sorry*. After a while, she began to say two phrases that she used as if they were single words, in a ritualized way: *stopit* and *nomore*.

Psychologists at the hospital did not really know how much she understood. Nor did they know how to evaluate whatever language she had: to what degree did it deviate from the standard pattern? They eventually asked Victoria A. Fromkin, a UCLA psycholinguist, to study Genie's language abilities. Fromkin brought along a graduate student, Susan Curtiss (now an assistant professor of linguistics at UCLA), who became so fascinated by Genie that she devoted much of the next seven years of her life to researching the girl's linguistic development.

Working with Genie was not an easy task. Although she had learned to walk with a jerky motion and became more or less toilet trained during her first seven months at Children's Hospital, Genie still had many disconcerting habits. She salivated and spat constantly, so much so that her body and clothing were filled with spit and "reeked of a foul odor," as Curtiss recounts. When excited or agitated, she urinated, leaving her companion to deal with the results. And she masturbated excessively.

Nevertheless, Genie was decidedly human, and her delight at discovering the world—as well as her obvious progress—made the struggle worthwhile. When Curtiss started working with Genie, she began by simply spending time with her or taking her to visit places, in order to establish a relationship. She took Genie to the supermarket, where Genie walked around the store and examined the meats and the plastic containers with some curiosity. Every house seemed exciting to Genie, who had spent so much of her life cooped up in one room; on walks she would often go up to the front doors of houses, hoping that someone would open the door and let her in.

During her first seven months of freedom, Genie had learned to recognize many new words—probably hundreds by the time Curtiss started investigating her knowledge of language systematically in June 1971. And she had begun to speak. On a visit with Curtiss to the home of one of the therapists, Genie eagerly explored every room, then picked up a decorator pillow; when asked what it was, she replied "pillow." Asked if she wanted to see the family cat, Genie

replied, "No. No. Cat," and shook her head vehemently. Most of the time, however, she said nothing.

At first Genie spoke only in one-word utterances, as toddlers do when they start to talk. Then in July of 1971, she began to string two words together on her own, not just while imitating what somebody else had said. She said "big teeth," "little marble," "two hand." A little later she produced some verbs: "Curtiss come," "Want milk." In November of the same year she progressed to occasional three-word strings: "small two cup," "white clear box."

Unlike normal children, however, Genie never asked questions, despite many efforts to train her to do so. Nor did she understand much grammar. And her speech development was abnormally slow. A few weeks after normal children reach the two-word stage, their speech generally develops so rapidly and explosively that it is difficult to keep track of or describe. No such explosion occurred for Genie. Four years after she began to put words together, her speech remained, for the most part, like a somewhat garbled telegram.

While Genie did not speak in a fully developed, normal way, she acquired some language after she was discovered. That contradicted one aspect of the theory that says language can be learned only during a critical period between two years of age and puberty.

On the other hand, Genie failed to learn the kind of grammatical principles that, according to Noam Chomsky, distinguish the language of human beings from that of animals. For example, she could not grasp the difference between various pronouns, or between active and passive verbs. In that sense, she appeared to suffer from having passed the critical period.

Her language deficiencies could not be attributed to a lack of teachers. Though at first it did not seem possible that she could ever attend any school, within a few months of her arrival at Children's Hospital she began going to nursery classes for normal children. She soon transferred to a special elementary school for handicapped children. Next, she spent several years in a city high school for the mentally retarded. Outside school, a speech therapist worked with her consistently for many years. Meanwhile, one of the therapists and his wife took Genie into their own home to live with their two teenage sons, a teenage daughter, a dog, and a cat. They tried to teach Genie to trace with her fingers the shape of sandpaper letters, to recognize words or work with Play-Doh, as well as deal with the demands of family life. She apparently had no trouble writing her name, and drew a number of pictures based on experiences she had had.

Nor did Genie's deficiencies appear to be inborn. Although many details of her early history are unclear, and Genie's mother has given contradictory accounts of them, Genie seems to have been a normal baby. She suffered from an Rh blood incompatibility, but received an exchange transfusion one day after birth. During her first year of life, before she was isolated from the rest of her family, she may have been on the road to language, since her mother reported that she heard Genie saying words right after she was locked up.

The gift of language has always been viewed as distinctively human, or even as proof of the existence of the soul. Its source has mystified human beings for millennia. In the 13th century, Frederick II, Emperor of the Holy Roman Empire, decided to perform an experiment to find out what kind of speech children would develop if left to their own devices in their early years; he wondered whether it would be Hebrew, Greek, Latin, or the language of their parents. He selected a few newborns and decreed that no one speak to them. The babies were suckled and bathed as usual, but songs and lullabies were strictly forbidden. Frederick II never got his answer, however, for the children all died. The experiment was never repeated.

In the early 19th century, Itard tried desperately to teach Victor, the wild boy of Aveyron, to speak. He began when Victor was about 12 years old—around the time of puberty, as with Genie.

However, Victor never spoke more than a few single words, perhaps because of an injury to his throat, where he had a scar.

Chomsky believes that human beings are born with a unique competence for language, built into their brains. But he adds that the innate mechanisms that underlie this competence must be activated by exposure to language at the proper time, which Chomsky speculates must occur before puberty.

Among human beings, four-week-old babies can recognize the difference between some 40 consonants that are used in human languages, as shown by how their sucking and heartbeats change when different consonant sounds are presented by audiotape. That ability seems to be innate, since babies respond to many more consonants than are used in their parents' language—English, for example, has only 24 consonant sounds, yet babies of English-speaking parents react to the consonants present in Japanese. Babies lose that ability as they grow up. By the age of six, when children enter school, their ability to hear the difference between sounds to which they have not been exposed in their own language is severely reduced. Feature detectors responsible for recognizing about a dozen consonant sounds have so far been inferred to exist in the human brain. They need to be triggered by the environment, however; if not, they appear to atrophy.

Had something similar happened to Genie's brain? Curtiss raised that possibility when she reported that Genie, unlike 99 percent of right-handed people, seemed to use the right hemisphere of her brain for language. Since the left hemisphere is predisposed for language in right-handed people, that could account for some of the strange features of Genie's language development.

On tests of "dichotic listening," for example, which involve presenting different sounds to both ears simultaneously and asking the subject to react to them, "Genie's left ear outperformed her right ear on every occasion," Curtiss reports in her book. (Sound from the left ear is linked to the right hemisphere; from the right ear, to the left hemisphere.) Furthermore, "the degree of ear advantage is abnormal: Genie's left ear performed at 100 percent accuracy, while the right ear performed at a level below chance." That indicated Genie was using her right hemisphere as consistently as do people in whom, because of damage or surgery, only the right hemisphere is functioning.

When Genie's brain-wave patterns were examined at the UCLA Brain Research Institute—first as she listened to different sentences, then as she looked at pictures of faces—the data suggested that Genie used her right hemisphere for both language and nonlanguage functions. Genie also proved to be particularly good at tasks involving the right hemisphere, such as recognizing faces. On the Mooney Faces Test, which requires the subject to distinguish real from "false" faces in which features are misplaced and to point out several features on each face, Genie's performance was "the highest reported in the literature for either child or adult," according to Curtiss.

From the very beginning, Genie's vocabulary revealed an extraordinary attention to the visual world, which is the special province of the right hemisphere—to color, shape, and size. All of her first two-word phrases were about static objects. While normal children usually start talking about people and actions or about the relations between people and objects, Genie spoke primarily about the attributes of things: "black shoe," "lot bread."

While summarizing the numerous tests made on Genie until 1979, Curtiss noted that Genie's performance had increased consistently over the years. For example, on the Leiter International Performance Scale, which was developed for use with deaf children and does not require verbal instructions, she had an IQ of 38 in 1971, an IQ of 53 in 1972, an IQ of 65 in 1974, and an IQ of 74 in 1977. However, she had made much less progress on tasks governed primarily by the left hemisphere. Even at the age of 20, she still performed at a three-year-old level on tests of

auditory memory (a left-hemisphere task); she scored at a 6- to 12-year-old level on tests of visual memory (which tap both hemispheres), and at an adult level on tests of Gestalt perception (a right-hemisphere task).

The theory of language learning recently offered by Curtiss is an attempt to explain Genie's dependence on her right hemisphere. Possibly, Curtiss wrote in a paper on cognitive linguistics published by UCLA, the acquisition of language is what triggers the normal pattern of hemispheric specialization. Therefore, if language is not acquired at the appropriate time, "the cortical tissue normally committed for language and related abilities may functionally atrophy," Curtiss wrote. That would mean that there are critical periods for the development of the left hemisphere. If such development fails, later learning may be limited to the right hemisphere.

Obviously Genie has many problems besides her lack of syntax or her dependence on the right hemisphere of her brain. During her most formative years—her entire childhood—she was malnourished, abused, unloved, bereft of any toys or companionship. Naturally, she is strange in many ways. Yet her language deficits remain particularly striking since she often found means of explaining what was important to her. She used gestures if necessary (starting in 1974, she received regular lessons in American Sign Language to complement her spoken language). Once she wanted an egg-shaped container that held panty hose that was made of chrome-colored plastic. She signaled her desire by making the shape of an egg with her hands, and then pointing to many other things with a chromium finish. In her book, Curtiss describes how Genie occasionally used her limited language to remember her past and to tell about details of her confinement. "Father hit arm. Big wood. Genie cry," she said once. Another time, when Curtiss took her into the city to browse through shops, Genie said, "Genie happy."

In 1978, Genie's mother became her legal guardian. During all the years of Genie's rehabilitation, her mother had also received help. An eye operation restored her sight, and a social worker tried to improve her behavior toward Genie. Genie's mother had never been held legally responsible for the child's inhuman treatment. Charges of child abuse were dismissed in 1970, when her lawyer argued that she "was, herself, a victim of the same psychotic individual"—her husband. There was "nothing to show purposeful or willful cruelty," he said.

Nevertheless, for many years the court assigned a guardian for Genie. Shortly after Genie's mother was named guardian, she astounded the therapists and researchers who had worked with Genie by filing a suit against Curtiss and the Children's Hospital among others—on behalf of herself and her daughter—in which she charged that they had disclosed private and confidential information concerning Genie and her mother for "prestige and profit" and had subjected Genie to "unreasonable and outrageous" testing, not for treatment, but to exploit Genie for personal and economic benefits. According to the *Los Angeles Times*, the lawyer who represents Genie's mother estimated that the actual damages could total $500,000.

The case has not yet come to court, but in the two years since it was filed, Genie has been completely cut off from the professionals at Children's Hospital and UCLA. Since she is too old to be in a foster home, she apparently is living in a board-and-care home for adults who cannot live alone. The *Los Angeles Times* reported that as of 1979 her mother was working as a domestic servant. All research on Genie's language and intellectual development has come to a halt. However, the research Genie stimulated goes on. Much of it concerns the relationship between linguistic ability and cognitive development, a subject to which Genie has made a significant contribution.

Apart from Chomsky and his followers, who believe that fundamental language ability is innate and unrelated to intelligence, most psychologists assume that the development of language is tied to—and emerges from—the development of nonverbal intelligence, as described by Piaget. However, Genie's obvious nonverbal intelligence—her use of tools, her drawings, her knowledge of causality, her mental maps of space—did not lead her to an equivalent competence in the grammar normal children acquire by the age of five.

Puzzled by the discrepancy between Genie's cognitive abilities and her language deficits, Curtiss and Fromkin wondered whether they could find people with the opposite pattern—who have normal language ability despite cognitive deficits. That would be further evidence of the independence of language from certain aspects of cognition.

In recent months, they have found several such persons among the mentally retarded, as well as among victims of Turner's syndrome, a chromosomal defect that produces short stature, cardiac problems, infertility, and specific learning difficulties in females. With help from the National Science Foundation (which had also funded some of Curtiss's research on Genie), Fromkin and Curtiss have identified and started working with some children and adolescents who combine normal grammatical ability with serious defects in logical reasoning, sequential ability, or other areas of thinking.

"You can't explain their unimpaired syntax on the basis of their impaired cognitive development," says Curtiss, who is greatly excited by this new developmental profile. She points out that in the youngsters studied, the purely grammatical aspect of language—which reflects Chomsky's language universals—seems to be isolated from the semantic aspect of language, which is more tied to cognition. "Language no longer looks like a uniform package," she declares. "This is the first experimental data on the subject." Thus the ordeal of an abused child may help us understand some of the most puzzling but important aspects of our humanity.

Chapter 13

The Concept of "Stages" in Piaget's Theory

ROLF E. MUUSS

Once upon a time, children were seen to be little more than imperfect adults. Under this view, socialization was the process by which, bit by bit, children came to acquire the beliefs and values typical of the adults in their culture. A revolution in the study of socialization occurred in the early 20th century, however, when a number of theorists—notably Sigmund Freud, George Herbert Mead, and Jean Piaget—began to claim that socialization proceeds in separate and discrete stages. The general idea is that while different individuals might proceed through these stages at different speeds, all individuals had to pass through the earlier stages to reach the later ones. These different theorists, however, had quite different ideas about what stages were central to the development of young children. In retrospect, Piaget's theory of "stages"—reviewed in this selection—has likely influenced the empirical study of childhood socialization more than any other.

For Piaget, developmental stages simply mean that a sequential progression in the cognitive structures, which underly problem-solving operations, takes place. Thus, stages emerge in an orderly, invariant sequential pattern, and no stage can be skipped. The earlier stages provide essential building material that the individual integrates and transforms in the process of moving to the next higher level. Significant is that the problem-solving skills that characterize a given stage are qualitatively distinguishable from those found in stages that precede as well as those that succeed it, e.g., elementary school children can solve the same problem when presented in concrete terms that high school students can solve when presented abstractly. And it is this qualitative change that elevates Piaget's theory from simply a description of age-related changes in reasoning to a stage theory. For example, adolescents deal with learning tasks and with their world in substantially different, more abstract, ways than elementary school children because their cognitive structure is different. The appeal of Piaget's stages is that they identify a comprehensive system of different features in the developmental progression of reasoning ability. Furthermore, the developmental progression identified by Piaget is characteristic of most individuals found in a broadly defined age range. The idea of a "stage" does not negate the well-known fact of the existence of intra-individual, interindividual, and intercultural differences; however, it does mean that a given stage-defining operation follows the same sequence in all individuals. In other words, each higher level stage integrates and builds upon the accomplishments and the underlying structure of the preceding stage.

The speed with which an individual progresses through these stages depends upon intellectual ability, educational experiences, cultural and social context, as well as other factors.

Source: Rolf E. Muuss, *Theories of Adolescence,* 6th Edition, McGraw-Hill, 1996. Reprinted by permission of the McGraw-Hill Companies.

However, the sequential progression through the stages itself is not a function of these factors, but is invariant. Children who possess low intelligence, come from preindustrial cultures or from dysfunctional families, or have limited educational experiences may progress at a slower rate and may not reach the final stages. The age levels suggested for these stages are not norms, but allow for considerable variations, and therefore, should be treated as approximations.

The landmarks of Piaget's stage-dependent theory, based on major qualitative advances in cognitive structure, are: sensorimotor, preoperational, concrete operational, and formal operational stages. Originally, the theory focused on infancy and childhood but was later expanded to include adolescence. The stage-dependent theory is the core of Piaget's initial systematic theory of development, and is by far the most widely known and most often discussed part of his theory.

THE SENSORIMOTOR STAGE

The *sensorimotor stage of development* (from birth to age 2) is subdivided into six developmental phases. The first phase (birth to 1 month), the *reflex phase*, consists primarily of exercising inborn reflexes such as the sucking reflex, which, as it becomes modified to meet the demands of different situations, becomes the sucking schema. During the second phase (1 to 4 months), which Piaget calls the phase of *primary circular reactions*, reflexes are slowly replaced by voluntary movements. Children may tirelessly practice an emerging schema, such as grasping, since they are motivated by "function pleasure"—a concept quite different from the behavioristic notion of "drive reduction" or "reinforcement." In the third phase (4 to 8 months), that of *secondary circular reactions*, infants begin to pursue objects and events unrelated to themselves—for example, following slow movements of an attractive toy. Or, if an infant learns through trial and error to grasp a cord and make a bell jingle, he or she

may repeat such behavior. That such an action can be repeated is evidence of the beginning of intentionality and even an incipient form of goal-directed behavior. The fourth phase (8 to 12 months), that of *coordination of secondary schemata*, is characterized by the emergence of an understanding of means-ends relationships. The child reaches for a box in order to obtain the toy that is inside. When the child begins to search for a toy hidden under a blanket, the concept of "object permanence" is beginning to emerge. During the fifth phase (12 to 18 months), *tertiary circular reactions*, the concept of "object permanence" becomes more stable. The child will search for and find the object even though in the process of hiding it, it may have been moved through a series of displacements. The last of the six phases (18 to 24 months) is that of *internalization of sensorimotor schemata*. The child begins to use foresight and symbolic representation in solving sensorimotor problems. For the first time, the child may investigate whether a hole is big enough before attempting to push an object through it, thus giving evidence that the strictly sensorimotor approach to problem solving is being replaced by thought. The progression from the primarily sensorimotor approach to life to the beginning use of thought is the qualitative difference between this and the preoperational stage.

THE PREOPERATIONAL STAGE

The second period of development (2 to 7 years), called the *preoperational stage*, is a transition period from the predominantly egocentric and sensorimotor stage of early childhood to rudimentary forms of social behavior and the beginning of conceptual thought. Children learn new concepts on the basis of direct, first-hand perceptual experiences—that is, they are still at the mercy of what they see and hear. Reality is what they perceive; other alternatives are not available to them. When a chocolate bar is broken into pieces, they think there is more chocolate, because the pieces look like more candy than the solid bar.

Preoperational children are too dependent on sensory impressions and they do not yet comprehend the *principle of conservation:* a given quantity remains the same, even though the way that quantity has been arranged has changed. One commonly used illustration is the pouring of water from a low but wide glass into a tall but narrow glass in full view of children. Even though they actually observe the water being poured, preoperational children think there is more water in the tall glass because it looks like more. They do not think in terms of a hierarchy of classes and supraclasses. A child may maintain, "We are not in Baltimore; we are in Maryland," without comprehending that one can be included in the other.

The judgments of preoperational children are still intuitive and subjective, but they are beginning to deal with more complex issues. Preoperational children manipulate objects, tools, and toys effectively, express thoughts, and ask questions. Nevertheless, accurate judgment and thought is limited by several factors:

1. Basically, children are still heavily dependent on sensory experiences.
2. They cannot consider two or more dimensions at the same time, rather, they focus on one aspect and consequently neglect to consider the other. A corollary is their directional thinking, also referred to as one-way mapping or one-way functioning, which interferes with mental reversibility.
3. They cannot rearrange or reorganize information in their minds.
4. They are quite limited in their ability to take the point of view of another person.

THE CONCRETE OPERATIONAL STAGE

At approximately age 7 or 8, a major qualitative shift in children's conceptual development takes place. They are now beginning to perform *concrete logical operations* in their mind. This period (from 7 or 8 to approximately puberty) is referred to as the *operational stage in logical thinking*.

During the operational stage, using concrete content, the child learns to master basic logical operations. "Concrete" in this context does not mean that the child can deal only with tangible objects, but that any problem has to be tied to reality. The major limitation evident in the thinking at this level is the child's inability to think abstractly about a problem. Since concrete operations can be performed mentally, overt trial and error becomes unnecessary. For the first time, the child begins to think in accordance with a model of logical reasoning. The important elements of concrete logical operations are:

1. *The logic of classes*, which is based on an understanding of whether or not an object belongs or does not belong in a given class. This enables children to solve problems of classification. They become concerned with the relationship between the parts and the whole. Understanding and classifying parts that belong together help children to gain a better understanding of the whole, the supraclass. Their ability to hold several pieces of information in mind and to reverse their thinking enables them to understand hierarchy of classes and supraclasses.
2. *The logic of relations*, which makes it possible to order and organize several objects in relationship to one another, according to specific criteria. In a test situation, the child is asked to order a series of objects, such as dolls or sticks, according to their size. Such an "operation of serialization" is similar to the classification of a hierarchy, since it involves some understanding of the structure of the whole: "There is no class without classification; there is no systematic relation without serialization" (Piaget, 1962: 126). The logic of relations receives elaboration when the child is asked to set

two series of objects into correspondence with one another. For example, matching a series of dolls of increasing size with a corresponding set of hats or sticks. Possessing the "logic of relations," the operational child is able to organize objects according to their size, height, or weight as long as objects are presented concretely. Not until adolescence can such operations be performed abstractly.

3. *The principle of conservation*, to which Piaget attached great importance, is probably the most extensively researched cognitive operation. Realizing that changing a clay ball into a sausage or flattening it out into a pancake does not change its mass, weight, or volume, the operational child now begins to develop an understanding of the principle of conservation.

At the same time that the concrete operations emerge, the child's language, which until approximately age 7 had been predominantly egocentric, has become primarily sociocentric. Sociocentric language implies a genuine effort to understand other people and to communicate thoughts objectively. Research does not substantiate the dramatic transformation from egocentric to sociocentric speech as neatly as the shift from preoperational to operational thought suggests, but research does support the more general idea that, with the beginning of schooling and with increasing age, the proportion of egocentric speech decreases and that of sociocentric speech increases.

The change from egocentric to sociocentric thought is not only reflected in children's language, but permeates their thought processes as well. Sociocentric children can place themselves in the situation of other persons and take those persons' points of view.

Piaget identifies the properties of concrete operations and applies the term *elementary groupings*, or *group-like structures*, to the different ways in which a child's thought process can manipulate classes and relations. Since Piaget postulates a direct relationship between logic and a child's cognitive processes, the concepts he introduces are conveyed in terms of logic and mathematics. An important set of four concrete group-like structures, follows:

Combinativity. Two or more classes can be combined into one larger, more comprehensive class. For example, all men and all women equal all adults. Logical relationships, such as A is larger than B and B is larger than C; therefore, A is larger than C, can be comprehended. The ability to understand classes and to combine subclasses into supraclasses is essential to assemble or disassemble a hierarchy of classifications.

Reversibility. Every operation is reversible. Every operation has an opposite operation that reverses it. Supraclasses can be taken apart so that the effect of combining subclasses is reversed: All adults except all women equals all men. The child's ability to reverse thought processes is an important indicator of cognitive development.

Associativity. Children whose operations have become associative can reach a goal in various ways. They can make detours in thought, but in such a fashion that the results obtained by these different routes remain the same. For example, $(3 + 6) + 4 = 13$, and $6 + (3 + 4) = 13$.

Identity or nullifiability. An operation that is combined with its opposite becomes nullified. Illustrations of nullifiability in mathematics are: give 3 and take 3 away results in null, or 5 times X divided by 5 equals X. If I drive one mile west and one mile east, I am where I started; my actions are nullified.

Primary groupings make combinativity, reversibility, and associativity in thought possible and thus aid a child in achieving a structural equilibrium that is considerably more mobile and flexible than the thought process of a preoperational child. Thus, the approach to problem solving is no longer intuitive or impulsive but rational and logical. However, reasoning is not yet integrated into a single total system of interrelated prepositions.

THE FORMAL OPERATIONS STAGE

The final stage of cognitive development of Piaget's theory is the *stage of formal operations*, which typically emerges during adolescence. Piaget's formal operations include, among others, the use of propositional thinking, combinatorial analysis, proportional reasoning, probabilistic reasoning, correlational reasoning, and abstract reasoning. The concept *formal* implies that what matters is form and logic rather than content. With the progression through these stages, mental operations become increasingly more abstract, more complex, more logical, and the boundaries of the mental structures become more permeable and thus, provide thought process with greater flexibility.

Adolescents not only think beyond the present but analytically reflect about their own thinking. Piaget calls this type of reasoning "second-degree thinking"; it involves operations that produce "thinking about thinking," "statements about statements," or more significantly, "operations on operations." Such operations allow a set of all possible combinations to emerge, which then make possible the construction of new knowledge out of previously acquired knowledge by way of propositional thinking. Thus, the interrelationship of actual observation, learning and vicarious learning, and the layering upon layering of knowledge eventually makes hypothetical reasoning possible and allows the construction of theories.

In their thoughts, adolescents can leave the real objective world behind and enter the world of ideas. They now can control events in their minds through logic deductions of possibilities and consequences. Even the directions of thought processes change. Preadolescents begin thinking about reality by attempting to extend thoughts toward possibility. Adolescents who have mastered formal operations begin by thinking of all logical possibilities and then considering them in a systematic fashion; reality becomes secondary to possibility because adolescents reduce reality to a subset of possibility. To emphasize this point further, one could say that, in operation thinking, reality is the foreground and possibility remains in the background. In formal operational thinking, this relationship is reversed—possibility has become the foreground and reality has become simply one of the many possibilities.

REFERENCES

Piaget, J. Three Lectures. *Bulletin of the Menninger Clinic,* 1962, 26, 120–145.

Chapter 14

Columbus and the Making of Historical Myth

BARBARA RANSBY

It's a story that most of us learned in school: A brave Christopher Columbus defied conventional wisdom, and the dangers of the Atlantic Ocean, and came to discover the New World. In this selection, Barbara Ransby compares the story of Columbus that appears in history textbooks with the historical record, and argues that, by virtue of what these textbooks emphasize and what they omit, they shape not only our view of the past but also our view of the present.

As the world approaches the quincentennial commemoration of Christopher Columbus's accidental 'discovery' of America, we are reminded that history is, in large part, a battle-ground upon which scholars and activists fight to define the lens through which we will view the past. There is also a struggle to define which historical actors will be immortalised as heroes and heroines and which events will be emblazoned into our collective memory as turning-points and historical landmarks. How the story of Christopher Columbus should be told is at the centre of one such intellectual battle. The manufactured, but widely accepted, myth of Columbus as the brave and noble visionary who set sail on an unknown course and discovered a whole new world belies the real legacy of Columbus: a bloody legacy of rape, pillage and plunder. But, it is a myth which is quite consistent with how most of US history is recounted by mainstream historians—as great deeds by great white men which resulted in great things for all humankind. More specifically, it is a myth which celebrates imperial conquest, male supremacy and the triumph of military might as necessary components of progress and civilisation.

As examination of the Columbus myth illustrates how elites are able to justify their exploits under the guise of 'necessary evil'. Moreover, a survey of the treatment of Columbus in North American children's textbooks is a further indication of exactly how historical myths are made, and when and where the seeds of the dominant culture are planted. To assess how most Americans are introduced to the story of Columbus in grade school, I examined thirty social studies textbooks published between 1966 and 1990 by major US publishers. Many of the newer texts are currently used in public schools throughout the US, the rest were the intellectual baby food of the current generation of college students.

In the overwhelming majority of writings about Columbus, particularly in children's books, there is a simplistic celebration of Columbus as a 'great discoverer [whose] courage opened a new world to Europeans', with little or no critical commentary.[1] In the majority of more 'enlightened' texts, however, there is an uncomfortable reconciliation of Columbus, the avaricious, slave-trading pirate, with Columbus, the brave and venturesome Italian mariner who

Source: "Columbus and the Making of the Historical Myth" by Barbara Ransby, from *Race & Class*, Volume 33, January–March 1992, pages 79–86. Used by permission of the Institute of Race Relations.

paved the way for the expansion of western civilisation. Implicitly, of course, a new way could not be paved without the removal of obtrusive roadblocks to progress. Those roadblocks included millions of indigenous people who had lived on the lands Columbus supposedly discovered some 25,000 years before his expedition arrived. They were people who had names, cultures, belief systems and a history. They lived in harmony with an entire eco-system which was harshly disrupted with the arrival of European invaders in the 1490s. But elementary schoolchildren are told very little about the Taino and Carib peoples, and even less about the bloody conquest of their civilisations by the European colonisers we now celebrate as national icons. It is a conflict with which mainstream historians are quite uneasy because it does not fit neatly into the panoramic sweep of progress which is how many of them opt to characterise North American history. Many of these writers are much more comfortable quoting selectively from Columbus's journal about how he admired the gentleness and generosity of the 'Indians', carefully omitting his conclusion that their kind and calm demeanour would make them easier to exploit and enslave.

Most children's textbooks also fail to mention that Columbus actually introduced the slave trade to the Americas. When he was unsuccessful in his desperate search for gold and other natural riches in the islands of the Caribbean, he began sending human cargo back to Spain instead. Hundreds of Taino and Carib Indians were torn from their homes and families and shipped to Europe to be sold as servants and slaves in the decades after Columbus's arrival. Social studies texts, for the most part, omit, gloss over or reconstruct this ignominious episode in early American history. One text euphemistically describes the six Tainos Columbus forcibly took back to Spain on his first return trip as his 'guests'.[2] Another text, which admits that the colonisers killed thousands of Indians, still describes the system of coerced labour set up by Columbus in the following terms: 'Columbus

tried to make use of the Indians by requiring them to bring him gold and to work for his colonies.'[3] This passage seems to suggest that the native people were idle and unproductive before Columbus's arrival and required his assistance in finding 'useful' and productive work.

Ultimately, the popular myths surrounding Columbus serve as subtle, and sometimes not so subtle, justifications for both male supremacy and white supremacy. Schoolchildren are taught, through omissions, euphemisms and outright distortions, that conquest is a heroic, masculine enterprise worthy of emulation, and that, when the casualties of such conquests are uncivilised people of colour, they are expendable. Three hundred and fifty years after Columbus's initial invasion of the Caribbean, US president Andrew Jackson, himself engaged in a campaign to finish off the process of Native American genocide begun by Columbus, summed up the necessity of the early conquest in these words: 'What good man would prefer a country covered with forests and ranged by a few thousand savages to our extensive republic, studded with cities, towns, and prosperous farms . . . filled with the blessings of liberty, civilisation, and religion?'[4] According to historian Ron Takaki, during the nineteenth century, the ruling elite of the US concluded that 'white violence was a necessary partial evil for the realisation of a general good—the extension of white civilisation and the transformation of the wilderness into an agrarian society'.[5]

Most Americans know, in some vague sense, the grim fate that befell the native populations of the Caribbean islands after Columbus's advent. Within fifty years of the arrival of the European invaders, a population of over 300,000 native people was wholly decimated, with not one member surviving by 1540.[6] This was due in part to disease and displacement, but much of it was due to outright brutality and savagery on the part of the invaders, who waged genocidal wars against those they perceived as obstructions to progress. Women were raped, the environment was ravaged and, eventually, most of what had existed before was destroyed. The land was cleared for the building of a new world. Columbus initially described the so-called Indians he met as 'gentle souls', but when they refused to acquiesce passively to his plans for their subjugation, he was relentless in his brutality against them. Columbus biographer Kirkpatrick Sale describes a scene near the colony of Isabela in 1495:

> to subdue the recalcitrant natives and tame the countryside . . . the soldiers mowed down dozens with point blank volleys, loosed the dogs to rip open limbs and bellies, chased fleeing Indians into the bush to skewer them on sword and pike, and 'with God's aid soon gained a complete victory, killing many Indians and capturing others who were also killed'. Of the valley that was Paradise they made a desert, and called it peace.[7]

Moreover, what happened in the Caribbean islands in the 1490s and early 1500s was only a dress rehearsal for what was to transpire on the North American mainland some 300 years later.

Even though most Americans do not know, or choose not to know, all the gory details of the Columbian conquest, there is a general awareness among most that genocide did occur and that a people was annihilated. Authors of children's texts about Columbus, as hard as they try to evade the brutal truth, are often forced to admit that 'the Indians were treated unfairly', and 'many Indians died'. Yet, both in popular myth and in written texts, authors have attempted to reconcile the good and the bad in the Columbian legacy, minimising the latter and highlighting the former. 'He had his faults, but . . . ' is the sentiment echoed throughout many of the writings about him.

The reticence of scholars to dethrone Columbus, despite the admitted atrocities he committed, is reflected in the following quote by the Columbian researcher and Pulitzer prize winner, John Noble Wilford:

> We do know he was an inept governor of the Spanish settlements in the Caribbean and had a

bloodied hand in the brutalisation of the native people and in the start of the slave trade. But we are left wondering if he is to be admired and praised, condemned—or perhaps pitied as a tragic figure.[8]

Despite his admission that Columbus murdered and enslaved Indian people, Wilford is still uncertain whether such behaviour really warrants condemnation. He speculates that perhaps the significance of such actions is outweighed by Columbus's own personal tragedies. Similarly, other texts mention Columbus's reprehensible deeds, but describe them in such dispassionate terms that they seem almost benign. One 1990 textbook casually refers to the genocidal conquest of the native peoples in this way: 'Though they had a keen interest in the peoples of the Caribbean, Columbus and his crews were never able to live peacefully among them.'[9] The author seems perplexed by the fact that the enslavement of native people and the theft of their land was any cause for tension between them and the European invaders. He is also reluctant to assign blame for the mysterious conflict, as indicated by his ambiguous and neutral choice of words. What such erroneous formulations effectively do is reduce the crimes against native people to footnotes in a larger, implicitly more important, text. The main story is about the greatness of western civilisation, the march of progress, the triumph of civilisation over savagery, Christianity over heathenism, and the imposition of order upon the chaos of the wilderness. This is a fundamentally racist formulation, consistent with the ways in which the subjugation and massacre of people of colour have been rationalised both by scholars and by ruling elites for generations. In fact, the rationalisation offered by the apologists for Native American genocide sounds frighteningly similar to the justification for the recent Gulf war. The murder of thousands of Iraqi civilians was described as an unfortunate but necessary action, taken in order to abate the greater evil of unchecked barbarism.

While the Columbian myth is both an American and a European one, it has a special significance in the context of US history and folklore. Even though Columbus was a European, and his first voyage predated the American revolution by nearly 300 years, he is revered by many as the first American hero. The nation's capital is named in his honour, as are several US cities, streets, parks and schools, including one of the country's oldest and most prestigious universities. His birthday is a federal holiday and the US government intends to spend millions of dollars in 1992 to commemorate the quincentenary of his initial transatlantic voyage. The legacy of Columbus has become an integral part of the annals of North American history because it fits so neatly into a larger scenario which celebrates the so-called pioneer spirit as that which has propelled the US to its current greatness. And, after all, Columbus was the first pioneer, followed by the Pilgrims, the cowboys, and US troops guarding the new frontiers of democracy around the globe today. Columbus was one among many great white explorers who courageously ventured into the darkness of the unknown, only to find a wilderness crying out to be tamed. The wilderness included both the land and its people. When the newly formed US began the process of constructing a national identity and culture, the memory of Christopher Columbus was resurrected as a symbol of the virtues of rugged individualism, stoic determination and a ruthless pioneer spirit which the young republic sought to instil in its citizens. It is no coincidence then that in 1692, the bicentennial of Columbus's fateful voyage, there were no great celebrations in the American colonies. But 100 years later, in the immediate wake of the American revolution, Columbus was lauded in commemorative festivities throughout the newly independent nation.[10]

It is also significant, and not all surprising, that the blatantly racist and sexist nature of the Columbian conquest has in no way diminished the great discoverer's status as an enduring and celebrated American hero. While most children's books essentially ignore the issue of gender and minimise the issue of race in re-telling the story of Columbus, both race and sex are integral features of the conquest of the Caribbean islands. The racist nature of the conquest is readily apparent. Repeatedly, in the descriptions of the world Columbus 'discovered', the native population is referred to as part of the natural landscape, nearly, indistinguishable from the other wild creatures who inhabited the islands. The following passage is typical: '[Columbus] returned to Spain taking with him a few of the curious copper-skinned natives, some birds, and some fish which he found'.[11] No distinction is made by this writer between Columbus's human and non-human souvenirs. Children reading such a passage could easily be left with the impression that the significance of those copper-skinned human beings was no greater than that of the captured fish or birds.

Initially, the native people were described by Columbus as generous and docile creatures. Later, when they got a taste of what their European visitors had in store for them and began to resist colonisation and 'progress', Columbus increasingly characterised them as 'cannibalistic savages' who had to be beaten into submission or extinction.[12] Columbus's animosity towards the native people was not the result of some innate aversion to people of colour or any xenophobic aversion to difference, as indicated by his initially favourable description of them. Rather, deeming them 'racially', socially and culturally inferior served as a convenient rationale for confiscating their land, usurping their labour and, eventually, annihilating them as a people. In fact, it was not their dark skin which Columbus alleged was an indicator of their inferiority, but their culture, their way of life and that fact that they did not embrace Christianity. After all, the Moors and Jews had just been expelled from Spain for the same reasons by Columbus's benefactor, Queen Isabella. So, as early as the fifteenth century, the notion of an inferior 'breed' of men and women served as reason for their exploitation and subjugation.

Columbus's legacy is not only that of racism and imperialism, but of sexual conquest as well. According to Kirkpatrick Sale, 'the women of America were as much a part of the bounty due the conquering Europeans as the other resources in which it luxuriated'.[13] native American women, like their African and African-American counterparts centuries later, were victims of sexual terrorism as a part of the larger scenario of conquest and colonisation. An Italian sailor, who was a part of Columbus's entourage when he invaded Santa Cruz island, described in his journal a scene that was probably typical:

> I captured a very beautiful Carib woman whom the Lord Admiral [Columbus] gave me, and with whom, having taken her into my cabin, she being naked according to their custom, I conceived desire to take pleasure [rape her]. I wanted to put my desire into execution but she did not want it and treated me with her finger nails in such a manner that I wished I had never begun . . . I took a rope and thrashed her well, for which she raised such unheard of screams that you would not have believed your ears.[14]

The rape of Indian women was not uncommon, but seems to have been systematic and routine. Another member of Columbus's crew described the situation in the colony of La Navidad in 1493: 'Bad feelings arose and broke out into warfare because of the licentious conduct of our men towards the Indian women.'[15]

Moreover, the story of Columbus's voyage is, above all, characterized as an adventure story in which men, more specifically European men, are the principal, if not the sole, cognisant actors. It is recounted as a romantic tale of fearless seamen who set out to explore the far reaches of the earth, only to stumble upon a treasure greater than they could have imagined, a new world. It was couched as a distinctly male adventure, a biased but favourable characterisation which

ignores and minimises the very real experiences of the native women who were some of the chief victims of the conquest and colonisation.

Schoolchildren in the US are encouraged to view Columbus as a great hero, the Admiral of the Ocean Sea. Most of them learn the familiar rhyme: 'In 1492, Columbus sailed the ocean blue', which firmly implants the legendary figure in their memories. They are even encouraged to learn from, and emulate, his example. One popular text urges teachers to highlight Columbus's virtues so that children see the benefits of patience and courage. And, since most public schools in western nations socialise children not to be critical thinkers, but to be good citizens, hard workers and, if need be, loyal soldiers, the myth of Columbus serves those purposes well. Moreover, openly to acknowledge the brutal and unsavoury origins of European influence in the western hemisphere would mean confronting the bloody traditions spawned from those beginnings. Therefore, Columbus's image has been scrubbed clean and sanitised by many generations of American historians so that he can now be offered up as a sterling example of the glorious era of discovery. His weaknesses, mistakes and horrid transgressions are all excused in the name of progress. The construction of the heroic myth and legend surrounding Columbus also belies the notion that the writing of history is an objective enterprise. And it further underscores the contention that history is ultimately written by the victors, and by those with the power and resources to publish, distribute and thus validate the version of history which best serves the interests of the status quo.

So, in 1992, it is a quite ignoble band of pioneers, with Columbus at the helm, that Americans will celebrate so lavishly on the occasion of the quincentenary. There will be travelling museum exhibitions, elaborate parades and commemorative ceremonies. In Puerto Rico, there will be a flotilla of ships bearing the names of the original three ships sailed by Columbus in 1492 and a re-enactment of the invasion, euphemistically referred to as the landing. And the government of the Dominican Republic is organising as 'archaeological reconstruction' of one of Columbus's unsuccessful Caribbean colonies established in 1494.[16] But, just as native people fought to defend their culture and their lives against imperialist hegemony five centuries ago, today progressive historians, activists and the political descendants of those first American freedom-fighters are struggling to resist yet another insult upon the memory of those who died.

American Indian Movement leader Russel Means once compared the legacy of Columbus to the legacy of Hitler. Native Americans and their allies throughout the Americas are determined that such a legacy not be celebrated without visible, vocal and militant opposition. Counter-demonstrations, days of mourning for the victims of genocide and de-commemoration ceremonies are planned throughout the year by groups ranging from the Women of All Red Nations to a multicultural group of educator-activists, called REPOhistory. An intercontinental run for peace and dignity is also planned which will include participants from north, central and south America. One set of runners will begin in Argentina, another in Alaska and the tour will culminate in a ceremony and rally in Mexico City. The general purpose is to link the native communities throughout the hemisphere and to celebrate a common history of resistance and survival—in spite of Columbus. These are but a few of the many efforts underway to reclaim, inch by inch, the confiscated territory which is our history.

REFERENCES

1. Allen Y. King, I. Dennis and F. Potter, *The United States and the Other Americas* (New York, 1978), p. 47. Other sources used for this article include R.C. Brown and H.J. Bass, *One Flag, One Nation* (Morristown, N.J., 1985); Christopher Columbus, *Journal of First Voyage* (New York, 1924); D.T. Gerace (ed), *Columbus and His World: proceedings of the first San Salvador conference* (Ft. Lauderdale, Fl., 1987); H.F. Graff, *America: the glorious republic* (Boston, 1986); H.F. Graff and P. Bohannan, *The Call of Freedom: the grand experiment* (New York, 1978); L.S. Kenworthy, *One Nation: the United States* (Lexington, 1972); S.E. Morison, *Admiral of the Sea* (Boston, 1942); P.E. Taviani, *Christopher Columbus: the grand design* (London, 1985).
2. George Shaftel, *Decisions in United States History* (Lexington, Mass., 1972), p. 19.
3. D. Buggey et al, *America, America* (Glenview, Il., 1977), p. 65.
4. Quoted in Ronald T. Takaki, *Iron Cages: race and culture in nineteenth century America* (Seattle, 1979), p. 103.
5. Ibid.
6. Buggey, op. cit., p. 65.
7. Kirkpatrick Sale, The Conquest of Paradise: Christopher Columbus and the Columbian legacy (New York, 1990), p. 154.
8. J.N. Wilford, 'Discovering Columbus', in *New York Times Magazine* (11 August 1991).
9. Clarence L. Ver Steeg, *The American Spirit: a history of the American people* (Englewood, N.J., 1990), p. 262.
10. Wilford, op. cit.
11. Heller and Potter, *One Nation Indivisible* (Columbus, Ohio, 1966), p. 8.
12. G. Shaftel, *Decisions in United States History* (Lexington, Mass., 1972).
13. Sale, op. cit., p. 141.
14. Ibid., p. 140.
15. Ibid., p. 139.
16. Ibid., p. 143.

PART 6
Family

Chapter 15
Changing Families

RODERIC BEAUJOT

This is a selection from Roderic Beaujot's *Earning & Caring in Canadian Families,* an award-winning book that pulls together in one place a wealth of information on the changes that have occurred—and not occurred—in connection with Canadian families over the last few decades. This section outlines trends associated with marriage, separation and divorce, remarriage, widowhood, and living alone. Other sections of the book—which cannot be reproduced here for reasons of space—deal with things like parenting, children, the family, and work. We have left out sections explaining in detail certain methodological techniques (such as "life table analysis") in order to focus on the conclusions reached. Although much of the discussion here is descriptive, Beaujot does present explanations for much of his data. For example, he explains the increasing recourse to divorce as reflecting, in part, the fact that (1) the family has lost many of its instrumental functions, and (2) the increasing emphasis on the family's expressive functions often leads people to expect more of marriage than was previously the case. As is always the case when explanations are presented to explain "discovered patterns" in the data, you need to ask yourself if there are other ways to explain the same data.

Until the beginning of the 20th century, marriage patterns involved a relatively advanced age at marriage and reflected significant proportions of the population who did not marry (Gee 1986). Over the first six or seven decades of the century, except for a slight reversal in the 1930s, marriages occurred earlier in people's lives and higher proportions of people were getting married. Then, suddenly, these trends reversed. In 1972 the median age at first marriage was 21.2 for brides and 23.4 for grooms, but by 1996 it had risen to ages comparable to those at the turn of the century, at 26.3 for women and 28.3 for men.

Not only is marriage occurring later in life, but it is also happening with less frequency. Using life-table techniques to combine the 1970–72 age-specific marriage rates implied that 90 percent of adults could be expected to marry at some point in their lives, compared to 75 percent in 1991. With achieved characteristics, particularly education and occupation, playing an increasing role in their lives, women are delaying the transition to marital relationships while they establish stable work careers. Women's greater economic independence allows them to search longer for the right person (Oppenheimer 1987). For both sexes, marriage has become less central to the transition to adulthood and to the set of roles defining adult status (Goldscheider and Waite 1986).

Still, the 1990 General Social Survey found that 80 percent of persons aged 18–29 expected to marry, and another 10 percent were uncertain about their prospects. The Survey showed that between the ages of 30 and 39, 90 percent of persons had been in a union at some point in their lives; the figure increased to 95 percent at ages 50–64.

Statistics show that individuals can expect to spend, on average, slightly less than half of their whole lives in the married state, with the average number of marriages per person being 1.3 for men and 1.2 for women. While the average duration of marriage had declined by the 1956–61 marriage cohort, it was still estimated to be above 30 years (Dumas and Péron 1992: 94).

Another important feature of marriage is the extent of *homogamy*, or people marrying others who are like themselves. In everyday conversations about mate selection, two contradictory principles often emerge: "opposites attract" and "like marries like." Clearly, most people do choose someone different from themselves in that they choose someone of the other sex. Beyond that, the idea that opposites attract receives little research support. On certain characteristics, such as religion, homogamy has declined, yet among marriages occurring in 1990, more than half of the people in each of the following groups married others of the same religion: Jewish, Mennonite, Pentecostal, Jehovah's Witness, Catholic, Eastern Orthodox, and other Christian and non-Christian. Even those whose religion was "unknown or not stated" were more likely to marry someone in the same category (Statistics Canada 1997b). U.S. data show that both education and social class remain important in mate selection, but that education has become more important than the social class of the parents (Kalmijn 1991) Homogamy by education, when both spouses are working outside the home, is connected to inequality across families: given couples who both have high education will have many combined advantages compared to other couples with less education.

It is probably in the age factor that marriage partners are most likely to be different. These differences are systematic, with women being on average younger than men. The difference in the age at first marriage is about two years—a figure that declined from a difference of about three years in the 1960s and four years in the early part of the century. The 1990 General Social Survey found that among the currently married population, in 51 percent of cases the man is two or more years older, and in 38 percent of cases he is three or more years older (McDaniel 1994: 21). In contrast, only 6 percent of women are two or more years older than their husbands. At the same time, 41 percent of couples are within two years in age.

Although a two-year gap may seem small, it can have considerable implications, at least for people marrying at young ages. A younger person is less likely to be experienced at taking responsibility and leadership, and more likely to have achieved less in life. Taken together, for most couples the *mating gradient*, or the differential status of the spouses, means that the wife will have a somewhat lower achieved status than the husband. In the average marriage the husband will tend to earn more money, partly because he is older and more established. As a result, for the benefit of the total family income his job may have a higher priority in the family life. The family is more likely to move for the sake of his job than for hers, and the wife is more likely to withdraw from the labour force for the sake of the children. The wife's slight disadvantage at the beginning of the marriage—established just because she was younger—can become entrenched over the course of the marriage.

Frances Goldscheider and Linda Waite (1986) analyzed the *propensities to marry* in light of the relative costs and benefits of marriage for the sexes. They found that, for the United States before 1980, long-term employment increased the likelihood of marriage for men but not for women. It seemed that women were more likely to use a higher personal income to "buy out of marriage," and that greater options outside of marriage reduced their relative preferences for marriage. In terms of benefits, women tended to gain financially from marriage while men gained more in terms of non-economic benefits, including enhanced survivorship—both mental and physical health. Goldscheider and Waite proposed that, leaving out finances, "his" marriage was more desirable than "hers" on many dimensions. Having gained other options for financial support, women would be less prone to marry. Also for men, the greater "access to wife-like social and sexual services outside of marriage" was reducing the "incentive to make longer-term commitments of financing and support" (p. 93). Still, Goldscheider and Waite expected these differential effects by sex to weaken with the transformation of the role of marriage as a factor in men's and women's transitions to adulthood.

At the same time, Goldscheider and Waite (1991) find that employment predicts marriage, especially for men, but also for women. Many people believe that a successful marriage these days calls for two jobs. The time needed to establish these two jobs may well be an important part of the delay of marriage. Analyzing the propensity to marry among U.S. cohorts marrying in the 1970s and 1980s, Megan Sweeney (1997) finds that economic prospects have become positively related to marriage for both men and women in the later cohort, suggesting, as Goldscheider and Waite (1986) had expected, that men and women have come to resemble one another in terms of the relationship between economic prospects and marriage.

SEPARATION AND DIVORCE

Although the rates of separation and divorce have increased since the 1960s, the most common situation is still for people to be married only once. For instance, 1990 statistics indicated that at ages 30–54, some 10 percent had never been married, another 10 percent were formerly married, 67 percent were married or cohabiting with no previous marriage, and 12 percent were married or cohabitating after a

previous marriage (Beaujot 1995: 42). In terms of family units, the 1995 General Social Survey found that 70 percent of families with children included both biological parents, while 22 percent had only one parent and 8 percent were stepfamilies with one biological parent and a step-parent (Statistics Canada 1997c).

Life-table techniques that extrapolate on the basis of the data from a given year suggest that between 1986 and 1991 the divorce rate stabilized at slightly more than 30 percent of marriages (Nault and Bélanger 1996: 18). The comparison of divorces by duration of marriage also suggests the beginnings of a decline in the propensity to divorce (Bélanger and Dumas 1998: 35). In part, this may be because marriages are becoming more selective, with more cohabitation and less marriage. Compared to other countries, Canadian divorce rates are higher than the rates in Japan, France, or Germany, roughly the same as those of Sweden and the United Kingdom, and considerably lower than in the United States.

Life-table techniques, on the basis of 1991 data, indicate an average age at divorce of 39 years for women and 42 for men, and an average of 21 and 15 years respectively spent in the divorced state. These statistics do not include the period of separation that often precedes an official divorce, nor do they include the period of cohabitation that sometimes follows divorce.

In their analysis of the *transition to divorce*, Goldscheider and Waite (1991: 104–6) found that the risk of divorce is greater when a partner's parents have separated, or when the parents of the partners have higher education. However, higher education for husbands reduces this risk, and higher earnings on the part of the husband both decrease divorce and hasten the transition to parenthood.

Canadian data show similar patterns (Balakrishnan, Lapierre-Adamcyk, and Krotki 1993). For instance, higher education is linked with higher divorce rates, but the presence of children reduces the rates. Higher men's incomes reduce divorce. Women with higher incomes have higher divorce prospects, but lower rates of dissolution of cohabitation. Divorce propensities are particularly high for those who married at a young age and had pre-marital births. Divorce is also higher for couples raising stepchildren, for those who have a larger age difference at marriage, and for persons whose parents had separated (Hall and Zhao 1995).

In analyzing "what holds marriage together," Jan Trost (1986) proposes that most of the standard bonds have declined. The state has redefined the legal bonds to permit divorce by mutual consent; and the trend to two-income families means less economic interdependency. The trend to fewer children means weaker bonds through parenthood. At the expressive and sexual levels, expectations are higher and consequently a higher likelihood exists that people fall short of their expectations.

DIVORCE TRENDS: INSTRUMENTAL, EXPRESSIVE, AND COMMITMENT FACTORS

The understanding of divorce trends can be placed in the context of instrumental and expressive factors in marriage and the changing nature of the marriage commitment. With the decrease in the *instrumental* functions fulfilled by families, families have less holding them together. This is particularly true in the economic domain, where families now experience less economic interdependence. A wife in particular has a much easier time getting out of an unhappy marriage if she is employed and living in a two-income family. Moreover, if the marriage no longer determines her status, the prospect of moving out is less negative. The greater independence of women makes the divorce alternative more viable.

Instrumental questions also explain several other patterns about the incidence of divorce. Divorces are less likely to occur when a family has young, dependent children, because that is the time when the family is most economically interdependent. Indeed, both childless couples and those in the empty-nest stage have higher risks of divorce (Rowe 1989; Hoem 1995).

Divorce rates are also higher at the lower levels of socio-economic status. A lower income means that the instrumental exchanges in the marriage are less rewarding, and consequently the prospect of divorce is not as negative.

The greater relevance of the *expressive* dimension is equally important in understanding the divorce trend. Given that marriage is now seen much more as an arrangement for the mutual gratification of participants, spouses expect more from families in terms of intimacy and interpersonal rewards, and they see individual well-being and self-fulfilment as significant values. Families are expected to serve individual needs, rather than individuals serving family needs. Divorce today, then, may be more prevalent because it represents a natural solution to marriages that do not serve the mutual gratification of the persons involved. In particular, 88 to 95 percent of respondents to the 1995 General Social Survey considered divorce to be justified if there was a "lack of love and respect from the partner," "unfaithful behaviour," or "abusive behaviour" (Frederick and Hamel 1998: 8). According to the survey, the most common grounds for divorce are abusive behaviour, infidelity, lack of love and respect, and excessive drinking by a partner—all factors at the expressive level. For Tamara Hareven (1983), high rates of divorce are proof that people care about marriage and about the quality of their relationships. Still, Anne-Marie Ambert and Maureen Baker (1988) found that significant numbers of people were regretting their decision to divorce. In a third of separations, the partners had no serious grounds for divorce. Some divorces happen because of circumstances that have little to do with the marriage, such as problems at work, mid-life crises, or continuing emotional problems. Other divorces are due to "taking a risk" with an affair that ultimately does not lead to a permanent relationship.

One of the most consistent findings in divorce research is that the probabilities of divorce are higher for those who get married at an early age. For women aged 35 to 49 in 1984, the probability of marital dissolution among those who married at 19 years of age or younger was almost twice as large (26 versus 14 percent) as for those who married at the age of 25 or older (Balakrishnan and Grindstaff 1988; Desrosiers and Le Bourdais 1991). The same applies to the risk of dissolution of common-law unions, which are higher for those entering unions at young ages or if there was a conception before the union (Turcotte and Bélanger 1997: 19–20). The higher divorce levels among those marrying young occur for several reasons, some of them related to instrumental questions. The lower income associated with youth means that the instrumental exchanges may be less rewarding. Furthermore, those marrying young are more likely to be downwardly mobile, especially if the wife is pregnant at the time of marriage, which detracts from the possibility of pursuing further education. On the expressive level, as these young married persons mature they may find that their spouses were poor choices for them, and that they are not receiving the expected gratification. It may even be that, for persons marrying at younger ages, emotional gratification is particularly important. Early marriage may have been a way of escaping an unrewarding situation in their families of origin. If the expressive dimension is especially important to them, they will show less hesitation about separating when that dimension is not working.

Obviously, divorce would be less common if everyone frowned on it and if the legal restrictions were formidable. But the attitudes toward divorce in Western societies have changed significantly. The social stigma attached to marital dissolution has lessened considerably, and people now accept that divorce occurs frequently for "normal" people. The definition of acceptable grounds for dissolving marital commitments has also changed. Until 1968 adultery was the only grounds for divorce in Canada. The 1968 Divorce Act extended the grounds for divorce to include both fault-related grounds and marriage-breakdown grounds. Fault-related grounds include adultery and other sexual offences, prolonged alcohol or drug addiction, and physical and mental cruelty. To obtain a divorce on these grounds there must be an injured party who brings the other spouse to trial, as well as a subsequent determination of guilt. As of 1986, divorce under marriage-breakdown grounds can occur after spouses have lived apart for one year, for whatever reason.

REMARRIAGE

Given the prevalence of divorce, more people are now marrying for the second time or living in postmarital consensual unions. Among persons getting married in 1990, 77 percent had never been married before, 20 percent had been divorced, and 3 percent were widowed. In a third of the marriages, at least one of the partners had previously been married. Under conditions implied in the 1991 life table of marriages, the average number of marriages per person marrying was 1.3.

The propensity of divorced persons to remarry has declined significantly, especially for women. Under conditions of the 1991 life table of marriages, 64 percent of divorced men and 52 percent of divorced women could be expected to remarry.

The lower proportions of remarriage, especially for women, probably relate to the changing costs and benefits. Given greater economic independence, people have less need to be married, and women who have been married may be more likely to conclude that the relative "costs of marriage" are not always to their benefit. Given age differences at marriage, and especially at remarriage, and the higher mortality of men, there are also less potentially available mates for older women.

WIDOWHOOD

Widowhood affects men and women differently. Although we can, and should, feel sorry for all the widowed women, the fact is that men have to die to produce these widows. Projections for the generation of persons born in 1921–36 imply that 60 percent of men will be married at the time of their deaths, compared with 20 percent of women (Péron and Légaré 1988).

The average age at widowhood is 74.1 for men and 71.2 for women. The average length of time spent in this state is 8.7 and 15.1 years respectively. Widowed persons are not likely to remarry: according to 1991 statistics, only 1 in 25 widowed women remarry, which is partly a result of the number of available men of comparable age.

NOT LIVING IN UNION AND LIVING ALONE

In 1991, 30 percent of women at ages 25–34 were neither married nor cohabiting, compared to 15 percent in 1971. For men at these ages and times, the proportion not in union has increased from 21 to 39 percent. That is, even when cohabitation is included, living in relationships is down compared to levels experienced over the last 50 years (Beaujot 1995: 40).

A larger proportion of people are now living alone. For the whole population aged 15 and over, 12 percent were living alone in 1996. By age group, the figures are 10 percent or lower until age 55, but they reach 48 percent at ages 85 and over (Statistics Canada 1997a:7). Between 1991 and 1996, the rate of living in union decreased for all age groups (Bélanger and Dumas 1998). Among the reasons suggested for increased singlehood are that young people are postponing living together, common-law relationships are breaking up much more frequently than marriages, marriages of young people are breaking up earlier than those of previous generations, and the tendency to remarry after divorce or widowhood is declining.

Living alone is particularly predominant among older women, including 42 percent of those over 65. But these elderly women are not necessarily isolated (Stone 1988). Only some 7 to 10 percent of the elderly have no surviving children (Péron and Légaré 1988). Even elderly who have never married usually have family and friends they are involved with in exchanges (Strain 1990). The evidence indicates that while the co-residence of elderly persons with their children has declined, older people do remain in contact with their families. Contact between siblings in later life is also important, especially for women, those who are not married, and those without children (Connidis 1989).

REFERENCES

Ambert, Anne-Marie and Maureen Baker. 1988. "Marriage Dissolution." In B. Fox, ed., *Family Bonds and Gender Divisions*. Toronto: Canadian Scholar's Press.

Balakrishnan, T.R. and Carl Grindstaff. 1988. "Early Adulthood Behaviour and Later Life Course Paths." Ottawa: Report for Review of Demography, Health and Welfare.

Balakrishnan, T.R., Evelyne Lapierre-Adamcyk, and Karol J. Krotki. 1993. *Family and Childbearing in Canada*. Toronto: University of Toronto Press.

Beaujot, Roderic. 1995. "Family Patterns at Mid-Life (Marriage, Parenting and Working)." In R. Beaujot, Ellen M. Gee, Fernando Rajulton, and Zenaida Ravanera, *Family over the Life Course*. Ottawa: Statistics Canada, cat. no. 91-543.

Bélanger, Alain and Jean Dumas. 1998. *Report on the Demographic Situation in Canada 1997*. Ottawa: Statistics Canada, cat. no. 91-209.

Connidis, Ingrid. 1989. "Contact between Siblings in Later Life." *Canadian Journal of Sociology* 14,4: 429–42.

Desrosiers, Hélène and Céline Le Bourdais. 1991. "The Impact of Age at Marriage and Timing of First Birth on Marriage Dissolution in Canada." *Canadian Studies in Population* 18,1: 29–51.

Dumas, Jean and Yves Péron. 1992. *Marriage and Conjugal Life in Canada.* Ottawa: Statistics Canada, cat. no. 91-534.

Frederick, Judith and Jason Hamel. 1998. "Canadian Attitudes to Divorce." *Canadian Social Trends* 48: 6–11.

Gee, Ellen. 1986. "The Life Course of Canadian Women: An Historical and Demographic Analysis." *Social Indicators Research* 18,3: 263–83.

Goldscheider, Frances and Linda J. Waite. 1986. "Sex Differences in the Entry into Marriage." *American Journal of Sociology* 92,1: 91–109.

———— 1991. *New Families, No Families?* Berkeley: University of California Press.

Hall, David R. and John Z. Zhao. 1995. "Cohabitation and Divorce in Canada: Testing the Selectivity Hypothesis." *Journal of Marriage and Family* 57,2: 421–27.

Hareven, Tamara K. 1983. "American Families in Transition: Historical Perspective on Change." In A.S. Skolnick and J.H. Skolnick, eds., *Family in Transition.* Boston: Little, Brown and Co.

Hoem, Jan. 1995. "Educational Capital and Divorce Risk in Sweden in the 1970s and 80s." Stockholm Research Reports in Demography, no. 95.

Kalmijn, Matthijs. 1991. "Status Homogamy in the United States." *American Journal of Sociology* 97,2: 496–523.

McDaniel, Susan. 1994. *Family and Friends.* Ottawa: Statistics Canada, cat. no. 11-612, no. 9.

Nault, François and Alain Bélanger. 1996. *The Decline of Marriage in Canada* 1981 to 1991. Statistics Canada, cat. no. 84-536.

Oppenheimer, Valerie K. 1988. "A Theory of Marriage Timing." *American Journal of Sociology* 94,3: 563–91.

Péron, Yves and Jacques Légaré. 1988. "L'histoire matrimoniale et parentale des générations atteignant le seuil de la vieillesse d'ici l'an 2000." Ottawa: Report for Review of Demography, Health and Welfare.

Rowe, Geoff. 1989. "Union Dissolution in a Changing Social Context." In J. Légaré, T.R. Balakrishnan, and R. Beaujot, eds., *The Family in Crisis: A Population Crisis?* Ottawa: Royal Society of Canada.

Statistics Canada. 1997a. "1996 Census: Marital Status, Common-Law Unions and Families." *The Daily* 14 October 1997.

———— 1997b. *Marriage and Divorce.* Ottawa: Statistics Canada, cat. no. 84-212.

———— 1997c. "Youth and the Labour Market." *Labour Force Update.* Ottawa: Statistics Canada, cat. no. 71-005.

Stone, Leroy O. 1988. *Family and Friendship Ties among Canada's Seniors.* Ottawa: Statistics Canada, cat. no. 89-508.

Strain, Laurel A. 1990. "Receiving and Providing Care: The Experiences of Never-Married Elderly Canadians." Presentation, XII World Congress of Sociology, Madrid, July 1990.

Sweeney, Megan. 1997. "Women, Men and Changing Families: The Shifting Economic Foundations of Marriage." University of Wisconsin-Madison: Center for Demography and Ecology, Working Paper, no. 97-14.

Trost, Jan. 1986. "What Holds Marriage Together." In J. Veevers, ed., *Continuity and Change in Marriage and Family.* Toronto: Holt, Rinehart and Winston.

Turcotte, Pierre and Alain Bélanger, 1997. "Moving in Together." *Canadian Social Trends* 47: 7–9.

Chapter 16

Update on Families

STATISTICS CANADA

This brief selection is useful because it presents some data on families from the 2001 Census that allow us to assess recent family-related trends. Some of the patterns identified (e.g., although most people still prefer "traditional" marriages, common-law unions and lone-parent families account for an increasing percentage of all families) will come as no surprise. Others might. For example, are you surprised by the finding that fewer than 10 percent of all seniors are in "health care institutions" *and* that this percentage has actually *declined* since 1981? As with the last selection, pay attention to what the report emphasizes and ignores. For example, it tries to explain the finding that more and more people in their early 20s are living with their parents by linking it to a number of variables. By contrast, no attempt is made to explain the finding that household size is shrinking and more and more people are living alone. Why the difference? Finally, the report concludes by suggesting that "family trends in the 21st century will continue to evolve." What does "evolve" mean in this context? What assumptions lie behind the use of this particular word as opposed to something more neutral, like "change"?

With the release of data from the 2001 Census, much new information on the state of Canadian families has become available. This update outlines the major changes that have occurred within families and their living arrangements over the last 20 years.

Canadians continue to marry and have children. However, marital histories are becoming more complex. Common-law unions, lone-parent families, smaller households and people living alone are on the rise.

In 2001, the proportion of "traditional families"—mom, dad and kids—continued to decline, while families with no children at home were on the rise. Married or common-law couples with children aged 24 and under living at home represented only 44% of all families in Canada, down from 55% in 1981. At the same time, couples who had no children living at home accounted for 41% of all families in 2001, up from 34% in 1981. In 2001, lone-parent families increased to 16% of all families from 11% in 1981.

Behind this shift in living arrangements are diverse factors, such as lower fertility rates, delayed childbearing or a rise in the number of childless couples. In addition, because life expectancy is increasing, couples have more of their lives to spend together as "empty-nesters" after their children have grown up and left home.

Source: "Update on Families," Statistics Canada publication *"Canadian Social Trends"*, Catalogue 11-008-XIE, Number 69, Summer 2003, pages 11–13. Available at http://www.statcan.ca/english/freepub/11-008-XIE/0010311-008-XIE.pdf

COMMON-LAW RELATIONSHIPS MORE FREQUENT, ESPECIALLY AMONG THE YOUNG

The proportion of couples who live in common-law arrangements is on the rise. In 2001, 16% of all couples lived common-law up from 6% in 1981. The rate in 2001 is substantially higher than that in the United States, where 8% of couples lived common-law, but is much lower than in Sweden (30%) and Norway (24%). The trend toward common-law was strongest in Quebec, where 30% of all couples lived in common-law unions in 2001, a rate similar to that in Sweden.

Although common-law relationships are most popular among the young, they are also becoming more acceptable among older generations. In 2001, 48% of 20- to 29-year-olds who lived as a couple were in a common-law union, compared with 5% of those aged 55 years or older. Common-law unions continue to be less stable than marriages. According to the 2001 General Social Survey (GSS), women whose first union was common-law were twice as likely to experience a separation as those whose first union was marriage.[1]

MORE CHILDREN LIVING IN COMMON-LAW AND LONE-PARENT FAMILIES THAN BEFORE

It has become more acceptable to bring up children in common-law relationships, although childbearing is still more common in marriages. In 2001, 46% of common-law families included children, whether born in the current union or in a previous relationship. In 1981, this percentage was 34%. In terms of children, about 13% of those under the age of 15 lived in a common-law family in 2001, compared with 3% in 1981. This national average, however, masks large differences between the provinces. While in Quebec, 29% of children under age 15 lived with common-law parents, only 8% of children in the rest of Canada had this living arrangement.

According to the National Longitudinal Survey of Children and Youth, children are experiencing parental separation at increasingly younger ages. Furthermore children born into common-law unions are more apt to see the separation of their parents. Research suggests that children who experience the separation or divorce of their parents during their childhood are more likely to separate themselves later in their adult lives.[2]

In 2001, about 19% of children did not live with both parents. Most of these children lived with a lone parent, the majority of whom were lone mothers. Only about 1% of children under age 15 lived with neither parent—these children usually stayed with other relatives.

HOUSEHOLDS BECOMING SMALLER

Canadian households continue to shrink as fewer people live in large households and more people live alone. In 2001, the average household size fell to 2.6 from 2.9 in 1981. One and two-person households have increased in the last two decades. By 2001, 13% of the population aged 15 and over lived alone compared with 9% in 1981.

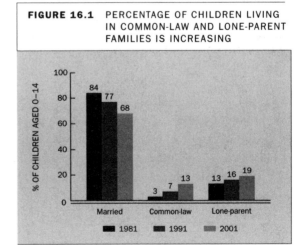

FIGURE 16.1 PERCENTAGE OF CHILDREN LIVING IN COMMON-LAW AND LONE-PARENT FAMILIES IS INCREASING

SENIORS MORE LIKELY TO LIVE ALONE AND LESS LIKELY TO LIVE IN HEALTH CARE INSTITUTIONS

In 2001, most senior men (61%) and about one-third (35%) of senior women lived with a spouse or partner and no children, little change from two decades earlier. The percentage of seniors residing with their adult children remained unchanged for men at 13%, but increased for women to 12% in 2001 from 9% in 1981.

Seniors were also more likely to live alone. In 2001, 35% of senior women and 16% of men aged 65 and over lived alone compared with 32% of women and 13% of men in 1981.

The percentage of seniors living in health care institutions has decreased to 9% in 2001 from 10% in 1981 for senior women and to 5% from 7% of senior men over the same time period.

YOUNG ADULTS LIVING WITH THEIR PARENTS

The new economy, with its intensified competition and rapid technological advances, has increased the need for higher skill levels and more education. More schooling, falling marriage rates, rising age at first marriage and the growth of common-law unions (which are more likely to dissolve than marriages) have extended the period during which young adults live with their parents. Young adults are increasingly remaining in or returning to the parental home. In 2001, 41% of 20- to 29-year-olds lived with their parents, a large increase from 27% in 1981. Young men in their early twenties are the most likely to live at home, with 64% doing so, compared with 52% of young women aged 20 to 24.

The fact that young adults continue to live with their parents has contributed to the decline in unions (marriage or common-law) among young adults. While the percentage of young

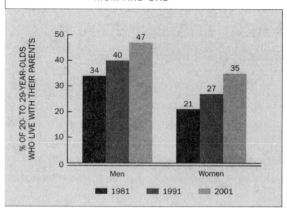

FIGURE 16.2   MORE YOUNG ADULTS LIVE WITH MOM AND DAD

adults in common-law unions has increased over the past 20 years, the percentage in marriages has declined by more, resulting in fewer unions among people in their twenties. In 2001, 35% of 20- to 29-year-olds were in a marriage or in a common-law union compared with 52% in 1981. Men in this age group are less likely to be married or in a common-law union than women.

STEPFAMILIES[3]

Many couples in new marriages or common-law unions have children from previous relationships. In 1998–99, nearly 7% of Canadian children under the age of 15 were living in a stepfamily.[4] Most of these children were part of a blended family,[5] which most often included the couple's biological children and the wife's children from a previous relationship.

SUMMARY

The Canadian family is continuing to be reshaped. More and more people are in common-law unions or form a lone-parent family. Children are increasingly being raised in these two types of families. The traditional family, although the single largest group, has declined in popularity from two decades ago. Family trends in the 21st century will continue to evolve. Stay posted.

NOTES

1. Statistics Canada. 2002. *Changing Conjugal Life in Canada* (Statistics Canada Catalogue no. 89-576-XIE). p. 6.
2. Statistics Canada. 2002. *Profile of Canadian Families and Households: Diversification Continues* (Statistics Canada Catalogue no. 96F0030XIE2001 003). p. 7.
3. Stepfamilies refer to families in which at least one child is from a previous relationship of one of the parents.
4. National Longitudinal Survey of Children and Youth, 1998–99.
5. Blended families contain children of both spouses from one or more previous unions, or one or more children from the current union and one or more children from previous unions.

Chapter 17

Experimental Family Organization: An Historico-Cultural Report on the Oneida Community*

WILLIAM M. KEPHART

Ours is a culture in which (1) the relationship between husband and wife is supposed to be characterized by emotional intimacy, and (2) parents are supposed to love their children as "special treasures." The fact that these things are not always true does not change the fact that they are cultural ideals. And yet, this has not always been the case in Western societies. Indeed, many commentators have noted that these two things did not emerge as cultural ideals in Western societies until after the 18th century. What is "family" life like in a society where monogamy and emotional intimacy between sexual partners is discouraged and where "special attachments" between individual parents and their children are discouraged? This selection presents some evidence that bears on that question by describing the Oneida Community. We might note that in the decades since this article was first published, some new materials on the Oneida Community have come to light that answer some of the questions that Kephart was not able to answer (see, for example, Spencer Klaw, *Without Sin: The Life and Death of the Oneida Community,* Penguin Books, 1993).

By way of background, it should be mentioned that the Community was founded in 1848 on the old Indian lands along the Oneida Creek in central New York State. John Humphrey Noyes, founder and long-time leader of the group, was a graduate of Yale Theological Seminary, although his theological views and Perfectionist philosophy had proved too heretical for the people of Putney, Vermont, where he had been preaching. Noyes' theology revolved around spiritual equality which, as he interpreted it, included both the economic and sexual spheres. In the Kingdom of God, all persons were to love and to share equally—a so-called Bible communism. Noyes gained some adherents, and in Putney the little group of Perfectionists actually started to practice what they preached. Predictably, however, there was little future for the group in an area that had been close to the heart of Puritanism, and Noyes and his followers were eventually run out of town.

Reassembling at Oneida, New York, they constructed a large Community Mansion House, and by expanding their efforts were able to increase the size of the group to several hundred

*Expanded version of paper read at the August 1962, meeting of the National Council on Family Relations, Storrs, Connecticut. The study was facilitated by a grant from the University of Pennsylvania Committee on the Advancement of Research. Although not included herein, an extensive list of bibliographical materials is available. Interested persons may write the author.

members. And for many decades the Oneida Community sustained one of the most unusual social experiments the world has ever seen. Economic communism, group marriage, scientific breeding, sexual equality—it couldn't happen here, but it did! Indeed, the Community flourished until around 1880, after which a business enterprise (Oneida, Ltd.) was set up and the stock apportioned among the members. It is hoped that the following remarks will shed some light on this very remarkable historico-cultural episode, one which—for some reason—has been neglected by both historians and sociologists.

SOCIAL ORGANIZATION AND FAMILY FUNCTIONS

What was there, in the elements of social organization, which successfully held the Community together in the face of both internal problems and external pressures? To begin with, much of the communality of action derived from the fact that the entire membership was housed under one roof. The original communal home was built in 1849, but because of the increase in members it was replaced in 1862 by a spacious brick building known as the Mansion House. In subsequent years, wings were added as needed. The building still stands, in its entirety; in fact, during my visit to Oneida, I stayed at the Mansion House and can attest to the fact that it is a striking architectural form, internally as well as externally. Noyes helped both in the planning and in the actual construction, and while sociologists might question the extent to which physical structure influences social organization, the Mansion House would seem to be a case in point.

Although each adult had a small room of his own, the building was designed to encourage a feeling of togetherness, hence the inclusion of a communal dining hall, recreation rooms, library, concert hall, outdoor picnic area, etc. It was in the Big Hall of the Mansion House that John Humphrey Noyes gave most of his widely-quoted home talks. It was here that musical concerts, dramas, readings, dances, and other forms of socializing were held. Community members

were interested in the arts, and were able to organize such activities as symphony concerts, glee club recitals, and Shakespearian plays, even though practically all the talent was home grown. Occasionally, outside artists were invited, but on a day-to-day basis the Community was more or less a closed group, with members seldom straying very far from home base. What might be called their reference behavior related entirely to the group. The outside community was, figuratively and literally, "outside," and was always referred to as the The World.

And, of course, it was the Mansion House itself which served as the structural base for practically all Community activity. Insofar as the Perfectionists were concerned, the totality of their existence lay within the walls of the Mansion House. The building was designed to encompass and facilitate this totality pattern, and from all accounts it served its purpose well.

Most of those interviewed were unable to separate the Old Community from the Mansion House. In their minds the two had become one, a fusion of the social and the structural, which, again, underscores the pervasiveness of the physical setting. Even today the building serves as a kind of community center. Most of the surviving members live there, and a good many of the direct descendants live within a block or two; in fact, as the descendants themselves age, they are likely to move into the Mansion House to spend their remaining years. In the words of one of the informants:

> We all love the old place. Many of our folks lived there, and most of us played there as kids. We know the building down to the last brick and board. It's odd, so many of the people who move away seem to come back when they get older and live in the Mansion House. It's because they had such good times and such happy memories.

It should not be thought that life in the old Community was a continual round of entertainment. The Oneidans built their own home, raised their own food, made all their own clothes (including shoes!), did their own laundry, ran their own school, and performed countless other collective tasks.

Virtually all of their activities were designed to accentuate the *we* rather than the *I*, and the economic sphere was no exception. Special abilities were recognized; indeed, wherever possible, occupational assignments were made on the basis of individual aptitudes. But at one time or another most of the work had to be rotated or shared, and so it was with Community life in general. The roles of the members were made crystal clear, and whether the activity in question was social, economic, sexual, or spiritual, the Oneida Perfectionists invariably turned against the *culte du moi* in favor of what to them was a selfless collectivism.

Human nature being what it is, of course, there were inevitable lapses on the part of certain members. Role conflicts sometimes did occur, and it was to counteract any tendency toward selfishness or ego-involvement that the much-publicized system of Mutual Criticism was inaugurated. Although details varied over the years, the general system involved a member who evidenced signs of personal aggrandizement being brought before a committee of peers who, frankly and objectively, attempted to pinpoint his social malfeasance. None of the persons talked with had undergone Mutual Criticism inasmuch as they were too young at the time. (Children were not included in this part of the Oneida program.) From all reports, however, the system of Mutual Criticism was well received. None of those interviewed could recall hearing of any adverse comments; in fact, it appears that as the membership increased, the system came to be applied not only to deviants but to any one who was seriously desirous of self-improvement. The following appeared during 1871–1872 in the *Oneida Circular*, the Community's weekly newspaper:

> I feel as though I had been washed; felt clean through the advice and criticism given. I would call the truth the soap; the critics the scrubbers; Christ's spirit the water.

The followers of John Humphrey Noyes were hard-working, well-behaved citizens, among whom crime and delinquency were virtually unknown. Because of this, they were generally respected by the surrounding community and by most every one else who came into actual contact with them. Nevertheless, the Oneidans were different. They knew it and The World knew it. By way of illustration, the Oneida women wore a very distinctive attire: in a period of floor-length skirts the Perfectionist ladies wore short ones (knee length) with loose trousers or "pantalettes" down to the shoes. I was shown some of the original dresses, and my impression was that they would create quite a stir even today. How must they have been viewed by outsiders 100 years ago! Moreover, all the Oneida women bobbed their hair, a custom which the Community instituted in 1848—and which was not introduced into The World until 1922 (by dancer Irene Castle). At any rate, it is easy to see why secular differentiation of this kind strengthened group identity. The following comment is illustrative:

> Your asking of sociological questions about what held the Community together reminds me of something my aunt used to tell. The old Oneidans kept pretty much to themselves, but during the summer months they would sometimes permit visitors. Some Sunday afternoons whole trainloads of visitors would come. They were served picnic-style on the lawn of the Mansion House. I think they were charged $1.00 for the whole thing. Of course, the visitors couldn't get over the way the Oneida women dressed, and they kept staring. My aunt always felt that the way outsiders always looked at them and talked about them had a great deal to do with their feelings of closeness.

Another measure which apparently helped to integrate Community membership was their widely-publicized system of economic communism. Personal ownership of wealth and private property of any kind were taboo, down to and including children's toys. Several of the informants mentioned the fact that in the early days of the Community the Oneidans had rough going; in fact, around 1850 their agricultural economy was in such poor shape that it was necessary for them to sell their watches in order to make ends meet. Fortunately, one of their members developed a steel trap, the manufacture of which involved a secret process of spring tempering. Demand for the traps proved great, and before long it was commonplace for the entire Community to turn out in order to meet the deadline for a large order.

From 1855 on, the Oneidans were without financial worry; in fact, when they broke up around 1880, the treasury showed a balance of some $600,000, no small sum for the period in question.

A final force which served to unite the Perfectionists was their religion and their spiritual devoutness; indeed, it would not be far from the mark to say that the Oneida Community was basically a religious organization. Their social, economic, and sexual beliefs all stemmed from the conviction that they were following God's word as expounded by John Humphrey Noyes. Noyes preached that Christ had already returned to earth and that redemption or liberation from sin was an accomplished fact. It followed, therefore, that the spiritual world was autonomous, free, and quite independent of the temporal order. From this perspective, it is easy to see why Noyes was often antagonistic to temporal or "external" law.

What was the net result of all of the above measures? From what was said, it appears that the Oneidans were able to maintain a remarkably cohesive form of family and social organization. Those interviewed were nearly unanimous in their belief that the old Oneida Community was an effectively organized, well integrated, and happy group. The following three comments speak for themselves:

I was a child in the old Community, and I can tell you that they were a happy group. Of course, I was only a child at the time—they disbanded before I was 10—and children like to glorify their childhood. Still, when anybody asks me about the old days, my dominant memory is one of contentment and happiness.

I was too young to remember much. But as I grew older and asked my relatives about the Community days, their faces would light up.

I was not born in the old Community, although many of my relatives were. But from the way they all talked about life in the Mansion House, they were living life to the fullest. They were able to combine the spiritual, the economic, and the social, and make it really work.

Sexual Practices

Although their family and social organization were unique, it was the Community's bizarre sexual system which attracted national and international attention. Just as Mormonism is invariably linked with polygyny, so the Oneida Community seems destined to be associated with group marriage. John Humphrey Noyes believed neither in romantic love nor in monogamous marriage, such manifestations being considered selfish and smacking of possessiveness. He taught that all men should love all women and that all women should love all men, and while no attempt was made to impose this reciprocality on The World, group marriage (or "Complex Marriage," as it was called) continued throughout the whole of the Community's existence.

Sex relations within the group were reportedly easy to arrange inasmuch as the men and women all lived in the Mansion House. If a man desired sexual intercourse with a particular woman, he was supposed to make his wish known to a Central Committee, who would convey his desire to the woman in question. If the latter consented, the man would go to her room at bedtime and spend an hour or so with her before returning to his own room. No woman was forced to submit to a sexual relationship which was distasteful to her, and the committee system presumably afforded her a tactful method for turning down unwelcome suitors. It was understood by all concerned that their sexual latitude did not carry with it the rights of parenthood. Only the select were permitted to have children, a point which will be discussed later.

Although respondents were agreed that the men readily adjusted to a plurality of women partners, they were generally silent on the question of how the Oneida females adjusted to a variety of male partners. It is unfortunate that so little information was available on this point, for this issue—in my opinion, at least—is a crucial one. In effect, the Oneida women were encouraged to have sex relations with a variety of men, but were not supposed to become emotionally involved with any of the men with whom they were having these relations! The woman of today tends to emotionalize and romanticize her sexual experience, and it would be hard for her to have any empathetic understanding of the Oneida system, wherein neither romance nor monogamous love were supposed to play any part in the sex act. As for the Oneida women, themselves, one can but conjecture.

One thin clue was the belief by four of the interviewees that at least in terms of overt behavior the female refusal rate was not high. Another male respondent stated that he had been informed by an old Community member that the latter "had never been refused." Two female interviewees had been told by an older woman member that the refusal rate was probably low.

The question whether the Oneida women ever took the initiative in requesting sexual relations drew a generally negative response. Several interviewees reported that they knew of some coquetry on the part of certain women, but that they had never heard of anything more direct.

The Eugenics Program

A vital component of the Oneida sexual system was the eugenics program, usually referred to as Stirpiculture. Noyes had been impressed with the writings of Darwin and Galton, and from the very beginning had decided that the Community should follow the principles of scientific propagation. Accordingly, he requested the Perfectionists to refrain from having children until such time as adequate financial resources were built up, and published accounts make much of the fact that during the 20 years it took to achieve economic self-sufficiency the Oneidans were successful in their efforts at fertility control. The type [of] birth control used was *coitus reservatus*, sexual intercourse up to but not including ejaculation. Male orgasm was permissible only with women who had passed menopause; in fact, it was with this group of females that the younger men were supposed to learn the necessary ejaculatory control. After the 20-year period, 53 women and 38 men were chosen to be parents, or stirps, and the eugenics program was officially inaugurated. During the ensuing ten years, 58 children were born into the Community, after which period the Perfectionists disbanded.

So much for the published accounts. From the information which could be pieced together, these accounts are somewhat inaccurate. To begin with, some children *were* born into the Community prior to 1869, the year the eugenics program was started. The technique of *coitus reservatus*, therefore, was not 100 per cent effective, though in view of its rather bizarre nature it seems to have worked reasonably well.[1]

The actual criteria and methods for selecting the stirps have never been revealed. It is known that committees were set up to make the selection, but what standards they used is something of a mystery. Noyes served on the committees, and it would seem that it was he who largely decided which of the Perfectionists were qualified for parenthood. It was said that Noyes, himself, fathered a dozen children, so that evidently he was not adverse to self-selection.

Whatever the criteria used, and whatever the relative contributions of heredity and environment, the Stirpiculture program was apparently a success. As a group, the children born of selected parents led a healthy and vigorous life. Their death rate was reportedly lower than that of the surrounding community;[2] in fact, as mentioned earlier, thirteen of the Stirpiculture children are still living, a figure substantially greater than actuarial expectancy. Interviews revealed that a number of the children had achieved eminence in the business and professional world, several had written books, and nearly all had in turn borne children who were a credit to the community.

It might be well at this point to clear up a misconception relative to the child-rearing program of the Community. It is true that the children were not raised by their parents. Infants were under the care of their mothers up to the age of 15 months, but thereafter were moved to the children's section of the Mansion House. And while the youngsters were treated with kindness by their parents, the Community made a conscious effort to play down feelings of sentimentality between parents and offspring, the feeling being that Perfectionists should treat all children as their own, and vice versa.

It is not true, however, that the child-rearing system was one of impersonality. Children were shown ample affection and kindness, and they apparently enjoyed the zest of group living; at least, all those interviewed felt certain that childhood in the Old Community was a happy and exhilarating experience. As one of the "children" put it:

> Well, I remember one little girl always wanted her mother. She'd stand outside her window and call to her, even though the mother wasn't supposed to answer. Other than that particular case, all the children seemed happy enough. Everybody was good to us. You know you were loved because it was like a big family. Also, there were so many activities for the youngsters, so many things to do, well—believe me— we were happy children. Everybody around here will give you the same answer on that!

As an example of historico-cultural investigation I have attempted to analyze an experimental

form of family organization. Other forms are available for parallel study: celibate groups such as the Father Divine Movement and the Shakers; polygynist groups such as the Mormon Fundamentalists (who continue their practice of plural marriage in spite of severe legal obstacles). Still other groups with unique forms of family or social organization would include the Amana Society, the Black Jews, the Hutterites, the House of David, the Llano Colonies, and the Old Order Amish.

To the best of my knowledge, the present account of the Oneida Community is the first ever to appear in any family journal. Most of the other groups mentioned above have yet to make such an appearance. It would seem, certainly, that they are over-due. Students of the family have made effective use of cross-cultural data, both for teaching purposes and for typologies in theory building. I submit that modern historico-cultural research—as focused, for example, on unique forms of family organization such as those mentioned above—would be similarly effective.

NOTES

1. It should be mentioned that in the minds of the Perfectionists the system was by no means bizarre. *Coitus Reservatus* was looked upon not only as an effective method of birth control but as a means of *emotionally elevating* sexual pleasure. Interestingly enough, in Aldous Huxley's recent best-selling *Island* (N.Y., Harper, 1962), *coitus reservatus* is the method used by the Utopian society of Pala: "Did you ever hear of the Oneida Community?" Ranga now asked. "Basically, *maithuna* is the same as what the Oneida people called *coitus reservatus*. . . . But birth control is only the beginning of the story. Maithuana is something else. Something even more important. Remember," he went on earnestly, "the point that Freud was always harping on . . . the point about the sexuality of children. What

we're born with, what we experience all through infancy and childhood, is a sexuality that isn't concentrated on the genitals; it's a sexuality diffused throughout the whole organism. That's the paradise we inherit. But the paradise gets lost as the child grows up.

Maithuana is the organized attempt to regain that paradise" (pp. 86–87).

2. H. H. and G. W. Noyes, "The Oneida Community Experiment in Stirpiculture," *Eugenics, Genetics and the Family*, 1 (1932), pp. 374–386.

PART 7
Gender and Sexuality

Chapter 18

Sex and Temperament

MARTHA C. WARD

The great value of anthropology is its ability to demonstrate that much of what we take as natural or innate in human beings in fact varies greatly from society to society. This is precisely why Margaret Mead's investigation of gender in three New Guinea societies has become one of the most-assigned readings in gender courses. Basically, what Mead found in New Guinea was one society (the Arapesh) where both males and females behaved in ways that might strike us as stereotypically feminine, a second society (the Mundugumor) where males and females behaved in ways that might strike us as stereotypically masculine, and a third society (the Tchambuli) where gender roles seemed to be a reversal of ours. This selection not only describes her findings in detail but also indicates some of the strengths and limitations of her analysis in light of later investigations. It also provides some insight (let's be honest: some *gossip*) about what can happen to Western anthropologists when they're thrown together in foreign climes.

From 1931 to 1933, Margaret Mead and Reo Fortune mounted an anthropological expedition to the Sepik River region of New Guinea. What happened during this trip is an incredible story about four cultures, three anthropologists, two genders, and one river. This story is enormously significant to what anthropologists know about women, men, and culture. In fact, the story has achieved its own mythic status in the history of science.

The Sepik River is a land of mosquitos, crocodiles, cannibals, and floating corpses, Mead would write. People ate tasteless flour laboriously processed from sago palms, yams, bananas, and other produce from their garden plots and fish from the Sepik and its tributaries. Until the Australian government imposed a colonial peace a few years earlier, the peoples of the river region had been cannibals and headhunters. But memories and the social organizations that supported these activities remained potent.

In the first group Mead studied, the Arapesh, both men and women acted in a mild, parental, and responsible manner—like the stereotypes about females at various times in human history. In the second group, the Mundugumor, both men and women were fierce, sexually charged, assertive, and loud—a view some people hold about males from time to time. And in the third, the Tchambuli, men gossiped about each other and worried about their hairstyles, pretty costumes, or whether any women would marry them. The women in this region of beautiful dark lakes were competent and no-nonsense business managers. These three groups showed Mead that a culture may impose personalities and patterns on one gender or both genders that are only a subset of the whole spectrum of possibilities available to human beings.

THE ARAPESH

When they first arrived in New Guinea, Margaret and Reo were not certain where to go or which group to study. They hired carriers from the interior to help them up the slippery trails and across the rivers; these workers even had to carry Margaret because her ankle was broken. The decision was made for them when their carriers simply stranded them, with six-months' supplies, in a mountain village.

In the steep hills above the flood plain of the Sepik, level land is scarce. Collecting enough firewood and food is difficult. The women carry loads of sixty to seventy pounds suspended from their foreheads, often with a nursing baby in a bark sling or bag. Precious pigs die easily and yams grow poorly in shallow tropical soils. Mead described the sexual division of labor as a necessity for survival. Men were freer to assume authority, a necessary but evil responsibility. Men worked desperately hard to keep the dangerous secrets of the men's houses; women were excluded from ceremonies to protect them and unborn children from malignant spirits.

Mead called the Arapesh cooperative, oriented to the needs of the next generation, gentle, responsive, carefully parental, and willing to subordinate themselves in caring for those who were younger and weaker. She noted that the Arapesh would probably find the Western notion of parenting and paternity repulsive. They said that a man and a woman cannot make a baby from a moment of passion or a simple act of intercourse. Rather, sex is the strong purposeful work of feeding and shaping a baby during the early weeks in its mother's womb. Since the child is the product of both father's semen and mother's blood, combined in equal parts in the beginning weeks, both parents must work diligently to make the child both desire. This arduous labor begins when menstruation ceases. When this hard work is done, intercourse

is strictly forbidden and a wide array of taboos are placed on the mother to protect the unborn child and insure a safe delivery.

An Arapesh man is strategically involved with various phases of his wife's labor. Immediately after birth and the careful disposal of the after-birth, he brings her a bundle of soft absorbent leaves to line the little net bag in which the baby is suspended through its waking time, curled up as though still in its mother's tummy. He brings water to wash the baby and sweet smelling leaves to keep evil influences from the hut. Putting his wooden pillow (which men use to protect their hair styles) beside his resting wife, he is "in bed having a baby." Together they fast and perform small rituals to help their baby grow safely. His maternal and nurturant tasks continue in diminishing degrees through the baby's first year of life. Arapesh parents observe what we call a **postpartum sex taboo:** They don't have intercourse with each other or with others until their baby is walking around; then it is strong enough to withstand its parents' renewed sexuality.

Mead's descriptions of mothers nursing their babies are one of the most authentic and enduring images from *Sex and Temperament.* The emotional content of the culture for her came through in these ordinary moments. Always a skillful observer, she related how mother and infant nursed together to how men and women have sex later in life. She tells how Arapesh mothers, like mothers everywhere, have to go back to work at some point. By the time her child is walking, it may be too heavy for a mother to carry on long trips to her garden. So she may leave it with its father or her sister or mother.

But what about Arapesh individuals who do not conform to these cultural patterns she described? Mead was deeply concerned about people who did not "fit in" their culture; the term she used was "deviant." If the Arapesh insisted that everyone was gentle, maternal, and not sexually aggressive, then they would have trouble with others who did not fit these patterns. In fact, Mead said that egocentric, possessive, or jealous women suffered most from their deviation from the norms of Arapesh society. They were likely to act out violently because there were no boundaries or acceptance for them as part of the continuum of human culture.

But Margaret Mead left the Arapesh disappointed. She had not found temperamental differences between women and men. So how could she examine the differences between the sexes if both had roughly the same temperament or social personality?

Moreover, Margaret and Reo had other frustrations. Her bad ankle kept her confined to the unstimulating Arapesh while her restless and volatile husband went off on trips. It is clear from her autobiography that she found Arapesh values of nurturing over aggression compatible with her own personality, while her husband found them particularly shapeless and offensive. She attributed their marital troubles to differences in their respective temperaments. Reo, it seems, was equally disgruntled with both the Arapesh and his wife.

THE MUNDUGUMOR

Their second field site was equally arbitrary. Margaret and Reo looked on a map and selected the nearest group accessible by water, patrolled by the government but not visited by missionaries. The river-dwelling Mundugumor were in sharp contrast to the Arapesh. Both males and females acted like stereotypes of men we would probably like to avoid. In fact, until the early 1930s, the Mundugumor had been cannibals and headhunters.

Mead called both men and women of the Mundugumor virile, actively masculine, positively sexed, jealous, violent, hard, and arrogant. She witnessed many episodes of angry defiance, mutual hostility, and ruthless individualism. She said they could be charming but hypocritical.

The Mundugumor lived on high, fertile land between swift and treacherous tributaries of the Sepik River. Their neighbors and trading partners spoke of them as ferocious and reckless, and

avoided crossing their lands. Rich by Sepik standards, the Mundugumor waterways were filled with fish, and with little effort, their gardens produced plenty of sago palms, coconut trees, and yams. The Mundugumor did not have to cooperate with each other to live well.

The rules of Mundugumor kinship and marriage were elaborate and harsh. In fact, they appeared made to be broken at the earliest opportunity. In their best possible kinship system, every man was supposed to acquire a wife by giving his sister in return for some other man's sister. But this principle never worked well. First of all, men wanted more than one wife; they also wanted to marry younger women who should have been properly married to a man in their sons' generation. So men competed with their sons for women because these young men wanted to use their sisters to make their own marriage alliances. Fathers used their daughters to make matches for themselves.

But Mundugumor women as sisters or daughters were never docile or cooperative in the marital schemes of their fathers or brothers. Furthermore, mothers plotted for themselves and against their daughters! A good Mundugumor mother wanted to see her daughter out of the way, replaced by a daughter-in-law living under her control. The best strategy of these two women was to become allies against their respective husbands. For obvious reasons, a Mundugumor woman preferred to have sons; a man preferred to have daughters.

The same atmosphere of jealousy and hostility prevailed after marriage. A man whose wife announced her pregnancy was a marked and unhappy man. He had to observe many public taboos while his peers taunted and teased him. He resented his wife and cursed the contraceptive magic which had so clearly failed him. A pregnant woman was deprived of sex and worried that her husband would desert her or take another wife altogether.

Mead wondered how any infant survived Mundugumor babyhood.

Mundugumor babies were not comforted with their mother's breasts; they were put in scratchy, harsh baskets until they learned to kick their way out of them. Once out of their baskets, they had to cling strongly to their mother's hair and make lots of noise to gain even the minimal attention necessary for survival. Mothers resented their smallest illness, accident, or weakness. Blows and cross words marked their weaning. They were surrounded by rules, a series of prohibitions: Don't go in the houses of your father's other wives and ask for food; don't cry or demand attention; don't wander out of sight, and so on.

It is not surprising that sex for Mundugumor adults potently mirrored their childhood experiences. Children who fought for every drop of milk and every ounce of nurturing would be unlikely candidates for romance, docility, or cooperation with parents' plans for arranged marriages. So girls put on their best jewelry or grass skirts and boys watched for the slightest sign of opportunity.

What would happen, Mead asked, to a Mundugumor couple who somehow invented long, languorous lovemaking, or to a Mundugumor man who rejoiced in his children's growth, or to a Mundugumor woman who cuddled and comforted her crying child? Too bad. They would be defined as deviates in Mundugumor society. While such individuals did not cause trouble in their communities, they were outsiders nonetheless. Who would marry a man who wished to be loyal or parental, or a woman who suckled a foster child?

The three months among the Mundugumor were troubled and discouraging for Mead. For starters, the group did not throw any light on her central theme of showing the contrast between female and male temperament since both sexes were so aggressive and assertive. As in the Arapesh, there were no behavioral styles that seemed to separate women and men. She hated the way they treated children and used them in conflict between the parents. The village flooded regularly and the mosquitos were even more hostile and aggressive than the Mundugumor.

Judging from her autobiography and their letters from the field, it is also clear that Margaret and Reo were getting on each other's nerves. She notes: "Reo was both repelled and fascinated by the Mundugumor. They struck some note in him that was thoroughly alien to me, and working with them emphasized aspects of his personality with which I could not empathize" (1976: 206). When she was ill with malaria, her husband offered no sympathy or assistance. When he was sick, he raged, fought the sickness, and climbed mountains.

So Margaret and Reo decided to leave this troubled field site. The government patrol boat took them upstream in time for Christmas. With the kind of luck, good and bad, that had so marked this trip, the boat deposited them on the doorstep of an English anthropologist named Gregory Bateson, who had been working in a dramatic culture called the Iatmul. This group set their tensions between the sexes into elaborate dances and ceremonials, using cross-dressing with costumes and makeup, and mock and ritual homosexuality.

THE TCHAMBULI

"You must be tired," Gregory said to Margaret tenderly as he pulled out a soft chair for her. She melted. Everything about this new anthropologist and the village was a relief for the aching ethnographer.

So Mead and Fortune decided to stay and finish their fieldwork with a group called the Tchambuli. They were neighbors to the Iatmul and had many similar practices. Both groups had splendid artistic traditions and complex cultures. Both lived in settled villages and traded fish with bush dwellers who made sago flour, the other staple of their diet. For both groups, women manufactured large, woven, mosquito-proof sleeping bags traded throughout the Sepik.

The Tchambuli lived on a blue-black lake. Small, sharp hills rose beyond the indistinct shores of the lake. In Mead's time a road wound near the lake margins. Men's houses, thirty to forty feet long, with painted, carved gables and figures of bird-men at the ends, lined the road. Paths ran from the ceremonial houses up the rocky hillsides to the women's houses. These were built to last three or four life-times and house three or four families.

For Mead, the Tchambuli dwelling house revealed the solidarity and solidity of women. Women, competent, collegial, and certain of themselves, occupied the center of the house. Men sat at the edges near the doors, uneasy, wary, ready to bolt back into their ceremonial houses. There they gathered their own firewood and cooked their own bachelor meals. While the women fished and wove, the men practiced dances, prepared extravagant costumes of feathers, fibers, and shells, or arranged each other's curls.

To men, the thing that mattered most in life was art. Every man knew at least one art: carving, weaving, painting, dancing, music, costume-making, drama productions, and the creation of a graceful pattern of social relations that allowed the unadorned women to draw sustenance and return to their work or trading activities. The women tolerated and even appreciated the games, dances, and theatricals the men staged. But the dance was valuable, not the dancer.

Tchambuli women weaned their children in the same careless, casual manner as they nursed them, stuffing their mouths with sweet delicacies to stop their crying.

Mead concluded that Tchambuli women had what she called dominance. She pointed out that the group practiced both patrilineal descent and polygyny (having two or more wives). These customs would seem to be oppressive or degrading to women. Yet these women had real power. While men bickered and reconciled, the women quietly carried on with their work. Mead spoke of women as impersonal, vigorous, and efficient.

Women, it is clear from her description, exercised their own choices for a mate despite patrilineal clans, polygyny, and a shallow mystique of arranged marriages.

Do not, however, be misled. Assuming that Mead presented a proper perspective on what she witnessed, women's freedom to ignore the rules of patriliny and arranged marriages still produced jealousy, conflicts, and soap opera dramas. For boys, there was a deeper discontinuity; a young man had no real training for his future role. By contrast, girls were thoroughly and practically trained in handicrafts, fishing, and the responsible, practical lives of women. The young men Mead saw in this society were confused; she says they were more maladjusted than any other group she had known. The patrilineal system justified a young man's wish or need to dominate, to initiate marriage choices, and to dictate economic decisions. But for reasons that are clear only in a later historic context, a man could not do these things. So some young men grew angry, violent, and neurotic. This was the primary example of deviancy she noted for the group.

DAUGHTERS OF SEX AND TEMPERAMENT

In the years that followed the publication of *Sex and Temperament*, many readers had trouble believing that within a 100-mile area of a remote and magnificent river region Mead conveniently found three societies that perfectly illustrated her points.

Mead always insisted that the sites selected for their three phases of fieldwork were only good luck. Ultimately, each was a theoretical bonus.

And, fortunately, we have the fieldwork of contemporary anthropologists, Nancy McDowell in the contemporary Mundugumor (now called the Biwat) and Deborah Gewertz among the Tchambuli (now called the Chambri). So we can ask these anthropologists and the host of excellent ethnographers who do fieldwork in this area: Was Margaret Mead losing it on the Sepik? Did she know what she was doing? Can we trust her conclusions? What can we really learn from studying sex and temperament in such settings?

Anthropologist Deborah Gewertz went to the Sepik River to do fieldwork in the early 1970s with the Chambri (Tchambuli). Although she was primarily concerned with trade and exchange networks, Deborah knew that she would be working in a group that had become an icon in women's studies. After all, Margaret Mead had labeled the women of Tchambuli "dominant."

Deborah concludes that Mead was essentially correct in what she saw, but she didn't stay long enough or have the viewpoint at that time to see the Chambri embedded in a long history of which 1933 was only a piece. Mead studied the Tchambuli as the group had just returned to the shores of the beautiful lake after a twenty-year exile in the hills above. While Mead was there, competition between males decreased temporarily while they rebuilt their base, the men's houses, the male rituals, and the symbolic equipment: slit drums, costumes, art and musical instruments. It is no wonder the men seemed strained and watchful, worried about marital prospects, or that they appeared preoccupied with artistic productivity and building activity. The women had already rebuilt their barter market system, trading fish for sago in the complementarity that ensured their food supply. So the women appeared "dominant."

According to Deborah Gewertz, Mead did not take complex regional histories into account nor push her own brilliant methodology to its fullest conclusions: She should have noted that women can move throughout a hierarchy without changing into men. Women can move through time taking on different attitudes and practices without losing basic functions. Sex roles (or gender roles) have enough flexibility to use in adjusting to changing circumstances. We cannot just label a group of women as dominant or submissive. Instead, we may find an underlying pattern of relationships that persists through time and provides us a range of negotiations for a complex variety of social situations.

With the blessings of Mead, anthropologist Nancy McDowell reworked the field notes from Margaret and Reo's sojourn among the Mundugumor in 1932 and compared them to her fieldwork with the group (now called the Biwat) in the early 1970s. Nancy concludes that "Mead's ethnographic skills, as well as her powers of observation and perception, were exceptional and clearly superseded the theory she espoused" "(McDowell 1991: 77). Unlike Mead, however, Reo Fortune never wrote up his notes from this trip. Margaret did some of them for him (as many academic wives have done for husbands), but the rest in his handwriting are useless.

What do we learn from these researchers? We see that gender roles are not fixed, rigid, or defined for all time. Sex roles are not divinely assigned nor inherent in something we call "nature." They are flexible; they can be used as problem-solving devices. For example, the Arapesh believed that women should avoid the yam gardens because the yams did not grow well around females; both women and gardens were believed to be protected by this belief. By contrast, Mundugumor couples took advantage of a similar mindset and deliberately copulated in other people's gardens just to ruin them.

What Mead called sex roles are only a script, not a prescription. She quoted Ruth Benedict, who said culture is "personality writ large." In Benedict's view, writes Mead,

> It is possible to see each culture, no matter how small and primitive or how large and complex, as having selected from the great arc of human potentialities certain characteristics and then having elaborated them with greater strength and intensity than any single individual could ever do in one lifetime. (Mead 1959: v)

Their view of culture as a pattern or configuration of homogenous and integrated elements, often linked with a unified theme, lacks the dimensions of contemporary theories. Now anthropologists think that culture is never simple, uniform, or well integrated. It is a messy, complicated, and often contradictory set of differences or oppositions that may exist side by side within the same group claiming the same territory, history, or worldview. This is why, today, we can talk of a female culture and a male culture within complex and contradictory ethnic, national, and world cultures.

REFERENCES

McDowell, Nancy. 1991. *The Mundugamor: From the Field Notes of Margaret Mead and Reo Fortune.* Washington, D.C.: Smithsonian Institution Press.

Mead, Margaret. 1972. *Blackberry Winter: My Earlier Years.* New York: William Morrow.

Mead, Margaret. 1959. "Preface" to Ruth Benedict, *Patterns of Culture.* New York: Mentor (originally published in 1934.)

Chapter 19

If Men Could Menstruate

GLORIA STEINEM

This selection is a classic in gender studies. Although meant to be funny, Steinem's brief essay makes a serious point: Although biology does not determine gender, it is often the case that cultural attitudes about gender shape attitudes about biology. In this case, she is suggesting that in a patriarchal society like ours, we would think quite differently about menstruation if it were associated with the dominant group (men) rather than the subordinate group (women). Are there other examples where we might feel differently about some biological process if it were associated with men rather than women (or with women rather than men)?

A white minority of the world has spent centuries conning us into thinking that a white skin makes people superior—even though the only thing it really does is make them more subject to ultraviolet rays and to wrinkles. Male human beings have built whole cultures around the idea that penis-envy is "natural" to women—though having such an unprotected organ might be said to make men vulnerable, and the power to give birth makes womb-envy at least as logical.

In short, the characteristics of the powerful, whatever they may be, are thought to be better than the characteristics of the powerless—and logic has nothing to do with it.

What would happen, for instance, if suddenly, magically, men could menstruate and women could not?

The answer is clear—menstruation would become an enviable, boastworthy, masculine event:

Men would brag about how long and how much.

Boys would mark the onset of menses, that longed-for proof of manhood, with religious rituals and stag parties.

Congress would fund a National Institute of Dysmenorrhea to help stamp out monthly discomforts.

Sanitary supplies would be federally funded and free. (Of course, some men would still pay for the prestige of commercial brands such as John Wayne Tampons, Muhammad Ali's Rope-a-dope Pads, Joe Namath Jock Shields "For Those Light Bachelor Days," and Robert "Baretta" Blake Maxi-Pads.)

Military men, right-wing politicians, and religious fundamentalists would cite menstruation ("*men*-struation") as proof that only men could serve in the Army ("you have to give blood to take blood"), occupy political office ("can women be aggressive without that steadfast cycle governed by the planet Mars?"), be priests and ministers ("how could a woman give her blood for our sins?"), or rabbis ("without the monthly loss of impurities, women remain unclean").

Male radicals, left-wing politicians, and mystics, however, would insist that women are equal, just different; and that any woman could enter their ranks if only she were willing to self-inflict a major wound every month ("you *must* give blood for the revolution"), recognize the preeminence of menstrual issues, or subordinate her selfness to all men in their Cycle of Enlightenment.

Street guys would brag ("I'm a three-pad man") or answer praise from a buddy ("Man, you lookin' *good*!") by giving fives and saying, "Yeah, man, I'm on the rag!"

TV shows would treat the subject at length. ("Happy Days": Richie and Potsie try to convince Fonzie that he is still "The Fonz," though he has missed two periods in a row.) So would newspapers. (SHARK SCARE THREATENS MENSTRUATING MEN. JUDGE CITES MONTHLY STRESS IN PARDONING RAPIST.) And movies. (Newman and Redford in "Blood Brothers"!)

Men would convince women that intercourse was *more* pleasurable at "that time of the month." Lesbians would be said to fear blood and therefore life itself—though probably only because they needed a good menstruating man.

Of course, male intellectuals would offer the most moral and logical arguments. How could a woman master any discipline that demanded a sense of time, space, mathematics, or measurement, for instance, without that in-built gift for measuring the cycles of the moon and planets—and thus for measuring anything at all? In the rarefied fields of philosophy and religion, could women compensate for missing the rhythm of the universe? Or for their lack of symbolic death-and-resurrection every month?

Liberal males in every field would try to be kind: the fact that "these people" have no gift for measuring life or connecting to the universe, the liberals would explain, should be punishment enough.

And how would women be trained to react? One can imagine traditional women agreeing to all these arguments with a staunch and smiling masochism. ("The ERA would force housewives to wound themselves every month": Phyllis Schlafly. "Your husband's blood is as sacred as that of Jesus—and so sexy, too!": Marabel Morgan.) Reformers and Queen Bees would try to imitate men, and *pretend* to have a monthly cycle. All feminists would explain endlessly that men, too, needed to be liberated from the false idea of Martian aggressiveness, just as women needed to escape the bonds of menses-envy. Radical feminists would add that the oppression of the nonmenstrual was the pattern for all other oppressions. ("Vampires were our first freedom fighters!") Cultural feminists would develop a bloodless imagery in art and literature. Socialist feminists would insist that only under capitalism would men be able to monopolize menstrual blood. . . .

In fact, if men could menstruate, the power justifications could probably go on forever.

If we let them.

Chapter 20

The National Conversation in the Wake of Littleton Is Missing the Mark

JACKSON KATZ AND SUT JHALLY

The high school may be in Littleton, Colorado, or Tabor, Alberta, but the pattern is now all too familiar: students with guns opening fire on other students. Naturally, we want to know the causes of this violence, and there has been no dearth of articles speculating on what those causes might be. The usual suspects include things like violent video games, social maladjustment, jock culture, a breakdown in family, and so on. In this selection Jackson Katz and Sut Jhally make an interesting point: Most discussions of these school shootings pay little or no attention to the one social pattern that is constant across cases—the shooters are male. At the very least, they suggest, we need to consider the possibility that the way our culture defines what it means to "be male" might be an important element in predisposing males toward this sort of violence. A useful supplement to this reading is the film *Tough Guise,* narrated by Jackson Katz and available from the Media Education Foundation.

The events at Columbine High School 12 days ago have plunged us into a national conversation about "youth violence" and how to stop it. Proposals came last week from all corners. That we are talking about the problem is good; but the way we are talking about it is misdirected.

It is tempting to look at the murderous attack in Littleton as a manifestation of individual pathologies, an isolated incident involving deeply disturbed teenagers who watched one too many video games. That explanation ignores larger social and historical forces, and is dangerously shortsighted. Littleton is an extreme case, but if we examine critically the cultural environment in which boys are being socialized and trained to become men, such events might not appear so surprising.

Political debate and media coverage keep repeating the muddled thinking of the past. Headlines and stories focus on youth violence, "kids killing kids," or as in the title of a CBS "48 Hours" special, "Young Guns." This is entirely the wrong framework to use in trying to understand what happened in Littleton—or in Jonesboro, Ark., Peducah, Ky., Pearl, Miss., or Springfield, Ore.

This is not a case of kids killing kids. This is boys killing boys and boys killing girls.

What these school shootings reveal is not a crisis in youth culture but a crisis in masculinity. The shootings—all by white adolescent males—are telling us something about how we are doing as a society, much like the canaries in coal mines, whose deaths were a warning to the miners that the caves were unsafe.

Consider what the reaction would have been if the perpetrators in Littleton had been girls. The first thing everyone would have wanted to talk about would have been: Why are girls—not kids—acting out violently? What is going on in the lives of girls that would lead them to commit such atrocities? All of the explanations would follow from the basic premise that being female was the dominant variable.

But when the perpetrators are boys, we talk in a gender-neutral way about kids or children, and few (with the exception of some feminist scholars) delve into the forces—be they cultural, historical, or institutional—that produce hundreds of thousands of physically abusive and violent boys every year. Instead, we call upon the same tired specialists who harp about the easy accessibility of guns, the lack of parental supervision, the culture of peer-group exclusion and teasing, or the prevalence of media violence.

All of these factors are of course relevant, but if they were the primary answers, then why are girls, who live in the same environment, not responding in the same way? The fact that violence—whether of the spectacular kind represented in the school shootings or the more routine murder, assault, and rape—is an overwhelmingly male phenomenon should indicate to us that gender is a vital factor, perhaps the vital factor.

Looking at violence as gender-neutral has the effect of blinding us as we desperately search for clues about how to respond.

The issue is not just violence in the media but the construction of violent masculinity as a cultural norm. From rock and rap music and videos, Hollywood action films, professional and college sports, the culture produces a stream of images of violent, abusive men and promotes characteristics such as dominance, power, and control as means of establishing or maintaining manhood.

Consider professional wrestling, with its mixing of sports and entertainment and its glamorization of the culture of dominance. It represents, in a microcosm, the broader cultural environment in which boys mature. Some of the core values of the wrestling subculture—dominant displays of power and control, ridicule of lesser opponents, respect equated with physical fear and deference—are factors in the social system of Columbine High, where the shooters were ridiculed, marginalized, harassed, and bullied.

These same values infuse the Hollywood action-adventure genre that is so popular with boys and young men. In numerous films starring iconic hypermasculine figures like Arnold Schwarzenegger, Sylvester Stallone, Wesley Snipes, Bruce Willis, and Mel Gibson, the cartoonish story lines convey the message that masculine power is embodied in muscle, firepower, and physical authority.

Numerous other media targeting boys convey similar themes. Thrash metal and gangsta rap, both popular among suburban white males, often express boys' angst and anger at personal problems and social injustice, with a call to violence to redress the grievances. The male sports culture features regular displays of dominance and one-upsmanship, as when a basketball player dunks "in your face," or a defensive end sacks a quarterback, lingers over his fallen adversary, and then, in a scene reminiscent of ancient Rome, struts around to a stadium full of cheering fans.

How do you respond if you are being victimized by this dominant system of masculinity? The lessons from Columbine High—a typical suburban "jockocracy," where the dominant male athletes did not hide their disdain for those who did not fit in—are pretty clear. The 17- and 18-year-old shooters, tired of being ridiculed or marginalized, weren't big and strong and so they used the great equalizer: weapons. Any discussion about guns in our society needs to include a discussion of their function as equalizers. In Littleton, the availability of weapons gave the shooters the opportunity to exact a twisted and tragic revenge: 15 dead, including themselves, and 23 wounded.

What this case reinforces is our crying need for a national conversation about what it means to be a man, since cultural definitions of manhood and masculinity are ever-shifting and are particularly volatile in the contemporary era.

Such a discussion must examine the mass media in which boys (and girls) are immersed, including violent, interactive video games, but also mass media as part of a larger cultural environment that helps to shape the masculine identities of young boys in ways that equate strength in males with power and the ability to instill fear—fear in other males as well as in females.

But the way in which we neuter these discussions makes it hard to frame such questions, for there is a wrong way and a right way of asking them. The wrong way: "Did the media (video games, Marilyn Manson, 'The Basketball Diaries') make them do it?" One of the few things that we know for certain after 50 years of sustained research on these issues is that behavior is too complex a phenomenon to pin down to exposure to individual and isolated media messages. The evidence strongly supports that behavior is linked to attitudes and attitudes are formed in a much more complex cultural environment.

The right way to ask the question is: "How does the cultural environment, including media images, contribute to definitions of manhood that are picked up by adolescents?" Or, "How does repeated exposure to violent masculinity normalize and naturalize this violence?"

There may indeed be no simple explanation as to why certain boys in particular circumstances act out in violent, sometimes lethal, ways. But leaving aside the specifics of this latest case, the fact that the overwhelming majority of such violence is perpetrated by males suggests that part of the answer lies in how we define such intertwined concepts as "respect," "power" and "manhood." When you add on the easy accessibility of guns and other weapons, you have all the ingredients for the next deadly attack.

Chapter 21

Fraternities and the Collegiate Rape Culture: Why Are Some Fraternities More Dangerous Places for Women?

A. AYRES BOSWELL AND JOAN Z. SPADE

Why do men rape women? Much popular thinking on the subject suggests that the men involved are psychological deviants of one sort or another. Possibly, but another view—and one commonly encountered in academic journals—is that there are few underlying psychological differences between rapist and nonrapists. According to this view, it is context and cultural values (in particular, the way we define what it means "to be male") that predispose some otherwise "normal" males to rape. This selection presents some evidence in support of this contention. After reading the article, you might want to discuss some of the issues and questions raised as they relate to your campus. For example, are there places on your campus where interactions between males and females are structured in ways that facilitate rape? What can be done to change that? Or how about the question that the authors themselves pose at the end of their article: "Why do men and women participate in activities that support a rape culture [even] when they see its injustices?"

Date rape and acquaintance rape on college campuses are topics of concern to both researchers and college administrators. Some estimate that 60 to 80 percent of rapes are date or acquaintance rape (Koss, Dinero, Seibel, and Cox 1988). Further, 1 out of 4 college women say they were raped or experienced an attempted rape, and 1 out of 12 college men say they forced a woman to have sexual intercourse against her will (Koss, Gidycz, and Wisniewski 1985).

Although considerable attention focuses on the incidence of rape, we know relatively little about the context or the *rape culture* surrounding date and acquaintance rape. Rape culture is a set of values and beliefs that provide an environment conducive to rape (Buchwald, Fletcher, and Roth 1993; Herman 1984). The term applies to a generic culture surrounding and promoting rape, not the specific settings in which rape is likely to occur. We believe that the

AUTHORS' NOTE: An earlier version of this article was presented at the annual meeting of the American Sociological Association, August 1993. Special thanks go to Barbara Frankel, Karen Hicks, and Jennifer Volchko for their input into the process and final version and to Judith Gerson, Sue Curry Jansen, Judith Lasker, Patricia Yancey Martin, and Ronnie Steinberg for their careful readings of drafts of this article and for many helpful comments.

specific settings also are important in defining relationships between men and women.

Some have argued that fraternities are places where rape is likely to occur on college campuses (Martin and Hummer 1989; O'Sullivan 1993; Sanday 1990) and that the students most likely to accept rape myths and be more sexually aggressive are more likely to live in fraternities and sororities, consume higher doses of alcohol and drugs, and place a higher value on social life at college (Gwartney-Gibbs and Stockard 1989; Kalof and Cargill 1991).

Instead of assuming that all fraternities provide an environment conducive to rape, we compare the interactions of men and women at fraternities identified on campus as being especially *dangerous* places for women, where the likelihood of rape is high, to those seen as *safer* places, where the perceived probability of rape occurring is lower.

The abusive attitudes toward women that some fraternities perpetuate exist within a general culture where rape is intertwined in traditional gender scripts. Men are viewed as initiators of sex and women as either passive partners or active resisters, preventing men from touching their bodies (LaPlante, McCormick, and Brannigan 1980). Rape culture is based on the assumptions that men are aggressive and dominant whereas women are passive and acquiescent (Buchwald et al. 1993; Herman 1984). What occurs on college campuses is an extension of the portrayal of domination and aggression of men over women that exemplifies the double standard of sexual behavior in U.S. society (Barthel 1988; Kimmel 1993).

Sexually active men are positively reinforced by being referred to as "studs," whereas women who are sexually active or report enjoying sex are derogatorily labeled as "sluts" (Herman 1984; O'Sullivan 1993). These gender scripts are embodied in rape myths and stereotypes such as "She really wanted it; she just said no because she didn't want me to think she was a bad girl!" (Burke, Stets, and Pirog-Good 1989; Jenkins and Dambrot 1987; Lisak and Roth 1988; Malamuth 1986; Muehlenhard and Linton 1987; Peterson and Franzese 1987). Because men's sexuality is seen as more natural, acceptable, and uncontrollable than women's sexuality, many men and women excuse acquaintance rape by affirming that men cannot control their natural urges (Miller and Marshall 1987).

Whereas some researchers explain these attitudes toward sexuality and rape using an individual or a psychological interpretation, we argue that rape has a social basis, one in which both men and women create and recreate masculine and feminine identities and relations. Based on the assumption that rape is part of the social construction of gender, we examine how men and women "do gender" on a college campus (West and Zimmerman 1987). We focus on fraternities because they have been identified as settings that encourage rape (Sanday 1990). By comparing fraternities that are viewed by women as places where there is a high risk of rape to those where women believe there is a low risk of rape as well as two local commercial bars, we seek to identify characteristics that make some social settings more likely places for the occurrence of rape.

METHOD

We observed social interactions between men and women at a private coeducational school in which a high percentage (49.4 percent) of students affiliate with Greek organizations. The university has an undergraduate population of approximately 4,500 students, just more than one third of whom are women; the students are primarily from upper-middle-class families. The school, which admitted only men until 1971, is highly competitive academically.

We used a variety of data collection approaches: observations of interactions between men and women at fraternity parties and bars, formal interviews, and informal conversations.

Observations focused on the four fraternities named most often as high-risk houses and the four identified as low-risk houses.

Throughout the spring semester, the first author observed at two fraternity parties each weekend at two different houses (fraternities could have parties only on weekends at this campus). She also observed students' interactions in two popular university bars on weeknights to provide a comparison of students' behavior in non-Greek settings. The first local bar at which she observed was popular with seniors and older students; the second bar was popular with first-, second-, and third-year undergraduates because the management did not strictly enforce drinking age laws in this bar.

In addition, 50 individuals were interviewed including men from the selected fraternities, women who attended those parties, men not affiliated with fraternities, and self-identified rape victims known to the first author. The first author approached men and women by telephone or on campus and asked them to participate in interviews. The interviews included open-ended questions about gender relations on campus, attitudes about date rape, and their own experiences on campus.

To assess whether self-selection was a factor in determining the classification of the fraternity, we compared high-risk houses to low-risk houses on several characteristics. In terms of status on campus, the high- and low-risk houses we studied attracted about the same number of pledges; however, many of the high-risk houses had more members. There was no difference in grade point averages for the two types of houses. In fact, the highest and lowest grade point averages were found in the high-risk category. Although both high- and low-risk fraternities participated in sports, brothers in the low-risk houses tended to play intramural sports whereas brothers in the high-risk houses were more likely to be varsity athletes. The high-risk houses may be more aggressive, as they had a slightly larger number of disciplinary incidents and their reports were more severe, often with physical harm to others and damage to property. Further, in year-end reports, there was more property damage in the high-risk houses. Last, more of the low-risk houses participated in a campus rape-prevention program. In summary, both high- and low-risk fraternities seem to be equally attractive to freshmen men on this campus, and differences between the eight fraternities we studied were not great; however, the high-risk houses had a slightly larger number of reports of aggression and physical destruction in the houses and the low-risk houses were more likely to participate in a rape prevention program.

RESULTS

The Settings

Fraternity Parties

We observed several differences in the quality of the interaction of men and women at parties at high-risk fraternities compared to those at low-risk houses. A typical party at a low-risk house included an equal number of women and men. The social atmosphere was friendly, with considerable interaction between women and men. Men and women danced in groups and in couples, with many of the couples kissing and displaying affection toward each other. Brothers explained that because many of the men in these houses had girlfriends, it was normal to see couples kissing on the dance floor. Coed groups engaged in conversations at many of these houses, with women and men engaging in friendly exchanges, giving the impression that they knew each other well. Almost no cursing and yelling was observed at parties in low-risk houses; when pushing occurred, the participants apologized. Respect for women extended to the women's bathrooms, which were clean and well supplied.

At high-risk houses, parties typically had skewed gender ratios, sometimes involving more men and other times involving more women. Gender segregation also was evident at these parties, with the men on one side of a room or in the bar drinking while women gathered in another area. Men treated women differently in the high-risk houses. The women's bathrooms in the high-risk houses were filthy, including clogged toilets and vomit in the sinks.

Men attending parties at high-risk houses treated women less respectfully, engaging in jokes, conversations, and behaviors that degraded women. Men made a display of assessing women's bodies and rated them with thumbs up or thumbs down for the other men in the sight of the women. Men behaved more crudely at parties at high-risk houses. At one party, a brother dropped his pants, including his underwear, while dancing in front of several women. Another brother slid across the dance floor completely naked.

The atmosphere at parties in high-risk fraternities was less friendly overall. With the exception of greetings, men and women rarely smiled or laughed and spoke to each other less often than was the case at parties in low-risk houses. The few one-on-one conversations between women and men appeared to be strictly flirtatious (lots of eye contact, touching, and very close talking). It was rare to see a group of men and women together talking. Men were openly hostile, which made the high-risk parties seem almost threatening at times.

Students at parties at the high-risk houses seemed self-conscious and aware of the presence of members of the opposite sex, an awareness that was sexually charged. Dancing early in the evening was usually between women. Close to midnight, the sex ratio began to balance out with the arrival of more men or more women. Couples began to dance together but in a sexual way (close dancing with lots of pelvic thrusts.)

As others have found, fraternity brothers at high-risk houses on this campus told about routinely discussing their sexual exploits at breakfast the morning after parties and sometimes at house meetings (cf. Martin and Hummer 1989; O'Sullivan 1993; Sanday 1990). During these sessions, the brothers we interviewed said that men bragged about what they did the night before with stories of sexual conquests often told by the same men, usually sophomores. The women involved in these exploits were women they did not know or knew but did not respect, or *faceless victims*. Men usually treated girlfriends with respect and did not talk about them in these storytelling sessions. Men from low-risk houses, however, did not describe similar sessions in their houses.

The Bar Scene

The bar atmosphere and social context differed from those of fraternity parties. The music was not as loud, and both bars had places to sit and have conversations. At all fraternity parties, it was difficult to maintain conversations with loud music playing and no place to sit. The volume of music at parties at high-risk fraternities was even louder than it was at low-risk houses, making it virtually impossible to have conversations. In general, students in the local bars behaved in the same way that students did at parties in low-risk houses with conversations typical, most occurring between men and women.

The first bar, frequented by older students, had live entertainment every night of the week. Some nights were more crowded than others, and the atmosphere was friendly, relaxed, and conducive to conversation. People laughed and smiled and behaved politely toward each other. The ratio of men to women was fairly equal, with students congregating in mostly coed groups. Conversation flowed freely and people listened to each other.

Although the women and men at the first bar also were at parties at low- and high-risk fraternities, their behavior at the bar included none of the blatant sexual or intoxicated behaviors observed at some of these parties. As the evenings wore on, the number of one-on-one conversations between men and women increased and conversations shifted from small talk to topics such as war and AIDS. Conversations did not revolve around picking up another person, and most people left the bar with same-sex friends or in coed groups.

The second bar was less popular with older students. Younger students, often under the legal drinking age, went there to drink, sometimes after leaving campus parties. This bar was much smaller and usually not as crowded as the first bar. The atmosphere was more mellow and relaxed than it was at the fraternity parties. People went there to hang out and talk to each other.

On a couple of occasions, however, the atmosphere at the second bar became similar to that of a party at a high-risk fraternity. As the number of people in the bar increased, they removed chairs and tables, leaving no place to sit and talk. The music also was turned up louder, drowning out conversation. With no place to dance or sit, most people stood around but could not maintain conversations because of the noise and crowds. Interactions between women and men consisted mostly of flirting. Alcohol consumption also was greater than it was on the less crowded nights, and the number of visibly drunk people increased. The more people drank, the more conversation and socializing broke down. The only differences between this setting and that of a party at a high-risk house were that brothers no longer controlled the territory and bedrooms were not available upstairs.

Gender Relations

Relations between women and men are shaped by the contexts in which they meet and interact. As is the case on other college campuses, *hooking up* has replaced dating on this campus, and fraternities are places where many students hook up. Hooking up is a loosely applied term on college campuses that had different meanings for men and women on this campus.

Most men defined hooking up similarly. One man said it was something that happens

> when you are really drunk and meet up with a woman you sort of know, or possibly don't know at all and don't care about. You go home with her with the intention of getting as much sexual, physical pleasure as she'll give you,

which can range anywhere from kissing to intercourse, without any strings attached.

The exception to this rule is when men hook up with women they admire. Men said they are less likely to press for sexual activity with someone they know and like because they want the relationship to continue and be based on respect.

Women's version of hooking up differed. Women said they hook up only with men they cared about and described hooking up as kissing and petting but not sexual intercourse. Many women said that hooking up was disappointing because they wanted longer-term relationships.

Whereas first-year women get tired of the hook-up scene early on, many men do not become bored with it until their junior or senior year.

Treatment of Women

Not all men held negative attitudes toward women that are typical of a rape culture, and not all social contexts promoted the negative treatment of women. When men were asked whether they treated the women on campus with respect, the most common response was "On an individual basis, yes, but when you have a group of men together, no." Men said that, when together in groups with other men, they sensed a pressure to be disrespectful toward women. A first-year man's perception of the treatment of women was that "they are treated with more respect to their faces, but behind closed doors, with a group of men present, respect for women is not an issue." One senior man stated, "In general, college-aged men don't treat women their age with respect because 90 percent of them think of women as merely a means to sex." Women reinforced this perception. A first-year woman stated, "Men here are more interested in hooking up and drinking beer than they are in getting to know women as real people." Another woman said, "Men here use and abuse women."

Characteristic of rape culture, a double standard of sexual behavior for men versus women was prevalent on this campus. As one Greek senior man stated, "Women who sleep around are sluts and get bad reputations; men who do are champions and get a pat on the back from their brothers." Women also supported a double standard for sexual behavior by criticizing sexually active women. A first-year woman spoke out against women who are sexually active: "I think some girls here make it difficult for the men to respect women as a whole."

One concrete example of demeaning sexually active women on this campus is the "walk of shame." Fraternity brothers come out on the porches of their houses the night after parties and heckle women walking by. It is assumed that these women spent the night at fraternity houses and that the men they were with did not care enough about them to drive them home. Although sororities now reside in former fraternity houses, this practice continues and sometimes the victims of hecklings are sorority women on their way to study in the library.

A junior man in a high-risk fraternity described another ritual of disrespect toward women called "chatter." When an unknown woman sleeps over at the house, the brothers yell degrading remarks out the window at her as she leaves the next morning such as "Fuck that bitch" and "Who is that slut?" He said that sometimes brothers harass the brothers whose girlfriends stay over instead of heckling those women.

Attitudes toward Rape

The sexually charged environment of college campuses raises many questions about cultures that facilitate the rape of women. How women and men define their sexual behavior is important legally as well as interpersonally. We asked students how they defined rape and had them compare it to the following legal definition: the perpetration of an act of sexual intercourse with a female against her will and consent, whether her will is overcome by force or fear resulting from the threat of force, or by drugs or intoxicants; or when, because of mental deficiency, she is incapable of exercising rational judgment. (Brownmiller 1975, 368).

When presented with this legal definition, most women interviewed recognized it as well as the complexities involved in applying it. A first-year woman said, "If a girl is drunk and the guy knows it and the girl says, 'Yes, I want to have sex,' and they do, that is still rape because the girl can't make a conscious, rational decision under the influence of alcohol." Some women disagreed. Another first-year woman stated, "I don't think it is fair that the guy gets blamed when both people involved are drunk."

The typical definition men gave for rape was "when a guy jumps out of the bushes and forces himself sexually onto a girl." When asked what date rape was, the most common answer was "when one person has sex with another person who did not consent." Many men said, however, that "date rape is when a woman wakes up the next morning and regrets having sex." Some men said that date rape was too gray an area to define. "Consent is a fine line," said a Greek senior man student. For the most part, the men we spoke with argued that rape did not occur on this campus. One Greek sophomore man said, "I think it is ridiculous that someone here would rape someone." A first-year man stated, "I have a problem with the word rape. It sounds so criminal, and we are not criminals; we are sane people."

Whether aware of the legal definitions of rape, most men resisted the idea that a woman who is intoxicated is unable to consent to sex. A Greek junior man said, "Men should not be responsible for women's drunkenness." One first-year man said, "If that is the legal definition of rape, then it happens all the time on this campus." A senior man said, "I don't care whether alcohol is involved or not; that is not rape. Rapists are people that have something seriously wrong with them." A first-year man even claimed that when women get drunk, they invite sex. He said, "Girls get so drunk here and then come on to us. What are we supposed to do? We are only human."

DISCUSSION AND CONCLUSION

The degradation of women as portrayed in rape culture was not found in all fraternities on this campus. Both group norms and individual behavior changed as students went from one place to another. Although individual men are the ones who rape, we found that some settings are more likely places for rape than are others. Our findings suggest that rape cannot be seen only as an isolated act and blamed on individual behavior and proclivities, whether it be alcohol consumption or attitudes. We also must consider characteristics of the settings that promote the behaviors that reinforce a rape culture.

Relations between women and men at parties in low-risk fraternities varied considerably from those in high-risk houses. Peer pressure and situational norms influenced women as well as men. Although many men in high- and low-risk houses shared similar views and attitudes about the Greek system, women on this campus, and date rape, their behaviors at fraternity parties were quite different.

Women who are at highest risk of rape are women whom fraternity brothers did not know. These women are faceless victims, nameless acquaintances—not friends. Men said their responsibility to such persons and the level of guilt they feel later if the hook-ups end in sexual intercourse are much lower if they hook up with women they do not know. In high-risk houses, brothers treated women as subordinates and kept them at a distance. Men in high-risk houses actively discouraged ongoing heterosexual relationships, routinely degraded women, and participated more fully in the hook-up scene; thus, the probability that women would become faceless victims was higher in these houses. The flirtatious nature of the parties indicated that women go to these parties looking for available

men, but finding boyfriends or relationships was difficult at parties in high-risk houses. However, in the low-risk houses, where more men had long-term relationships, the women were not strangers and were less likely to become faceless victims.

These findings suggest that a more conducive environment for conversation can promote more positive interactions between men and women. Simple changes would provide the opportunity for men and women to interact in meaningful ways such as adding places to sit and lowering the volume of music at fraternity parties or having parties in neutral locations, where men are not in control. The typical party room in fraternity houses includes a place to dance but not to sit and talk. The music often is loud, making it difficult, if not impossible, to carry on conversations; however, there were more conversations at the low-risk parties, where there also was more respect shown toward women.

Alcohol consumption was a major focus of social events here and intensified attitudes and orientations of a rape culture. Although pressure to drink was evident at all fraternity parties and at both bars, drinking dominated high-risk fraternity parties, at which nonalcoholic beverages usually were not available and people chugged beers and became visibly drunk. A rape culture is strengthened by rules that permit alcohol only at fraternity parties. Under this system, men control the parties and dominate the men as well as the women who attend. As college administrators crack down on fraternities and alcohol on campus, however, the same behaviors and norms may transfer to other places such as parties in apartments or private homes where administrators have much less control. At commercial bars, interaction and socialization with others were as important as drinking, with the exception of the nights when the bar frequented by under-class students became crowded. Although one solution is to offer nonalcoholic social activities, such events receive little support on this campus. Either these alternative events lacked the prestige of the fraternity parties or the alcohol was seen as necessary to unwind, or both.

Students on this campus were aware of the context in which they operated and the choices available to them. They recognized that, in their interactions, they created differences between men and women that are not natural, essential, or biological (West and Zimmerman 1987). Not all men and women accepted the demeaning treatment of women, but they continued to participate in behaviors that supported aspects of a rape culture. Many women participated in the hook-up scene even after they had been humiliated and hurt because they had few other means of initiating contact with men on campus. Men and women alike played out this scene, recognizing its injustices in many cases but being unable to change the course of their behaviors.

Although this research provides some clues to gender relations on college campuses, it raises many questions. Why do men and women participate in activities that support a rape culture when they see its injustices? What would happen if alcohol were not controlled by groups of men who admit that they disrespect women when they get together? What can be done to give men and women on college campuses more opportunities to interact responsibly and get to know each other better? These questions should be studied on other campuses with a focus on the social settings in which the incidence of rape and the attitudes that support a rape culture exist.

Our findings indicate that a rape culture exists in some fraternities, especially those we identified as high-risk houses. College administrators are responding to this situation by providing counseling and educational programs that increase awareness of date rape including campaigns such as "No means no." These strategies are important in changing attitudes, values, and behaviors; however, changing individuals is not enough. The structure of campus life and the impact of that structure on gender relations on campus are highly determinative. To eliminate campus rape culture, student leaders and administrators must examine the situations in which women and men meet and restructure these settings to provide opportunities for respectful interaction. Change may not require abolishing fraternities; rather, it may require promoting settings that facilitate positive gender relations.

REFERENCES

Barthel, D. 1988. *Putting on appearances: Gender and advertising.* Philadelphia: Temple University Press.

Boeringer, S. B., C. L. Shehan, and R. L. Akers, 1991. Social contexts and social learning in sexual coercion and aggression: Assessing the contribution of fraternity membership. *Family Relations* 40: 58–64.

Brownmiller, S. 1975. *Against our will: Men, women and rape.* New York: Simon & Schuster.

Buchwald, E., P. R. Fletcher, and M. Roth, eds. 1993. *Transforming a rape culture.* Minneapolis, MN: Milkweed Editions.

Burke, P., J. E. Stets, and M. A. Pirog-Good. 1989. Gender identity, self-esteem, physical abuse and sexual abuse in dating relationships. In *Violence in dating relationships: Emerging social issues,* edited by M. A. Pirog-Good and J. E. Stets. New York: Praeger.

Gwartney-Gibbs, P., and J. Stockard. 1989. Courtship aggression and mixed-sex peer groups. In *Violence in dating relationships: Emerging social issues,* edited by M. A. Pirog-Good and J. E. Stets. New York: Praeger.

Herman, D. 1984. The rape culture. In *Women: A feminist perspective,* edited by J. Freeman, Mountain View, CA: Mayfield.

Holland, D. C., and M. A. Eisenhart. 1990. *Educated in romance: Women, achievement, and college culture.* Chicago: University of Chicago Press.

Horowitz, H. L. 1988. *Campus Life: Undergraduate cultures from the end of the 18th century to the present.* Chicago: University of Chicago Press.

Hunter, F. 1953, *Community power structure.* Chapel Hill: University of North Carolina Press.

Jenkins, M. J., and F. H. Dambrot. 1987. The attribution of date rape: Observer's attitudes and sexual experiences and the dating situation. *Journal of Applied Social Psychology* 17: 875–95.

Janis, I. L. 1972, *Victims of groupthink.* Boston: Houghton Mifflin.

Kalof, L., and T. Cargill. 1991. Fraternity and sorority membership and gender dominance attitudes. *Sex Roles* 25: 417–23.

Kimmel, M. S. 1993. Clarence, William, Iron Mike, Tailhook, Senator Packwood, Spur Posse, Magic . . . and us. In *Transforming a rape culture,* edited by E. Buchwald, P. R. Fletcher, and M. Roth. Minneapolis, MN: Milkweed Editions.

Koss, M. P., T. E. Dinero, C.A. Seibel, and S. L. Cox. 1988. Stranger and acquaintance rape: Are there differences in the victim's experience? *Psychology of Women Quarterly* 12: 1–24.

Koss, M. P., C. A. Gidycz, and N. Wisniewski. 1985. The scope of rape: Incidence and prevalence of sexual aggression and victimization in a national sample of higher education students. *Journal of Consulting and Clinical Psychology* 55: 162–70.

LaPlante, M. N., N. McCormick, and G. G. Brannigan. 1980. Living the sexual script: College students' views of influence in sexual encounters. *Journal of Sex Research* 16: 338–55.

Lisak, D., and S. Roth. 1988. Motivational factors in nonincarcerated sexually aggressive men. *Journal of Personality and Social Psychology* 55: 795–802.

Malamuth, N. 1986. Predictors of naturalistic sexual aggression. *Journal of Personality and Social Psychology* 50: 953–62.

Martin, P. Y., and R. Hummer. 1989. Fraternities and rape on campus. *Gender & Society* 3: 457–73.

Miller, B., and J. C. Marshall. 1987. Coercive sex on the university campus. *Journal of College Student Personnel* 28: 38–47.

Moffat, M. 1989. *Coming of age in New Jersey: College Life in American culture.* New Brunswick, NJ: Rutgers University Press.

Muehlenhard, C. L., and M. A. Linton. 1987. Date rape and sexual aggression in dating situations: Incidence and risk factors. *Journal of Counselling Psychology* 34: 186–96.

O'Sullivan, C. 1993. Fraternities and the rape culture. In *Transforming a rape culture,* edited by E. Buchwald, P. R. Fletcher, and M. Roth. Minneapolis, MN: Milkweed Editions.

Peterson, S. A., and B. Franzese. 1987. Correlates of college men's sexual abuse of women. *Journal of College Student Personnel* 28: 223–28.

Sanday, P. R. 1990. *Fraternity gang rape: Sex, brotherhood, and privilege on campus.* New York: New York University Press.

West, C., and D. Zimmerman. 1987. Doing gender. *Gender & Society* 1: 125–51.

Chapter 22

The Signs of Cybersex Addiction

ANNIE RUTH C. SABANGAN

Cybersex—what's next? For many people, cybersex is a part of their lives, and that has profound effects. This news article points to students staying up all night in cybersex chat rooms and flunking from school, throwing away their work days, or even becoming like hard drug addicts and giving their lives to online sex. The article explores why people might engage in cybersex, observes when it becomes a problem, and discusses some of the abusive sides to the behaviour. Should we think of this as deviance? Should we treat it like alcoholism and other forms of addiction? Is this an individual and private activity, or is it really a social one with social consequences? Is there a need to control the Internet as more of the negative sides of this technology become clearer? You decide.

The day has just begun. Quezon City's silent roads have waken to the honking of horns, stifling smog and a motley crowd. Outside a two-story commercial building in the city, vendors have started to ply their trade, beggars occupy their usual pitches, pedestrians fill the sidewalks.

But on the second floor of that building, eight people, mostly young adult men, are doing things discordant with the turns of the biological clock. They have skipped one Friday night of sleep. Their minds are superactive, as if driven by a dose of cocaine.

They have stayed at the building's cybercafé, huddled in cubicles, from dusk to dawn. All of them are immersed in cybersex chats made more interactive by web cameras.

A few blocks from the building is the University of the Philippines. At the U.P. College of Engineering a male student has become infamous among his batch mates.

They say he has become a walking zombie, often staying up late at night chatting, most of the time in Internet sex rooms. His foray sometimes lasts for 12 hours. He often goes to school spaced out. He has become so oblivious to grooming that he has neglected to bathe. His tangled hair reeks of a pungent smell down to his body. He flunked his exams and failed to graduate.

If these people would be subjected to a psychological assessment, it wouldn't be hard to diagnose that their lifestyles are symptomatic of an emerging psychological disorder called cybersex addiction—a phenomenon extensively studied by psychologists in First World countries but which remains unexplored in the Philippines.

Nevertheless, cybersex addiction can be compared to other types of addiction, like substance abuse, gambling or sexual abuse in its corporeal sense, explains Joseph H. Puyat, professor of psychology at the University of the Philippines.

Source: Sabangan, Annie Ruth. "The Signs of Cybersex Addiction." Special Report on Cybersex: Part 4 of 5. *The Manila Times.* Accessed at http://www.manilatimes.net/others/special/2003/oct/17/20031017spe1.html on October 17, 2003.

"Someone is addicted to something when he or she is no longer under control of his or her behavior. If it is an activity, the activity is already controlling that person. It becomes one's obsession," he adds.

FOUR SIGNS OF CYBERSEX ADDICTION

Puyat says addiction is generally characterized by at least four abnormal signs of behavior—anxiety and/or personal distress, maladaptability, statistical frequency and deviance from social norms.

An addict feels anxiety and/or personal distress when he cannot engage in cybersex.

"If you don't do it, you feel that your day is not complete. You feel distressed, and relief comes only when you engage in cybersex," Puyat says.

"Maladaptive" behaviors manifest themselves when cybersex hobbles a person from performing his or her regular routine or from being productive in other aspects of his or her life.

Maladaptability arises from cybersex through these examples: when one's working hours in a regular job are eaten up by cybersex, when a student's time for his or her homework is consumed by Internet activities leading to gross irresponsibility or when males addicted to cybersex no longer look at women as persons but "think of them in terms of breasts and vaginas."

When these maladaptive behaviors are reflected in a person's attitude and ways of interaction, they become not only a personal problem but a societal burden, Puyat says. Maladaptive personal problems arising from cybersex addiction infect society when, for instance, Puyat says, "the activity already controls your behavior and you cannot control your impulses that you either start to harass people, tell them [sexual] jokes that they don't like or give them unwelcome remarks that discomfit them."

Statistical frequency is measured, albeit subjectively, by the level of engagement of a population to an activity.

To determine disorder in cybersex, one must take a representative sample of who are into it, determine the usual Internet use of the sample population and get the average number of people engaged in that kind of use. If individuals are found using the Internet divergent from the common use, one is led to conclude their behavior is abnormal.

Deviance from social norms happens when a person's lifestyle runs counter to the values of his community so that it looks perverse in the social mirror.

Puyat considers statistical frequency and deviance from social norms superficial. "These standards are subjective. If, for example, an ordinary person strips in public, people would interpret that as a sign of lunacy. But when 'bold' stars—say Katya Santos or Diana Zubiri—do that, it's no longer abnormal," explains Puyat.

ADDICTS AND NONADDICTS

Not all drinkers become alcoholics. Similarly, not all cybersex chatters become cybersex addicts.

The difference lies in wanting or indulging in the activity. A man may have had engaged in Internet sex chat at one time or another, but he would never make it a part of his everyday life, much less the center of his life. A husband who has had a passing interest in pornographic photographs of young women on the Internet would not be an avid visitor of the site and eventually solicit a quick sex fix.

There's nothing wrong in thinking about sex most of the time, says Puyat. "It's normal for some people at some stage in their lives. Like for teenage boys. It's something biological."

Sexual fantasies are also normal, he observes. "What differentiates normal from abnormal people is that normal people do not act out their fantasies. It's like the Ally McBeal type of fantasy that after you fantasize, that's it," he says.

However, between two people facing a situation conducive to abnormal sexual behavior—one who is not into cybersex and the other often engaging into it—Puyat says it is easy to surmise that the one preoccupied with cybersex would engage in actual sex. "But then again, it's just a presumption and it stops there," he points out.

Cherrie Joy F. Billedo, a psychology instructor at U.P., says the literature on Internet addiction set a clear distinction between addicts and nonaddicts.

She notes that people who often get addicted to the Internet are into a "synchronous form" of online interaction like chatting.

FACADES AND EXCUSES

Like other addicts, most cybersex dependents do not admit their addiction although their behavior indicates otherwise. "Either addicts don't admit it or they don't recognize they have it," says Puyat.

Dr. Robert Weiss, founder and clinical director of the Sexual Recovery Institute in Los Angeles, thinks cybersex is dangerous because "it reinforces and normalizes sexual disorders."

The Times' online interviews with cybersex chatters and research on Internet sex websites elucidate this point. *The Times* notes that most of those who are hooked on cybersex either believe or pretend nothing's wrong with what they do.

For instance, an Internet editorial written by a Filipino cybersex buff made it appear that cybersex is all fun and safe.

Some of the advantages of cybersex that the writer noted were: (1) no sexually transmitted disease and no unwanted pregnancies, (2) hooking with someone is easy; you'll go to the same chatroom so it is expected that everyone is horny, (3) you don't have to pay for a good day, (4) cybersex partners never complain if you want another; sexual partners do, (5) cybersex doesn't make you feel like a loser; you can be what you want to be, (6) you are allowed to have sex with a 16-year-old girl on the Internet; in real life

you'll be sentenced to life and (7) you can do it in the office without having to wait until everyone has gone.

Getting beyond these facades, rationalizations and excuses on engaging in cybersex would, however, disclose deep cuts in the inner feelings of an addict, according to Weiss.

The inner feelings of sexual addicts (including cybersex addicts), Weiss noted, could fall into one of three categories: shameful, secretive or abusive.

He says shame is characterized by "a feeling of inner worthlessness or despair about ever being good enough."

"[Shameful acts] become the hidden inner core of feelings, which end up sabotaging relationships, careers and self-esteem."

Secrecy, on the other hand, he says, is the "hallmark of sexual addiction." Sex addicts often compartmentalize their lives because they hide their sexual behavior. Consistently wrapped in a "web of lies and manipulations," addicts often hide from those who are close to them "while using justifications, rationalizations and outright denial to lie to themselves."

The abusive behavior of sex addicts "can run the gamut from manipulations to lying in order to be sexual," says Weiss.

"Potential sexual partners are being abused when invited into situations they don't fully understand, when there is a clear inequity of power in a relationship or when the right of sexual choice is taken away," Weiss noted.

NOT THE CAUSE

Is the use of the Internet the cause of cybersex addiction? Puyat and Billedo say it's not. Most of the people who engage in cybersex, they say, already have unresolved problems before they indulged in the activity.

Finding themselves in a deadlock and in very stressful situations, these people look for ways to rid themselves of their burden until they develop compulsive behaviors.

"That's how addictive behaviors develop. You engage, for instance, in cybersex in response to a stressful situation and because that behavior helped you resolve the stress you engage in it again and again to resolve your stress," explains Puyat.

Billedo says the Internet acts like a facilitator—much like a peddler making the drug more accessible to the user.

Like other forms of addiction, cybersex cannot be resolved overnight. "Although the original problem has been resolved," Puyat says, "most of the time the addiction stays."

PART 8

Aging

Chapter 23

Population and Politics: Voodoo Demography, Population Aging, and Canadian Social Policy

ELLEN M. GEE

It seems like such a straightforward and commonsensical argument: As baby boomers pass into retirement, they will increasingly and quite unfairly come to be subsidized by younger generations who themselves are struggling to make ends meet. The very reasonableness of this argument probably explains why it is so often encountered in the popular press. And yet, as this selection demonstrates (at least with regard to Canada), it's an argument that does not hold up under close scrutiny. Partly this is because it implies things (most retired Canadians are well-off) that are simply wrong. But mainly this commonly encountered argument is misguided because it sees "demography" to be the primary cause of things (e.g., lack of pension funds, dramatic increases in the costs of health care) that have really been caused mostly by other things. Note the author's contention that this is not the first time that "demographics" has been seen as a threat to society. It also happened in the early 20th century and gave rise to the eugenics movement. The author suggests that people who saw high birth rates among non-Nordic populations as a threat to society were as flawed in their thinking as people who today see aging baby boomers as a threat. At the end of the day, does she convince you of this?

We are constantly bombarded with words and images informing us that our changing demographics—in particular, our aging population—are the cause, and will continue to be the cause, of a leaner and meaner Canada. These words and images reflect the ideology of voodoo—or apocalyptic—demography[1] that has come to frame Canadians' views of their society, now and in the future. What is voodoo/apocalyptic demography? It is the oversimplified idea that population aging has catastrophic consequences for a society. More specifically, it embraces the view that increasing numbers (or 'hordes') of older people will bankrupt a society, due to their incessant demands on the health-care system and on public pensions. A closely aligned idea is that an aging society exacts an unfair price on younger segments of the population who have to pay to meet the needs of the burgeoning numbers of elders. This idea has come to be labeled 'intergenerational equity' (or 'inequity') (Longman, 1987). Intertwined in the intergenerational equity concept is an image of the elderly as well-off leisurers who golf and cruise, partly at public expense, and who have no regard for the situation of younger people. This

Source: Excerpts from "Population and Politics: Voodoo Demography. Population Aging, and Canadian Public Policy," by Ellen Gee, from *The Overselling of Population Aging: Apocalyptic Demography, Intergenerational Challenges, and Social Policy,* edited by Ellen M. Gee and Gloria M. Gutman. Copyright © Oxford University Press Canada 2000. Reprinted by permission of Oxford University Press Canada.

image, too, comes with a label—the elderly are 'greedy geezers' (Binstock, 1994). Also, this generational unfairness is viewed as leading to intergenerational conflict, straining the Canadian social fabric.

My analysis of apocalyptic demography will encompass both its numerical or data side and its political consequences and agenda. However, as a preface, I present actual examples of it, as culled from Canadian newspapers.

Painful Decisions Must Be Made to Ensure Future of Social Programs

If you think we are having a hard time affording our social programs today, just wait a few years. What is little understood is how the demographic clock is working against us and how fast it is ticking.

Peter Hadekel, *Montreal Gazette*,
10 Dec. 1994

Grandma! Grandpa! Get Back to Work!

Retirement isn't a birthright. Those who enjoy it haven't earned it. Canadians enjoy retirement, and why not? Most retirees are having the time of their lives: long, lazy summers at the cottage, gambling jaunts to Vegas in the winter, golf all year round.

Peter Shawn Taylor, *Saturday Night*, June 1995

Raise Seniors' Taxes

Ottawa should hit older people and their estates with new taxes to pay down the national debt, says a top lawyer. Seniors have benefited from a lifetime of economic growth boosted by government spending and it is now time for them to pay the country back. . . . The $400 billion federal debt 'belongs' to older Canadians, but younger generations are being asked to pay for it.

Toronto Star, 11 Nov. 1994

Greyer Horizons

. . . the deal between the generations is under severe threat, as the costs of state pensions rise.

Many countries are running out of people to pay those contributions. . . . But the argument between the generations is not just about pensions. Medical expenses, too, will burgeon as people get older.

Barbara Beck, *Globe and Mail*,
29 Dec. 1995

Value for Money

Canadians have rarely received so few benefits for their tax dollars, and the difficult times are just beginning. The consequences of this will be profound: tense interregional conflict, *clashes between young and old people*, and, if things get really bad, class warfare. [italics added]

Edward Greenspoon, *Globe and Mail*,
3 Oct. 1996

Pension Plan Pins Prospects on Market

Faced with the daunting demographic challenges of an aging baby-boom . . . Canadians—younger ones in particular—are skeptical . . . the CPP will be around for their retirement. And they have every reason to worry.

Shawn McCarthy and Rob Carrick,
Globe and Mail, 11 Apr. 1998

Paying for the Boomers

Blame it on the baby boomers. Last week, Finance Minister Paul Martin announced that Canada Pension Plan contributions will increase to 9.9 percent of pensionable earnings.

Maclean's, 24 Feb. 1997

Letter to the Editor

The old women lugging their pension-laden purses from store to store aren't suffering. It's the people who are too young for the pension who are hard up.

Toronto Star, 5 Dec. 1994

At least five themes can be detected in this material. One theme is the *homogenization* of persons on the basis of age, e.g., old people are basically the same—they are comfortably well off. A second theme is *age-blaming*. A third theme is that the shifting age structure is considered to be a significant *social problem* (e.g., 'a daunting demographic challenge'; 'the demographic clock is working against us'). A fourth, and very prominent, theme is *intergenerational injustice*—an aging population exacts an unfair toll on its younger members. The last theme is the *intertwining of population aging and social policy* concerns: for example, demographic aging will make it hard for us to afford our social programs; the federal debt is the fault of seniors; public pension sustainability is threatened by the baby boomers.

POPULATION AND POLITICS

Apocalyptic demography demonstrates that population can become intertwined with politics to serve a political agenda. This is not the first time that this unhappy mixture has occurred; in this century, two other examples come to mind. One is the cause of the eugenics movement in Canada, in which the control of reproduction was viewed as a way to preserve and improve the white race. Non-whites and less 'socially desirable' whites became the target of a campaign to lower their fertility. This movement gained its impetus from scientists and physicians; for example, E.W. McBride, McGill University's Strathcona Professor of Zoology in the early 1900s, wrote that 'All attempts to favour the slum population by encouraging their habits of reckless reproduction is throwing the support of their children on the State [which] places a heavier burden on the shoulders of the Nordic race, who form the bulk of the taxpayers' (McLaren, 1990:24).

These ideas may seem foolish to us now, but their transformation into legislation is much more difficult to brush off. The eugenics movement led to sterilization legislation in British Columbia and Alberta that remained on the books until 1972 in both provinces. The Alberta legislation was more stringent, and we only have hard data for that province (because of lost and destroyed files in BC). We know that between 1928 and 1971, nearly 3,000 sterilizations occurred in Alberta; that teenage girls were the most likely to be sterilized; that Anglo-Saxons were underrepresented among those sterilized; and that in the last 27 years of the legislation, Indians and Métis, who comprised 2.5 per cent of Alberta's population, accounted for more than 25 per cent of the persons who were sterilized (ibid.).

At first glance, all of this may seem very remote from the issues involved in apocalyptic demography. But there are important points of parallelism: the problems of the day were conceptualized in strictly demographic terms, these demographic problems were deemed to be costly to the public purse; and, accordingly, 'remedies' were sought to lower public costs.

A second example of the intertwining of population and politics can be found in the formulation of the 'population bomb' problem in the three decades or so after World War II. It is true that populations in many Third World countries were growing rapidly after the war—largely due to the introduction of technologies that lowered the death rate. However, it was the industrialized North that defined the problem as a 'bomb' that had to be detonated, with massive birth control aid as the detonating device. Millions of Western dollars (both public and private monies, with the private sources large US-based foundations like the Rockefeller Foundation) were spent on the delivery of birth control to (largely) women in Third World countries, based on the assumption that lower rates of population growth would positively influence economic development.

APOCALYPTIC DEMOGRAPHY AND SOCIAL POLICY

Let us now turn to some of the direct ways in which apocalyptic demography has informed

Canadian public policy—and how these claims stack up against empirical evidence.

Pensions and Population Aging

Most of the public debate around population aging has focused on pensions. The pension area brings out two of the strongest images of apocalyptic demography—the elderly as well-heeled 'greedy geezers' and the intergenerational injustice that will be brought on by the baby boomers.

Income and income security in later life are a huge topic. Here, I just want to highlight important points with regard to apocalyptic demography.

First, the 'greedy geezer' stereotype is unwarranted. While we do have a small portion of highly visible well-off seniors, the Canadian aged as a whole are not rich. In a recent analysis of 1996 Survey of Consumer Finance data, Lochhead (1998) shows that 20 per cent of Canadian senior-headed households have less than $65 in annual pre-transfer income, i.e., income before the Old Age Security (OAS), Guaranteed Income Supplement (GIS), and Canada/Quebec Pension Plan (C/QPP), and that 40 per cent have less than $5,179 in pre-transfer income. It should also be remembered that the GIS was put in as a temporary measure in the late 1960s and was expected not to be needed when the C/QPP matured. However, the incomes of many seniors have remained so low that the GIS has never been rescinded and it is important in keeping many older Canadians out of poverty. Nearly 40 per cent of the elderly have such meager incomes that they qualify for the GIS, and the combined OAS/GIS benefit does not lift the elderly living in larger cities out of poverty, and it barely does for others. As well, poverty continues to plague older unattached women, of whom nearly one-half live below the poverty line (Gee and Gutman, 1995).

Contribution rates to the Canada Pension Plan (shared equally by employers and employees) were increased in January 1998, with the goal of creating a five-year fund of money. This change has been presented as necessitated by our changing demographics. Let's see if the reason really is demographic.

The CPP operates on a 'pay-go' principle, with the contributions of today's workers paying the benefits of today's seniors, so there has never been a CPP fund in the same sense as there is with private pension plans. But there has been a potential fund, that is, the difference between what workers are contributing and what seniors are receiving. But that fund has been depleted over the years, not because of excessive benefits paid to seniors, but rather due to the borrowing of these funds by the provinces—at very low interest rates and generally not repaid—for all manner of things, such as building bridges and schools and preserving parks (Finlayson, 1988).

Thus, one problem is the transfer of potential pension benefits to other areas. This is not illegal; in fact, it was built into the original CPP legislation at the insistence of Ontario, which would not agree to sign this new pension scheme unless provincial borrowing was allowed. Such is the nature of Canadian federalism. Another problem is that the original contribution rates were set very low; in Myles's (1996:55) words, our contribution rates are 'pitiably low' and 'by international and even American standards Canada is not even in the ballpark.'

These comments are not meant to imply that some increases in CPP contribution rates will not be required as the population ages. This is surely to be the case, and has been known for many years. The problem is that other causes are not mentioned. Another concern, highlighted by Prince (1996), is the political shift in pension reform from a focus on expanding coverage to one of 'heading for cover'. The federal government now concentrates on affordability, neglecting issues of expansion in benefits (desperately needed by many, as data on seniors' incomes show), as well as problems with private pensions, such as increasingly inadequate coverage, especially in the private sector, and lack of indexation. The Senior's Benefit would have done little, except save the federal government money. It would have added 17 cents a day to the incomes of poorer seniors and was projected to save the government $2.1 billion in 2011 and $8.2 billion in 2030 (Brown, 1997).

Clearly, the message is that we are not to depend on public pensions and must save for our own retirement. The preferred vehicle is RRSPs—a partially privatized system that benefits the highly paid—although all evidence suggests that RRSPs will not play a key role for many Canadians in replacing pre-retirement income (Baldwin, 1996). McDonald (1995: 451) warns that our pension reforms are placing us on 'the brink of entrenching a two-tiered retirement system: one for the rich and one for the poor'. Our model of later-life income as social insurance is being replaced with a social welfare model. The pension reforms that will affect tomorrow's elderly are being driven by a neo-conservative ideology that will create hardship. The issue is not demography; rather, it is the failure of our policy-makers to recognize that the market-driven solutions that may have worked in the past will not work now. One could say that apocalyptic policy accompanies apocalyptic demography.

Today's workforce faces unemployment, downsizing and restructuring, and increased contract and part-time labour. As Marshall (1995: 48) states, 'rational individual-level planning for retirement is virtually impossible, [therefore] we must try to reverse the current trend of placing more and more responsibility for providing income security in retirement onto individuals.' This sentiment is echoed by demographers Rosenberg and Moore (1996), the authors of the 1991 Canadian census monograph on population aging. In my words, pension policy and economic realities for workers are on a collision course for reasons quite independent of demography. In more creative language, McDaniel (1996b) refers to the problem as one of 'serial employment and skinny government'.

Apocalyptic Demography and Health Care

There is no simple relationship between population age structure and health-care costs. While it seems obvious/intuitive that the older a population is, the more expensive are its health costs, the research evidence does not support this. For example, if we compare Canadian health costs and age structure with those of other developed countries, we see that while the Canadian population is quite 'young', we spend a higher proportion of our GDP on health than do many other 'much older' countries (Binstock, 1993).

Nevertheless, health-care costs have been escalating in the last few decades in Canada. The reason is not population aging. Barer et al. (1995) estimate that less than 5 per cent of the increase in BC health-care costs over a 12-year period is due to our changing age structure and that, overall, annual growth rates in the GDP of 1–2 per cent per year could accommodate the increases in costs. A major factor is increasing use of the health-care system. These increases have been substantial for all age groups, but have risen the most for persons aged 75 and over. Some ask if older people are receiving 'unnecessary' health care. Some evidence suggests that this might be the case, for example, Black et al. (1995), using Manitoba data for the period 1971–83, found that around one-half of the increase in consultations to specialist physicians was due to increased visits by elders in (self-reported) good health. But all gerontologists know that a very high proportion of the aged self-report they are in good health, meaning they are in good health 'for their age' (Gutman et al., 1999). Certainly, any 'overuse' of the medical/health system by elders (and others) should be curtailed, but we must be clear about what constitutes overuse and how much savings would be entailed. For example, one US–based study (Emanuel and Emanuel, 1994) finds that only 1 percent of total national health-care expenditures would be saved if all aggressive treatment, hospice care, and advance directives were eliminated for persons aged 65 and over in their last year of life. Marshall (1997) argues that health-care reform aimed at reducing unnecessary use should be targeted at servicing patterns and not at the elderly *per se*.

But let us not forget two things. First, the Canadian health-care system is—despite, not because of, our demographics—very expensive. (This is in direct contrast to our income security system, which has minimal administrative costs; see Brown, 1997). The reasons for this are complex, having to do with the multiple linkages among needs, delivery, financing, organization, and management (Angus, 1996). This topic is outside the realm of what is being addressed here, but one point is important to emphasize. Available evidence shows that the successful control of health-care expenditures is more likely to occur in centralized health-care fiscal systems (ibid.). However, Canada and its provinces are committed to decentralization in health care, so we will have to be very careful that we are not making a costly policy error.

Second, despite our expensive formal health-care system, the large bulk of health care to the elderly is provided informally, largely by women. Attempts to reduce the formal costs of caring will thus place an even greater burden on women, who may themselves be frail and lack the financial resources to cope. Rosenthal (1994) argues that the health-care reform that is shifting elder care from institutions to the community carries along with it the yet unaddressed need for support for caregivers—support in the workplace, support in the form of formal services, and support with regard to available and high-quality institutions. And Aronson (1992) reminds us that many women caregivers really do not have a choice in the matter, given the prevailing gendered division of care labour. Health-care reform that traps and overworks women in an effort to save government dollars is not much of a bargain.

CONCLUSION

It is important to recognize voodoo/apocalyptic demography (and its components) for what it is—an ideology based on beliefs that do not hold up to the test of empirical research and that is leading us in regressive policy directions. It is attractive because (1) it provides a simple and intuitively plausible explanation for present-day problems and (2) it places blame on inexorable demographic change that we cannot do anything about. Together, these two qualities allow us to take what seems to be a simple path, even though it may be a path that creates a much degraded Canadian society. In many ways, voodoo demography can be considered as a kind of 'moral panic' (Thompson, 1998)—the consequences of population aging are being exaggerated to serve a political agenda.

NOTE

1. The terms 'voodoo demography' and 'apocalyptic demography' are used synonymously.

REFERENCES

Angus, Douglas E. 1966. 'Future Horizons for Health and Health Care: A Policy Perspective', in Canadian Federation of Demographers, *Towards the XXIst Century: Emerging Socio-Demographic Trends and Policy Issues in Canada*. Ottawa: Canadian Federation of Demographers, 11–22.

Aronson, Jane. 1992. 'Women's Sense of Responsibility for the Care of Old People: "But Who Else is Going to Do It?"', *Gender and Society* 6: 8–29.

Baldwin, Bob. 1996. 'Income Security Prospects for Older Canadians', in A. Joshi and E. Berger, eds., *Aging Workforce, Income Security, and Retirement: Policy and Practical Implications*. Hamilton, Ont.: Office of

Gerontological Studies, McMaster University, 69–74.

Barer, Morris L., Robert G. Evans, and Clyde Hertzman. 1995. 'Avalanche or Glacier?: Health Care and Demographic Rhetoric', *Canadian Journal of Aging* 14: 193–224.

Bengtson, Vern L., and R. A. Harootyan. 1994. *Intergenerational Linkages: Hidden Connections in American Society.* New York: Springer.

Binstock, Robert H. 1993. 'Healthcare Costs Around the World: Is Aging a Fiscal "Black Hole"?', *Generations* 17, 4: 37–42.

———. 1994. 'Changing Criteria in Old-Age Programs: The Introduction of Economic Status and Need for Services', *Gerontologist* 34: 726–30.

Black, Charlene, P. Noralou Roos, Betty Havens, and Linda McWilliam. 1995. 'Rising Use of Physician Services by the Elderly: The Contribution of Morbidity', *Canadian Journal on Aging* 14: 225–44.

Brown, Robert L. 1997. 'Economic Security for an Aging Canadian Population', Ph.D. thesis, Simon Fraser University.

Clark, R. L., and J. J. Spengler. 1980. 'Dependency Ratios: Their Use in Economic Analyses', in J.L. Simon and J. DaVanzo, eds, *Research in Population Economics,* vol. 2. Greenwich, Conn.: JAI Press, 63–76.

Corak, Miles, ed. 1998. Government Finances and Generational Equity. Ottawa: Statistics Canada Catalogue No. 68-513-XPB.

Denton, Frank T., Christine H. Fever and Bryon G. Spencer. 1998. "The Future Population of Canada: Its Age Distribution and Its Dependency Relations", *Canadian Journal on Aging* 17: 83–109.

Emanuel, E. J. and L. L. Emanuel. 1994. "The Economics of Dying: The Illusion of Cost Savings at the End of Life," *New England Journal of Medicine* 330: 540–4.

Finlayson, Anne. 1988. *Whose Money Is It Anyway? The Showdown on Pensions.* Markham, Ont.: Viking/Penguin.

Foot, David K. 1989. 'Public Expenditure, Population Aging and Economic Dependency in Canada, 1921–2021', *Population Research and Policy Review* 8: 97–117.

Fortin, Pierre. 1996. 'The Canadian Fiscal Problem: The Macroeconomic Connection', in Osberg and Fortin (1996a) 26–38.

Gee, Ellen M., and Gloria M. Gutman. 1995. 'Introduction', Gee and Gutman, eds., *Rethinking Retirement.* Vancouver: Geronology Research Centre, Simon Fraser University, 1–12.

Gillespie, W. Irwin. 1996. 'A Brief History of Government Borrowing in Canada', in Osberg and Fortin (1996a: 1–25).

Good, Christopher. 1995. 'The Generational Accounts of Canada', *Fraser Forum* (Aug.: special issue). Vancouver: Fraser Institute.

Gutman, G.M., A. Stark, A. Donald, and B.L. Beattie. 1999. 'The Contribution of Self-reported Health Ratings to Predicting Frailty, Institutionalization and Death Over a 5 Year Period', unpublished paper.

Hodgson, Dennis. 1988. 'Orthodoxy and Revisionism in American Demography', *Population and Development Review.* 14: 541–69.

Hunsley, Terrance. 1997. *Lone Parent Incomes and Social Policy Outcomes: Canada in International Perspective.* Kingston, Ont.: Queen's University School of Policy Studies.

Kotlikoff, Lawrence J. 1993. *Generational Accounting: Knowing Who Pays, and When, For What We Spend.* New York: Free Press.

Kronebusch, Karl, and Mark Schlesinger. 1994. 'Intergenerational Transfers', in Bengtson and Harootyan (1994: 112–51).

Longman, Philip. 1987. *Born to Pay: The New Politics of Aging in America.* Boston: Houghton Mifflin.

Lochhead, Clarence. 1998. 'Who Benefits from Canada's Income Security Programs," *Insight* 21, 4: 9–12.

McDaniel, Susan A. 1996a. 'At the Heart of Social Solidarity', *Transition* 9 (Sept.): 9–11.

———. 1996b. 'Serial Employment and Skinny Government: Reforming Caring and Sharing in Canada at the Millennium', in Federation of Canadian Demographers, *Towards the XXIst Century: Emerging Socio-Demographic Trends and Policy Issues in Canada.* Ottawa: Canadian Federation of Demographers.

———. 1997. 'Intergenerational Transfers, Social Solidarity, and Social Policy: Unanswered Questions and Policy Challenges', *Canadian Journal on Aging/Canadian Public Policy* (Supplement): 1–21.

McDonald, Lynn. 1995. 'Retirement for the Rich and Retirement for the Poor: From Social Security to Social Welfare', *Canadian Journal on Aging* 14: 447–51.

McLaren, Angus. 1990. *Our Own Master Race: Eugenics in Canada, 1845–1945.* Toronto: McClelland & Stewart.

McMullin, Julie A., and Victor W. Marshall. 1995. 'Social Integration: Family, Friends and Social Support', in Marshall, Mullin, P. J. Ballantyne, J. F. Daciuk, and B. T. Wigdor, eds, *Contributions to Independence Over the Life Course.* Toronto: Centre for Studies in Aging, University of Toronto.

Marshall, Victor W. 1995. 'Rethinking Retirement: Issues for the Twenty-First Century', in E. M. Gee and G. M. Gutman, eds, *Rethinking Retirement.* Vancouver: Gerontology Research Centre, Simon Fraser University, 31–50.

———. 1997. 'The Generations: Contributions, Conflict, Equity', prepared for the Division of Aging and Seniors, Health Canada.

Murphy, Michael. 1996. 'Implications of and Aging Society and Changing Labour Market: Demographics', *Roundtable on Canada's Aging Society and Retirement Income System.* Ottawa: Caledon Institute of Social Policy.

Myles, John. 1995. 'Pensions and the Elderly', *Review of Income and Wealth* 41: 101–6.

———. 1996. 'Challenges Facing the Welfare State: Putting Pension Reform in Context', in A. Joshi and E. Berger, eds, *Aging Workforce, Income Security and Retirement Policy and* *Practical Implications.* Hamilton, Ont.: Office of Gerontological Studies, McMaster University, 51–6.

Osberg, Lars. 1998. 'Meaning and Measurement in Intergenerational Equity', in M. Corak, ed., *Government Finances and Generational Equity.* Ottawa: Statistics Canada Catalogue No. 68–513–XPB, 131–9.

——— and Pierre Fortin, eds. 1996a. *Unnecessary Debts.* Toronto: James Lorimar.

——— and ——— Pierre Fortin. 1996b. 'Credibility Mountain', in Osberg and Fortin (1996a: 157–72).

Pozo, Susan, ed. 1996. Exploring the Underground Economy: Studies of Illegal and Unreported Activity. Kalamazoo, Mich.: W.E. Upjohn Institute for Employment Research.

Prince, Michael J. 1996. 'From Expanding Coverage to Heading for Cover: Shifts in the Politics and Policies of Canadian Pension Reform', in A. Joshi and E. Berger, eds. *Aging Workforce, Income Security and Retirement Policy and Practical Implications.* Hamilton, Ont.: Office of Gerontological Studies, McMaster University, 57–67.

——— and Neena L. Chappell. 1994. Voluntary Action by Seniors in Canada. Victoria, BC: Centre on Aging, University of Victoria.

Robertson, Ann. 1997. 'Beyond Apocalyptic Demography: Towards a Moral Economy of Interdependence', *Ageing and Society* 17: 425–26.

Rosenberg, Mark W., and Eric G. Moore, 1996. 'Transferring the Future of Canada's Aging Population', in Federation of Canadian Demographers, *Towards the XXIst Century: Emerging Socio-Demographic Trends and Policy in Canada.* Ottawa: Canadian Federation of Demographers, 35–41.

Rosenbluth, Gideon. 1996. 'The Debt and Canada's Social Programs', in Osberg and Fortin (1996a: 90–111).

Rosenthal, Carolyn J. 1994. 'Long-term Care Reform and "Family" Care: A Worrisome Combination', *Canadian Journal of Aging* 13: 419–27.

Statistics Canada. 1998. *The Daily.* http://www.statcan.ca/Daily/English/980512/d980512.pdf

Thompson, Kenneth. 1998. *Moral Panics.* London: Routledge.

US Department of Commerce. 1993. *An Aging World II.* Washington: Government Printing Office: International Population Report Series P-95 (Feb.).

Van Audenrode, Marc. 1996. 'Some Myths about Monetary Policy', in Osberg and Fortin (1996a: 112–23).

Wolfson, M. C., G. Rowe, X. Lin, and S. F. Gribble. 1998. 'Historical Generational Accounting with Heterogeneous Populations', in M. Corak, ed., *Government Finances and Generational Equity.* Ottawa: Statistics Canada Catalogue No. 68–513–XPB, 107–25.

Chapter 24

Aging Around the World: The Aged as Teachers

DONALD O. COWGILL

In some ways, this selection likely reinforces something that most readers already believe: In many traditional societies, the elderly are treated with respect (read: more respect than is associated with the elderly in our society) because they are repositories of valued knowledge. Certainly, the many examples presented here—drawn overwhelmingly from the anthropological literature—suggest that this common belief is well grounded. On the other hand, there are also other lessons to be learned from this selection. For example, it seems clear that "storytelling" in traditional societies is a well-developed art, and that the process of storytelling binds together grandparents and grandchildren in a way that does not happen in our society. Why? Partly, it likely is that the elderly in our society are less likely to have valuable knowledge to transmit, but it also seems obvious that there are other factors at work, e.g., grandchildren are less likely to live near their grandparents; the "storytelling function" has been taken over by the mass media; and so on. Generally, this selection can serve as the starting point for thinking about the *many* reasons that the elderly in our society have lost ground relative to the elderly in traditional societies.

Almost forty years ago, Simmons (1945:40) asserted: "Few generalizations concerning the aged in primitive societies can be made with greater confidence than that they have almost universally been regarded as the custodians of knowledge *par excellence* and the chief instructors of the people." Maxwell and Silverman (1970) hypothesized that control of useful knowledge is a primary basis of the high esteem in which older people are held in such societies. Later, Watson and Maxwell (1977) confirmed this hypothesis after correlating an information control scale with a scale for esteem of elderly in 26 societies. This implies that control of useful information partially explains the high esteem of the elderly in primitive societies, but, conversely, the loss of such control in modern societies helps explain the decline in the status of the elderly in these societies.

Among the Aleuts in the late nineteenth century, every village reportedly had one or two men whose special function was to educate the children (Elliot, 1886). In many societies this becomes the particular prerogative of grandparents. Thus it is the grandparents, not the parents, who represent the chief transgenerational conveyors of a society's culture (Tomashevich, 1981:21). So it is among the !Kung Bushman, where the grandparents care for small children while their mothers are away on their gathering forays (Biesele and Howell, 1981:89). The elder generation spends much of its time in teaching the grandchildren the skills, traditions, and values of the society. In fact the

Baganda define a good grandparent as "one who teaches, loves and cares for his or her grandchildren" (Nahemow, 1983:112). This is true also in Dahomean society, where older people spend much of their time educating their grandchildren, using storytelling as the chief medium (Tomashevich, 1981:28). But this is neither a matter of convenience nor of blood relationship; it is very much a matter of age and experience. Age and wisdom are so closely identified.

It is natural that such wise persons should be advisors as well as teachers.

Another area in which the knowledge of older people is extensive and relevant is the physical environment within which the people live. Fuller notes (1972:59) that among the Zulu, information supplied by him about the natural environment was distrusted because he "was not old enough to know." The only credible information came from their own elderly. The elderly of the Maori are a veritable storehouse of nature lore. The names of all living things are known and this represents only a fragment of the information stored in the memories of elderly Maori people (Simmons, 1945:138). The older men among the Aranda of Australia teach the young the tracks of various animals and the location of the best sources of food.

Perhaps even more notable among the teaching skills of the elderly are those in the realm of arts and crafts. These range broadly through music, art, pottery, weaving, tanning, dance, flower arranging, and calligraphy. Among them are the best technicians, the older women in pottery and basketry and the older men in weaving and tanning. In Japan the folk arts in which older people excel and which they in turn teach to the young include calligraphy, flower arranging, the tea ceremony, *bonsai* horticulture, and several stylized forms of poetry (Maeda, 1978:66–67). Among the Bantus of southern Africa, an elderly male or female usually initiated a dance, performing the first steps, and an elder began the first drumming (Fuller, 1972:63). The treasured knowledge of the elders of the Coast Salish included methods of construction and canoe making (Amoss, 1981a:227).

A favorite medium through which the elderly carry out their educator role is storytelling. Some develop this to a high art, and the education is at the same time amusement and entertainment. Such was the case with the old men of the Asmat tribe. Beginning at about the age of eight, boys would gather at the fireplace of their grandfather to listen to the adventures of fictional characters, or of animals. In the course of such stories, the children would learn much about their jungle environment and the natural resources of the area (Van Arsdale 1981b:116–117). The young defer to the elderly among the !Kung Bushmen, and the elderly take great delight in telling and retelling stories of their own exploits or those of mythical beings (Biesele and Howell, 1981:88–89). Oratory is a prized art form in Samoa, and the young orator chiefs often gather in the evening to listen to their elders as they discuss myths, legends, customs, family history, and genealogy. The aged are considered storehouses of information, and this is the customary method of imparting it (Holmes and Rhoads, 1983:123).

I observed an interesting variation in the use of older people for oral history in China in 1978. Here the elderly were encouraged to tell about their lives before the Revolution of 1949. The intent was the opposite of most oral history; instead of glorifying the past, the purpose was to portray the horrible conditions that obtained in China before the revolution and in the process to justify it and attest to the progress since then. The elderly often visit schools to tell their "bitterness stories." In performing this role, the elderly are presented as heroes in Chinese society (Missine, 1982:7).

What do older people get in return for these activities? Often the returns are very tangible and very practical. In fact the simplest answer to the question is: they get a living. In some societies this is supplied in a quid pro quo exchange;

that is, in return for a given bit of valued information, the elder may receive definite remuneration. Aged men among the Navaho charged high prices for information about cures, sacred names, legends, secrets, and songs (Simmons, 1945:135). They were paid in sheep, cattle, or horses.

In other instances the exchange was less explicit and less crassly economic. Marshall (1976) reports that among the !Kung Bushmen, a hunter is expected to share any kill with his parents and with his wife's parents.

But apart from the economic rewards, which may be specific and explicit or quite general and implicit, there are other rewards. When the information imparted is valued, its possessors and teachers will also be valued, and this implies some other intangible dividends in the form of prestige, honor, respect, and a sense of importance to the community. The feeling of being a significant member of the society and having a secure and accepted role in it is certainly a part of the role of the aged in the preindustrial societies. It is a role that tends to be eroded in the process of modernization.

The fact of the matter is that rapid social change, such as the contemporary process of modernization, renders older people obsolete. Their classic role as conservators and transmitters of vital information is destroyed. Much that they know is no longer pertinent, and much that they don't know is essential.

The acceleration of social change—along with the developing technology of recording, storing, and retrieving information—has largely destroyed the traditional role of the elderly as teachers. The pace of social change is now so swift that one's knowledge and skills are obsolete by the time one is old, unless of course he or she participates in lifelong learning, as a few are belatedly coming to do. But even here the emphasis is upon the renewal of technical skills or the development of idiosyncratic forms of personal expression. There does not appear to be anything on the education horizon that would renew the grandparent-to-grandchild teaching-learning relationship.

BIBLIOGRAPHY

Amoss, Pamela T. 1981a. "Coast Salish Elders." Pp. 227–47 in P. T. Amoss and S. Harrell (eds.), *Other Ways of Growing Old*. Stanford, CA: Stanford University Press.

Biesele, Megan, and Nancy Howell. 1981. "The Old People Give You Life: Aging Among !Kung Hunter Gatherers." Pp. 77–98 in P. Amoss and S. Harrell (eds.), *Other Ways of Growing Old: Anthropological Perspectives*. Stanford, CA: Stanford University Press.

Elliott, H. W. 1886. *Our Arctic Province: Alaska and the Seal Islands*. New York: Scribner's.

Fuller, Charles Edward. 1972. "Aging Among Southern African Bantu." Pp. 51–72 in D. O. Cowgill and L. D. Holmes (eds.), *Aging and Modernization*. New York: Appleton-Century-Crofts.

Holmes, Lowell D., and Ellen C. Rhoads. 1983. "Aging and Change in Modern Samoa." Pp. 119–29 in J. Sokolovsky (ed.), *Growing Old in Different Cultures*. Belmont, CA: Wadsworth.

Maeda, Daisaku. 1978. "Ageing in Eastern Society." Pp. 45–72 in D. Hobman (ed.), *The Social Challenge of Ageing*. New York: St. Martin's Press.

Marshall, Lorna. 1976. "Sharing, Talking and Giving." Pp. 349–71 in R. B. Lee and I. DeVore (eds.), *Kalahari Hunter Gatherers: Studies of !Kung San and Their Neighbors*. Cambridge: MA: Harvard University Press.

Maxwell, Robert J., and Philip Silverman. 1970. "Information and Esteem: Cultural Considerations in the Treatment of the Elderly." *Aging and Human Development* 1: 361–92.

Missine, Leo E. 1982. "Elders Are Educators." *Perspective on Aging* 11 (No. 6, November–December): 5–8.

Nahemow, Nina. 1983. "Grandparenthood in Baganda: Role Option in Old Age?" Pp. 104–15 in J. Sokolovsky (ed.), *Growing Old in Different Societies: Cross-Cultural Perspectives.* Belmont, CA: Wadsworth.

Simmons, Leo. 1945. *The Role of the Aged in Primitive Society.* London: Oxford University Press.

Tomashevich, George Vid. 1981. "Aging and the Aged in Various Cultures." Pp. 17–41 in G. Falk, U. Falk, and G. V. Tomashevich (eds.), *Aging in America and Other Cultures.* Saratoga, CA: Century Twenty One Publishing.

Van Arsdale, Peter W. 1981. "The Elderly Asmat of New Guinea." Pp. 111–23 in P. T. Amoss and S. Harrell (eds.), *Other Ways of Growing Old: Anthropological Perspectives.* Stanford, CA: Stanford University Press.

Watson, Wilbur H., and Robert J. Maxwell (eds.). 1977. *Human Aging and Dying: A Study in Sociocultural Gerontology.* New York: St. Martin's Press.

PART 9
Deviance

Chapter 25

On Being Sane in Insane Places

DAVID L. ROSENHAN[1]

It sounds like a movie: Sane people get admitted to mental institutions to investigate the bad guys only to find that nobody believes them when they say that they are sane and try to get out. In fact, the sane patients who sought admission to mental hospitals in the experiment reported here did all get out. Rosenhan's concern, however, is to use the data that they recorded in these hospitals to document the profound effect that the label of "insane" had on the hospital professionals. As those data demonstrate, staff reactions to the simplest behaviours (like asking a question) differed dramatically from what happens outside the hospital. These particular "patients," being part of an experiment, did not have to carry their label with them when they left the hospital. Unfortunately, real patients typically do not have that option. Is Rosenhan correct in suggesting that the mentally ill have become the modern equivalent of lepers in our society?

If sanity and insanity exist, how shall we know them?

The question is neither capricious nor itself insane. However much we may be personally convinced that we can tell the normal from the abnormal, the evidence is simply not compelling. It is commonplace, for example, to read about murder trials wherein eminent psychiatrists for the defense are contradicted by equally eminent psychiatrists for the prosecution on the matter of the defendant's sanity. More generally, there are a great deal of conflicting data on the reliability, utility, and meaning of such terms as "sanity," "insanity," "mental illness," and "schizophrenia." (*1*) Finally, as early as 1934, Benedict suggested that normality and abnormality are not universal (*2*). What is viewed as normal in one culture may be seen as quite aberrant in another. Thus, notions of normality and abnormality may not be quite as accurate as people believe they are.

To raise questions regarding normality and abnormality is in no way to question the fact that some behaviors are deviant or odd. Murder is deviant. So, too, are hallucinations. Nor does raising such questions deny the existence of the personal anguish that is often associated with "mental illness." Anxiety and depression exist. Psychological suffering exists. But normality and abnormality, sanity and insanity, and the diagnoses that flow from them may be less substantive than many believe them to be.

At its heart, the question of whether the sane can be distinguished from the insane (and

[1] The author is professor of psychology and law at Stanford University, Stanford, California 94305. Portions of these data were presented to colloquiums of the psychology departments at the University of California at Berkeley and at Santa Barbara; University of Arizona, Tucson; and Harvard University, Cambridge, Massachusetts.

Source: D.L. Rosenhan, "On being sane in insane places," *Science*, New Series, Vol. 179, No. 4070 (Jan. 19, 1973). Reprinted with permission from AAAS.

whether degrees of insanity can be distinguished from each other) is a simple matter: Do the salient characteristics that lead to diagnoses reside in the patients themselves or in the environments and contexts in which observers find them? The belief has been strong that patients present symptoms, that those symptoms can be categorized, and, implicitly, that the sane are distinguishable from the insane. More recently, however, this belief has been questioned. Based in part on theoretical and anthropological considerations, but also on philosophical, legal, and therapeutic ones, the view has grown that psychological categorization of mental illness is useless at best and downright harmful, misleading, and pejorative at worst. Psychiatric diagnoses, in this view, are in the minds of observers and are not valid summaries of characteristics displayed by the observed (*3–5*).

Gains can be made in deciding which of these is more nearly accurate by getting normal people (that is, people who do not have, and have never suffered, symptoms of serious psychiatric disorders) admitted to psychiatric hospitals and then determining whether they were discovered to be sane and, if so, how. If the sanity of such pseudopatients were always detected, there would be prima facie evidence that a sane individual can be distinguished from the insane context in which he is found. Normality (and presumably abnormality) is distinct enough that it can be recognized wherever it occurs, for it is carried within the person. If, on the other hand, the sanity of the pseudopatients were never discovered, serious difficulties would arise for those who support traditional modes of psychiatric diagnosis. Given that the hospital staff was not incompetent, that the pseudopatient had been behaving as sanely as he had been outside of the hospital, and that it had never been previously suggested that he belonged in a psychiatric hospital, such an unlikely outcome would support the view that psychiatric diagnosis betrays little about the patient but much about the environment in which an observer finds him.

This article describes such an experiment. Eight sane people gained secret admission to 12 different hospitals (*6*). Their diagnostic experiences constitute the data of the first part of this article; the remainder is devoted to a description of their experiences in psychiatric institutions.

PSEUDOPATIENTS AND THEIR SETTINGS

The eight pseudopatients were a varied group. One was a psychology graduate student in his 20's. The remaining seven were older and "established." Among them were three psychologists, a pediatrician, a psychiatrist, a painter, and a housewife. Three pseudopatients were women, five were men. All of them employed pseudonyms, lest their alleged diagnoses embarrass them later. Those who were in mental health professions alleged another occupation in order to avoid the special attentions that might be accorded by staff, as a matter of courtesy or caution, to ailing colleagues. (*7*) With the exception of myself (I was the first pseudopatient and my presence was known to the hospital administration and chief psychologist and, so far as I can tell, to them alone), the presence of pseudopatients and the nature of the research program was not known to the hospital staffs (*8*).

The settings were similarly varied. In order to generalize the findings, admission into a variety of hospitals was sought. The 12 hospitals in the sample were located in five different states on the East and West coasts. Some were old and shabby, some were quite new. Some were research-oriented, others not. Some had good staff-patient ratios, others were quite understaffed. Only one was a strictly private hospital. All of the others were supported by state or federal funds or, in one instance, by university funds.

After calling the hospital for an appointment, the pseudopatient arrived at the admissions office complaining that he had been hearing voices. Asked what the voices said, he replied that they were often unclear, but as far as he could tell they said "empty," "hollow," and "thud." The voices were unfamiliar and were of the same sex as the pseudopatient. The choice of these symptoms was occasioned by their apparent similarity to existential symptoms. Such symptoms are alleged to arise from painful concerns about the perceived meaninglessness of one's life. It is as if the hallucinating person were saying, "My life is empty and hollow." The choice of these symptoms was also determined by the absence of a single report of existential psychoses in the literature.

Beyond alleging the symptoms and falsifying name, vocation, and employment, no further alterations of person, history, or circumstances were made. The significant events of the pseudopatient's life history were presented as they had actually occurred. Relationships with parents and siblings, with spouse and children, with people at work and in school, consistent with the aforementioned exceptions, were described as they were or had been. Frustrations and upsets were described along with joys and satisfactions. These facts are important to remember. If anything, they strongly biased the subsequent results in favor of detecting sanity, since none of their histories or current behaviors were seriously pathological in any way.

Immediately upon admission to the psychiatric ward, the pseudopatient ceased simulating *any* symptoms of abnormality. In some cases, there was a brief period of mild nervousness and anxiety, since none of the pseudopatients really believed that they would be admitted so easily. Indeed, their shared fear was that they would be immediately exposed as frauds and greatly embarrassed. Moreover, many of them had never visited a psychiatric ward; even those who had, nevertheless, had some genuine fears about what might happen to them. Their nervousness, then, was quite appropriate to the novelty of the hospital setting, and it abated rapidly.

Apart from that short-lived nervousness, the pseudopatient behaved on the ward as he "normally" behaved. The pseudopatient spoke to patients and staff as he might ordinarily. Because

there is uncommonly little to do on a psychiatric ward, he attempted to engage others in conversation. When asked by staff how he was feeling, he indicated that he was fine, that he no longer experienced symptoms. He responded to instructions from attendants, to calls for medication (which was not swallowed), and to dining-hall instructions. Beyond such activities as were available to him on the admissions ward, he spent his time writing down his observations about the ward, its patients, and the staff. Initially these notes were written "secretly," but as it soon became clear that no one much cared, they were subsequently written on standard tablets of paper in such public places as the dayroom. No secret was made of these activities.

The pseudopatient, very much as a true psychiatric patient, entered a hospital with no foreknowledge of when he would be discharged. Each was told that he would have to get out by his own devices, essentially by convincing the staff that he was sane. The psychological stresses associated with hospitalization were considerable, and all but one of the pseudopatients desired to be discharged almost immediately after being admitted. They were, therefore, motivated not only to behave sanely, but to be paragons of cooperation. That their behavior was in no way disruptive is confirmed by nursing reports, which have been obtained on most of the patients. These reports uniformly indicate that the patients were "friendly," "cooperative," and "exhibited no abnormal indications."

THE NORMAL ARE NOT DETECTABLY SANE

Despite their public "show" of sanity, the pseudopatients were never detected. Admitted, except in one case, with a diagnosis of schizophrenia, (9) each was discharged with a diagnosis of schizophrenia "in remission." The label "in remission" should in no way be dismissed as a formality, for at no time during any hospitalization had any question been raised about any pseudopatient's simulation. Nor are there any indications in the hospital records that the pseudopatient's status was suspect. Rather, the evidence is strong that, once labeled schizophrenic, the pseudopatient was stuck with that label. If the pseudopatient was to be discharged, he must naturally be "in remission"; but he was not sane, nor, in the institution's view, had he ever been sane.

The uniform failure to recognize sanity cannot be attributed to the quality of the hospitals, for, although there were considerable variations among them, several are considered excellent. Nor can it be alleged that there was simply not enough time to observe the pseudopatients. Length of hospitalization ranged from 7 to 52 days, with an average of 19 days. The pseudopatients were not, in fact, carefully observed, but this failure speaks more to traditions within psychiatric hospitals than to lack of opportunity.

Finally, it cannot be said that the failure to recognize the pseudopatients' sanity was due to the fact that they were not behaving sanely. While there was clearly some tension present in all of them, their daily visitors could detect no serious behavioral consequences—nor, indeed, could other patients. It was quite common for the patients to "detect" the pseudopatient's sanity. During the first three hospitalizations, when accurate counts were kept, 35 of a total of 118 patients on the admissions ward voiced their suspicions, some vigorously. "You're not crazy. You're a journalist, or a professor (referring to the continual note-taking). You're checking up on the hospital." While most of the patients were reassured by the pseudopatient's insistence that he had been sick before he came in but was fine now, some continued to believe that the pseudopatient was sane throughout his hospitalization (10). The fact that the patients often recognized normality when staff did not raises important questions.

Failure to detect sanity during the course of hospitalization may be due to the fact that physicians operate with a strong bias toward what statisticians call the Type 2 error (5). This is to say that physicians are more inclined to call a healthy person sick (a false positive, Type 2) than a sick person healthy (a false negative, Type 1). The reasons for this are not hard to find: it is clearly more dangerous to misdiagnose illness than health. Better to err on the side of caution, to suspect illness even among the healthy.

But what holds for medicine does not hold equally well for psychiatry. Medical illnesses, while unfortunate, are not commonly pejorative. Psychiatric diagnoses, on the contrary, carry with them personal, legal, and social stigmas (11). It was therefore important to see whether the tendency toward diagnosing the sane insane could be reversed. The following experiment was arranged at a research and teaching hospital whose staff had heard these findings but doubted that such an error could occur in their hospital. The staff was informed that at some time during the following three months, one or more pseudopatients would attempt to be admitted into the psychiatric hospital. Each staff member was asked to rate each patient who presented himself at admissions or on the ward according to the likelihood that the patient was a pseudopatient. A 10-point scale was used, with a 1 and 2 reflecting high confidence that the patient was a pseudopatient.

Judgments were obtained on 193 patients who were admitted for psychiatric treatment. All staff who had had sustained contact with or primary responsibility for the patient—attendants, nurses, psychiatrists, physicians, and psychologists—were asked to make judgments. Forty-one patients were alleged, with high confidence, to be pseudopatients by at least one member of the staff. Twenty-three were considered suspect by at least one psychiatrist. Nineteen were suspected by one psychiatrist and one other staff member. Actually, no genuine pseudopatient (at least from my group) presented himself during this period.

The experiment is instructive. It indicates that the tendency to designate sane people as insane can be reversed when the stakes (in this case, prestige and diagnostic acumen) are high.

But what can be said of the 19 people who were suspected of being "sane" by one psychiatrist and another staff member? Were these people truly "sane" or was it rather the case that in the course of avoiding the Type 2 error the staff tended to make more errors of the first sort—calling the crazy "sane"? There is no way of knowing. But one thing is certain: any diagnostic process that lends itself too readily to massive errors of this sort cannot be a very reliable one.

THE STICKINESS OF PSYCHODIAGNOSTIC LABELS

Beyond the tendency to call the healthy sick—a tendency that accounts better for diagnostic behavior on admission than it does for such behavior after a lengthy period of exposure—the data speak to the massive role of labeling in psychiatric assessment. Having once been labeled schizophrenic, there is nothing the pseudopatient can do to overcome the tag. The tag profoundly colors others' perceptions of him and his behavior.

As far as I can determine, diagnoses were in no way affected by the relative health of the circumstances of a pseudopatient's life. Rather, the reverse occurred: the perception of his circumstances was shaped entirely by the diagnosis. A clear example of such translation is found in the case of a pseudopatient who had had a close relationship with his mother but was rather remote from his father during his early childhood. During adolescence and beyond, however, his father became a close friend, while his relationship with his mother cooled. His present relationship with his wife was characteristically close and warm. Apart from occasional angry exchanges, friction was minimal. The children had rarely been spanked. Surely there is nothing especially pathological about such a history. Indeed, many readers may see a similar pattern in their own experiences, with no markedly deleterious consequences. Observe, however,

how such a history was translated in the psychopathological context, this from the case summary prepared after the patient was discharged.

> This white 39-year-old male . . . manifests a long history of considerable ambivalence in close relationships, which begins in early childhood. A warm relationship with his mother cools during his adolescence. A distant relationship with his father is described as becoming very intense. Affective stability is absent. His attempts to control emotionality with his wife and children are punctuated by angry outbursts and, in the case of the children, spankings. And while he says that he has several good friends, one senses considerable ambivalence embedded in those relationships also . . .

The facts of the case were unintentionally distorted by the staff to achieve consistency with a popular theory of the dynamics of a schizophrenic reaction (*12*). Nothing of an ambivalent nature had been described in relations with parents, spouse, or friends. To the extent that ambivalence could be inferred, it was probably not greater than is found in all human relationships. It is true the pseudopatient's relationships with his parents changed over time, but in the ordinary context that would hardly be remarkable—indeed, it might very well be expected. Clearly, the meaning ascribed to his verbalizations (that is, ambivalence, affective instability) was determined by the diagnosis: schizophrenia. An entirely different meaning would have been ascribed if it were known that the man was "normal."

All pseudopatients took extensive notes publicly. Under ordinary circumstances, such behavior would have raised questions in the minds of observers, as, in fact, it did among patients. Indeed, it seemed so certain that the notes would elicit suspicion that elaborate precautions were taken to remove them from the ward each day. But the precautions proved needless. The closest any staff member came to questioning those notes occurred when one pseudopatient asked his physician what kind of medication he was receiving and began to write down the response. "You needn't write it," he was told gently. "If you have trouble remembering, just ask me again."

If no questions were asked of the pseudopatients, how was their writing interpreted? Nursing records for three patients indicate that the writing was seen as an aspect of their pathological behavior. "Patient engaged in writing behavior" was the daily nursing comment on one of the pseudopatients who was never questioned about his writing. Given that the patient is in the hospital, he must be psychologically disturbed. And given that he is disturbed, continuous writing must be behavioral manifestation of that disturbance, perhaps a subset of the compulsive behaviors that are sometimes correlated with schizophrenia.

One tacit characteristic of psychiatric diagnosis is that it locates the sources of aberration within the individual and only rarely within the complex of stimuli that surrounds him. Consequently, behaviors that are stimulated by the environment are commonly misattributed to the patient's disorder. For example, one kindly nurse found a pseudopatient pacing the long hospital corridors. "Nervous, Mr. X?" she asked. "No, bored," he said.

The notes kept by pseudopatients are full of patient behaviors that were misinterpreted by well-intentioned staff. Often enough, a patient would go "berserk" because he had, wittingly or unwittingly, been mistreated by, say, an attendant. A nurse coming upon the scene would rarely inquire even cursorily into the environmental stimuli of the patient's behavior. Rather, she assumed that his upset derived from his pathology, not from his present interactions with other staff members. Occasionally, the staff might assume that the patient's family (especially when they had recently visited) or other patients had stimulated the outburst. But never were the staff found to assume that one of themselves or the structure of the hospital had anything to do with a patient's behavior. One psychiatrist pointed to a group of patients who were sitting outside the cafeteria entrance half an hour before lunchtime. To a group of young residents he indicated that such behavior was characteristic of the oral-acquisitive nature of the syndrome. It seemed not to occur to him that there were very few things to anticipate in a psychiatric hospital besides eating.

A psychiatric label has a life and an influence of its own. Once the impression has been formed that the patient is schizophrenic, the expectation is that he will continue to be schizophrenic. When a sufficient amount of time has passed, during which the patient has done nothing bizarre, he is considered to be in remission and available for discharge. But the label endures beyond discharge, with the unconfirmed expectation that he will behave as a schizophrenic again. Such labels, conferred by mental health professionals, are as influential on the patient as they are on his relatives and friends, and it should not surprise anyone that the diagnosis acts on all of them as a self-fulfilling prophecy. Eventually, the patient himself accepts the diagnosis, with all of its surplus meanings and expectations, and behaves accordingly (5).

THE EXPERIENCE OF PSYCHIATRIC HOSPITALIZATION

The term "mental illness" is of recent origin. It was coined by people who were humane in their inclinations and who wanted very much to raise the station of (and the public's sympathies toward) the psychologically disturbed from that of witches and "crazies" to one that was akin to the physically ill. And they were at least partially successful, for the treatment of the mentally ill has improved considerably over the years. But while treatment has improved, it is doubtful that people really regard the mentally ill in the same way that they view the physically ill. A broken leg is something one recovers from, but mental illness allegedly endures forever (13). A broken leg does not threaten the observer, but a crazy schizophrenic? There is by now a host of evidence that attitudes toward the mentally ill are characterized by fear, hostility, aloofness, suspicion, and dread (*14*). The mentally ill are society's lepers.

That such attitudes infect the general population is perhaps not surprising, only upsetting. But that they affect the professionals—attendants, nurses, physicians, psychologists and social workers—who treat and deal with the mentally ill is more disconcerting. Negative attitudes are there too and can easily be detected. Such attitudes should not surprise us. They are the natural offspring of the labels patients wear and the places in which they are found.

Consider the structure of the typical psychiatric hospital. Staff and patients are strictly segregated. Staff have their own living space, including their dining facilities, bathrooms, and assembly places. The glassed quarters that contain the professional staff, which the pseudopatients came to call "the cage," sit out on every dayroom. The staff emerge primarily for caretaking purposes—to give medication, to conduct therapy or group meeting, to instruct or reprimand a patient. Otherwise, staff keep to themselves, almost as if the disorder that afflicts their charges is somehow catching.

So much is patient-staff segregation the rule that, for four public hospitals in which an attempt was made to measure the degree to which staff and patients mingle, it was necessary to use "time out of the staff cage" as the operational measure. While it was not the case that all time spent out of the cage was spent mingling with patients (attendants, for example, would occasionally emerge to watch television in the dayroom), it was the only way in which one could gather reliable data on time for measuring.

The average amount of time spent by attendants outside of the cage was 11.3 percent (range, 3 to 52 percent). This figure does not represent only time spent mingling with patients, but also includes time spent on such chores as folding laundry, supervising patients while they shave, directing ward cleanup, and

sending patients to off-ward activities. It was the relatively rare attendant who spent time talking with patients or playing games with them. It proved impossible to obtain a "percent mingling time" for nurses, since the amount of time they spent out of the cage was too brief. Rather, we counted instances of emergence from the cage. On the average, daytime nurses emerged from the cage 11.5 times per shift, including instances when they left the ward entirely (range, 4 to 39 times). Later afternoon and night nurses were even less available, emerging on the average 9.4 times per shift (range, 4 to 41 times). Data on early morning nurses, who arrived usually after midnight and departed at 8 a.m., are not available because patients were asleep during most of this period.

Physicians, especially psychiatrists, were even less available. They were rarely seen on the wards. Quite commonly, they would be seen only when they arrived and departed, with the remaining time being spent in their offices or in the cage. Consequently, it is understandable that attendants not only spend more time with patients than do any other members of the staff—that is required by their station in the hierarchy—but, also, insofar as they learn from their superior's behavior, spend as little time with patients as they can. Attendants are seen mainly in the cage, which is where the models, the action, and the power are.

I turn now to a different set of studies, those dealing with staff response to patient-initiated contact. It has long been known that the amount of time a person spends with you can be an index of your significance to him. If he initiates and maintains eye contact, there is reason to believe that he is considering your requests and needs. If he pauses to chat or actually stops and talks, there is added reason to infer that he is individuating you. In four hospitals, the pseudopatients approached the staff member with a request which took the following form: "Pardon me, Mr. [or Dr. or Mrs.] X, could you tell me when I will be eligible for grounds privileges?" (or " . . . when I will be presented at the staff meeting?" or

TABLE 25.1 SELF-INITIATED CONTACT BY PSEUDOPATIENTS WITH PSYCHIATRISTS AND NURSES AND ATTENDANTS, COMPARED TO CONTACT WITH OTHER GROUPS

CONTACT	PSYCHIATRIC HOSPITALS		UNIVERSITY CAMPUS (NONMEDICAL)	UNIVERSITY MEDICAL CENTER PHYSICIANS		
	Psychiatrists	Nurses and attendants	Faculty	"Looking for a psychiatrist"	"Looking for an internist"	No additional comment
Responses						
Moves on, head averted (%)	71	88	0	0	0	0
Makes eye contact (%)	23	10	0	11	0	0
Pauses and chats (%)	2	2	0	11	0	10
Stops and talks (%)	4	.5	100	78	100	90
Mean number of questions answered (out of 6)	*	*	6	3.8	4.8	4.5
Respondents (No.)	13	47	14	18	15	10
Attempts (No.)	185	1283	14	18	15	10

* Not applicable.

". . . when I am likely to be discharged?"). While the content of the question varied according to the appropriateness of the target and the pseudopatient's (apparent) current needs the form was always a courteous and relevant request for information. Care was taken never to approach a particular member of the staff more than once a day, lest the staff member become suspicious or irritated. In examining these data, remember that the behavior of the pseudopatients was neither bizarre nor disruptive. One could indeed engage in good conversation with them.

The data for these experiments are shown in Table 25.1, separately for physicians (column 1) and for nurses and attendants (column 2). Minor differences between these four institutions were overwhelmed by the degree to which staff avoided continuing contacts that patients had initiated. By far, their most common response consisted of either a brief response to the question, offered while they were "on the move" and with head averted, or no response at all.

The encounter frequently took the following bizarre form: (pseudopatient) "Pardon me, Dr. X. Could you tell me when I am eligible for grounds privileges?" (physician) "Good morning, Dave. How are you today?" (Moves off without waiting for a response.)

It is instructive to compare these data recently obtained at Stanford University. It has been alleged that large and eminent universities are characterized by faculty who are so busy that they have no time for students. For this comparison, a young lady approached individual faculty members who seemed to be walking purposefully to some meeting or teaching engagement and asked them the following six questions.

1. "Pardon me, could you direct me to Encina Hall?" (at the medical school: ". . . to the Clinical Research Center?").
2. "Do you know where Fish Annex is?" (there is no Fish Annex at Stanford).
3. "Do you teach here?"
4. "How does one apply for admission to the college?" (at the medical school: ". . . to the medical school?")
5. "Is it difficult to get in?"
6. "Is there financial aid?"

Without exception, as can be seen in Table 25.1 (column 3), all of the questions were answered.

No matter how rushed they were, all respondents not only maintained eye contact, but stopped to talk. Indeed, many of the respondents went out of their way to direct or take the questioner to the office she was seeking, to try to locate "Fish Annex," or to discuss with her the possibilities of being admitted to the university.

Similar data, also shown in Table 25.1 (columns 4, 5, and 6), were obtained in the hospital. Here too, the young lady came prepared with six questions. After the first question, however, she remarked to 18 of her respondents (column 4), "I'm looking for a psychiatrist," and to 15 others (column 5), "I'm looking for an internist." Ten other respondents received no inserted comment (column 6). The general degree of cooperative responses is considerably higher for these university groups than it was for pseudopatients in psychiatric hospitals. Even so, differences are apparent within the medical school setting. Once having indicated that she was looking for a psychiatrist, the degree of cooperation elicited was less than when she sought an internist.

POWERLESSNESS AND DEPERSONALIZATION

Eye contact and verbal contact reflect concern and individuation; their absence, avoidance and depersonalization. The data I have presented do not do justice to the rich daily encounters that grew up around matters of depersonalization and avoidance. I have records of patients who were beaten by staff for the sin of having initiated verbal contact. During my own experience, for example, one patient was beaten in the presence of other patients for having approached an attendant and told him, "I like you." Occasionally, punishment meted out to patients for misdemeanors seemed so excessive that it could not be justified by the most rational interpretations of psychiatric cannon. Nevertheless, they appeared to go unquestioned. Tempers were often short. A patient who had not heard a call for medication would be roundly excoriated, and the morning attendants would often wake patients with, "Come on, you m_ _ _ _ _ f _ _ _ _ _ s, out of bed!"

Neither anecdotal nor "hard" data can convey the overwhelming sense of powerlessness which invades the individual as he is continually exposed to the depersonalization of the psychiatric hospital. It hardly matters which psychiatric hospital—the excellent public ones and the very plush private hospital were better than the rural and shabby ones in this regard, but, again, the features that psychiatric hospitals had in common overwhelmed by far their apparent differences.

Powerlessness was evident everywhere. The patient is deprived of many of his legal rights by dint of his psychiatric commitment (*15*). He is shorn of credibility by virtue of his psychiatric label. His freedom of movement is restricted. He cannot initiate contact with the staff, but may only respond to such overtures as they make. Personal privacy is minimal. Patient quarters and possessions can be entered and examined by any staff member, for whatever reason. His personal history and anguish is available to any staff member (often including the "grey lady" and "candy striper" volunteer) who chooses to read his folder, regardless of their therapeutic relationship to him. His personal hygiene and waste evacuation are often monitored. The water closets have no doors.

At times, depersonalization reached such proportions that pseudopatients had the sense that they were invisible, or at least unworthy of account. Upon being admitted, I and other pseudopatients took the initial physical examinations in a semipublic room, where staff members went about their own business as if we were not there.

On the ward, attendants delivered verbal and occasionally serious physical abuse to patients in the presence of others (the pseudopatients) who were writing it all down. Abusive behavior, on the other hand, terminated quite abruptly when other staff members were known to be coming. Staff are credible witnesses. Patients are not.

A nurse unbuttoned her uniform to adjust her brassiere in the presence of an entire ward of viewing men. One did not have the sense that she was being seductive. Rather, she didn't notice us. A group of staff persons might point to a patient in the dayroom and discuss him animatedly, as if he were not there.

THE CONSEQUENCES OF LABELING AND DEPERSONALIZATION

How many people, one wonders, are sane but not recognized as such in our psychiatric institutions? How many have been needlessly stripped of their privileges of citizenship, from the right to vote and drive to that of handling their own accounts? How many have feigned insanity in order to avoid the criminal consequences of their behavior, and, conversely, how many would rather stand trial than live interminably in a psychiatric hospital—but are wrongly thought to be mentally ill? How many have been stigmatized by well-intentioned, but nevertheless erroneous, diagnoses? On the last point, recall again that a "Type 2 error" in psychiatric diagnosis does not have the same consequences it does in medical diagnosis. A diagnosis of cancer that has been found to be in error is cause for celebration. But psychiatric diagnoses are rarely found to be in error. The label sticks, a mark of inadequacy forever.

Finally, how many patients might be "sane" outside the psychiatric hospital but seem insane in it—not because craziness resides in them, as it were, but because they are responding to a bizarre setting.

SUMMARY AND CONCLUSIONS

It is clear that we cannot distinguish the sane from the insane in psychiatric hospitals. The hospital itself imposes a special environment in which the meaning of behavior can easily be misunderstood. The consequences to patients hospitalized in such an environment—the powerlessness, depersonalization, segregation, mortification, and self-labeling—seem undoubtedly counter-therapeutic.

REFERENCES AND NOTES

1. P. Ash, J. *Abnorm. Soc. Psychol.* 44, 272 (1949); A. T. Beck, *Amer. J. Psychiat.* 119, 210 (1962); A. T. Boisen, *Psychiatry* 2, 233 (1938); N. Kreitman, *J. Ment. Sci.* 107, 876 (1961); N. Kreitman, P. Sainsbury, J. Morrisey, J. Towers, J. Scrivener, *ibid.*, p. 887; H. O. Schmitt and C. P. Fonda, *J. Abnorm. Soc. Psychol.* 52, 262 (1956); W. Seeman, *J. Nerv. Ment. Dis.* 118, 541 (1953). For an analysis of these artifacts and summaries of the disputes, see J. Zubin, *Annu. Rev. Psychol.* 18, 272 (1967); L. Phillips and J. G. Draguns, *ibid.* 22, 447 (1971).

2. R. Benedict, *J. Gen. Psychol.,* 10 59 (1934).

3. See in this regard H. Becker, *Outsiders: Studies in the Sociology of Deviance* (Free Press, New York, 1963); B. M. Braginsky, K. Ring, *Methods of Madness: The Mental Hospital as a Last Resort* (Holt, Reinhart & Winston, New York, 1969); G. M. Crocetti and P. V. Lemkau, *Amer. Sociol. Rev.* 30, 577 (1965); E. Goffman, *Behavior in Public Places* (Free Press, New York, 1964); R. D. Laing, *The Divided Self: A Study of Sanity and Madness* (Quadrangle, Chicago, 1960); D. L. Phillips, *Amer. Sociol. Rev.* 28, 963 (1963); T. R. Sarbin, Psychol. Today 6, 18 (1972); E. Schur, *Amer. J. Sociol.* 75, 309 (1969); T. Szasz, *Law, Liberty and Psychiatry* (Macmillan, New York, 1963); *The Myth of Mental Illness: Foundations of a Theory of Mental Illness* (Hoeber-Harper, New York, 1963). For a critique of some of these views, see W. R. Gove, *Amer. Sociol. Rev.* 35, 873 (1970).

4. E. Goffman, *Asylums* (Doubleday, Garden City, NY, 1961).

5. T. J. Scheff, *Being Mentally Ill: A Sociological Theory* (Aldine, Chicago, 1966).

6. Data from a ninth pseudopatient are not incorporated in this report because, although his sanity went undetected, he falsified aspects of his personal history, including his marital status and parental relationships. His experimental behaviors therefore were not identical to those of the other pseudo-patients.

7. Beyond the personal difficulties that the pseudopatient is likely to experience in the hospital, there are legal and social ones that, combined, require considerable attention before entry. For example, once admitted to a psychiatric institution, it is difficult, if not impossible, to be discharged on short notice, state law to the contrary notwithstanding. I was not sensitive to these difficulties at the outset of the project, nor to the personal and situational emergencies that can arise, but later a writ of habeas corpus was prepared for each of the entering pseudopatients and an attorney was kept "on call" during every hospitalization. I am grateful to John Kaplan and Robert Bartels for legal advice and assistance in these matters.

8. However distasteful such concealment is, it was a necessary first step to examining these questions. Without concealment, there would have been no way to know how valid these experiences were; nor was there any way of knowing whether whatever detections occurred were a tribute to the diagnostic acumen of the hospital's rumor network. Obviously, since my concerns are general ones that cut across individual hospitals and staffs, I have respected their anonymity and have eliminated clues that might lead to their identification.

9. Interestingly, of the 12 admissions, 11 were diagnosed as schizophrenic and one, with the identical symptomatology, as manic-depressive psychosis. This diagnosis has more favorable prognosis, and it was given by the private hospital in our sample. On the relations between social class and psychiatric diagnosis, see A. deB. Hollingshead and F.C. Redlich, *Social Class and Mental Illness: A Community Study* (New York: John Wiley, 1958).

10. It is possible, of course, that patients have quite broad latitudes in diagnosis and therefore are inclined to call many people sane even those whose behavior is patently aberrant. However, although we have no hard data on this matter, it was our distinct impression that this was not the case. In many instances, patients not only singled us out for attention, but came to imitate our behaviors and styles.

11. J. Cumming and E. Cumming, *Community Ment. Health* 1, 135 (1965); A. Farina and K. Ring, *J. Abnorm. Psychol.* 70, 47 (1965); H. E. Freeman and O. G. Simmons, *The Mental Patient Comes Home* (Wiley, New York, 1963); W. J. Johannsen, *Ment. Hygiene* 53, 218 (1969); A. S. Linsky, *Soc. Psychiat.* 5, 166 (1970).

12. For an example of a similar self-fulfilling prophecy, in this instance dealing with the "central" trait of intelligence, see R. Rosenthal and L. Jacobson, *Pygmalion in the Classroom* (Holt, Rinehard & Winston, New York, 1968).

13. The most recent and unfortunate instance of this tenet is that of Senator Thomas Eagleton.

14. T. R. Sarbin and J. C. Mancuso, *J. Clin. Consult. Psychol.* 35, 159 (1970); T. R. Sarbin, ibid. 31, 447 (1967); J. C. Nunnally, Jr., *Popular Conceptions of Mental Health* (Holt, Rinehart & Winston, New York, 1961).

15. D. B. Wexler and S. E. Scoville, *Ariz. Law Rev.* 13, 1 (1971).

Chapter 26

Obedience to Authority: An Experimental View

STANLEY MILGRAM

The "Milgram experiment" is one of the best-known experiments in social science. The goal was to find out how difficult it is to get otherwise decent people to obey an order to harm another human being. It turns out, as this selection from Milgram's book makes clear, that it is not difficult at all. A few simple experimental manipulations and people who would "never" think of doing harm in fact obey an order (over and over again) to do just that. Milgram (as he himself points out) had the image of Nazi Germany and the death camps firmly in mind when designing this experiment, but Nazi Germany is an extreme example of something that is really quite common. Those in authority in democratic regimes have also given orders to do harm and those orders have been obeyed. Milgram wrote at the time of the Vietnam War and used examples from that war to make his point here. What examples might he use were he writing today? Postscript: Research studying "obedience" à la Milgram long ago came to a screeching halt in social science because ethics review committees deemed such research unethical given the possible consequences for the naïve subjects involved. What are the pros and cons of this position? What have we gained and lost?

Obedience, because of its very ubiquitousness, is easily overlooked as a subject of inquiry in social psychology. But without an appreciation of its role in shaping human action, a wide range of significant behavior cannot be understood.

The person who, with inner conviction, loathes stealing, killing, and assault may find himself performing these acts with relative ease when commanded by authority. Behavior that is unthinkable in an individual who is acting on his own may be executed without hesitation when carried out under orders.

The dilemma inherent in obedience to authority is ancient, as old as the story of Abraham. What the present study does is to give the dilemma contemporary form by treating it as subject matter for experimental inquiry, and with the aim of understanding rather than judging it from a moral standpoint.

THE DILEMMA OF OBEDIENCE

Obedience, as a determinant of behavior, is of particular relevance to our time. It has been reliably established that from 1933 to 1945 millions of innocent people were systematically slaughtered on command. Gas chambers were built, death camps were guarded, daily quotas of corpses were produced with the same efficiency as the manufacture of appliances. These inhumane policies may have originated in the mind

Source: Pages xi, 1–6, 14, 22–24, 32–36, 179–180, 188–189 from *Obedience to Authority: An Experimental View,* by Stanley Milgram. Copyright © 1974 by Stanley Milgram. Reprinted by permission of HarperCollins Publishers Inc.

of a single person, but they could only have been carried out on a massive scale if a very large number of people obeyed orders.

The Nazi extermination of European Jews is the most extreme instance of abhorrent immoral acts carried out by thousands of people in the name of obedience. Yet in lesser degree this type of thing is constantly recurring: ordinary citizens are ordered to destroy other people, and they do so because they consider it their duty to obey orders.

In order to take a close look at the act of obeying, I set up a simple experiment at Yale University. Eventually, the experiment was to involve more than a thousand participants and would be repeated at several universities, but at the beginning, the conception was simple. A person comes to a psychology laboratory and is told to carry out a series of acts that come increasingly into conflict with conscience. The main question is how far the participant will comply with the experimenter's instructions before refusing to carry out the actions required of him.

But the reader needs to know a little more detail about the experiment. Two people come to a psychology laboratory to take part in a study of memory and learning. One of them is designated as a "teacher" and the other a "learner." The experimenter explains that the study is concerned with the effects of punishment on learning. The learner is conducted into a room, seated in a chair, his arms strapped to prevent excessive movement, and an electrode attached to his wrist. He is told that he is to learn a list of word pairs; whenever he makes an error, he will receive electric shocks of increasing intensity.

The real focus of the experiment is the teacher. After watching the learner being strapped into place, he is taken into the main experimental room and seated before an impressive shock generator. Its main feature is a horizontal line of thirty switches, ranging from 15 volts to 450 volts, in 15-volt increments. There are also verbal designations which range from SLIGHT SHOCK to DANGER—SEVERE SHOCK. The

teacher is told that he is to administer the learning test to the man in the other room. When the learner responds correctly, the teacher moves on to the next item; when the other man gives an incorrect answer, the teacher is to give him an electric shock. He is to start at the lowest level (15 volts) and to increase the level each time the man makes an error, going through 30 volts, 45 volts, and so on.

The "teacher" is a genuinely naïve subject who has come to the laboratory to participate in an experiment. The learner, or victim, is an actor who actually receives no shock at all. The point of the experiment is to see how far a person will proceed in a concrete and measurable situation in which he is ordered to inflict increasing pain on a protesting victim. At what point will the subject refuse to obey the experimenter?

Conflict arises when the man receiving the shock begins to indicate that he is experiencing discomfort. At 75 volts, the "learner" grunts. At 120 volts he complains verbally; at 150 he demands to be released from the experiment. His protests continue as the shocks escalate, growing increasingly vehement and emotional. At 285 volts his response can only be described as an agonized scream.

Observers of the experiment agree that its gripping quality is somewhat obscured in print. For the subject, the situation is not a game; conflict is intense and obvious. On one hand, the manifest suffering of the learner presses him to quit. On the other, the experimenter, a legitimate authority to whom the subject feels some commitment, enjoins him to continue. To extricate himself from the situation, the subject must make a clear break from authority. The aim of this investigation was to find when and how people would defy authority in the face of a clear moral imperative.

A reader's initial reaction to the experiment may be to wonder why anyone in his right mind would administer even the first shocks. Would he not simply refuse and walk out of the laboratory? But the fact is that no one ever does. Since the subject has come to the laboratory to aid the experimenter, he is quite willing to start off with the procedure. There is nothing very extraordinary in this, particularly since the person who is to receive the shocks seems initially cooperative, if somewhat apprehensive. What is surprising is how far ordinary individuals will go in complying with the experimenter's instructions. Indeed, the results of the experiment are both surprising and dismaying. Despite the fact that many subjects experience stress, despite the fact that many protest to the experimenter, a substantial proportion continue to the last shock on the generator.

Many subjects will obey the experimenter no matter how vehement the pleading of the person being shocked, no matter how painful the shocks seem to be, and no matter how much the victim pleads to be let out. This was seen time and again in our studies and has been observed in several universities where the experiment was repeated. It is the extreme willingness of adults to go to almost any lengths on the command of an authority that constitutes the chief finding of the study and the fact most urgently demanding explanation.

A commonly offered explanation is that those who shocked the victim at the most severe level were monsters, the sadistic fringe of society. But if one considers that almost two-thirds of the participants fall into the category of "obedient" subjects, and that they represented ordinary people drawn from working, managerial, and professional classes, the argument becomes very shaky. Indeed, it is highly reminiscent of the issue that arose in connection with Hannah Arendt's 1963 book, *Eichmann in Jerusalem*. Arendt contended that the prosecution's effort to depict Eichmann as a sadistic monster was fundamentally wrong, that he came closer to being an uninspired bureaucrat who simply sat at his desk and did his job. For asserting these views, Arendt became the object of considerable scorn, even calumny. Somehow, it was felt that the monstrous deeds carried out by Eichmann required a brutal, twisted, and sadistic personality, evil incarnate. After witnessing hundreds of

ordinary people submit to the authority in our own experiments, I must conclude that Arendt's conception of the *banality of evil* comes closer to the truth than one might dare imagine. The ordinary person who shocked the victim did so out of a sense of obligation—a conception of his duties as a subject—and not from any peculiarly aggressive tendencies.

This is, perhaps, the most fundamental lesson of our study: ordinary people, simply doing their jobs, and without any particular hostility on their part, can become agents in a terrible destructive process. Moreover, even when the destructive effects of their work become patently clear, and they are asked to carry out actions incompatible with fundamental standards of morality, relatively few people have the resources needed to resist authority. A variety of inhibitions against disobeying authority come into play and successfully keep the person in his place.

OBTAINING PARTICIPANTS FOR THE STUDY

To recruit subjects, an advertisement was placed in a local newspaper. It called for people of all occupations to take part in a study of memory and learning, and it offered $4 payment and 50 cents carfare for one hour of participation.

FEEDBACK FROM THE VICTIM

In all conditions the learner gave a predetermined set of responses to the word-pair test, based on a schedule of approximately three wrong answers to one correct answer.

The victim's responses were a key element in the situation and needed to be worked out carefully. In pilot studies, at first no vocal feedback from the victim was used. It was thought that the verbal and voltage designations on the control panel would create sufficient pressure to curtail the subject's obedience. However, this proved not to be the case. In the absence of protests from the learner, virtually every subject in the pilot study, once commanded, went blithely to the end of the board, seemingly indifferent to the verbal designations. This deprived us of an adequate basis for measuring obedient tendencies. A force had to be introduced that would strengthen the subject's resistance to the experimenter's commands, and reveal individual differences in terms of a distribution of breakoff points.

This force took the form of protests from the victim. Initially, mild protests were used, but these proved inadequate. Subsequently, more vehement protests were inserted into the experimental procedure. To our consternation, even the strongest protests from the victim did not prevent many subjects from administering the harshest punishment ordered by the experimenter. But the protests did lower the mean of maximum shocks somewhat and created some spread in the subject's performance; therefore, the victim's cries were recorded on tape and incorporated into the regular experimental procedure.

Each vocal response of the victim was coordinated to a particular voltage level on the shock generator. It is difficult to convey on the printed page the full tenor of the victim's responses, for we have no adequate notation for vocal intensity, timing, and general qualities of delivery. In general, however, the victim indicated no discomfort until the 75-volt shock was administered, at which time there was a little grunt. Similar reactions followed the 90- and 105-volt shocks, and at 120 volts the victim shouted to the experimenter that the shocks were becoming painful. Painful groans were heard on administration of the 135-volt shock, and at 150 volts the victim cried out "Experimenter, get me out of here! I won't be in the experiment any more! I refuse to go on!" Cries of this type continue with generally rising intensity, so that at 180 volts the victim cried out "I can't stand the pain" and by 270 volts his response to the shock was definitely an agonizing scream. Throughout, from 150 volts on, he insisted that he be let out of the experiment. At 300 volts the victim shouted in

desperation that he would no longer provide answers to the memory test.

At this juncture, it was found, subjects would usually turn to the experimenter for guidance. The experimenter would instruct the subject to treat the absence of a response as a wrong answer, and to shock the subject according to the usual schedule. He advised the subjects to allow 5 to 10 seconds before considering no response as a wrong answer, and to increase the shock level one step each time the learner failed to respond correctly. At 315 volts, after a violent scream, the victim reaffirmed vehemently that he was no longer a participant. He provided no answers, but shrieked in agony whenever a shock was administered. After 330 volts he was not heard from, nor did his answers reappear on the four-way signal box.

MEASURES

The main measure for any subject is the maximum shock he administers before he refuses to go any further. In principle this may vary from 0 (for a subject who refuses to administer even the first shock) to 30 (for a subject who administers the highest shock on the generator).

INTERVIEW AND DEBRIEFING

An important aspect of the procedure occurred at the end of the experimental session. A careful postexperimental treatment was administered to all subjects. The exact content of the session varied from condition to condition and with increasing experience on our part. At the very least every subject was told that the victim had not received dangerous electric shocks. Each subject had a friendly reconciliation with the unharmed victim and an extended discussion with the experimenter. The experiment was explained to defiant subjects in a way that supported their decision to disobey the experimenter. Obedient subjects were assured that their behavior was entirely normal and that their feelings of conflict or tension were shared by other participants. Subjects were told that they would receive a comprehensive report at the conclusion of the experimental series. In some instances, additional detailed and lengthy discussions of the experiment were also carried out with individual subjects.

CLOSENESS OF THE VICTIM

Now let us look at the actual performance of subjects in the experiment. To begin, we shall consider the results of the Remote-Feedback variation (Experiment 1). It differs slightly from the usual situation in that no vocal complaint is heard from the victim. He is placed in another room where he cannot be seen by the subject, nor can his voice be heard; his answers flash silently on the signal box. However, at 300 volts the laboratory walls resound as he pounds in protest. After 315 volts, no further answers appear, and the pounding ceases.

Of the 40 subjects, 26 obeyed the orders of the experimenter to the end, proceeding to punish the victim until they reached the most potent shock available on the generator. After the 450-volt shock was administered three times, the experimenter called a halt to the session.

BRINGING THE VICTIM CLOSER

If the victim were rendered increasingly more salient to the subject, would obedience diminish? A set of four experiments was designed to answer this question. We have already described the Remote condition.

Experiment 2 (Voice-Feedback) was identical to the first except that vocal protests were introduced. As in the first condition, the victim was placed in an adjacent room, but his complaints could be heard clearly through the walls of the laboratory.

Experiment 3 (Proximity) was similar to the second, except that the victim was placed in the same room as the subject, a few feet from him.

Thus he was visible as well as audible, and voice cues were provided.

Experiment 4 (Touch-Proximity) was identical to the third, with this exception: the victim received a shock only when his hand rested on a shock plate. At the 150-volt level the victim demanded to be let free and refused to place his hand on the shock plate. The experimenter ordered the subject to force the victim's hand onto the plate. Thus obedience in this condition required that the subject have physical contact with the victim in order to give him punishment at or beyond the 150-volt level.

Forty adult subjects were studied in each condition. The results revealed that obedience was significantly reduced as the victim was rendered more immediate to the subject.

Thirty-five percent of the subjects defied the experimenter in the Remote condition, 37.5 percent in Voice-Feedback, 60 percent in Proximity, and 70 percent in Touch-Proximity.

EPILOGUE

The dilemma posed by the conflict between the conscience and authority inheres in the very nature of society and would be with us even if Nazi Germany had never existed.

Some dismiss the Nazi example because we live in a democracy and not an authoritarian state. But, in reality, this does not eliminate the problem. For the problem is not "authoritarianism" as a mode of political organization or a set of psychological attitudes but authority itself. Authoritarianism may give way to democratic practice, but authority itself cannot be eliminated as long as society is to continue in the form we know.

In democracies, men are placed in office through popular elections. Yet, once installed, they are no less in authority than those who get there by other means. And, as we have seen repeatedly, the demands of democratically installed authority may also come into conflict with conscience. The importation and enslavement of millions of black people, the destruction of the American Indian population, the internment of Japanese Americans, the use of napalm against civilians in Vietnam, all are harsh policies that originated in the authority of a democratic nation, and were responded to with the expected obedience. In each case, voices of morality were raised against the action in question, but the typical response of the common man was to obey orders.

Now let us return to the experiments and try to underscore their meaning. The behavior revealed in the experiments reported here is normal human behavior but revealed under conditions that show with particular clarity the danger to human survival inherent in our make-up. And what is it we have seen? Not aggression, for there is no anger, vindictiveness, or hatred in those who shocked the victim. Men do become angry; they do act hatefully and explode in rage against others. But not here. Something far more dangerous is revealed: the capacity for man to abandon his humanity, indeed, the inevitability that he does so, as he merges his unique personality into larger institutional structures.

Each individual possesses a conscience which to a greater or lesser degree serves to restrain the unimpeded flow of impulses destructive to others. But when he merges his person into an organizational structure, a new creature replaces autonomous man, unhindered by the limitations of individual morality, freed of humane inhibition, mindful only of the sanctions of authority.

What is the limit of such obedience? At many points we attempted to establish a boundary. Cries from the victim were inserted; they were not good enough. The victim claimed heart trouble; subjects still shocked him on command. The victim pleaded to be let free, and his answers no longer registered on the signal box; subjects continued to shock him. At the outset we had not conceived that such drastic procedures would be needed to generate disobedience, and each step was added only as the ineffectiveness of the earlier techniques became clear. The final effort to establish a limit was the Touch-Proximity condition. But the very first subject in this condition subdued the victim on command, and proceeded to the highest shock level. A quarter of the subjects in this condition performed similarly.

The results, as seen and felt in the laboratory, are to this author disturbing. They raise the possibility that human nature, or—more specifically—the kind of character produced in American democratic society, cannot be counted on to insulate its citizens from brutality and inhumane treatment at the direction of malevolent authority. A substantial proportion of people do what they are told to do, irrespective of the content of the act and without limitations of conscience, so long as they perceive that the command comes from a legitimate authority.

Chapter 27

The CSI Effect: Fact or Fiction?

ANDREW THOMAS

What's the relationship between the popularity of a TV show and "real life?" It seems obvious that some shows are popular because they represent escapist fantasies that bear little resemblance to the lives of their viewers. In other cases, however, the relationship is not as obvious as it seems. Consider an example that goes back several decades. During the 1950s and early 1960s, many of the most popular sitcoms involved middle-class (white) families where dads went off to work each weekday and wives stayed home to care for the kids and maintain the home. Why were these shows so popular? You might think that it was because the shows reflected cultural norms regarding the family and gender roles that prevailed at the time. In fact, it was during the mid-1950s that middle-class wives began entering the workforce in record numbers. In other words, sitcoms featuring the "traditional nuclear family" were popular at precisely the moment in North American history when that family type was crumbling. Now fast-forward to the very popular *CSI* shows that are the focus of this selection. As this article demonstrates, many viewers take the procedures and techniques on these shows at face value, and this structures what they say and do when they act as jurors—even though the behaviour and procedures used by real-life police and prosecutors are often quite different from those seen on TV. But if these shows don't really reflect what police and prosecutors do, why are these shows so popular? One possibility is that they create an image of the justice system that appeals to people. After all, science is "objective," and so when science is merged with police work (which is what these shows do), the wrongly accused are always vindicated, the guilty are proven guilty beyond any doubt, and things like racial and class bias (of the sort discussed in the selection by Daniel Lazare) never, but never distract lead investigators like Gil Grissom or Horatio Caine as they pursue evildoers.

As chief prosecutor for Maricopa County, which includes the city of Phoenix, my office prosecutes about 40,000 felonies each year and includes a staff of 300 prosecutors. In June 2005, we surveyed 102 of those attorneys,[1] all of whom had trial experience, and they reported that the *CSI* effect is no myth: Of the prosecutors we surveyed, 38% believed they had at least one trial that resulted in either an acquittal or hung jury because forensic evidence was not available, even though prosecutors believed the existing testimony was sufficient by itself to sustain a

Source: Andrew P. Thomas, *The CSI Effect: Fact or Fiction*, 115 YALE L.J. POCKET PART 70 (2006), http://www.thepocketpart.org/2006/02/Thomas.html.

Responding to Tom R. Tyler, *Viewing* CSI *and the Threshold of Guilt: Managing Truth and Justice in Reality and Fiction*, 115 YALE L.J. 1050 (2006).

conviction. In about 40% of these prosecutors' cases, jurors have asked questions about evidence like "mitochondrial DNA," "latent prints," "trace evidence," or "ballistics"—even when these terms were not used at trial.

On television, if the *CSI* people do their job right, the jurors will have little choice but to convict. In real life, the false expectation of plentiful scientific evidence can create a bias in the jury if this issue is not properly addressed at trial. The investigative techniques portrayed on *CSI* are not always available or even reasonable. Yet almost eight out of ten Maricopa County prosecutors believe that jurors are disappointed in the lack of forensic evidence presented at trial.

All of the prosecutors we surveyed had jury trial experience. Sixty-four had more than ten jury trials and thirty-eight had more than thirty trials. Our prosecutors frequently talk to jurors after their verdicts about the cases they just decided. On the basis of these conversations with juries, 74% of our prosecutors maintained that they have prosecuted a case in which the jury "expected to be presented with scientific evidence," and that when both scientific and nonscientific evidence existed, 45% of our prosecutors felt "the jury focused so much on presented scientific evidence that they paid too little attention to unscientific evidence" like witnesses and police testimony.

In one drug case, the officer saw the defendant throw down a baggie of drugs. The baggie was not fingerprinted by the time of trial because there was a backlog for laboratory testing that was up to six months. As Deputy County Attorney Kristen Knudsen explained: "After the trial, the jury complained that the lack of fingerprint evidence suggested that the baggie could have been there all along."

Even statements by defendants themselves have failed to persuade some juries. In *State v. James Calloway*, Arizona Department of Corrections officers found a syringe in a cell with a note signed by "Jimbo" attached to it. Inmate "Jimbo" was found with a fresh mark on his arm consistent with syringe use, and admitted the syringe was his when he retrieved it from prison officials and signed the receipt. The jury criticized the prosecution because there was no DNA or fingerprint analysis on the syringe, and the jurors wanted a handwriting comparison on the note and the receipt.

Real prosecutors' offices are constrained by their limited resources. While some jurisdictions have access to some of the "bells and whistles" equipment depicted in television dramas, those resources are usually reserved for the most serious crimes. In Maricopa County, as in other counties, most felonies do not involve high-profile crimes and lengthy trials. The majority of prosecutions are for lower-level offenses like auto theft, drug possession, and assault. These cases often do not yield irrefutable physical or scientific evidence of guilt or innocence.

What may be of greatest concern is what goes on in the jury room, after arguments have been made. In 72% of cases, prosecutors suspect that jurors who watch shows like *CSI* claim a level of expertise during jury deliberations that sways other jurors who do not watch those shows.

In *State v. Everett Black*, the defendant was caught with drugs that were in a cigarette pack in defendant's pocket. He admitted that the pack was his but denied that the drugs were his or that he knew the drugs were there. The foreperson later said he watched *CSI* and that investigators should have done extensive fingerprinting, DNA testing, and other forensics, and that he did not think the prosecutors did enough. He had convinced the entire panel that on television they do so much more and that the police officers did not do a good job.

This is the kind of example that makes prosecutors worried that justice is not being done. Although verdicts have not yet noticeably changed from guilty to not guilty, prosecutors have had to take more and more preemptive steps to divert juries from reliance on television-style expectations.

Maricopa County prosecutors have begun to counter the *CSI* effect through voir dire, opening and closing arguments, and presentation of other evidence and testimony. While the defense often questions the work of investigators, prosecutors can restore balance to the criminal justice system by pointing out the reasons why there is no forensic evidence in a certain case.

Court officials could also take action to preserve the opportunity for fair trials. More judges could actively acknowledge the existence of the *CSI* effect and take steps during voir dire to prevent biased jurors from improperly influencing the jury. When they instruct juries before deliberations, judges could also mention that jurors should not use outside standards like those presented in forensic crime television shows.

These solutions are temporary, but as *CSI* continues to grow in popularity, and as more shows continue to follow its lead, these steps may soon be inadequate.

Andrew P. Thomas is Maricopa County Attorney, the chief prosecutor for Maricopa County, Arizona. Maricopa County is the fourth most populous county in the United States, with 3.5 million people in the greater Phoenix area. Mr. Thomas is a graduate of Harvard Law School and the author of four books.

NOTE

1. Maricopa County Attorney's Office, CSI: Maricopa County: The CSI Effect and its Real-Life Impact on Justice (June 30, 2005), http://www.maricopacountyattorney.org/Press/PDF/CSIReport.pdf.

PART 10

Religion

Chapter 28

Social Science Theories of Religion

ANDREW M. GREELEY

Andrew Greeley is a bit more colourful than most sociologists. For decades he has studied and written about religion in the modern world. His analyses of survey data gathered from populations in both North America and Europe are especially well known. He is also a Catholic priest who takes his pastoral duties very seriously. Finally, he is one of the best-selling novelists in North America. (Go into any bookstore in Canada and ask for the latest book by Andrew Greeley; given the rate at which he writes, a new book will come out every year you're in school.) In this selection, which Greeley wrote as an introduction to one of his books on religion, he provides a succinct review of the theories of religion developed by the classical theorists in sociology.

Serious, critical, and nontheological reflection on religion has presumably gone on as long as there has been religion. But such reflection as a formal activity that preoccupied many thinkers and writers was a late nineteenth-century phenomenon. The men who engaged in such reflection, all of them brilliant and some of them geniuses, provided the raw materials out of which came contemporary social science.

One could divide them into two categories—those who sought to explain religion and those who sought to explain it away. Marx and Freud and perhaps Durkheim can be included in the latter category while Weber belongs in the former.

Many of them were concerned about the persistence of religion, its ability to survive despite the onslaught of science. Some, most notably Freud, thought religion would slowly disappear. Others, Durkheim for example, thought it would survive but with a very limited area of competence. Still others, like Weber, found it hard to imagine a world without religion.

The search for the meaning of religion in these classic thinkers (as interpreted and clarified by their contemporary disciples) continues to define the terms of sociology's attempt to understand religion. They are to be read, not because they were right, not because what they said is the last word, but because it is within the context of the questions they ask—perennial questions perhaps—that our search continues.

OPIATE OF THE PEOPLE: KARL MARX

Karl Marx (1818–1883) was a dialectical materialist; he combined the Hegelian notion that reality emerges from an endless series of contradictions with Ludwig Feuerbach's materialism, the belief that matter was the only and ultimate reality. Hegel was wrong, Marx argued, not about dialectics but about making the dialectic spiritual. The ultimate reality is not spirit (or Spirit) but matter. Political and social reality is

Source: *Religion as Poetry,* by Andrew M. Greeley, Transaction Publishers, 1995. Reprinted with permission.

shaped by struggles between social classes over control of the material means of production.

Since there is no such thing as spirit, religion must be an illusion, part of the "superstructure" of reality generated by underlying reality of the material substructure. It is one of the techniques that the ruling class (whoever controls the means of production) uses to keep the subject class under control. It is an opiate, a drug that immobilizes the subject class with the hope of a spiritual reward as a substitute for material possessions.

Obviously, Marx was not completely wrong. Religion has often been a tool in the hands of rulers and a means for cowing people into submission. However, religion has also frequently been a motivating force for those people who feel that they are oppressed: the Fundamentalist Shiite Muslims in Iran, the new religious right in the United States, Solidarity in Poland, the civil rights movement in this country.

Marx owed his popularity to the incisiveness of his historical analysis, the toughness of his materialism, and the enthusiasm of his vision. Precisely because he admitted only material reality, his doctrine was considered to be scientific; and precisely because of the seeming inevitability of the dialectic he described, those who followed his faith believed that they would triumph.

After the collapse of the Iron Curtain in 1990, the weaknesses of Marxism were revealed to everyone. But Marx's notion that religion was a means of social domination and control can stand alone and does not need the rest of his philosophical system to sustain it. Religion still seems to promise "Pie in the sky when you die" as a substitute for social justice while you are still alive. Much of the skepticism of many intellectuals about religion is based on an implicit Marxist premise: men and women would like to believe in God and therefore they do. In fact, however, these observers would say, religion is nothing more than wish fulfillment, and indeed wish fulfillment that blinds men and women to injustice.

Reading Marx's attack on religion as the opiate of the people (in his essay, "Contributions to the Critique of Hegel's Theory of Right"), one is struck by how "unscientific" it is by the standards of contemporary social science. He asserts but does not prove. He attacks but does not provide evidence. He argues fiercely but his arguments are aprioristic and deductive. If science requires the possibility of falsification for verification to become possible then Marx's comments on religion are hardly scientific. But the passion of his moral outrage can still stir the emotions.

RELIGION AS NEUROSIS: SIGMUND FREUD

In a certain sense Freud and Marx are at the opposite ends of the argument about human suffering. Marx saw suffering as the result of the oppression of one social class by another. Freud (1856–1939) saw it as the result of unresolved childhood conflicts. Marx called for revolution, Freud for psychoanalysis. Marx wanted the workers to throw off the chains of bourgeoisie oppression. Freud wanted the patient to throw off the domination of the neurotic superego. Marx exhorted his followers to social action, Freud prescribed long and painful self-examination.

But both were atheists, both were materialists, both rejected the spiritual, both believed that materialism was necessary for science and that their respective analyses were "scientific," indeed the only possible science. Both began movements that often have looked like substitute religions, even substitute churches. Both often looked and acted like the Moses of their new faiths. Both have had enormous influence on how men and women, including many who are anything but Marxists or Freudians, think about religion.

For Freud religion is essentially neurotic, a regression to childhood behavior patterns of guilt and dependency, based either on humankind's collective guilt about the murder of a father by the primal horde (in *Totem and Taboo*) or on the human need to transfer control of life to a father figure (as in *Moses and Monotheism*). Religion therefore reinforces the control of the superego—the childish self with its feelings of guilt—over the reality principle, the mature self. In the process of discharging guilt and breaking free of dependency, psychoanalysis should free a person from the religious illusion.

Freud no more proved the truth of this analysis of religion than Marx proved the truth of his analysis. The brilliance of his insight is taken to be sufficient proof, a posture that no responsible modern scientist could possibly accept. Yet it is certainly clear to both clinicians who must work everyday with the emotionally troubled and to ordinary people that religion is often the focus if not the cause of much neurosis, especially if religion is linked to conflicts with one's parents. God becomes the father, the Church becomes the mother, and guilt over one's failures to be what parents want one to be becomes the source of neurotic feelings of "sinfulness."

The question remains, however, of whether that is all religion does. Is religion ever radical instead of reactionary? Are religious men and women ever relatively free of neurosis? Freud never really bothered to try to respond to the latter question just as Marx never bothered to respond to the former question. For both men the questions never arose because on apriori grounds there was no point in asking them.

RELIGION AS SOCIETY'S SELF-WORSHIP: EMILE DURKHEIM

Marxism and Freudianism in attenuated forms pervade the atmosphere of modern thought and shape, however implicitly, the response of many men and women to religion: it is an illusion, created either by the infrastructure of society (the means of production) or the superstructure of the self (the rigid, controlling superego). Emile

Durkheim (1858–1917) is not so well known and certainly not so influential. But among sociologists who study religion, Durkheim is far more influential than either Marx or Freud. The latter two discuss religion in passing as part of their larger theories of the human condition and dismiss it as an illusion. Durkheim, however, made religion the central concern of his sociology and can be considered in many respects the founder of not only sociology of religion but also empirical sociology. In his book *Suicide* (1897) he begins with an empirical question: why are suicide rates lower for Catholics than for Protestants? His answer is that Catholicism as a community exerts stronger social control than does Protestantism. Catholic suicide rates are, by the way, still lower than Protestant rates, almost a century after Durkheim's analysis.

In his *Elementary Forms of the Religious Life* (1915) he considers the religion of the Australian aborigines and asks what role it plays in their lives. Durkheim's startling, original, and creative explanation of religion is that it is society worshiping itself as it experiences itself in the "effervescence"—the emotional enthusiasm of religious rituals. The experience of the ritual creates religion instead of vice versa.

Durkheim calls these rituals "collective representations" because in them the community becomes conscious of itself as a reality that transcends the personality of the individual members—as, for example, in a football pep rally. The energies released in such situations become or seem to become a reality distinct from that of the participants. When the rituals are religious—a Catholic Mass, a Jewish high holy day ceremony, a Protestant revival service—the celebrants encounter what seems to be a religious reality and assume that it is a "supernatural" figure. In fact they merely encounter society as a collective agent, generating enthusiasm and fervor. Thus, Durkheim says, worship of God is nothing more than society worshiping itself. Durkheim has had a tremendous impact on both sociologists and anthropologists. Religions with strong ritual systems have more control on the behavior of their members than do other religions. Thus, Eider (1992), in a study of elderly people, showed that those who practiced Catholicism or Judaism (as opposed to Protestantism) had better health and that Jews and Catholics even "postponed" their deaths until after their important religious festivals (Christmas and Easter, high holy days and Passover). Durkheim established beyond any possibility of doubt that ritual and imagery were of enormous religious importance and that to a very considerable extent they shaped religion and religious response.

Like Marx before him and Freud after him, Durkheim was ultimately a reductionist: in explaining religion he explained it away. Unlike Marx and Freud, however, Durkheim was not hostile to religion. Quite the contrary, he was perfectly prepared to see religion as useful and necessary. It could and should continue, though it should abandon the field of explanations about the world to science. He seemed unwilling to face the fact that those who, like himself, saw what religion really was—society's self-worship—would have an insidious effect on the faith of less sophisticated people. It is fair to say that religion as something more than ritual has survived despite Durkheim's analysis. While no serious social science student of religion today can ignore Durkheim's conclusions, there are relatively few who accept his analysis without considerable qualification.

THE FUNCTION OF FUNERALS: BRONISLAW MALINOWKSI

Bronislaw Malinowski (1884–1942) was a Polish anthropologist who worked in the Tobriand Islands in South Pacific during the First World War. His approach to religion is "functionalism." He was not so much concerned with explaining religion as a global phenomenon as he was with describing the function of specific religious activities in society. His description of a funeral ritual is a classic in social research and could as easily be applied to a funeral service in a contemporary American church or synagogue as to a primitive people in Melanesia. The ritual reintegrates the social network after the trauma of loss and enables life to continue. Malinowski built on the work of Durkheim who also described funeral rites, though not so precisely or powerfully, but he did not fall into reductionism. The dangers of functionalism are that the analyst plays God, explaining what people are doing from the point of view of one who understands their "real" if unperceived motivations. In unskilled hands, functionalism can become supercilious and arrogant. However, Malinowksi was far too sophisticated to succumb to such a temptation. His "primitives" are more or less deliberately creating emotions that reintegrate society. Their ritual is not so much producing a "supernatural" that they can adore, but attempting to heal wounds in the social fabric.

The Irish wake—now infrequent in Ireland but persisting in somewhat more modest form in the United States—is a spectacular example of "mortuary ritual." The drinking and singing and dancing in the cottage where the dead body rests (described in the Dublin ballad "Tim Finnegan's Wake") to say nothing of the love making in the fields around the cottage were deliberate acts of defiance aimed at death. The social network was reintegrated by shouting at the top of one's lungs, "screw you, death!" It is one way to deal with grief.

A REPLY TO MARX: MAX WEBER

Max Weber (1864–1920), according to most sociologists, is the giant who did more to shape contemporary sociology than any other of the founding geniuses. Much of his life's work was an implicit dialogue with Karl Marx in which Weber argued against materialistic determinism. His best known work *The Protestant Ethic and the Spirit of Capitalism* (1922) argues that while religion may be shaped by social institutions (such as the means of production), it also shapes them. The "work ethic" ("inner-worldly asceticism") is perhaps the result of capitalism but also shapes it. Capitalism is in part the product of a religious ethic.

Weber believed that there was an affinity between the kind of work habits that capitalism requires and the ethical emphasis of certain kinds of Protestantism, particularly Calvinism. This affinity created a situation in which those who possessed such an ethic would become leaders in the capitalist enterprise and to some extent shape its development. Eventually the ethic (which Weber did not like) would become so powerful and pervasive in capitalist society that it would no longer correlate with religion.

His analysis then is cautious, complex, and low-key. Marx said the economic organization of society shaped religion, that the latter was little more than an epiphenomenon. Weber did *not* reply that the truth was the other way around. Rather he replied that matters were more complicated and that both religion and economic organization were capable to some extent of shaping one another.

Such an analysis does not provide the sort of rallying cry around which revolutions are organized. But it does correspond to the gray, problematic nature of ordinary reality and to what a common sense answer would be to the question of whether religion shapes economic structure or economic structure shapes religion.

Weber's reply, in language much simpler than the heavy Teutonic academic rhetoric that he would have preferred, is that both are capable of influencing each other. It is an insight that seems so self-evident as to be trivial except that since Marx, millions of people have rejected it. Moreover, it completely recasts the issue of religion in modern society. In Weber's view religion was not merely the result of collective experiences of higher powers (though it surely could be that, too). Religion was also a road map which explained the meaning of life and provided directions for how men and women ought to live.

It is fair to say that this understanding of religion has shaped sociology and the sociology of religion ever since. There are still reductionists, men and women who insist that religion is "nothing but . . ." However, after Max Weber that position is a difficult one to take.

RATIONAL CHOICE MODELS

A more recent approach to the sociology of religion is the so-called "rational choice" model advocated, for example, by Iannacone (1991), Finke and Stark (1992), and Warner (1993). These theorists propose a model of "religious competition" to account for the fact that religion prospers in countries with religious pluralism (like the United States) and does not prosper in countries where there is either an established Church or a religious quasi-monopoly. The model, which Warner proposes as a replacement for the secularization model that he considers bankrupt, does not try to explain away religion but rather to explain why it is stronger in some parts of the world than in others.

The "rational choice" model, based on a convergence of concerns between economics and sociology, is used at the present time as a paradigm for the consideration of many traditional sociological problems. It will not serve my purpose in this book to address the controversy over the general use of a "rational choice" approach to sociology. Its great merit when applied to religion (and to the rationality of churches trying harder when they are forced to compete) is that it does not attempt to explain religion away but, forsaking the secularization ideology, address itself to a specific empirical question without prejudice based on the presumed disappearance of religion.

REFERENCES

Eider, Ellen. 1992. Religion, disability, depression, and the time of death. *American Journal of Sociology* 97 (January).

Finke, Roger and Rodney Stark. 1992. The Churching of America, 1776–1990: *Winners and Losers in Our Religious Economy.* New Brunswick, NJ: Rutgers University Press.

Iannacone, Laurence. 1991. The consequences of religious market structure: Adam Smith and the economics of religion. *Rationality and Society* 3 (April): 156–77.

Warner, H. Steven. 1993. Work in progress toward a new paradigm for the sociological study of religion in the United States. *American Journal of Sociology* 98, no. 5: 1044–93.

Chapter 29

American Religious Exceptionalism

RODNEY STARK AND ROGER FINKE

In the last selection, Andrew Greeley pointed out that "rational choice" models of religion are especially popular in sociology today. Unfortunately, he didn't provide much detail on what the "rational choice" theory is. The basic idea is very simple: If we think of churches as "business firms," then the same principles that govern success in the business world will govern success in the religious realm. Thus, just as "monopoly" breeds laziness and lack of creativity in business, it will have the same effect on churches; by contrast, just as competition motivates sales personnel to work harder and be creative, it too will have the same effect on ministers. The final result, which is really a prediction, is that the more competition between churches, the higher the rates of religious participation. Here Stark and Finke use this prediction to explain why rates of religious participation in the United States are so much higher than in Europe (or, for that matter, in Canada).

For more than 150 years, European visitors have remarked on the popularity of religion in the United States, and especially on the immense level of voluntary support Americans give to their churches. Thus, in 1818, William Cobbett wrote home to his neighbors in the English town of Botley about the density of churches in America and how well supported they were:

> Here are plenty of Churches. No less than three Episcopal (or English) Churches; three Presbyterian Churches; three Lutheran Churches; one or two Quaker Meeting-houses; two Methodist places; all within *six miles* of the place where I am sitting. And, these, mind, not poor shabby Churches; but each of them larger and better built and far handsomer than Botley Church, with the church-yards kept in the neatest order, with a head-stone to almost every grave. As to the Quaker Meeting-house, it

would take Botley Church into its belly, if you were first to knock off the steeple. (Cobbett 1818, 229)

During his travels in the United States during 1830–31, Alexis de Tocqueville had a similar response, noting that "there is not a country in the world where the Christian religion retains a greater influence over the souls of men than in America" ([1835–39] 1956, 314). At mid-century, the Swiss theologian Philip Schaff (1855, 91) observed that attendance at Lutheran Churches was far higher in New York than in Berlin.

If European visitors marveled at American religiousness, Americans who traveled in Europe were equally surprised by the lack of religious participation they observed. Thus, Robert Baird, the first major historian of American religion, reported after an eight-year sojourn on the

Source: Rodney Stark and Roger Finke, *Acts of Faith: Explaining the Human Side of Religion*, University of California Press, 2000. Copyright © 2000 The Regents of the University of California.

Continent, that nowhere in Europe did church attendance come close to the level taken for granted by Americans (1844, 188).

Today, no one disputes that religious participation has long been far higher in America than in Europe. What is in dispute, is *why*. The answer to that question seemed obvious to many Europeans who wrote about American religion during the nineteenth century. Almost unanimously, they stressed the powerful competitive forces unleashed by a free market religious economy.

In the 1850s, Karl T. Griesinger, a militantly irreligious German, complained that the separation between church and state fueled religious efforts, observing: "Clergymen in America [are] like other businessmen; they must meet competition and build up a trade, and it is their own fault if their income is not large enough. Now it is clear why heaven and hell are moved to drive the people to the churches, and why attendance is more common here than anywhere else in the world" (1858; translated in Handlin 1949, 261).

Some twenty years earlier, the Austrian journalist Frances Grund had made similar points, noting that establishment makes the clergy "indolent and lazy" because

> a person provided for cannot, by the rules of common sense, be supposed to work as hard as one who has to exert himself for a living. . . . Not only have Americans a greater number of clergymen than, in proportion to the population, can be found either on the Continent or in England; but they have not one idler amongst them; all of them are obliged to exert themselves for the spiritual welfare of their respective congregations. Americans, therefore, enjoy a threefold advantage: they have more preachers; they have more active preachers, and they have cheaper preachers than can be found in any part of Europe. (1837; quoted in Powell 1967, 77–80)

Wittingly or not, these visitors echoed Adam Smith's penetrating analysis of the weaknesses of established churches, which, he said, inevitably produce a clergy content to repose "themselves upon their benefices [while neglecting] to keep up the fervour of faith and the devotion in the great body of the people; and having given themselves up to indolence, were become altogether incapable of making any vigorous exertion in defence even of their own establishment" ([1776] 1981:789).

However, by the turn of the twentieth century, awareness of the invigorating consequences of religious competition was fading rapidly. Smith's writings on religions were of so little interest that they were (and are) deleted from most editions of *The Wealth of Nations*. For a century, the received wisdom was that pluralism harms religion because competing religious bodies undercut one another's credibility. Eventually these views were formulated into elegant sociology by Peter Berger (1967; 1979), who repeatedly argued that pluralism inevitably destroys the plausibility of all religions and only where one faith prevails can there exist a "sacred canopy" able to inspire universal confidence and assent. It was not until the 1980s that anyone challenged Berger's claims (Finke 1984; Stark 1985; Finke and Stark 1988). Nevertheless, this view of the corrosive effects of pluralism was and is utterly inconsistent with the American experience. If competition erodes the plausibility of religions, why is the most pluralistic nation on earth among the most religious?

Indeed, having now had more than two centuries to develop under free market conditions, the American religious economy surpasses Adam Smith's wildest dreams about the creative forces of a free market (Moore 1994). There are more than 1,500 separate religious "denominations" (Melton 1989), many of them very sizable—24 have more than 1 million members each. Each of these bodies is entirely dependent on voluntary contributions, and American religious donations currently total more than $60 billion per year or more than $330 per person over age 18. These totals omit many contributions to church construction funds (new church construction amounted to $3 billion in 1993), as well as most donations to religious schools, hospitals, and foreign missions. In 1996, more than $2.3 billion was donated to support missionaries and a significant amount of this was spent on missionaries to Europe (Siewert and Valdez 1997).

Not only do Americans donate huge sums to their churches, many denominations are quite dependent on volunteer labor. Some, including the Mormons and Jehovah's Witnesses, rely entirely on an unpaid clergy and many more depend on volunteers to perform all of the needed clerical and maintenance services.

Thus, it is obvious to all American denominations that they are as subject to market forces as in any commercial firm, and that they live or die depending on their ability to attract, hold, and motivate members.

COMPETITION AND COMMITMENT IN AMERICA

It is frequent in science for important results to first be reported by investigators who failed to recognize their implications. So it was in the 1920s when a dedicated opponent of pluralism discovered that religious competition greatly increased community levels of participation. In an effort to show that rural America was "lamentably overchurched" and in dire need of consolidated churches, Edmund deS. Brunner conducted a series of exceptionally well executed studies of religious life in 138 small towns and villages. As can be seen in Table 29.1, in places where his proposed standard of no more than one church per 1,000 population was met, church membership and Sunday school enrollments were low. And as the number of churches competing for followers per 1,000 increased, so did religious participation.

That Brunner's findings were entirely contrary to the received wisdom that religious competition weakens faith went unremarked for more than sixty years (Finke and Stark 1992). In 1987, Kevin Christiano also reported positive effects of pluralism in an analysis based on American cities at the start of the twentieth cen-

TABLE 29.1 COMPETITION AND COMMITMENT IN AMERICAN TOWNS AND VILLAGES, 1923–25

| | CHURCHES PER 1,000 POPULATION | | | |
	One	Two	Three	Four or More
Percentage who belong to a church	27.4	36.0	34.8	43.4
Percentage enrolled in Sunday schools	15.8	22.3	25.2	37.4

SOURCE: Adapted from Brunner 1927, 74.

tury, noting that the "Protestant denominations may have grown in *conjunction with*, and in spite of, increases in internal differentiation [pluralism]" (1987, 128–29). Christiano recognized that his findings were entirely contrary to the prevailing theory that the proliferation of religious groups would speed secularization, but did not pursue the issue.

So much for hindsight. The first published findings on the positive effects of pluralism and competition presented in conjunction with a new theoretical view appeared the next year (Finke and Stark 1988). Based on an analysis of data for the 150 largest American cities in 1906, the study proposed to test the thesis that the "more pluralism, the greater the religious mobilization . . . the more highly specialized and aggressive the churches are, the greater the odds that any given individual will be activated" (ibid., 43). When the percentage of Catholics was controlled for, the results were strong and as hypothesized—the more diverse the local religious economy, the higher the percentage of the population who belonged to a church. Subsequently, these findings were replicated when data for 1890, 1916, and 1926 were substituted for the 1906 data (Finke 1992).

In *The Churching of America* (1992), we used the growth of a competitive, free market religious economy to explain the dramatic rise in American church membership over the past two centuries. It is instructive that European visitors did not begin to remark on the unusual religiousness of America until about forty years after the Revolution, because in the beginning there was nothing remarkable about American religion. In 1776, about 17 percent of Americans belonged to a church, about the same percentage as in England at that time. And it may have been even lower in earlier days, if we can credit the judgment by the Church of England's Society for the Propagation of the Gospel, which, in 1701, decried the lack of "Publick Worshipp of God" and widespread "Infidelity" in America (Pascoe 1901, I:87).

However, as free market conditions developed and dozens of vigorous new denominations appeared, church membership and attendance soared. By 1850, about 34 percent of Americans were church members, or twice the percentage in Britain that year. By 1900, half of Americans were churched, and today nearly two-thirds are enrolled in a specific local congregation (Finke and Stark 1992). It is this that requires explanation. And the most plausible and best-tested explanation is the rise of a free-market religious economy wherein eager and efficient firms compete for support.

In 1776, the Church of England was the subsidized and official church in the Colony of New York, having supplanted the Dutch Reformed Church as the established faith when the English seized the colony from Holland. In addition to these denominations, there were nine other active religious bodies in the colony, most of them very new and very small. As would be expected, religious participation was very low; only about 15 percent of the New York population belonged to a church. Having backed the losing side in the American Revolution, the Church of England lost its established status and free market conditions soon prevailed. Subsequently, the New York State census of 1865 revealed a church membership rate of 34 percent, spread across 53 active denominations, and 26 percent of New York's residents attended church weekly.

Precisely as hypothesized, analysis of data for the 942 towns and cities of New York State

TABLE 29.2 PLURALISM AND WEEKLY CHURCH ATTENDANCE IN 900 NEW YORK STATE TOWNS, 1865

PLURALISM INDEX SCORE	PERCENTAGE WHO ATTENDED WEEKLY	NUMBER OF TOWNS
0	10.6	86
.001–.549	22.9	233
.550–.699	29.9	293
.700–.799	33.6	231
.800+	33.9	57

SOURCE: New York, Secretary of State, *Census of the State of New York for 1865* (Albany: C. Van Benthuysen & Sons, 1867).

found that both the membership rate and the weekly attendance rate rose very substantially with the degree of pluralism. Of perhaps even greater interest is the fact that the increase in average weekly church attendance attenuates as the pluralism index reaches very high levels as can be seen in Table 29.2. This is the *saturation effect* mentioned earlier. The largest increase is between *no* pluralism (the town has only one denomination) and *some* diversity—the percentage who attend weekly more than doubles. The next increase in pluralism results in a significant, but rather smaller, increase in church attendance. But above that level, additional pluralism has little or no effect on attendance. That is to be expected, since any market has a saturation point.

REFERENCES

Baird, Robert. 1844. *Religion in America; or, An Account of the Origin, Progress, Relation to the State, and Present Condition of the Evangelical Churches in the United States.* New York: Harper & Bros.

Berger, Peter. 1967. *The Sacred Canopy.* New York: Doubleday.

———. 1979. *The Heretical Imperative: Contemporary Possibilities of Religious Affiliation.* New York: Doubleday.

Brunner, Edmund deS. 1927. *Village Communities.* New York: George H. Doran.

Christiano, Kevin. 1987. *Religious Diversity and Social Change: American Cities, 1890–1906.* New York: Cambridge University Press.

Cobbett, William. 1818. *Journal of a Year's Residence in the United States of America.* Reprint. London: Centaur, 1964.

Finke, Roger. 1984. "The Churching of America, 1850–1980." Ph.D. diss., University of Washington, Seattle.

———. 1992. "An Unsecular America." In *Religion and Modernization: Sociologists and Historians Debate the Secularization Thesis,* edited by Steve Bruce. Oxford: Clarendon Press.

Finke, Roger, and Rodney Stark. 1988. "Religious Economies and Sacred Canopies: Religious Mobilization in American Cities, 1906." *American Sociological Review* 53: 41–49.

———. 1992. *The Churching of America, 1776–1990: Winners and Losers in Our Religious Economy.* New Brunswick, N.J.: Rutgers University Press.

Handlin, Oscar. ed. 1949. *This Was America.* Cambridge, Mass.: Harvard University Press.

Melton, J. Gordon. 1989. *The Encyclopedia of American Religions.* 3d ed. Detroit: Gale Research.

Moore, R. Lawrence. 1994. *Selling God: American Religion in the Marketplace of Culture.* New York: Oxford University Press.

Pascoe, C.F. 1901. *Two Hundred Years of the SPG.* 2 vols. London: SPG.

Powell, Milton B., ed., 1967. *The Voluntary Church: Religious Life, 1740–1860, Seen through the Eyes of European Visitors.* New York: Macmillan.

Schaff, Philip. 1961 [1855]. *America: A Sketch of Its Political, Social, and Religious Character.* Cambridge, Mass.: Harvard University Press, Belknap Press.

Siewert, John A., and Edna G. Valdez, eds. 1997. *Mission Handbook.* 17th ed. Monrovia, Calif.: MARC.

Smith, Adam. [1776] 1981. *An Inquiry into the Nature and Causes of the Wealth of Nations.* 2 vols. Indianapolis: Liberty Fund.

Stark, Rodney. 1985. "From Church-Sect to Religious Economies." In *The Sacred in a Post-Secular Age,* edited by Phillip E. Hammond, 139–49. Berkeley and Los Angeles: University of California Press.

Stark, Rodney, and William Sims Bainbridge. 1985. *The Future of Religion: Secularization, Revival, and Cult Formation.* Berkeley and Los Angeles: University of California Press.

Tocqueville, Alexis de. [1835–39] 1956. *Democracy in America.* 2 vols. New York: Vintage Books.

Chapter 30

The New Story about What's Happening in the Churches

REGINALD W. BIBBY

This is a selection from Reginald Bibby's *Restless Gods,* the third in a series of books that he has written on the state of religion in Canada using data gathered specially for this purpose. Like many investigators, Bibby notes that there has been a long-term decline in the popularity of mainstream Protestant groups. However, as he makes clear, this has not been the result of defection to fundamentalist groups (as the press often suggest) but rather of a fairly dramatic increase in "religious nones" (i.e., people who say "none" when asked their religion). In this latest installment, however, Bibby claims to catch sight of something important: The decades-old decline in the popularity of mainstream religion is showing signs of "bottoming out." Bibby suggests that this is a possible prelude to a resurgence of interest in mainstream religion. If such resurgence does come to pass at this point in Canadian history, what do you think might be some of the likely causes?

Historically, proponents of religion have claimed that the gods have chosen to make contact with humans by using groups. Those groups, in the form of followers, churches, congregations, and the like, have seen themselves as the bearers of revelation and the custodians of tradition. They have maintained ongoing contact with the gods, gathered people together for things like worship, education, and social support, and seen themselves as entrusted to carry out some of the work of the gods on earth.

At first it may sound like an audacious claim. But sociologically speaking, the argument for the necessity of the group makes pretty good sense. Ideas and activities do not exist in a vacuum. Social psychologists, dating back to the likes of George Herbert Mead and Charles Cooley, have reminded us that ideas are socially instilled and socially sustained. Virtually all the ideas we hold can be traced back to social sources that include family, friends, authors, media, and, very frequently, religious groups. It can also be convincingly argued that the interdependence of life means we need other people in order to have our basic emotional and physical needs met, as well as to accomplish goals of almost any kind. Not surprisingly, then, religions have not existed without explicit group components. From a theist's perspective, it could all be part of a divine plan.

Source: *Restless Gods: The Renaissance of Religion in Canada,* by Reginald W. Bibby, Stoddart Publishing Co., 2002. Reprinted by permission.

An examination of religious identification in Canada over time reveals two distinct patterns: the stable dominance of established Christian groups and the difficulty new entries have had in cracking that monopoly.

- Between 1891 and 1991 the Catholic share of the Canadian population grew from 42% to 47%. The Protestant share was 56% in 1891 and 52% in 1941, but it slipped to 36% by 1991. The drop, however, was not because of significant proportional growth among other older and newer groups. It was rather because the percentage of "Religious Nones" grew from less than 1% through 1971 to 12% by 1991—reflecting, in part, the methodological fact that "No Religion" had not been an acceptable option in census surveys prior to 1971.

- The percentage-of-population growth of groups such as Jehovah's Witnesses and Latter-Day Saints between 1951 and 1991, during the period when Roman Catholic and Protestant bodies were experiencing declines, was minuscule.

- Further, as of the early 1990s—at the point when the country's well-established groups had been in numerical decline for some two decades—the membership totals of would-be competitors were very, very small. For all the media hype about disenchanted and disaffiliated Canadians turning to a wide range of religious options, relatively few people were actually identifying with the available alternatives. In a nation of close to 30 million people, fewer than 6,000 individuals identified with any of such highly publicized religions as Wicca, Scientology, or New Age. To put things in perspective, the 1991 census found that Canadians describing their religion as New Age numbered 480 in B.C., 150 in Ontario, and 15 in Quebec.[1]

These data suggest that what we have in Canada is an extremely tight "religious market" dominated by Catholic and Protestant "companies." New entries find the going extremely tough. In November of 2001, an evangelical organization held a conference in Montreal entitled "Igniting Our Passion for the Lost." It featured two prominent American evangelical speakers and included an emphasis on "renewed commitment to the harvest in Quebec."[2] Such organizations keep trying. They also find market gains slow in coming.

An important footnote needs to be added concerning the "No Religion" category. Claims that Religious Nones are booming need to be interpreted with caution. Apart from some important methodological issues—including the fact that the option was not a bona fide possibility until 1971—it seems clear that being "nothing" is a temporary status for many people. Canadians who indicate that they have no religion tend to be somewhat younger than others. In fact, the 1991 census showed that just over 40% of Nones were under the age of 25 and some 80% were under 45. About one in three had not yet married, and almost half had not yet had children.

My research and that of others suggests that many of these people will turn to religious groups when they want "rites of passage" relating to marriage and the birth of children; in the process, considerable numbers will "re-acquire" the Catholic and Protestant identities of their parents.[3] In fact, since at least the mid-80s, when the Canadian census began uncovering Nones, about 20% have said they anticipate turning to religious groups for weddings, 15% for birth-related ceremonies, and 35% for funerals. In addition, as we will see shortly, marriages involving Nones and others tend to result in children more frequently being raised "something" than the reverse—where children of "somethings" are raised "nothing." In succinct terms, the people residing in the "Religious None" category often have short stays.

These findings for Canada provide little indication that the preferred suppliers are changing. Instead, the established Roman Catholic and Protestant churches continue to monopolize the religion market.

Simply put, well-established religious groups can be expected to go down only so far before they bottom out. They may be at a low point for a while. But as new people with new ideas take on positions of influence, and as human and financial resources are put in place, these companies can be expected to stir and, to varying degrees, begin to rise again.

It's not a question of if; it's a question of when.

This revitalization argument does not assume that all well-established religious groups are going to show new signs of life at the same time or at the same pace. On the contrary, a necessary condition will be the appearance of leaders and laity who see the need for change, are able to envision what is needed to bring about change, and are capable of operationalizing and implementing ideas.

At such time as organizational resurgence begins to occur, it should be evident in the numbers of people the resurgent groups are attracting. An examination of attendance trends indicates that such a turnaround may in fact be starting to take place in Canada.

CIRCULATION–PLUS AMONG CONSERVATIVES

Dating back to the first Canadian census in 1871, the proportion of Canadians who have been identifying with Conservative Protestants has remained steady at about 8%. Research shows three important features about the Conservative Protestant numerical pool.

- First, evangelical groups have had to work extremely hard just to stay where they are. Smaller religious groups typically lose far more people to larger groups than they gain through intermarriage. The success of Conservative Protestants in remaining at about 8% of the population suggests that they have exhibited considerable vitality.[4] Further, with growth in the national population, holding at 8% translates into notable numerical growth—about 2.5 million people today,

compared to 1.1 million in 1950 and 277,000 in 1867.

- Second, their success in sustaining numbers is due primarily to their ability to retain their children, as well as their capacity to hold on to their geographically mobile members—two critically important sources of addition and attrition. Contrary to widespread belief, additions through evangelistic outreach, by comparison, have been relatively small.

- Third, people who identify with Conservative Protestant groups tend to be far more likely than other Canadians to be actively involved in their churches. Their levels of attendance have exceeded those of Mainline Protestants since at least the 1950s, as well as those of Roman Catholics since about the mid-80s. Currently, some six in ten people identifying with Conservative groups claim to be attending services almost every week or more, up from five in ten in 1990.

The net result of these vitality, retention, switching, and participation characteristics has been numerical growth at congregational levels. To look at evangelical Protestants in Canada is to see considerable energy, life, and growth.

REMNANT RESILIENCE IN THE MAINLINE

From the 1960s through about 1990, Canada's four Mainline Protestant denominations seemed to be in a numerical freefall. For starters, census data show that *the proportion of Canadians identifying with each group shrank*—the United Church from 20% to 11%, the Anglicans from 13% to 8%, and the Presbyterians and Lutherans from about 4% to 2% each. Together, this meant that the Mainline Protestant "religious family" that included 41% of the Canadian population in 1961 had dropped to 23% by 1991.

This old story about Canada's Mainline Protestants is the one that many people are continuing to tell. And with the residential school lawsuits exacerbating their resource problems—to put it mildly—few observers have seen much hope for renewed vitality within the country's Mainline denominations.

However, during the 1990s, an important development occurred: the decline in the proportion of Mainliners attending services weekly stopped, remaining steady at around 15%. There are fewer people in the Mainline population pool than in the past, but those who are still there are showing signs of life. For the first time in three decades, the proportion of the "Mainline remnant" who are active in these four Protestant groups remained fairly constant between 1990 and 2000.

This finding that regular weekly attendance has remained stable overall means that, in contrast to the stereotype of most Mainline congregations declining, there is a measure of vitality and numerical growth in many settings. The fact that roughly 15% of the people identifying with these four denominations have continued to be actively involved means that younger adults have been taking the place of older adults in sufficient numbers to at least sustain their collective 15% level.

There is also some very important news in this context about young people: the *Project Teen Canada* national surveys have found that the patterns of lower levels of identification and stable levels of attendance seen among adults have also been taking place among teenagers:

- Between 1984 and 1992, the proportion of 15-to-19-year-olds who identified with Mainliners dropped from 22% to 11%, and currently stands at only 8%.
- However, among "the teenage remnant" who continue to identify themselves as Mainliners, weekly attendance rose to 23% in 2000, up from 16% in 1992 and 17% in 1984.

In light of these findings, the reports "from the pews" about what is happening in Mainline congregations is particularly interesting to examine. The results are consistent with the attendance trends: one in three people who are involved in Mainline churches say their congregations have been growing in recent years, one in three that they have stayed about the same, and the remaining one in three that they have been declining in size. These are not exactly the unified cries of people on a boat that is sinking.

There's no question that the sizes of the affiliation pools of the four Mainline denominations have been declining. Participation also continues to be highest among the older members in this religious family. Still, these findings point to considerable life among the remnants, including younger people. To paraphrase Mark Twain, rumours of the death of Mainline Protestantism in Canada appear to have been greatly exaggerated.

SOLID STABILITY AND LATENT LIFE AMONG CATHOLICS

Roman Catholicism in Quebec and outside Quebec has been buoyed up over the years by tremendous growth in its affiliate pools through birth and immigration. As a proportion of the Canadian population, Roman Catholics have succeeded in holding their own over time. Census data show they made up 43% of the population in 1871, 42% in 1941, and about 45% in 2001. With growth in the national population, such proportional stability has meant that Catholics have grown from 1.5 million in 1871 to 4.8 million in 1941 to around 14 million today, with just under half—about six million—living in Quebec.

In addition, despite the dramatic drop in weekly attendance among Roman Catholics since the 1960s, the number of active participants has remained remarkably stable, at least outside Quebec. Although attendance has declined beyond Quebec's borders from 75% in the 1950s to a current level of 32%, population growth has meant that those figures have translated into about 3 million active churchgoers in the mid-50s, as well as about 2.5 million weekly attenders today.

Clearly, some local congregations are flourishing, some are holding their own, and others are decreasing in size. Corroborating such realities, almost equal proportions of Roman Catholics outside Quebec who are involved in their parishes reported in the *Project Canada* 2000 survey that their churches have been growing, staying about the same, or declining in size in recent years—almost identical proportions, incidentally, to those reported by Mainline Protestants. In short, outside Quebec, the size of the active Catholic core has continued to be significant, while the number of marginal and inactive Catholics has grown substantially.

Quebec has presented a different story. The weekly attendance drop from 88% in the mid-1950s to 20% today has represented a "people drop" from about 3.6 million to 1.2 million—a 67% loss in 50 years. However, there are some signs that the sleeping Roman Catholic giant in Quebec is beginning to stir:

- While the attendance attrition was dramatic between the 1950s and 1970s, coinciding with the Quiet Revolution and Vatican II, it has slowed down significantly, with the absolute numbers involved obviously bolstered by increases in Quebec's population. As a result, the 28% weekly attendance level of 1990 translated into about 1.6 million Catholics; today's 20%, as noted, represents about 1.2 million people.
- Currently, about 6 million Quebeckers see themselves as Roman Catholics, compared to only 4 million in the 1950s. What this means is that the Catholic Church in Quebec doesn't lack for Catholics; it lacks for involved Catholics.

I am not trying to make a case for new life if the new life is not there. At minimum, these data indicate that the resurgence of the Roman Catholic Church in Quebec is lagging far behind that of both Conservative and Mainline Protestants. And as I said earlier, to postulate organizational revitalization is not to suggest that timelines will be identical for all well-established religious groups. In Quebec, the leadership and resources required may simply not yet be in place on the scale needed for the Church's re-emergence to be more widespread and visible.

VITALITY AMONG OTHER FAITH GROUPS

Other religious groups, including Muslims, Buddhists, Hindus, and Sikhs, have experienced numerical growth in the post-1960s, primarily as a result of accelerated immigration from Asia and the Middle East. These Other Faith groups, when combined with Jews and people with ties to Eastern Orthodoxy, have a pool of affiliates that has jumped in size from under 500,000 in the mid-50s to about two million as of 2000. New arrivals have typically displayed high levels of religious commitment and enthusiasm, and these most recent cohorts are no exception. They have been socially and politically active and have raised the profile of major world religions in this country while expanding Canada's religious diversity.

The hurdle for new religious groups, past and present, lies in being able to sustain and increase numbers in a Canadian religious marketplace where Catholic and Protestant groups have held a virtual monopoly. Over time, smaller religious groups have encountered considerable difficulty retaining their offspring, many of whom "defect" to Catholicism and Protestantism through acculturation and assimilation. For example, 6% of current teens between the ages of 15 and 19 who have a Buddhist, Hindu, Muslim, or Sikh parent already see themselves as Protestants or Catholics; conversely, less than 1% of teens with a Catholic or Protestant parent identify with any of those four Other Faith traditions. There is also little doubt that many young people who come from Other Faith

TABLE 30.1 RELIGIOUS IDENTIFICATION OF CANADIANS, 1871–2000

	1871	1901	1931	1961	1991	2000
Roman Catholic	42%	42%	41%	47%	46%	45%
Protestant	56	56	54	49	36	32
Eastern Orthodox	<1	<1	1	1	2	1
Jewish	<1	<1	1	1	1	1
Other Faiths	2	2	2	1	3	4
No Religion	<1	<1	<1	<1	12	20

SOURCE: Statistics Canada; 2000 estimated.

homes will marry people outside their traditions. And Statistics Canada data through 1991 suggest that when they do, they more often than not will raise their children in the tradition of their Catholic or Protestant—or even their No Religion—partner.[5] That's the primary reason that faiths other than Christianity have had difficulty making significant proportional gains in Canada over time.

Despite their problems with sustaining growth, major global religions have experienced new visibility and vitality in Canada in the post-1960s. The immigrants who have helped bolster previously low numbers have brought with them new energy and new resources that have intensified religious diversity in Canada. To the extent that some of the immigrants or their children have opted for Protestantism or Catholicism, they have added further cultural diversity to those groups.

In sum, "the rise" of Other Faiths in the post-1960s and their influence on Canadian life and the Canadian religious scene has been an important part of the new story about what's been happening to organized religion in Canada. Their vitality can be seen in our survey findings on youth—surveys that provide us with sample sizes three times that of usual adult surveys, giving us a rather unique look at the role religious groups, both newer and older, play in the lives of Canada's young people.

These overall findings about the churches suggest that some important new developments are taking place in a variety of religious group

settings and among young people—that there is something of a renaissance of organized religion in Canada. To varying degrees, Canada's well-established groups show signs of slowing, halting, and even beginning to reverse the downward numerical trends of the second half of the 20th century. As well-established groups in particular continue to make changes and to re-emerge, such patterns can be expected to become even more pronounced over the next few decades.

Quebec stands out as the current exception. We have seen some important indications—including ongoing identification, occasional attendance, receptivity to greater involvement, and the increase in demand for rites of passage—that suggest there will soon be much more to the Quebec story. Indeed, one of the most interesting questions concerning religion in Canada in the new century is not *will* the Roman Catholic Church in Quebec rebound, but rather *when* will clear signs of such rejuvenation begin to appear?

ENDNOTES

1. Statistics Canada, 1993: 16–17.
2. Church Planting Canada brochure, 2001: 2.
3. See, for example, Bibby, 1993: 148–51, 157–59.
4. For details, see Bibby, 1993: 40–46 and 1997.
5. See Bibby, 1997b and 2000.

BIBLIOGRAPHY

Statistics Canada. 1993. Religions in Canada. Ottawa: Industry, Science and Technology Canada. 1991 Census of Canada. Catalogue no. 93-319

Church Planting Canada brochure, 2001: 2.

Bibby, Reginald W. 1993. *Unknown Gods: The Ongoing Story of Religion in Canada.* Toronto: Stoddart.

Bibby, Reginald W. 1997. "The Persistence of Christian Religious Identification in Canada." *Canadian Social Trends* (Spring): 24–28.

Bibby, Reginald W. 2000. "Canada's Mythical Religious Mosaic: Some Census Findings." *Journal for the Scientific Study of Religion* 39: 235–39.

PART 11
Media and Globalization

Chapter 31

Interview with Noam Chomsky

DAVID BARSAMIAN

There are a great many ways in which we acquire our opinions and, more generally, our way of "seeing" the world—and few would deny that the mass media play a role in that process. The exact nature of the role played by the media in shaping our perception of the world, however, is a matter of some debate. In one particularly well-known argument, Noam Chomsky and Edward Hermann argue that the mass media function to "manufacture consent." What this means, they suggest, is that the mass media, by virtue of what it pays attention to and what it ignores, and by virtue of the ways it frames stories, generates in ordinary people ways of seeing the world that function to benefit elites (and *not* the general public). Chomsky and Hermann call it a "propaganda" model of the media. In this selection, Chomsky discusses the history of the mainstream press's involvement in propaganda, and the continuing relevance of the propaganda model in understanding the press's coverage of current events. How do you go about deciding who is more correct, Chomsky or the mainstream views that he is critiquing? Note: *Z Magazine* is an online magazine and carries lists of publications by Chomsky and Hermann.

Noam Chomsky is Institute Professor in the Department of Linguistics and Philosophy at MIT. He is the author of scores of books—his latest are *Power and Terror* and *Middle East Illusions*. His book *9-11* was an international bestseller.

BARSAMIAN: In recent years, the Pentagon, and then the media, have adopted this term "collateral damage" to describe the death of civilians. Talk about the role of language in shaping and forming people's understanding of events.

CHOMSKY: Well, it's as old as history. It has nothing much to do with language. Language is the way we interact and communicate, so, naturally, the means of communication and the conceptual background that's behind it, which is more important, are used to try to shape attitudes and opinions and induce conformity and subordination. Not surprisingly, it was created in the more democratic societies.

The first coordinated propaganda ministry, called the Ministry of Information, was in Britain during World War I. It had the task, as they put it, of controlling the mind of the world. What they were particularly concerned with was the mind of America and, more specifically, the mind of American intellectuals. They thought if they could convince American intellectuals of the nobility of the British war effort, then American intellectuals could succeed in driving the basically pacifist population of the United

Source: David Barsamian, "Interview with Noam Chomsky," *Z Magazine*, July/August 2003, Volume 16, Number 7/8. Reprinted with permission.

States, which didn't want to have anything to do with European wars, rightly, into a fit of fanaticism and hysteria, which would get them to join the war. Britain needed U.S. backing, so Britain had its Ministry of Information aimed primarily at American opinion and opinion leaders. The Wilson administration reacted by setting up the first state propaganda agency here, called the Committee on Public Information.

It succeeded brilliantly, mainly with liberal American intellectuals, people of the John Dewey circle, who actually took pride in the fact that for the first time in history, according to their picture, a wartime fanaticism was created, and not by military leaders and politicians but by the more responsible, serious members of the community, namely, thoughtful intellectuals. And they did organize a campaign of propaganda, which within a few months did succeed in turning a relatively pacifist population into raving anti-German fanatics who wanted to destroy everything German. It reached the point where the Boston Symphony Orchestra couldn't play Bach. The country was driven into hysteria.

The members of Wilson's propaganda agency included people like Edward Bernays, who became the guru of the public relations industry, and Walter Lippmann, the leading public intellectual of the 20th century, the most respected media figure. They very explicitly drew from that experience. If you look at their writings in the 1920s, they said, We have learned from this that you can control the public mind, you can control attitudes and opinions. That's where Lippmann said, "We can manufacture consent by the means of propaganda." Bernays said, "The more intelligent members of the community can drive the population into whatever they want" by what he called "engineering of consent." It's the "essence of democracy," he said.

From that come enormous industries, ranging from advertising to universities, all committed very consciously to the conception that you must control attitudes and opinions because the people are just too dangerous.

It's particularly striking that it developed in the more democratic societies. They tried to duplicate it in Germany and Bolshevik Russia and South Africa and elsewhere. But it was always quite explicitly a mostly American model. There is a good reason for that. If you can control people by force, it's not so important to control what they think and feel. But if you lose the capacity to control people by force, it becomes more necessary to control attitudes and opinions.

That brings us right up to the present. By now the public is no longer willing to accept state propaganda agencies, so the Reagan Office of Public Diplomacy was declared illegal and had to go in roundabout ways. What took over instead was private tyrannies, basically, corporate systems, which play the role of controlling opinion and attitudes, not taking orders from the government, but closely linked to it, of course. That's our contemporary system. Extremely self-conscious. You don't have to speculate much about what they're doing because they're kind enough to tell you in industry publications and also in the academic literature.

So you go to, say, the 1930s, perhaps the founder of a good bit of modern political science. A liberal Wilsonian, Harold Lasswell, in 1933 wrote an article called "Propaganda" in the *Encyclopedia of Social Sciences*, a major publication, in which the message was, "We should not [all of these are quotes, incidentally] succumb to democratic dogmatisms about men being the best judges of their own interests." They're not, we are. And since people are too stupid and ignorant to understand their best interests, for their own benefit—because we're great humanitarians— we must marginalize and control them. The best means is propaganda. There is nothing negative about propaganda, he said. It's as neutral as a pump handle. You can use it for good or for evil.

And since we're noble, wonderful people, we'll use it for good, to ensure that the stupid, ignorant masses remain marginalized and separated from any decision-making capacity.

The Leninist doctrines are approximately the same. There are very close similarities. The Nazis also picked it up. If you read *Mein Kampf*, Hitler was very impressed with Anglo-American propaganda. He argued, not without reason, that that's what won World War I and vowed that next time around the Germans would be ready, too, and developed their own propaganda systems modeled on the democracies. The Russians tried it, but it was too crude to be effective. South Africa used it; others, right up to the present. But the real forefront is the United States, because it's the most free and democratic society, and it's just much more important to control attitudes and opinions.

You can read it in the *New York Times*. They ran an interesting article about Karl Rove, the president's manager—basically his minder, the one who teaches him what to say and do. It describes what Karl Rove is doing now. He was not directly involved in the war planning, but neither was Bush. This was in the hands of other people. But his goal, he says, is to present the president as a powerful wartime leader, aimed at the next presidential election, so that the Republicans can push through their domestic agenda, which is what he concentrates on, which means tax cuts—they say for the economy, but they mean for the rich—tax cuts and other programs which he doesn't bother enumerating, but which are designed to benefit an extremely small sector of the ultra-wealthy and privileged and will have the effect of harming the mass of the population. But more significant than that—it's not outlined in the article—is to try to destroy the institutional basis for social support systems, try to eliminate things like schools and Social Security and anything that is based on the conception that people have to have some concern for one another. That's a horrible idea, which has

to be driven out of people's minds. The idea that you should have sympathy and solidarity, you should care whether the disabled widow across town is able to eat, that has to be driven out of people's minds.

Clearly, there is a huge gap on the Iraq war between U.S. public opinion and the rest of the world. Do you attribute that to propaganda?

There is just no question about it. The campaign about Iraq took off last September [2002]. This is so obvious it's even discussed in mainstream publications, like the chief political analyst for UPI, Martin Sieff, has a long article describing how it was done. In September, which happened to be the opening of the midterm congressional campaign, that's when the drumbeat of wartime propaganda began. It had a couple of constant themes. One big lie was that Iraq was an imminent threat to the security of the United States. We have got to stop them now or they're going to destroy us tomorrow. The second big lie was that Iraq was behind September 11. Nobody says it straight out; it's kind of insinuated.

Take a look at the polls. They reflected the propaganda very directly. The propaganda is distributed by the media. They don't make it up, they just distribute it. You can attribute it to high government officials or whatever you like. But the campaign was reflected very quickly in the polls. By September and since then, roughly 60 percent, oscillating around that, of the population believes that Iraq is a threat to our security. Congress, if you look at the declaration of October, when they authorized the president to use force, said Iraq is a threat to the security of the United States. By now about half the population, maybe more by now, believes that Iraq was responsible for September 11, that Iraqis were on the planes, that they are planning new ones.

There is no one else in the world that believes any of this; there is no country where Iraq is regarded as a threat to their security. Kuwait and

Iran, which were both invaded by Iraq, don't regard Iraq as a threat to their security. Iraq is the weakest country in the region, and as a result of the sanctions, which have killed hundreds of thousands of people—about probably two-thirds of the population is on the edge of starvation—the country has the weakest economy and the weakest military force in the region. Its economy and its military-force expenditures are about a third those of Kuwait, which has 10 percent of its population, and well below others.

But only in the United States is there fear or any of these beliefs. You can trace the growth of the beliefs to the propaganda. It's interesting that the United States is so susceptible to this. There is a background, a cultural background, which is interesting. But whatever the reasons are for it, the United States happens to be a very frightened country by comparative standards. Levels of fear here of almost everything, crime, aliens, you pick it, are just off the spectrum. You can argue, you can inquire into the reasons, but the background is there.

What is it that makes it susceptible to propaganda?

That's a good question I don't say it's more susceptible to propaganda; it's more susceptible to fear. It's a frightened country. The reasons for this—I don't, frankly, understand them, but they're there, and they go way back in American history. It probably has to do with conquest of the continent, where you had to exterminate the native population; slavery, where you had to control a population that was regarded as dangerous, because you never knew when they were going to turn on you. It may just be a reflection of the enormous security. The security of the United States is beyond anyone else. The United States controls the hemisphere, it controls both oceans, it controls the opposite sides of both oceans, never been threatened. The last time the U.S. was threatened was the War of 1812. Since then it just conquers others. And somehow this

engenders a sense that somebody is going to come after us. So the country ends up being very frightened.

There is a reason why Karl Rove is the most important person in the administration. He is the public relations expert in charge of crafting the images. So you can drive through the domestic agendas, carry out the international policies by frightening people and creating the impression that a powerful leader is going to save you from imminent destruction. The *Times* virtually says it because it's very hard to keep hidden. It is second nature.

One of the new lexical constructions that I'd like you to comment on is "embedded journalists."

That's an interesting one. It is interesting that journalists are willing to accept it. No honest journalist would be willing to describe himself or herself as "embedded." To say "I'm an embedded journalist" is to say "I'm a government propagandist." But it's accepted. And it helps implant the conception that anything we do is right and just; so therefore, if you're embedded in an American unit, you're objective. Actually, the same thing showed up, in some ways even more dramatically, in the Peter Arnett case. Peter Arnett is an experienced, respected journalist with a lot of achievements to his credit. He's hated here precisely for that reason. The same reason Robert Fisk is hated.

Fisk being British, Arnett is originally from New Zealand.

Fisk is by far the most experienced and respected Middle East journalist. He's been there forever, he's done excellent work, he knows the region, he's a terrific reporter. He's despised here. You barely ever see a word of his. If he's mentioned, he's denounced somehow. The reason is he's just too independent. He won't be an embedded journalist. Peter Arnett is condemned because he gave an interview on Iraqi television. Is anybody condemned for giving an interview on U.S. television? No, that's wonderful.

The attack on Afghanistan in October 2001 generated a couple of these interesting terms, and you've commented on them. One was the Operation Enduring Freedom and the other is "unlawful combatant." Truly an innovation in international jurisprudence.

It's an innovation since the post-war period. After World War II there was a relatively new framework of international law established, including the Geneva Conventions. And they do not permit any such concept as enemy combatant in the way it's used here. You can have prisoners of war, but there is no new category. Actually, it's an old category, pre–World War II, when you were allowed to do just about anything. But under the Geneva Conventions, which were established to criminalize formally the crimes of the Nazis, this was changed. So prisoners of war are supposed to have special status. The Bush administration, with the cooperation of the media and the courts, is going back to the pre–World War II period, when there was no serious framework of international law dealing with crimes against humanity and crimes of war and is declaring not only to carry out aggressive war, but also to classify people it bombs and captures as some new category who are entitled to no rights.

They have gone well beyond that. The Administration has now claimed the right to take people here, including American citizens, to place them in confinement indefinitely without access to families and lawyers, and to keep them there with no charges until the president decides that the war against terror, or whatever he wants to call it, is over. That's unheard of. And it's been to some extent accepted by the courts. And they're, in fact, going beyond the new, what's sometimes called PATRIOT 2 Act, which is so far not ratified. It's inside the Justice Department, but it was leaked. By now there are a couple of articles by law professors and others about it in the press. It's astonishing. They're

claiming the right to remove citizenship, the fundamental right, if the Attorney General infers—they don't have to have any evidence—just infers that the person is involved somehow in actions that might be harmful to the United States. You have to go back to totalitarian states to find anything like this. An enemy combatant is one. The treatment of people—what's going on in Guantanamo is a gross violation of the most elementary principles of international humanitarian law since World War II, that is, since these crimes were formally criminalized in reaction to the Nazis.

You were an active and early dissident in the 1960s opposing U.S. intervention in Indochina. You have now this perspective of what was going on then and what is going on now. Describe how dissent has evolved in the United States.

Actually, there is another article in the *New York Times* that describes how the professors are antiwar activists, but the students aren't. Not like it used to be, when the students were antiwar activists. What the reporter is talking about is that around 1970—and it's true—by 1970 students were active antiwar protesters. But that's after eight years of a U.S. war against South Vietnam, which by then had extended to all of Indochina, which had practically wiped the place out. In the early years of the war—it was announced in 1962—U.S. planes are bombing South Vietnam, napalm was authorized, chemical warfare to destroy food crops, and programs to drive millions of people into "strategic hamlets," which are essentially concentration camps. All public. No protest. Impossible to get anybody to talk about it. For years, even in a place like Boston, a liberal city, you couldn't have public meetings against the war because they would be broken up by students, with the support of the media. You would have to have hundreds of state police around to allow the speakers like me to escape unscathed. The protests came after years and years of war. By then, hundreds of thousands of people had been killed, much of

Vietnam had been destroyed. Then you started getting protests.

But all of that is wiped out of history, because it tells too much of the truth. It involved years and years of hard work of plenty of people, mostly young, which finally ended up getting a protest movement. Now it's far beyond that. But the *New York Times* reporter can't understand that.

I'm sure the reporter is being very honest. The reporter is saying exactly what I think she was taught—that there was a huge antiwar movement because the actual history has to be wiped out of people's consciousness. You can't learn that dedicated, committed effort can bring about significant changes of consciousness and understanding. That's a very dangerous thought to allow people to have.

Chapter 32

An Introduction to McDonaldization

GEORGE RITZER

George Ritzer's work on the "McDonaldization of society" has proven to be enormously popular with undergraduate students over the last few years. Clearly, it is an idea that resonates with the experience of a great many people. Basically, Ritzer's core argument is that the principles that guide the fast-food industry, McDonald's in particular, are coming to dominate more and more aspects of social life generally. These principles include efficiency, calculability, predictability, and control. In this selection, taken from the first chapter of his book, Ritzer outlines this core argument and traces the success of McDonald's itself. In later chapters, he details how each of these principles has come to pervade education, health care, and the workplace. You might want to think about the ways in which the emphasis on these four things (efficiency, calculability, predictability, and control) shape your own daily experiences. On the other hand, critics might argue that the very appeal of Ritzer's book with undergraduates is itself evidence of McDonaldization. After all, it's a simple argument that can be applied with cookie-cutter efficiency and little imagination to one area of life after another. Does this contribute to the argument's appeal?

Ray Kroc, the genius behind the franchising of McDonald's restaurants, was a man with big ideas and grand ambitions. But even Kroc could not have anticipated the astounding impact of his creation. McDonald's is one of the most influential developments in twentieth-century America. Its reverberations extend far beyond the confines of the United States and the fast-food business. It has influenced a wide range of undertakings, indeed the way of life, of a significant portion of the world. And that impact is likely to expand at an accelerating rate.[1]

However, this is *not* a book about McDonald's, or even the fast-food business, although both will be discussed frequently throughout these pages. Rather, McDonald's serves here as the major example, the "paradigm," of a wide-ranging process I call *McDonaldization*, that is,

> the process by which the principles of the fast-food restaurant are coming to dominate more and more sectors of American society as well as of the rest of the world.

McDonaldization affects not only the restaurant business, but also education, work, health care, travel, leisure, dieting, politics, the family, and virtually every other aspect of society. McDonaldization has shown every sign of being an inexorable process by sweeping through seemingly impervious institutions and parts of the world.

McDonald's success is apparent: in 1993 its total sales reached $23.6 billion with profits of almost $1.1 billion.[2] The average U.S. outlet has total sales of approximately $1.6 million in a year.[3] McDonald's, which first began franchising in 1955, opened its 12,000th outlet on March 22, 1991. By the end of 1993, McDonald's had almost 14,000 restaurants worldwide.

The impact of McDonaldization has been manifested in many ways:

- The McDonald's model has been adopted not only by other budget-minded hamburger franchises such as Burger King and Wendy's, but also by a wide array of other low-priced fast-food businesses.

- The McDonald's model has also been extended to "casual dining," that is, more "upscale," higher-priced restaurants with fuller menus. For example, Outback Steakhouse and Sizzler sell steaks, Fuddrucker's offers "gourmet" burgers, Chi-Chi's and Chili's sell Mexican food, The Olive Garden proffers Italian food, and Red Lobster purveys . . . you guessed it.

- McDonald's is making increasing inroads around the world.[4] In 1991, for the first time, McDonald's opened more restaurants abroad than in the United States. As we move toward the next century, McDonald's expects to build twice as many restaurants each year overseas than it does in the United States.[5] By the end of 1993, over one-third of McDonald's restaurants were overseas; at the beginning of 1995, about half of McDonald's profits came from its overseas operations. McDonald's has even recently opened a restaurant in Mecca, Saudi Arabia.[6]

- Other countries with their own McDonaldized institutions have begun to export them to the United States. For example, the Body Shop is an ecologically sensitive British cosmetics chain with 893 shops in early 1993, 120 of which were in the United States, with 40 more scheduled to open that year. Furthermore, American firms are now opening copies of this British chain, such as The Limited, Inc.'s Bath and Body Works.

- Other types of business are increasingly adapting the principles of the fast-food business to their needs. Said the vice chairman of Toys "Я" Us, "We want to be thought of as a sort of McDonald's of toys."[7] Other chains with similar ambitions include Jiffy-Lube, AAMCO Transmissions, Midas Muffler & Brake Shops, Hair Plus, H & R Block, Pearle Vision Centers, Jenny Craig, Home Depot, Barnes & Noble, Petstuff, and Wal-Mart (the nation's largest retailer with about 2,500 stores and almost $55 billion in sales.)[8]

McDonald's has achieved its exalted position because virtually all Americans, and many others, have passed through its golden arches on innumerable occasions. Furthermore, most of us have been bombarded by commercials extolling McDonald's virtues, commercials that are tailored to different audiences. Some play to young children watching Saturday-morning cartoons. Others solicit young adults watching prime-time programs. Still others coax grandparents to take their grandchildren to McDonald's. In addition, these commercials change as the chain introduces new foods (such as breakfast burritos), creates new contests, and ties its products to things such as new motion pictures. These ever-present commercials, combined with the fact that people cannot drive very far without having a McDonald's pop into view, have served to embed McDonald's deep in popular consciousness. A poll of school-age children showed that 96% of them could identify Ronald McDonald, second only to Santa Claus in name recognition.[9]

Over the years, McDonald's has appealed to people in many ways. People are even led to believe that they contribute, at least indirectly, to charities such as the Ronald McDonald Houses for sick children.

THE LONG ARM OF MCDONALDIZATION

McDonald's has strived to continually extend its reach within American society and beyond.

As the company chairman said, "Our goal: to totally dominate the quick service restaurant industry worldwide. . . . I want McDonald's to be more than a leader. I want McDonald's to dominate."[10]

McDonald's began as a phenomenon of suburbs and medium sized towns, but in recent years it has moved into big cities and smaller towns.[11] You can now find fast-food outlets in New York's Times Square as well as on the Champs Elysees in Paris. Soon after it opened in 1992, the McDonald's in Moscow sold almost 30,000 hamburgers a day and employed a staff of 1,200 young people working two to a cash register.[12] In early 1992, Beijing witnessed the opening of the world's largest McDonald's, with 700 seats, 29 cash registers, and nearly 1,000 employees. On its first day of business, it set a new one-day record for McDonald's by serving about 40,000 customers.[13]

Small satellite, express, or remote outlets, opened in areas that cannot support full-scale fast-food restaurants. They have begun to appear in small store fronts in large cities and in nontraditional settings such as department stores, service stations, and even schools.

No longer content to dominate the strips that surround many college campuses, fast-food restaurants have moved onto many of those campuses. The first fast-food restaurant opened at the University of Cincinnati in 1973. Today, college cafeterias often look like shopping-mall food courts. In conjunction with a variety of "branded partners" (for example, Pizza Hut and Subway), Marriott now supplies food to almost 500 colleges and universities.[14] The apparent approval of college administrations puts fast-food restaurants in a position to further influence the younger generation.

In other sectors of society, the influence of fast-food restaurants has been subtler, but no less profound. Though McDonald's and other fast-food restaurants have begun to appear in high schools and trade schools,[15] few lower-grade schools as yet have in-house fast-food restaurants. However, many have had to alter school cafeteria menus and procedures to make fast food readily available.[16] The attempt to hook school-age children on fast food reached something of a peak in Illinois where McDonald's operated a program called, "*A* for Cheeseburger." Students who received *A*'s on their report cards received a free cheeseburger, thereby linking success in school with rewards from McDonald's.[17]

The military has also been pressed to offer fast food on both bases and ships. Despite the criticisms by physicians and nutritionists, fast-food outlets increasingly turn up *inside* hospitals.

As powerful as it is, McDonald's has not been alone in pressing the fast-food model on American society and the rest of the world. Other fast-food giants, such as Burger King and Kentucky Fried Chicken, have played a key role, as have innumerable other businesses built on the principles of the fast-food restaurant.

Even the derivatives of McDonald's and the fast-food industry in turn exert their own influence. For example, the success of *USA TODAY* has led many newspapers across the nation to adopt, for example, shorter stories and color weather maps. As one *USA TODAY* editor put it, "The same newspaper editors who call us McPaper have been stealing our McNuggets."[18]

The expansion deep into the newspaper business suggests that McDonaldization may be inexorable and may therefore come to insinuate itself into every aspect of society and people's private lives. In the movie *Sleeper*, Woody Allen not only created a futuristic world in which McDonald's was an important and highly visible element, but he also envisioned a society in which even sex underwent the process of McDonaldization. The denizens of his future world were able to enter a machine called an "orgasmatron," which allowed them to experience an orgasm without going through the muss and fuss of sexual intercourse.

Sex actually has, like virtually every other sector of society, undergone a process of McDonaldization. "Dial-a-porn" allows people to have intimate, sexually explicit, even obscene conversations with people they have never met and probably never will meet.[19] Those who answer the phones mindlessly and repetitively follow "scripts" that have them saying such things as, "Sorry, tiger, but your Dream Girl has to go . . . Call right back and ask for me."[20] Escort services advertise a wide range of available sex partners. People can see highly specialized pornographic movies at urban multiplexes and can rent them from local video stores for viewing in the comfort of their living rooms. In New York City, an official called a three-story pornographic center "the McDonald's of sex" because of its "cookie-cutter cleanliness and compliance with the law."[21] These examples suggest that no aspect of people's lives is immune to McDonaldization.

THE DIMENSIONS OF MCDONALDIZATION

Why has the McDonald's model proven so irresistible? Four alluring dimensions lie at the heart of the success of this model and, more generally, of McDonaldization. In short, McDonald's has succeeded because it offers consumers, workers, and managers efficiency, calculability, predictability, and control.[22]

First, McDonald's offers *efficiency*, or the optimum method for getting from one point to another. For consumers, this means that McDonald's offers the best available way to get from being hungry to being full. Other institutions, fashioned on the McDonald's model, offer similar efficiency in losing weight, lubricating cars, getting new glasses or contacts, or completing income-tax forms. In a society where both parents are likely to work, or where there may be only a single parent, efficiently satisfying the hunger and many other needs of people is very attractive. In a society where people rush, usually by car, from one spot to another, the efficiency of a fast-food meal, perhaps even without leaving their cars by wending their way along the drive-through lane, often proves impossible to resist. The fast-food model offers people, or at least appears to offer them, an efficient method for satisfying many needs.

Like their customers, workers in McDonaldized systems function efficiently. They are trained to work this way by managers, who watch over them closely to make sure they do. Organizational rules and regulations also help ensure highly efficient work.

Second, McDonald's offers *calculability*, or an emphasis on the quantitative aspects of products sold (portion size, cost) and service offered (the time it takes to get the product). Quantity has become equivalent to quality; a lot of something, or the quick delivery of it, means it must be good. As two observers of contemporary American culture put it, "As a culture, we tend to believe deeply that in general 'bigger is better.'"[23] Thus, people order the *Quarter Pounder*, the *Big Mac*, the *large* fries. More recently, there is the lure of the "double this" (for instance, Burger King's "Double Whopper With Cheese") and the "triple that." People can quantify these things and feel that they are getting a lot of food for what appears to be a nominal sum of money. This calculation does not take into account an important point: the extraordinary profitability of fast-food outlets and other chains, which indicates that the owners, not the consumers, get the best deal.

People also tend to calculate how much time it will take to drive to McDonald's, be served the food, eat it, and return home; then, they compare that interval to the time required to prepare food at home. They often conclude, rightly or wrongly, that a trip to the fast-food restaurant will take less time than eating at home. This sort of calculation particularly supports home-delivery franchises.

Some McDonaldized institutions combine the emphasis on time and money. Domino's promises pizza delivery in half an hour, or the pizza is free. Pizza Hut will serve a personal pizza in five minutes, or it, too, will be free.

Workers at McDonaldized systems also tend to emphasize the quantitative rather than the qualitative aspects of their work. Since the quality of the work is allowed to vary little, workers focus on such things as how quickly tasks can be accomplished. In a situation analogous of that of the customer, workers are expected to do a lot of work, very quickly, for low pay.

Third, McDonald's offers *predictability*, the assurance that their products and services will be the same over time and in all locales. The Egg McMuffin in New York will be, for all intents and purposes, identical to those in Chicago and Los Angeles. Also, those eaten next week or next year will be identical to those eaten today.

The workers in McDonaldized systems also behave in predictable ways. They follow corporate rules as well as the dictates of their managers. In many cases, not only what they do, but also what they say, is highly predictable. McDonaldized organizations often have scripts that employees are supposed to memorize and follow whenever the occasion arises. This scripted behavior helps create highly predictable interactions between workers and customers.

Fourth, *control*, especially through the *substitution of nonhuman for human technology*, is exerted over the people who enter the world of McDonald's. A *human technology* (a screwdriver, for example) is controlled by people; a *nonhuman technology* (the assembly line, for instance) controls people. The people who eat in fast-food restaurants are controlled, albeit (usually) subtly. Lines, limited menus, few options, and uncomfortable seats all lead diners to do what management wishes them to do—eat quickly and leave. Further, the drive-through (in some cases walk-through) window leads diners to leave before they eat. In the Domino's model, customers never come in the first place.

The people who work in McDonaldized organizations are also controlled to a high degree, usually more blatantly and directly than customers. They are trained to do a limited number of things in precisely the way they are told to do them. The technologies used and the way the organization is set up reinforce this control. Managers and inspectors make sure that workers toe the line.

McDonald's also controls employees by threatening to use, and ultimately using, nonhuman technology to replace human workers. No matter how well they are programmed and controlled, workers can foul up the system's operation. A slow worker can make the preparation and delivery of a Big Mac inefficient. A worker who refuses to follow the rules might leave the pickles or special sauce off a hamburger, thereby making for unpredictability. And a distracted worker can put too few fries in the box, making an order of large fries seem skimpy. For these and other reasons, McDonald's has felt compelled to steadily replace human beings with non-human technologies, such as the soft-drink dispenser that shuts itself off when the glass is full, the french-fry machine that rings and lifts itself out of the oil when the fries are crisp, the preprogrammed cash register that eliminates the need for the cashier to calculate prices and amounts. This technology increases the corporation's control over workers. Thus, McDonald's can assure customers that their employees and service will be consistent.

THE ADVANTAGES OF MCDONALDIZATION

This discussion of four of the fundamental characteristics of McDonaldization makes it clear that there are good, solid reasons why McDonald's has succeeded so phenomenally and why the process of McDonaldization is moving ahead so dramatically.

McDonaldization has undoubtedly led to positive changes. Here are a few specific examples:

- There is a far greater availability of goods and services than before.
- This wider range of goods and services is available to a much larger portion of the population.

- People are able to get what they want or need almost instantaneously.
- It is far more convenient to get what they want or need.
- Goods and services are of a far more uniform quality; at least some people get even better goods and services than before McDonaldization.
- Far more economical alternatives to high-priced, customized goods and services are widely available; therefore, people can afford things they could not previously afford.
- Fast, efficient goods and services are available to a population that is working longer hours and has fewer hours to spare.
- In a rapidly changing, unfamiliar, and seemingly hostile world, there is comfort in the comparatively stable, familiar, and safe environment of a McDonaldized system.
- Because of quantification, consumers can more easily compare competing products.
- People can do things, such as obtain money or a bank balance in the middle of the night, that were impossible before.
- It is now safer to do things (for example, diet) in a carefully regulated and controlled system.
- People are more likely to be treated similarly, no matter what their race, gender, or social class.
- Organizational and technological innovations are more quickly and easily diffused through networks of identical operators.
- The products of one culture are more easily diffused to others.

More specifically, McDonald's itself offers many praiseworthy programs, such as its Ronald McDonald Houses, which permit parents to stay with children undergoing treatment for serious medical problems; job-training programs for teenagers; programs to help keep its employees in school; efforts to hire and train the handicapped; the McMasters program, aimed at hiring senior citizens; and an enviable record of hiring and promoting minorities.

A CRITIQUE OF McDONALDIZATION: THE IRRATIONALITY OF RATIONALITY

Though McDonaldization offers powerful advantages, it has a downside. Efficiency, predictability, calculability, and control through nonhuman technology can be thought of as the basic components of a *rational* system.[24] However, rational systems inevitably spawn irrationalities.

For example, McDonaldization has produced a wide array of adverse effects on the environment. Take just one example: the need to grow uniform potatoes to create those predictable french fries that people have come to expect from fast-food restaurants. It turns out that the need to grow such potatoes has adversely affected the ecology of the Pacific Northwest. The huge farms that now produce such potatoes rely on the extensive use of chemicals. The need to produce a perfect fry means that much of the potato is wasted, with the remnants either fed to cattle or used for fertilizer. However, the underground water supply is now showing high levels of nitrates that may be traceable to the fertilizer and animal wastes.[25] There are, of course, many other ecological problems associated with the McDonaldization of society—the forests felled to produce paper, the damage caused by polystyrene and other materials, the enormous amount of food needed to produce feed cattle, and so on.

Another unreasonable effect of the fast-food restaurant is that it is often a dehumanizing setting in which to eat or work. Customers lining up for a burger or waiting in the drive-through line and workers preparing the food often feel as though they are part of an assembly line. Hardly amenable to eating, assembly lines have been shown to be inhuman settings in which to work.

The increase in the number of people, the acceleration of technological change, the increasing pace of life—all this and more make it impossible to go back to the nonrationalized world, if it ever existed, of home-cooked meals, traditional restaurant dinners, high-quality foods, meals loaded with surprises, and restaurants populated only by chefs free to fully express their creativity.

While one basis for a critique of McDonaldization is the past, another is the future.[26] The future in this sense is defined as human potential, unfettered by the constraints of McDonaldized systems. This critique holds that people have the potential to be far more thoughtful, skillful, creative, and well-rounded than they are now. If the world were less McDonaldized, people would be better able to live up to their human potential. This critique is based not on what people were like in the past, but on what they could be like in the future.

REFERENCES

1. For a similar but narrower viewpoint to the one expressed here, see Benjamin R. Barber. "Jihad Vs. McWorld." *The Atlantic Monthly,* March 1992, pp. 53–63.

2. These and other data on McDonald's come from its most recent (1993) annual report, *The Annual.*

3. Cynthia Rigg. "McDonald's Lean Units Beef up NY Presence." *Crain's New York Business,* October 31, 1994, p. 1.

4. Bill McDowall. "The Global Market Challenge." *Restaurants & Institutions,* vol. 104, no. 26, November 1, 1994, pp. 52ff.

5. Eben Shapiro in "Overseas Sizzle for McDonald's." *New York Times,* April 17, 1992, pp. D1, D4.

6. "Investors with Taste for Growth Looking to Golden Arches." *Tampa Tribune,* January 11, 1995, Business and Finance, p. 7.

7. Timothy Egan. "Big Chains Are Joining Manhattan's Toy Wars." *New York Times,* December 8, 1990, p. 29.

8. Paul Gruchow. "Unchaining America: Communities Are Finding Ways to Keep Independent Entrepreneurs in Business." *Utne Reader,* January–February 1995, pp. 17–18.

9. Steven Greenhouse. "The Rise and Rise of McDonald's." *New York Times,* June 8, 1986, section 3, p. 1.

10. Richard L. Papiernik. "Mac Attack?" *Financial World,* April 12, 1994, p. 30.

11. Laura Shapiro. "Ready for McCatfish?" *Newsweek,* October 15, 1990, pp. 76–77; N. R. Kleinfeld. "Fast Food's Changing Landscape." *New York Times,* April 14, 1985, section 3, pp. 1, 6.

12. Louis Uchitelle. "That's Funny, Those Pickles Don't Look Russian." *New York Times,* February 27, 1992, p. A4.

13. Nicholas D. Kristof. "'Billions Served' (and That Was Without China)." *New York Times,* April 24, 1992, section 3, p. A4.

14. Carole Sugarman. "Dining Out on Campus." *Washington Post/Health,* February 14, 1995, p. 20.

15. Mark Albright. "INSIDE JOB: Fast-Food Chains Serve a Captive Audience." *St. Petersburg Times,* January 15, 1995, p. 1H.

16. Mike Berry. "Redoing School Cafeterias to Favor Fast-Food Eateries." *Orlando Sentinel,* January 12, 1995, p. 11.

17. "Grade 'A' Burgers." *New York Times,* April 13, 1986, pp. 12, 15.

18. Peter Prichard. *The Making of McPaper: The Inside Story of USA TODAY.* Kansas City, MO: Andrews, McMeel, and Parker, 1987, pp. 232–233.

19. Nicholas D. Kristof. "Slicing, Dicing News to Attract the Young. *New York Times,* October 15, 1986, section 1, p. 16.

20. Cited in Robin Leidneer. *Fast Food, Fast Talk: Service Work and the Routinization of Everyday Life.* Berkeley: University of California Press, 1993, p. 9.

21. Martin Gottlieb. "Pornography's Plight Hits Times Square." *New York Times,* October 5, 1986, section 3, p. 6.

22. Max Weber. *Economy and Society.* Totowa, NJ: Bedminster Press, 1921/1968; Stephen Kalberg. "Max Weber's Types of Rationality:

Cornerstones for the Analysis of Rationalization Processes in History." *American Journal of Sociology* 85 (1980): 1145–1179.

23. Ian Mitroff and Warren Bennis. The Unreality Industry: The Deliberate Manufacturing of Falsehood and What It is Doing to Our Lives. New York: Birch Lane Press, 1989, p. 142.

24. It should be pointed out that the words *rational, rationality,* and *rationalization* are being used differently here and throughout the book than they are ordinarily employed. For one thing, people usually think of these terms as being largely positive; something that is rational is usually considered to be good. However, they are used here in a generally negative way. The positive term in this analysis is genuinely human "reason" (for example, the ability to act and work creatively), which is seen as being denied by inhuman, rational systems such as the fast-food restaurant. For another, the term *rationalization* is usually associated with Freudian theory as a way of explaining away some behavior, but here it describes the increasing pervasiveness of rationality throughout society. Thus, in reading this book, you must be careful to interpret the terms in these ways rather than in the ways they are conventionally employed.

25. Timothy Egan. In Land of French Fry, Study Finds Problems." *New York Times,* February 7, 1994, p. A10.

26. In this sense, this resembles Marx's critique of capitalism. Marx was not animated by a romanticization of precapitalist society, but rather by the desire to produce a truly human (communist) society on the base provided by capitalism. Despite this specific affinity to Marxist theory, this book is, as you will see, premised far more on the theories of Max Weber.

PART 12
Sociology of Work

Chapter 33

McJobs: McDonaldization and Its Relationship to the Labor Process

GEORGE RITZER

In this selection, Ritzer wants to expand on his core arguments regarding McDonaldization. For example, while it's easy to understand how, say, the process by which food is produced in fast-food restaurants has been shaped by an emphasis on efficiency, calculability, predictability, and control, what's less obvious but nevertheless true is that even the interactions between workers and customers are also shaped by these emphases. In some cases, Ritzer points out, these emphases function to blur the line between "worker" and "customer" so that customers become unpaid workers. Finally, he confronts what might be a puzzle: Why is there so little discontent among the workers whose lives have been affected by McDonaldization? Ritzer's answer is that any discontent that might arise in some particular organization is blunted by the fact that we live in a society that is being McDonaldized at so many different levels. Do you agree that McDonaldization produces little discontent? Isn't the popularity of Ritzer's argument itself some evidence to the contrary?

In recent years the spread of McDonaldized systems has led to the creation of an enormous number of jobs. Unfortunately, the majority of them can be thought of as McDonaldized jobs, or "McJobs." While we usually associate these types of positions with fast-food restaurants, and in fact there are many jobs in that setting, McJobs have spread throughout much of the economy....

It is worth outlining some of the basic realities of employment in the fast-food industry in the United States since those jobs serve as a model for employment in other McDonaldized settings. The large number of people employed in fast-food restaurants accounts for over 40 percent of the approximately 6 million people employed in restaurants of all types. Fast-food restaurants rely heavily on teenage employees—almost 70 percent of their employees are 20 years of age or younger. For many, the fast-food restaurant is likely to be their first employer. It is estimated that the first job for one of every 15 workers was at McDonald's; one of every eight Americans has worked at McDonald's at some time in his or her life. The vast majority of employees are part-time workers: the average workweek in the fast-food industry is 29.5 hours. There is a high turnover rate: Only slightly more than half the employees remain on the job for a year or more. Minorities are overrepresented in these jobs—almost two-thirds of employees are women and nearly a quarter are non-white. These are low-paid occupations, with many earning the minimum wage or slightly more. As a result, these jobs are greatly affected by changes in the minimum wage: An upward revision has an important effect on the income of these workers. However, there is a real danger that many workers would lose their positions as a result of such increases, especially in economically marginal fast-food restaurants. . . .

McJobs are characterized by the . . . dimensions of McDonaldization. The jobs tend to involve a series of simple tasks in which the emphasis is on performing each as efficiently as possible. Second, the time associated with many of the tasks is carefully calculated and the emphasis on the quantity of time a task should take tends to diminish the quality of the work from the point of view of the worker. That is, tasks are so simplified and streamlined that they provide little or no meaning to the worker. Third, the work is predictable; employees do and say essentially the same things hour after hour, day after day. Fourth, many nonhuman technologies are employed to control workers and reduce them to robot-like actions. Some technologies are in place, and others are in development, that will lead to the eventual replacement of many of these "human robots" with computerized robots. Finally, the rationalized McJobs lead to a variety of irrationalities, especially the dehumanization of work. The result is the extraordinarily high turnover rate described above and difficulty in maintaining an adequate supply of replacements.

The claim is usually made by spokespeople for McDonaldized systems that they are offering a large number of entry-level positions that help give employees basic skills they will need in order to move up the occupational ladder within such systems (and many of them do). This is likely to be true in the instances in which the middle-level jobs to which they move—for example, shift leader in or assistant manager or manager of a fast-food restaurant—are also routinized and scripted. . . . However, the skills acquired in McJobs are not likely to prepare one for, help one to acquire, or help one to function well in, the far more desirable postindustrial occupations which are highly complex and require high levels of skill and education. Experience in routinized actions and scripted interactions do not help much when occupations require thought and creativity. . . .

McJobs are not simply the de-skilled jobs of our industrial past in new settings; they are jobs that have a variety of new and distinctive characteristics. . . . There have also emerged many distinctive aspects of the control of these workers. Industrial and McDonaldized jobs both tend to be highly routinized in terms of what people do on the job. However, one of the things that is distinctive about McDonaldized jobs, especially since so many of them involve work that requires interaction and communication, especially with consumers, is that what people *say* on the job is also highly routinized. To put this another way, McDonaldized jobs are tightly scripted: They are characterized by *both* routinized actions . . . and scripted interactions (examples include "May I help you?"; "Would you like a dessert to go with your meal?"; and "Have a nice day!"). Scripts are crucial because many of the workers in McDonaldized systems are interactive service workers. This means that they not only produce goods and provide services, but they often do so in interaction with customers.

The scripting of interaction leads to new depths in the de-skilling of workers. Not only have employee actions been de-skilled; employees' ability to speak and interact with customers is now being limited and controlled. There are not only scripts to handle general situations but also a range of subscripts to deal with a variety of contingencies. Verbal and interactive skills are being taken away from employees and built into the scripts in much the same way that manual skills were taken and built into various technologies. At one time distrusted in their ability to *do* the right thing, workers now find themselves no longer trusted to *say* the right thing. Once able to create distinctive interactive styles, and to adjust them to different circumstances, employees are now asked to follow scripts as mindlessly as possible. . . .

McDonaldized systems have little interest in how their mainly part-time, short-time employees feel about and see themselves. These systems are merely interested in controlling their employees' overt behavior for as long as they work in such a system.

One very important, but rarely noted, aspect of the labor process in the fast-food restaurant and other McDonaldized systems is the extent to which customers are being led, perhaps even almost required, to perform a number of tasks without pay that were formerly performed by paid employees. For example, in the modern gasoline station the driver now does various things for free (pumps gas, cleans windows, checks oil, and even pays through a computerized credit card system built into the pump) that were formerly done by paid attendants. In these and many other settings, McDonaldization has brought the customer *into* the labor process: The customer *is* the laborer! This has several advantages for employers, such as lower (even nonexistent) labor costs, the need for fewer employers, and less trouble with personnel problems: Customers are far less likely to complain about a few seconds or minutes of tedious work than employees who devote a full workday to such tasks. Because of its advantages, as well as because customers are growing accustomed to and accepting of it, I think customers are likely to become even more involved in the labor process.

This is the most revolutionary development, at least as far as the labor process is concerned, associated with McDonaldization. . . . The analysis of the labor process must be extended to what customers do in McDonaldized systems. The distinction between customer and employee is eroding, or in postmodern terms "imploding," and one can envision more and more work settings in which customers are asked to do an increasing amount of "work." More dramatically, it is also likely that we will see more work settings in which there are no employees at all! In such settings, customers, in interaction with non-human technologies, will do *all* of the human labor. A widespread example is the ATM in which customers (and the technology) do all of the work formerly done by bank tellers.

In a sense, a key to the success of McDonaldized systems is that they have been able to supplement the exploitation of employees with the exploitation of customers. In Marxian terms, customers create value in the tasks they perform for McDonaldized systems. And they are not simply paid less than the value they produce, they are paid *nothing at all*. In this way, customers are exploited to an even greater degree than workers. As is true of the exploitation of workers, owners are unaware of the fact that they are exploiting customers. But knowledge of exploitation is not a prerequisite to its practice.

While we have been focusing on the exploitation of customers in McDonaldized systems, this is not to say that employers have lost sight of the need to exploit workers. Beyond the usual exploitation of being paid less than the value of what they produce, McDonald's employees are often not guaranteed that they will work the number of hours they are supposed to on a given day. If business is slow, they may be sent home early in order that the employer can economize on labor costs: This reduces their take-home pay. As a result, employees often find it hard to count on a given level of income, meager as it might be, each week. In this way, and many others, employees of McDonaldized systems are even more exploited than their industrial counterparts.

This discussion brings together the two great theories in the history of sociology—Weber's theory of rationalization and Marx's theory of capitalist expansion and exploitation. Rationalization is a process that serves the interest of capitalists. They push it forward (largely unconsciously) because it heightens the level of exploitation of workers, allows new agents (e.g., customers) to be exploited and brings with it greater surplus value and higher profits. . . . We can see here how rationalization not only enhances control but also heightens the level and expands the reach of exploitation.

In various ways, McDonaldization is imposed on employees and even customers. They often have no choice but to conform, even if they would prefer things to be done in other ways. However, it would be a mistake to look at McDonaldization as simply being imposed on workers and customers. As discussed above, the basic ideas associated with McDonaldization are part of the value system. Many workers and customers have internalized them and conform to them of their own accord.

The emphasis on the McDonaldization of work (like that on de-skilling) tends to emphasize only one side of the dialectic between structural changes, especially those imposed by management, and the significance of the responses of employees, which are consistently downplayed. But . . . the employees of McDonaldized systems often exhibit a considerable amount of independence, perhaps even creativity, on the job. . . . Also, . . . in our rush to condemn, we must not ignore the advantages to both employees and customers of the routinization, even the scripting, of work. . . .

There is also a dialectic between living one's life in a McDonaldized society and working in a McDonaldized job. These are mutually reinforcing, and the net result is that if most of one's life is spent in one McDonaldized system or another, then one is less likely to feel dissatisfied with either one's life or one's job. This helps to account for . . . [the] finding that McDonald's workers do not evidence a high level of dissatisfaction with their work. This, perhaps, is one of the most disturbing implications of the McDonaldization thesis. If most of one's life is spent in McDonaldized systems, then there is little or no basis for rebellion against one's McDonaldized job since one lacks a standard against which to compare, and to judge, such a job.

This also undermines one of Marx's fundamental assumptions that when all is said and done workers remain at odds with the kind of work that is being imposed on them and are a threat to those who are imposing the work.

To Marx, there is a creative core (species being, for example) lying just below the surface that is ever-ready to protest, or rebel against, the rationalized and exploitative character of work. However, can that creative core survive intact, or even at all, in the face of growing up in a McDonaldized world, being bombarded by media messages from McDonaldized systems, and being socialized by and educated in McDonaldized schools?

It has been argued that the kinds of trends discussed above and in Marx's work are occurring not only among the lower layers in the occupational hierarchy but also among the middle layers. McDonaldization is something that those at the top of any hierarchy seek to avoid for themselves but are willing and eager to impose on those who rank below them in the system. Initially, it is the lowest level employees who have their work McDonaldized, but it . . . eventually creeps into those middle layers.

While guilty of exploiting and controlling employees, franchise operators are, in turn, controlled and exploited by franchise companies. Many franchise operators have done well, even becoming multimillionaires controlling perhaps hundreds of franchises, but many others have staggered or failed as a result of high start-up costs and continuing fees to the franchise companies. (The inducement to the franchisor to open as many outlets as possible threatens the profitability and even the continued existence of extant franchise owners.) The operators take much of the financial risk, while the franchise companies sit back and (often) rake in the profits. In addition, the franchise companies frequently have detailed rules, regulations, and even inspectors that they use to control the operators.

While no class within society is immune to McDonaldization, the lower classes are the most affected. They are the ones who are most likely to go to McDonaldized schools; live in inexpensive, mass-produced tract houses; and work in McDonaldized jobs. Those in the upper classes have much more of a chance of sending their children to non-McDonaldized schools, living in custom-built homes, and working in occupations in which they impose McDonaldization on others while avoiding it to a large degree themselves.

Also related to the social class issue is the fact that the McDonaldization of a significant portion of the labor force does not mean that all, or even most, of the labor force is undergoing this process. In fact, the McDonaldization of some of the labor force is occurring at the same time that another large segment is moving in a postindustrial, that is, more highly skilled, direction. Being created in this sector of society are relatively high-status, well-paid occupations requiring high levels of education and training. McDonaldization and postindustrialization tend to occur in different sectors of the labor market. However, the spread of McJobs leads us to be dubious of the idea that we have moved into a new postindustrial era and have left behind the kind of de-skilled jobs we associated with industrial society.

It could be argued, as many have, that the focus in modern capitalism has shifted from the control and exploitation of consumption. While that may well be true, the fact is that capitalists do not, and will not, ignore the realm of production. . . . The nature of work is changing and capitalists are fully involved in finding new ways of controlling and exploiting workers. Further, they have discovered that they can even replace paid employees not only with machines, temporary workers, and so on but also with customers who are seemingly glad do the work for nothing! Here, clearly, is a new gift to the capitalist. Surplus value is now not only to be derived from the labor time of the employee but also from the leisure time of the customer. McDonaldization is helping to open a whole new world of exploitation and growth to the contemporary capitalist.

Chapter 34

Alienated Labour

KARL MARX

This will likely be a difficult selection. We have included it, however, so that you can read firsthand something written by Karl Marx, someone who undeniably has had a tremendous influence on sociology. As a start, take note of what's missing from this essay: In contrast to popular images of Marx, there's no call here for revolution, no telling workers to rise up and seize the factories, and so on. Marx's goal here, as in most of his writing in fact, is to *analyze.* In this case, he wants to understand how the logic of work under capitalism has impoverished the human experience. Perhaps the best way to read this selection is to make a list of the things that (according to Marx) workers confront as "alien" (separate and distinct from themselves and over which they have little or no control), and then ask why Marx believes these "alien" things might diminish us as human beings.

We shall begin from a *contemporary* economic fact. The worker becomes poorer the more wealth he produces and the more his production increases in power and extent. The worker becomes an ever cheaper commodity the more goods he creates. The *devaluation* of the human world increases in direct relation with the increase *in value* of the world of things. Labour does not only create goods; it also produces itself and the worker as a *commodity*, and indeed in the same proportion as it produces goods.

This fact simply implies that the object produced by labour, its product, now stands opposed to it as an *alien being*, as a *power independent* of the producer. The product of labour is labour which has been embodied in an object and turned into a physical thing; this product is an *objectification* of labour. The performance of work is at the same time its objectification. The performance of work appears in the sphere of political economy as a *vitiation* of the worker, objectification as a *loss* and as *servitude to the object*, and appropriation as *alienation*.

So much does the performance of work appear as vitiation that the worker is vitiated to the point of starvation. So much does objectification appear as loss of the object that the worker is deprived of the most essential things not only of life but also of work. Labour itself becomes an object which he can acquire only by the greatest effort and with unpredictable interruptions. So much does the appropriation of the object appear as alienation that the more objects the worker produces the fewer he can possess and the more he falls under the domination of his product, of capital.

All these consequences follow from the fact that the worker is related to the *product of his labour* as to an *alien* object. For it is clear on this presupposition that the more the worker expends himself in work the more powerful becomes the world of objects which he creates in

Source: *Karl Marx: Early Writings* translated and edited by T. B. Bottomore, McGraw-Hill Book Company, 1963. Reproduced with permission of The McGraw-Hill Companies.

face of himself, the poorer he becomes in his inner life, and the less he belongs to himself. The worker puts his life into the object, and his life then belongs no longer to himself but to the object. The greater his activity, therefore, the less he possesses. What is embodied in the product of his labour is no longer his own. The greater this product is, therefore, the more he is diminished. The *alienation* of the worker in his product means not only that his labour becomes an object, assumes an *external* existence, but that it exists independently, *outside himself*, and alien to him, and that it stands opposed to him as an autonomous power. The life which he has given to the object sets itself against him as an alien and hostile force.

Let us now examine more closely the phenomenon of *objectification*, the worker's production and the *alienation* and *loss* of the object it produces, which is involved in it. The worker can create nothing without *nature*, without the *sensuous external world*. The latter is the material in which his labour is realized, in which it is active, out of which and through which it produces things.

But just as nature affords the *means of existence* of labour, in the sense that labour cannot *live* without objects upon which it can be exercised, so also it provides the *means of existence* in a narrower sense; namely the means of physical existence for the *worker* himself. Thus, the more the worker appropriates the external world of sensuous nature by his labour the more he deprives himself of *means of existence*, in two respects: first, that the sensuous external world becomes progressively less an object belonging to his labour or a means of existence of his labour, and secondly, that it becomes progressively less a means of existence in the direct sense, a means for the physical subsistence of the worker.

In both respects, therefore, the worker becomes a slave of the object; first, in that he receives an *object of work*, i.e. receives *work*, and secondly, in that he receives *means of subsistence*. Thus the object enables him to exist, first as a *worker* and secondly, as a *physical subject*. The

culmination of this enslavement is that he can only maintain himself as a *physical subject* so far as he is a *worker*, and that it is only as a *physical subject* that he is a worker.

(The alienation of the worker in his object is expressed as follows in the laws of political economy: the more the worker produces the less he has to consume; the more value he creates the more worthless he becomes; the more refined his product the more crude and misshapen the worker; the more civilized the product the more barbarous the worker; the more powerful the work the more feeble the worker; the more the work manifests intelligence the more the worker declines in intelligence and becomes a slave of nature.)

Political economy conceals the alienation in the nature of labour in so far as it does not examine the direct relationship between the worker (work) and production. Labour certainly produces marvels for the rich but it produces privation for the worker. It produces palaces, but hovels for the worker. It produces beauty, but deformity for the worker. It replaces labour by machinery, but it casts some of the workers back into a barbarous kind of work and turns the others into machines. It produces intelligence, but also stupidity and cretinism for the workers.

The direct relationship of labour to its products is the relationship of the worker to the objects of his production. The relationship of property owners to the objects of production and to production itself is merely a consequence of this first relationship and confirms it. We shall consider this second aspect later.

Thus, when we ask what is the important relationship of labour, we are concerned with the relationship of the *worker* to production.

So far we have considered the alienation of the worker only from one aspect; namely, *his relationship with the products of his labour*. However, alienation appears not merely in the result but also in the *process of production*, within *productive activity* itself. How could the worker stand in an alien relationship to the product of his activity if he did not alienate himself in the act of production itself? The product is indeed only the *résumé* of activity, of production. Consequently, if *the product of labour is alienation, production* itself *must be active alienation*—the alienation of activity and the *activity of alienation*. The alienation of the object of labour merely summarizes the alienation in the work activity itself.

What constitutes the alienation of labour? First, that the work is *external* to the worker, that it is not part of his nature, and that, consequently, he does not fulfil himself in his work but denies himself, has a feeling of misery rather than well-being, does not develop freely his mental and physical energies but is physically exhausted and mentally debased. The worker, therefore, feels himself at home only during his leisure time, whereas at work he feels homeless. His work is not voluntary but imposed, *forced labour*. It is not the satisfaction of a need, but only a *means for satisfying other needs*. Its alien character is clearly shown by the fact that as soon as there is no physical or other compulsion it is avoided like the plague. External labour, labour in which man alienates himself, is a labour of self-sacrifice, of mortification. Finally, the external character of work for the worker is shown by the fact that it is not his own work but work for someone else, that in work he does not belong to himself but to another person.

We arrive at the result that man (the worker) feels himself to be freely active only in his animal functions—*eating*, *drinking* and *procreating*, or at most also in his *dwelling* and in *personal* adornment—while in his human functions he is reduced to an animal. The *animal becomes human* and the *human becomes animal*.

Eating, drinking and procreating are of course also genuine human functions. But abstractly considered, apart from the environment of human activities, and turned into final and sole ends, they are animal functions.

We have now considered the act of alienation of practical human activity, labour, from two aspects: (1) the relationship of the worker to the *product of labour* as an alien object which

dominates him. This relationship is at the same time the relationship to the sensuous external world, to natural objects, as an alien and hostile world; (2) the relationship of labour to the *act of production* within *labour*. This is the relationship of the worker to his own activity as something alien and not belonging to him, activity as suffering (passivity), strength as powerlessness, creation as emasculation, the *personal* physical and mental energy of the worker, his personal life (for what is life but activity?), as an activity which is directed against himself, independent of him and not belonging to him. This is self-alienation as against the above mentioned alienation of the thing.

We have now to infer a third characteristic of *alienated labour* from the two we have considered.

Man is a species being not only in the sense that he makes the community (his own as well as those of other things) his object both practically and theoretically, but also (and this is simply another expression for the same thing) in the sense that he treats himself as the present, living species, as a universal and consequently free being.[1]

Species-life, for man as for animals, has its physical basis in the fact that man (like animals) lives from inorganic nature, and since man is more universal than an animal so the range of inorganic nature from which he lives is more universal. Plants, animals, minerals, air, light, etc. constitute, from the theoretical aspect, a part of a human consciousness as objects of natural science and art; they are man's spiritual inorganic nature, his intellectual means of life, which he must first prepare for enjoyment and perpetuation. So also, from the practical aspect, they form a part of human life and activity. In practice man lives only from these natural products, whether in the form of food, heating, clothing, housing, etc. The universality of man appears in practice in the universality which makes the whole of nature into his inorganic body: (1) as a direct means of life; and equally (2) as the material object and instrument of his life activity. Nature is the inorganic body of man; that is to say nature, excluding the human body itself. To say that man *lives* from nature means that nature is his *body* with which he must remain in a continuous interchange in order not to die. The statement that the physical and mental life of man, and nature, are interdependent means simply that nature is interdependent with itself, for man is a part of nature.

Since alienated labour: (1) alienates nature from man; and (2) alienates man from himself, from his own active function, his life activity; so it alienates him from the species. It makes *species-life* into a means of individual life. In the first place it alienates species-life and individual life, and secondly, it turns the latter, as an abstraction, into the purpose of the former, also in its abstract and alienated form.

For labour, *life activity*, *productive life*, now appear to man only as *means* for the satisfaction of a need, the need to maintain his physical existence. Productive life is, however, species-life. It is life creating life. In the type of life activity resides the whole character of a species, its species-character; and free, conscious activity is the species-character of human beings. Life itself appears only as a *means of life*.

The animal is one with its life activity. It does not distinguish the activity from itself. It is *its activity*. But man makes his life activity itself an object of his will and consciousness. He has a conscious life activity. It is not a determination with which he is completely identified. Conscious life activity distinguishes man from the life activity of animals. Only for this reason is he a species-being. Or rather, he is only a self-conscious being, i.e. his own life is an object for him, because he is a species-being. Only for this reason is his activity free activity. Alienated labour reverses the relationship, in that man because he is a self-conscious being makes his life activity, his *being*, and only a means for his *existence*.

The practical construction of an *objective world*, the *manipulation* of inorganic nature, is the confirmation of man as a conscious species-being, i.e., a being who treats the species as his own being or himself as a species-being. Of course, animals also produce. They construct nests, dwellings, as in the case of bees, beavers, ants, etc. But they only produce what is strictly necessary for themselves or their young. They produce only in a single direction, while man produces universally. They produce only under the compulsion of direct physical needs, while man produces when he is free from physical need and only truly produces in freedom from such need. Animals produce only themselves, while man reproduces the whole of nature. The products of animal production belong directly to their physical bodies, while man is free in face of his product. Animals construct only in accordance with the standards and needs of the species to which they belong, while man knows how to produce in accordance with the standards of every species and knows how to apply the appropriate standard to the object. Thus man constructs also in accordance with the laws of beauty.

It is just in his work upon the objective world that man really proves himself as *a species-being*.

NOTE

1. In this passage Marx reproduces Feuerbach's argument in *Das Wesen des Christentums*.

Chapter 35
Motherhood and Paycheques

MARIE DROLET

This selection is useful because it presents some recent data on what happens when married women in Canada "delay" the birth of their first child (i.e., wait longer than average to have their first child). Basically, these data show that women who delay the birth of their first child earn more than other married women of the same age. This wage gap is largest for younger married women. However, this article is instructive for other reasons. Notice that it takes the focus on married *women* as entirely unproblematic and makes no reference whatsoever to the effects of "delaying the birth of your first child" on wages for married *men.* The pattern here is not unfamiliar. For example, we have lots of studies that look at the effects of a mother working outside the home on children but few or none on the effects of a father working outside the home on children. What assumptions about "motherhood" and "fatherhood" in our culture underlie the decisions that social scientific investigators make when deciding what is or is not important to study?

MEASURING DELAYS IN MOTHERHOOD

The concept of "delaying motherhood" refers to the difference between a mother's actual age at the birth of her first child and an average age for giving birth for the first time. It is calculated by taking into account factors such as education level, major field of study, urban size and birth year of the mother. **Delaying** children refers to postponing the birth of the first child for at least one full year *after* the predicted age for having children. Having children **early** refers to having children at least one full year *before* the predicted age for the birth of a first child.

Current trends in marriage and fertility patterns suggest that young Canadian women are delaying having families while they concentrate on developing their careers. In 1979, the average age of women at their first marriage was 22; by 1996 it had increased to 27. A comparable trend exists in the fertility patterns of Canadian women. In 1970, the fertility rate (the average number of live births per woman) was 2.3; by 1993, the rate had declined to 1.7.

At the same time, the labour force participation rate among married women aged 25 to 44 increased from 50% in 1976 to 78% in 1998. Family commitments, however, may limit women's participation in the labour force and result in different work histories for women than men. Women with children are more likely to work part-time, for example. This study uses data from the 1998 Survey of Labour and Income Dynamics to first examine the effects of

Source: "Motherhood and Paycheques," from the Statistics Canada publication *Canadian Social Trends,* Catalogue 11-008-XIE, Number 68, Spring 2003, pages 19–21. Available on http://www.statcan.ca/english/freepub/11-008-XIE/0040211-008-XIE.pdf

motherhood on the wages of Canadian women and then whether mothers' wages are affected by the age at which they have children.

DOES MOTHERHOOD AFFECT WOMEN'S WAGES?

In 1998, women with children spent less time working full-year, full-time (68% of their years of potential work experience) than women without children (87% of their years of potential work experience).[1] At the same time, the average hourly wages of mothers were 2% less, overall, than those of women who did not have children.

When comparing the wages of mothers and non-mothers by age group, the differences between them were much higher for older women. For women born before 1948, those who had no children had an average hourly wage rate in 1998 that was 23% greater than those who had children. For women born between 1948 and 1960, the difference was 16%, but for women born after 1960, the wage gap had largely disappeared. In 1998, the average hourly wage rate for this youngest group of women was $14.38 for those without children and $14.41 for those with children.

At the same time, with each successive generation of women, the proportion of potential work experience spent working full-year, full-time increased for mothers. Mothers born prior to 1948 spent 63% of their years of potential work experience working full-year, full-time compared to 73% for mothers born between 1948 and 1960, and 77% for those born after 1960.

DELAYING MOTHERHOOD MAKES FOR HIGHER WAGES

A significant portion of real lifetime earnings growth occurs during the first years after graduation,[2] which often coincide with decisions regarding marriage and children. The timing of labour force withdrawals related to children, then, may have important long-run implications for the earnings of women. In other words, the *timing* of family formation may affect women's earnings.

In 1998, the average hourly wages of women who delayed having children were 17% higher than those who had children early. Part of this variation is due to the differences in the labour force history of women who postpone family formation. Compared with women who had children early, women who delayed childbirth had averaged roughly 1.7 more years of full-year, full-time work experience, and a larger proportion (77% versus 66%) of their years of potential work experience was spent working full-year, full-time. A similar pattern is observed for the various age cohorts. For each cohort, the average hourly wages and full-year, full-time employment of women who delayed family formation were greater than that of women who had children early. While the wage advantage of mothers who delayed parenthood persisted after the birth of their first child, it decreased as their children grew older.

When differences in work experience are taken into account along with other factors,[3] women who delayed having children earned at least 6% more than women who had children early. However, the size of the gap differs depending on the age of the mother. The timing of motherhood seemed to have had little impact on the wages of older mothers. However, the wages of young mothers (those born after 1960) who postponed motherhood were at least 10% higher than the wages of those who had children early.

WHY THE WAGE GAP?

There are several possible reasons for the wage gap between mothers who interrupted their careers early to have children and those who waited until later. As noted earlier, the wage gap between mothers who delayed having children and those who had children early was greatest among younger women. This may reflect changes in the types of careers available to

TABLE 35.1 MOTHERS BORN BEFORE 1960 EARN LESS THAN OTHER MOTHERS

	ALL WOMEN		WOMEN BORN BEFORE 1948		WOMEN BORN BETWEEN 1948 AND 1960		WOMEN BORN AFTER 1960	
	Children	No children	Children	No children	Children	No children	Children	No children
Hourly wage rate	$15.61	$15.87	$15.39	$18.93	$16.47	$19.17	$14.41	$14.38
Age	42	33	55	54	44	43	32	28
Number of years of schooling	14	15	13	14	14	15	14	15
Years of potential work experience	24	13	37	34	24	22	12	7
Actual years of full-time, full-year work experience	16	12	23	31	18	21	9	7
Percentage of potential work experience spent working full-year, full-time	68	87	63	89	73	94	77	96

SOURCE: Statistics Canada, Survey of Labour and Income Dynamics, 1998.

women born at different times. For example, from 1971 to 1991, the number of women working in previously male-dominated fields such as management, natural sciences, engineering and mathematics grew considerably. Also, wage growth and promotion opportunities are substantial early in one's career; if women miss this stage due to child-raising, they may not recover. Women who postpone childbirth may be leaving the work force at a time when interruptions are less critical for their careers, and consequently may have higher wages in the longer run.

Furthermore, women who do not have children early in their careers may be more flexible about making decisions concerning training, promotions, travel and other factors that affect job advancement. Those who have children early may find their choices more restricted because of family commitments. Additionally, it is worthwhile to consider that women who postpone children may be inherently more career-oriented and/or may have had higher wages at the beginning of their careers than those women who had children early.

SUMMARY

Current trends in marriage and fertility patterns suggest that young Canadian women are delaying family formation and concentrating on developing their careers. The timing of motherhood appears to have a significant bearing on the wages of Canadian women. The work experience of women who postpone motherhood is different from that of women who have children early: in 1998, women who postponed having a family averaged roughly 1.7 more years of full-year,

TABLE 35.2 DELAYING MOTHERHOOD IS GOOD FOR THE PAYCHEQUE

Had children	MOTHERS BORN BEFORE 1948			MOTHERS BORN BETWEEN 1948 AND 1960			MOTHERS BORN AFTER 1960			ALL MOTHERS		
	Early	On Time	Delayed	Early	On Time	Delayed	Early	On Time	Delayed	Early	On Time	Delayed
Hourly wage rate	$14.42	$15.96	$16.89	$14.79	$15.71	$16.34	$15.47	$16.74	$17.64	$12.39	$15.25	$16.16
Age	42	42	42	55	55	55	44	44	44	31	32	33
Number of years of schooling	13	14	14	12	13	13	13	14	14	13	14	13
Years of potential work experience	23	22	22	37	37	36	24	24	24	12	11	13
Actual years of full-time, full-year work experience	15	15	17	23	21	25	17	18	19	8	9	11
Percentage of potential work experience spent working full-year, full-time	66	70	77	63	57	67	68	75	80	66	80	86

SOURCE: Statistics Canada, Survey of Labour and Income Dynamics, 1998.

full-time work experience, and spent a larger proportion of potential years working full-year and full-time.

The wages of women who postponed motherhood were also different from those of women who had children early. Women who had postponed having children until later in life earned at least 6% more in 1998 than women who had their children early. This observation takes into account important differences in work histories and education.

NOTES

1. Years of potential work experience is defined as age minus number of years of schooling minus five.
2. Murphy, K. and F Welsh. 1990. "Empirical Age-Earnings Profiles." *Journal of Labour Economics* 8, 2: 202–289.
3. A variety of wage-determining characteristics were used in the analysis, including actual labour market experience, education, field of study, part-time status, region, and urban class size.

PART 13
Race, Ethnicity, and Inequality

Chapter 36

Ethnic Heroes and Racial Villains in American Social Science

STEPHEN STEINBERG

Why are some ethnic groups in our society more successful than others? In the late 19th and early 20th centuries, it was common to suggest that biology was the critical factor. Some groups were more successful than others, it was argued, because of their brain size, genes, and so on. Biological explanations of this sort have increasingly fallen from favour, to be replaced, this selection argues, by cultural arguments. Under this newer thinking, the cultural values shared by the members of some groups promote success, just as the cultural values shared within other groups inhibit success. Steinberg argues that both arguments have a tendency to locate the cause of a group's success or failure in something that is "inside" the members of that group. Such an approach, he argues, leads us to ignore a range of structural processes in society at large that can affect how well a group "does" in society. He illustrates his theory by considering the "myth of Asian success."

Myths die hard, as the saying goes. To be sure, myths about race and ethnicity are deep-seated and often appear immune to change, but this is not because of some inherent potency or appeal. Myths are socially constructed. They arise in specific times and places, in response to identifiable circumstances and needs, and they are passed on through a process that can be readily observed. Whether a myth prospers or withers is always problematic; most, in fact, are relinquished or forgotten. To explain why some myths persist, we have to explore the relationship that these myths have to larger social institutions that promote and sustain them, and that in turn are served by them.

This book has dealt with myths that purport to explain why racial and ethnic groups occupy higher or lower places in the class system—why,

in the popular idiom, "we have made it and they have not." The popular explanation, translated into respectable academic language by mainstream social scientists, is that "we" had the cultural virtues and moral fiber that "they" are lacking. If this theory were predicated on fact alone, it would be fairly easy to dispense with—for example, by showing that Jews, the archetype of ethnic success, arrived with occupational experiences and skills that gave them a headstart relative to other immigrants from eastern and southern Europe, that these latter groups were favorably positioned relative to blacks, who were excluded from industrial employment altogether during the critical early phases of industrialization, and that racial minorities—blacks in particular—have been encumbered by discriminatory barriers across generations that constitute the chief reason for their current economic plight. However compelling these facts might be, even when fully documented and analyzed, they are overpowered by other assumptions and beliefs that are almost universally shared in American society and that pervade American social science as well.

A problem also arises when success is equated with virtue, and failure with sin and personal inadequacy. Not only does this individualize success or failure, thus obscuring the whole issue of social justice, but it also treats virtue and its opposite as a matter of personal endowment, rather than as traits that need to be explained in terms of their historical and social sources.

If the United States is an open society where the individual is not irreparably handicapped by "birth, family, and class," then how is racial hierarchy to be explained? The thrust of previous research had been to find in the cephalic index or in intelligence tests clear evidence of a biological inferiority that predestined blacks to subordinate status. The discrediting of scientific racism is unquestionably one of the great triumphs of liberal social science. However, subsequent theorists developed a social-scientific variant of scientific racism that essentially substituted culture for genes. Now it was held that groups that occupy the lowest strata of society are saddled by cultural systems that prevent them from climbing the social ladder. As before, failure is explained not in terms of societal structures, but in terms of traits endemic to the groups themselves.

For the exponents of social-scientific racism, furthermore, culture is almost as immutable as the genes themselves. Ethnic heroes and racial villains are merely an updated version of traditional folklore that pitted rugged cowboys against treacherous Indians (which also had racist overtones).

Nor is this racist folklore, masked as social science, politically innocent. Its covert ideological function is to legitimize existing racial inequalities. By placing cultural blame on the victims, the nation's vaunted ideals are reconciled with patently undemocratic divisions and inequities. By projecting collective Horatio Algers, in the unlikely forms of Jews and Asians, it is demonstrated that "success" is attainable to everyone, without regard to "birth, family, and class." Like all myths, the ethnic myth has an implicit moral: "we" are not responsible, morally or politically, for "their" misfortune.

NEW HEROES: ASIANS

Social science's enchantment with the success myth, replete with its cast of heroes and villains, has been renewed in recent years with the arrival of millions of immigrants, the majority of whom are Asians. That these new immigrants have generally settled in cities with large concentrations of poverty-stricken blacks has only highlighted the contrast between upwardly mobile immigrants and inner-city blacks. Invidious comparisons have been common in the popular press, and social scientists have churned out more spurious scholarship extolling cultural virtue and reciting the stock tale of triumph over adversity. That these new heroes—Asians—belong to racial minorities has thickened the plot, since it demonstrates, according to these scholars, that "race" is not an insurmountable obstacle and cannot explain why so many blacks are still mired in poverty.

THE MYTH OF ASIAN SUCCESS

In 1986 the five top recipients of the prestigious Westinghouse Science Talent Search were of Asian descent. This prompted a spate of articles in magazines and newspapers seeking to explain how a tiny minority, representing less than 2 percent of the national population, could achieve such bewildering success. The question, as framed by Malcolm Browne in an op-ed piece in the *New York Times*, is: "Do Asians have genetic advantages, or does their apparent edge in scientific skills stem from their special cultural tradition?"[1] Thus are we offered a choice between genes and culture as explanations for the academic excellence among Asians. Browne rejects genetic determinism, but has no such qualms with respect to cultural determinism. Paraphrasing an unnamed Westinghouse spokesman, he writes: "Tightly-knit families and high respect for all forms of learning are traditional characteristics of Asian societies . . . as they are for Jewish societies; in the past a very high proportion of top Westinghouse winners were Jewish." Of course, as Browne himself remarks, "the odd thing is that until the twentieth century, real science scarcely existed in Asia." Undaunted by this apparent contradiction, he argues that Asian children are endowed with "an underlying devotion to scholarship—the kind of devotion imprinted on Asian children by a pantheon of ancestors"—that has made them receptive to Western scientific thought. Thus is a theory bent to accommodate inconvenient facts.

Two years later the *New York Times* ran another piece under the heading, "Why Do Asian Pupils Win Those Prizes?"[2] The author, Stephen Graubard, a professor of history at Brown University and editor of *Daedalus*, opines that Asians, who were eleven of the fourteen Westinghouse finalists from Cardozo High School in Queens, New York, have the advantage of stable families and Asian mothers who rear their children for success. With an air of resignation, he then turns the question onto blacks and Puerto Ricans: "What is to be done for those hundreds of thousands of other New York children, many of illegitimate birth, who live with one parent, often in public housing, knowing little outside their dilapidated and decaying neighborhoods?" Since Graubard does not believe that the schools can do much to compensate for the defective culture of children from poverty backgrounds, these children are presumably condemned to languish in the cultural wasteland.

The same single-minded preoccupation with culture is found in yet another article in *The New York Times Magazine* on "Why Asians Succeed

Here." The author, Robert Oxnam, president of the prestigious Asia Society, writes as follows:

> The story of these new immigrants goes far beyond the high school valedictorians and Westinghouse Science scholars we read about in our newspapers. It is the story of a broader cultural interaction, a pairing of old Asian values with American individualism, Asian work ethics with American entrepreneurship. And, where those cultural elements have collided, it has also been a story of sharp disappointments and frustration.[3]

Once again, culture is the fulcrum of success. Like the other writers quoted above, Oxnam identifies "the strong family ties and powered work ethics of Asian cultures" as "key factors in Asian-American achievement."

This theory of Asian success is a new spin on earlier theories about Jews, to whom Asians are explicitly compared. As with the theory of Jewish success, there are a number of conceptual and empirical problems that throw the theory into question:

1. The theory of "Asian" success lumps together some twenty-five nationalities that are very disparate in history and culture. It is only in the United States that they are assumed to share a common "Asian" heritage. Little or no evidence is put forward to substantiate claims that they share common values with respect to family and work, that these values are significantly different from those found among non-Asian groups, or that these values are the key factors in explaining which Asians get ahead or why more Asians do so than others. Here is classic case of circular reasoning. Values are not measured independently, but inferred from success, and then posited as the cause of success.

2. Theories of Asian success gloss over the fact that large segments of the Asian populations in the United States are far from prosperous. Alongside dramatic and visible success, touted in the popular media, are deep pockets of

poverty, exploitation, and despair. Moreover, if successful Asians are presumed to owe their success to distinctively Asian values with respect to family and work, then are we to assume that less affluent Asians are deficient in these values? Are they therefore less "Asian"?

3. As in the case of Jewish success, the prevailing theory of Asian success overlooks the operation of premigration class factors that go a long way toward explaining the destinies of these immigrants after their arrival. The issue here has to do with selective migration—that is, with who decides to emigrate and who is permitted entry. As Ezra Vogel, a scholar of China and Japan, has noted, Asian immigrants "are a very biased sample, the cream of their own societies."[4] They are drawn disproportionately from the intellectual and professional elites that, for one reason or another, have restricted opportunity in their home countries. Many of them have been admitted under the occupational preferences built into the new immigration law. In short, they are "successful" even before their arrival in America.

Data collected by the Immigration and Naturalization Service demonstrate the class character of Asian immigration. Table 36.1 reports the percentage of immigrant workers classified as professionals.[5] In the case of Indians, over three-quarters of immigrants with occupations are professionals; this reached a high point in 1969–71 when nine out of every ten Indians with occupations were professionals. Among Filipinos, Koreans, and Japanese the figures range between half and three-quarters; among Chinese, the figures are somewhat lower, but still much higher than for non-Asians. The influx of professionals of all nationalities reached a peak between 1969 and 1971, and declined thereafter. Nevertheless, the evidence is clear that a major segment of Asian immigration represents an educational and occupational elite.

Other data indicate that between 1965 and 1981 some 70,000 medical professionals—physicians, nurses, and pharmacists—came from the Philippines, South Korea, and India.[6] Another major source of immigrants has been students who enter the United States with student visas and then do not return to their home country. Of the 70,000 Chinese students from Taiwan between 1950 and 1983, it is estimated that 90 percent remained in the United States. The same is true of tens of thousands of students from Hong Kong, Korea, and other Asian countries. What these figures indicate is not a dramatic success story, but merely the transfer of intellectual and professional elites from less developed nations.

TABLE 36.1 PERCENTAGE OF PROFESSIONALS AMONG ASIAN IMMIGRANTS WITH OCCUPATIONS

	1961–65	1966–68	1969–71	1971–74	1975–77
China	31%	35%	47%	37%	31%
India	68	67	89	84	73
Japan	44	50	45	37	28
Korea	71	75	70	51	38
Philippines	48	60	70	63	47
All Asians	40	52	62	54	44
All Immigrants	20	25	29	27	25

SOURCE: Adapted from Morrison G. Wong and Charles Hirschman, "The New Asian Immigrants," in *Culture, Ethnicity, and Identity*, ed. William McCready (New York: Academic Press: 1983), pp. 395–397.

These immigrants start out with the educational and occupational resources that are generally associated with educational achievement in the next generation. To put the cultural theory to a fair empirical test, one would have to compare the children of Asian professionals to the children of other professionals. Only in this way could we assess the significance of distinctive ethnic factors. It is hardly valid to compare the children of upper-middle-class Asian professionals to the children of unemployed black workers, as is done when "Asians" are compared to "blacks."[7]

Not all Asian immigrants, however, come from advantaged backgrounds. Indeed, in recent years the flow of immigrants has included large numbers of uneducated and unskilled workers. These are the "downtown Chinese," as Peter Kwong calls them in his recent book, *The New Chinatown*.[8] These immigrants have difficulty finding employment in the racially segmented labor market outside of Chinatown, and are forced to accept jobs, commonly in sweatshops and restaurants, that match their nineteenth-century counterparts in their debasing exploitation. It has yet to be demonstrated that the children of these super-exploited workers are part of an Asian success story. Indeed, the outbreak of gang violence among Chinatown youth has exploded another myth that had great currency in the 1950s; namely, that because of their close-knit families, delinquency is virtually nonexistent among the Chinese.[9]

In demystifying and explaining Asian success, we come again to a simple truth: that what is inherited is not genes, and not culture, but class advantage and disadvantage. If not for the extraordinary selectivity of the Asian immigrant population, there would be no commentaries in the popular press and the social science literature extolling Confucian values and "the pantheon of ancestors" who supposedly inspire the current generation of Asian youth. After all, no such claims are made about the Asian youth who inhabit the slums of Manila, Hong Kong, and Bombay, or, for that matter, San Francisco and New York.

NOTES

1. Malcolm W. Browne, "A Look at Success of Young Asians," *New York Times* (March 25, 1986), p. A31.
2. Stephen G. Graubard, "Why Do Asian Pupils Win Those Prizes?" *New York Times* (January 29, 1988), p. A35.
3. Robert B. Oxnam, "Why Asians Succeed Here," *New York Times Magazine* (November 30, 1986), p. 70.
4. Quoted in Fox Butterfield, "Why Asians Are Going to the Head of the Class," Education Supplement, *New York Times* (August 3, 1986), section 12, p. 20.
5. These percentages are based on the number of immigrants who report having a job, thereby excluding nonworking women, as well as the old and young.
6. Illsoo Kim, "Ethnic Class Division among Asian Immigrants: Its Implications for Social Welfare Policies," unpublished paper presented at the Conference on Asian American Studies, Cornell University, October 24, 1986, p. 3.
7. If there is a distinctively ethnic factor in patterns of Asian mobility, it is that like Jews of earlier generations, Asians realize that their channels of opportunity are restricted by prejudice. Closed off from the corporate fast lane, they are drawn to the professions. The sciences are particularly attractive to individuals who lack fluency in English. Data reporting SAT scores indicate that Asian American students score far above average on the math test, but far below average on the verbal test. *New York Times,* Section 12: "Education Life" (August 3, 1986), p. 3.
8. Peter Kwong, *The New Chinatown* (New York: Hill & Wang, 1987), pp. 5–6.
9. For example, see Henry Beckett, "How Parents Help Chinese Kids Stay Out of Trouble," series in the *New York Post* (July 11–13, 1955), and Betty Lee Sung, *The Story of the Chinese in America* (New York: Collier, 1971), p. 156.

Chapter 37

Visible Minority Workers Are at Greater Economic Risk

CANADIAN HERITAGE

Are some Canadians disadvantaged because of their ethnicity or colour? The following article on visible minority workers argues that this is the case. In its review of research, Canadian Heritage concludes that black families experience considerable financial problems even where they have equal education to non-black families. Read the article and decide whether you agree. The article simply states some findings, but you must ponder the causes and possible solutions.

DISADVANTAGED COMMUNITIES

In 1997, Professor James L. Torczyner of McGill University conducted a study of the major problems affecting the Black communities of Canada (1). After analysing both community and census data, he concluded that *"Black families in Canada may be experiencing considerable stress and change—both financial and emotional"* (1:2). Despite the fact that Black workers had almost comparable levels of educational attainment as non-Blacks (one in five Black adults was either attending university or at least had completed a Bachelor's degree), the Black workforce tended to have higher percentages of unemployed workers than the Canadian population as a whole: 15% to 10%. Black workers earned less money than Canadian workers as a whole (their average income was 15% less than those of the average Canadian worker: $20,617 to $24,001). Black women earned an equivalent of 71% of the average earnings of Black men. *"Almost 160,000 Black persons lived in poverty in 1991. More than three out of ten Blacks in Canada lived below the poverty line in 1991"* (1:11). Only 16% of Canadians did so in the same year. Women and children were, economically, the most vulnerable population segments.

EARNING GAPS AND LIFE-CYCLE LOSSES

Several studies of ethnic and racial discrimination in labour markets have been conducted in Canada. One common finding of these econometric studies is that a significant proportion of the existing wage gap between white and non-white workers is not directly attributable to demographic, educational or occupational characteristics of workers. It may be the product of racial discrimination practised by employers in the hiring and promotion of their workers.

After conducting an econometric analysis of 1991 census data, economist Robert Swidinsky of the University of Guelph (2) concluded that *"individual minority groups have to contend with significant wage and occupational discrimination in their labour market activities"* (2:38). Black immigrants encountered the most serious labour

Source: "Visible Minority Workers are at Greater Economic Risk," Evidence Series, Vol. 2, July 21, 1998, Department of Canadian Heritage. Reproduced with the permission of the Minister of Public Works and Government Services Canada, 2008.

market disadvantages. A similar study carried out by Pendakur and Pendakur found, after partialling out human capital related factors, that *"among men, the earnings penalties faced by Aboriginals and visible minorities are large and present in both native-born and immigrant populations"* (3:18). Visible minority males born in Canada were earning, on the average, 9% less income than similarly qualified white males. Among male immigrants, the income penalty was in the range of 15%. Although few differences in incomes were observed between visible and non-visible minority Canadian-born women, visible minority immigrant women faced a 7% wage penalty compared to their non-visible minority counterparts. Previously, in an econometric analysis, Da Silva and Dougherty had found that *"about a third of the offered earnings differential is attributable to discrimination"* (4:15).

Visible minority workers experience substantial income losses over their life-cycle earnings compared to non-visible minority workers. Using census data, economist Ather Akbari of Saint Mary's University found that *"the life cycle earnings of such a worker are 13% lower than those of a worker of European ethnicity. If such workers had not faced any discrimination in earnings, better productivity (education, number of weeks worked during the year, etc.) would have resulted in a 2% advantage"* (5:1). Discrimination, however, offset this advantage by causing an earnings decline of 15%. A year of work experience acquired by a non-European origin worker was valued significantly lower in Canadian labour markets than that acquired by a comparable European origin worker.

Wage gaps between visible and non-visible minority workers have also been studied in light of the educational credentials held by Canadian and foreign-born workers. A report produced by Wright and McDade, on behalf of the Institute for Research in Public Policy (IRPP), concluded that *"employers may be taking advantage of an opportunity to, for example, pay lower wages and salaries under the pretense of the non-recognition of credentials"* (6:77). Both discrimination and the non-recognition of credentials may be occurring at the same time. Differences in the rates of income return were more pronounced for men born in developing countries, particularly for those of visible minority backgrounds.

RACISM IN HIRING

Important field studies in the area of racism and hiring practices in Metropolitan Toronto were carried out by anthropologist Frances Henry and colleagues (7,8,9). In 1984, in-person and phone applications to 191 jobs were made by equally qualified applicants differing only in their ethnic and racial backgrounds. Henry and Ginzberg summarize the main finding of this study by saying that *"the results of the study clearly indicate that there is very substantial racial discrimination affecting the ability of members of racial minority groups to find employment"* (7:52). Whites had "3 job prospects for every one of Blacks" (7:51). Black applicants were also subject to more discourteous and negative treatment during the course of the job application. South Asians had to make at least 20 calls to pass the screening out procedures. The 1989 study found small differences between person-job offers for Whites and Blacks but the latter were generally treated differently. In at least 23% of the job contacts, Black applicants were treated rudely. *"In cases where applicants did not receive job offers, Black applicants were treated rudely four times more often than White applicants"* (9:18). Indo-Pakistanis and Blacks had to make, on average, approximately 19 to 20 calls to get a favourable job prospect.

REFERENCES

James L. Torczyner: "Diversity, Mobility and Change: The Dynamics of Black Communities in Canada," McGill Consortium for Ethnicity and Strategic Planning, executive summary presented to the Multiculturalism Branch, Department of Canadian Heritage, Ottawa, 1997.

Robert Swidinsky: "White-Visible Minority Earnings Differentials: A Comparison of Immigrant and Native Born Canadians," paper presented to Canadian Research Employment Forum (CERF) 1997, Richmond, B.C.

Krishnan Pendakur and Ravi Pendakur: "The Colour of Money: Earning Differentials Among Ethnic Groups in Canada," *Strategic Research and Analysis Publication* SRA-34B, Department of Canadian Heritage, 1996.

Arnold Da Silva: "Earnings of Immigrants: A Comparative Analysis" by Economic Council of Canada, March 1992.

Ather Akbari: "Ethnicity and Earnings Discrimination in Canadian Labour Markets: Some Evidence of the 1986 Census," report presented to Multiculturalism and Citizenship Canada, 1991.

Robert Wright and Kathryn McDade: "Barriers to the Recognition of the Credentials of Immigrants in Canada: An Analysis Using Census Data," report presented to the Secretary of State, Health and Welfare Canada, Institute for Research in Public Policy, Ottawa, June 1992.

Frances Henry and Effie Ginzberg: "Who Gets the Work: A Test of Racial Discrimination in Employment," Urban Alliance on Race Relations in Employment and Social Planning Council of Metropolitan Toronto publication, January 1985.

Frances Henry: "Race Relations Research in Canada Today: A State of the Art Review," report presented to the Canadian Human Rights Commission, September 25, 1986.

Frances Henry and Carol Tator: "Who Gets the Work in 1989?," report prepared for the Economic Council of Canada, 1989.

Chapter 38

Aboriginal Well-Being: Canada's Continuing Challenge

JERRY WHITE AND DAN BEAVON

You've likely read a news report suggesting that Canada has consistently scored at or near the top of the UN's Human Development Index. Such a result suggests that Canada is a great place to live. But suppose that the standard of living here deteriorated so that Canada fell from the top of the list to, say, 48th in the world. Would that be a cause for concern? Of course it would! This selection about Aboriginal well-being in Canada discusses how Aboriginal peoples have a much lower standard of living, have lower educational attainment, and suffer a host of inequalities in comparison to other Canadians. This selection demonstrates, using the very same measure that suggests that the standard of living in Canada (generally) is so high, that a clearly identifiable segment of the Canadian population—Registered Indians—does rank 48th in the world. It also suggests that if this inequality persists it will undermine every Canadian's standard of living; it may lead to social unrest and tear at the fabric of this country. The authors argue that we can not afford to shut our eyes to the problems any longer.

As you read this chapter please consider the following questions:

1) Is it reasonable that a group in Canada can have a common experience of disadvantage?
2) Is it important to address this relative disadvantage directly and if so how?

Canada was founded on the principles of peace, order and good government.[1] It would be fair to say that most Canadians view our society as peaceful, civil, and just. As Canadians, we are often shocked or dismayed when we see civil unrest in other countries, particularly when police or military force are used against civil populations in order to quell popular uprisings or to restore order. When we see such events unfolding in the news, we breathe a collective sigh of relief and count our blessings that we live where we do. However, it may be that our collective memories are quite short and our knowledge of history quite limited because police

forces and the military have intervened thousands of times against many different segments of civil society in Canada. Some of these interventions have been against protestors (e.g., the police action during 1997 Asia-Pacific Economic Cooperation summit meeting in Vancouver), unruly sports fans (e.g., the 1955 Rocket Richard riot in Montreal), unions (e.g., the 1919 Winnipeg general strike), and sometimes against Aboriginal peoples.

Some of the more recent and notable police and military interventions against Aboriginal peoples would include: Oka (1990), Gustafsen Lake (1995), and Ipperwash (1995). The Oka

Source: White, J. & Beavon, D. (2007). Chapter 1. *Aboriginal Well-Being: Canada's Continuing Challenge.* Toronto: Thompson Educational Publishers.

crisis of 1990[2] is particularly noteworthy because it represents the last time in Canadian history that the military was used against a segment of civil society.[3] The Oka crisis resulted in the death of Sûreté du Québec Corporal Marcel Lemay and it led to the Royal Commission on Aboriginal Peoples.[4] The Gustafsen Lake siege represented the largest paramilitary operation in the history of British Columbia,[5] and the incident at Ipperwash resulted in the death of Aboriginal protestor Dudley George.

Usually these police and military interventions are the result of Aboriginal occupations and protests. As the Ipperwash inquiry noted (Linden, 2007, p. 15):

> Aboriginal occupations and protests can be large or small, short or long, peaceful or violent. They occur in urban areas, rural areas, and in the remote north . . . The immediate catalyst for most major occupations and protests is a dispute over a land claim, a burial site, resource development, or harvesting, hunting and fishing rights. The fundamental conflict, however, is usually about land.

Aboriginal occupations and protests are quite common and the vast majority of these events are resolved peacefully, without violence or property damage.[6] Many of these incidents, however, garner considerable media coverage, especially when these events expose major fault lines within Canadian society. For example, the Burnt Church crisis of 1999 and 2000 resulted in angry non-Aboriginal fishermen damaging and destroying a number of Mi'kmaq lobster traps. The local Mi'kmaq retaliated by destroying non-Aboriginal fishing boats and buildings. The Caledonia dispute (2006 and on-going at press time) has been the catalyst for several confrontations between Aboriginal protestors, local non-Aboriginal residents, and the Ontario Provincial Police. While such incidents make for good news stories, they often expose the underlying racist underbelly that still permeates some segments of Canadian society. While many critics may question the economic effectiveness of

Aboriginal occupations and protests, they clearly do not understand the intrinsic value that Aboriginal peoples place on their traditional lands and how this attachment is integral to their culture and identity (Burrows, 2005).

While Aboriginal occupations of land will continue in the foreseeable future, Canadians witnessed an entirely new type of Aboriginal protest on June 29, 2007. On this date, the Assembly of First Nations (AFN) organized a National Day of Action. This one-day event was part of a broader strategy of the AFN, launched in the fall of 2006 to create awareness of First Nations issues; more specifically, it was a call for action against poverty.[7] This book deals with this same issue, not from an advocacy or political viewpoint, but from an empirical and scientific perspective.

The "Make Poverty History for First Nations" campaign was initiated to highlight the struggles facing First Nations people and communities. The "National Day of Action" was unique for several reasons.

First, the event was one of the largest rallies in Canadian history based on the sheer number of events and locations across the country.

Second, the event was peaceful. There was considerable tension before the event, and some in the media and less sympathetic groups were anticipating confrontations between the Aboriginal peoples and the general public or police. But many of the anticipated tensions were reduced prior to the event through a series of actions. Minister Prentice made a major announcement for an action plan to reform and speed up the specific claims process. The slow pace with which specific claims were resolved has often created tensions between many First Nations and the government. He also defused the threat of blockades at one potential hot spot, by conferring official reserve status to 75 acres of land recently purchased by the Roseau River First Nation in Manitoba. AFN Grand Chief Phil Fontaine also did his part to calm the waters. He repeatedly urged Aboriginal people to make the Day of Action a peaceful demonstration aimed at generating public awareness of, and support for, Aboriginal issues. Chief Fontaine also signed a protocol between the AFN and the RCMP that set out ground rules for dealing with any crisis that might occur during the day of action. In summary, the event was so peaceful that it was anticlimactic.

Third, the event was not an occupation of a specific piece of land. In fact, the protest was not really about land at all. What we witnessed was a shift from a *rights-based agenda* (e.g., specific and comprehensive claims, self-determination, self-government, Indian status, membership, citizenship), which have dominated the Aboriginal political landscape over the last thirty years, to a *needs-based agenda*. While all of these latter rights-based issues are important, there is no direct evidence to suggest that the disproportionate attention that has been paid to them has improved the quality of life of Aboriginal people or their communities. That is not to say we will not see improvements coming from these actions, but to date such gains have not been measurable. . . .

Aboriginal issues will clearly present Canada with some of its most complex challenges in the twenty-first century. Will this century be the one where we finally address the issues of poverty, lack of educational attainment, poor health, and social problems that beset Aboriginal peoples? Or, will it be one that replicates the past, maintains the status quo, and condemns the next generation of Aboriginal children to a life of mediocrity, suicides, substance abuse, and poverty?

The National Day of Action reminded us that there is a growing understanding and impatience with respect to the relative deprivation that Aboriginal peoples face in Canada. The well-being of the general population far exceeds that of its Aboriginal population. Now instead of turning that inequality into despair and internal violence, it is being channelled outward.

We decided to title this book *Aboriginal Well-being: Canada's Continuing Challenge*. We had even considered calling it *Canada's Shameful Legacy*; however, shame is not what is needed. What is needed is better policies developed from solid research evidence created in partnership with the Aboriginal peoples themselves.

In our 2003 book *Aboriginal Conditions*, we said that "we need to develop better measures of the First Nation communities and tailor our programs and policies to match the reality of the country." In that book we discussed our preliminary attempts to adapt the United Nations Human Development Index (HDI) to the First Nations in Canada (Beavon and Cooke, 2003). We also presented a "Community Capacity Index" which aimed to assess the relative capacity of Aboriginal communities to accept and handle their socio-economic development. As we have repeatedly argued we cannot download programs to communities that have not got the capacity to take them on. It serves no one's interests to dump programs as fast as people can fail at managing them (Maxim and White, 2003).

We also argued that there are real differences between Aboriginal communities. Some are thriving and relatively self-reliant, while others are facing or have suffered virtual collapse. Within many communities there are vast differences in the resources that families have available. In *Aboriginal Conditions* we also presented research on the intra-Aboriginal inequalities that plague the populations. We concluded that we needed better ways of understanding capacity and well-being and that we also needed to develop Canada-wide initiatives that target the intra-Aboriginal differences.

This book is our next generation of models and tools that are developed to give us a better understanding of the levels of development and well-being of the Aboriginal peoples of Canada. Some might ask why we are doing this (see Salée, 2006). We would argue that it is our responsibility, as social scientists, to try and improve our understanding of the world. That in itself is true. However, we have a selfish reason as well. Our own well-being is tied to the well-being of the others who inhabit this great country. In order to keep the high standards of living, level of prosperity, relative social calm, and exceptional living conditions, we have to recognize that there is an important, on-going disadvantage that is experienced by the Aboriginal peoples of Canada. Unless we address this central problem, Aboriginal relative deprivation will lead to the erosion of the well-being of all those living in Canada.

WHAT IS AT STAKE IN THIS RELATIVE DEPRIVATION?

One of the most powerful of human motivators is relative deprivation. Sociologists, have argued that relative differences in well-being and resources, including wealth, are often more important than the absolute differences in determining the perceived quality of life (Gurr, 1970; Griffin, 1988). This means that policies that increase the societal wealth but leave relative inequalities may not actually increase the overall well-being of a country.

An understanding of deprivation develops as people compare themselves to those around them. If the comparison group is reasonable, then people will react to differences. It is not some absolute level that is used in comparisons. Inequalities that remain even as the absolute levels of prosperity increase still lead to group resistance. If we think of a village of subsistence farmers that has only their crops and a small amount of generated income to live on, it may be that they develop a lifestyle where they are happy despite limited resources. If that village is moved to the outskirts of a big city or is integrated through digital means to the wider world, it will begin to assess its relative position. In this case the villagers will become angry about their circumstances and may begin to protest.

Feeling deprived as an individual differentiates from feeling deprived as a group . . . particularly if there are strong identifiers for that group (see Walker and Smith, 2002). We also know that social identity, social comparison, and understandings of distributive justice are involved in relative deprivation (ibid). These are

collective or social theories and when we integrate them with relative deprivation we get what we call integrated relative deprivation theory.

This integrated theory is important because it captures how a group sees itself, how an individual belongs or identifies their place in the group, whether there is or could be any explanation for their similar treatment and whether there is a measure of fairness or lack of fairness in their deprivation.

We have argued in other works (White and Beavon, 2003) that understanding the collective identity of Aboriginal peoples is important. The world today is composed of peoples bound together in groups that share some characteristics that create bonds between them. These groups coalesce for a variety of reasons. More often than not, these bonds of cohesion have some relationship to cultural and physical similarities. Social scientists have spent countless research hours studying these ethnic and racial ties. Ties that bind groups together also create differences with others. These differences between collectivities can often involve the development of hierarchies and inequalities. Socio-economic conditions, sometimes measured and sometimes assumed, are used to rank peoples. The roots of some of the most complex social problems are the differential development of ethnic groups and the social ranking that comes with these variations. Public policy in this era of human development is confronted by these social problems and the set of questions that issue from them.

If we look at this racialized and ethnicized understanding of differences in resources and resulting hierarchies and overlay this understanding with an appreciation of the integrated relative deprivation theory we can understand the import of the current situation. Aboriginal people, seeing and experiencing the differences in their lives in comparison with other groups in Canada, will inevitably draw conclusions about their relative worth. At an individual level this can result in a lack of respect for themselves, which leads to intra-group violence and self-abuse (drugs, alcohol, suicide, marital violence, etc.). The individual might blame society and strike out individually against that society (through crime or violence). Most assuredly, over time, the ties that create the collective identity will assert themselves in a collective understanding. Those who share history, culture, territory, and common understandings, who become bound together in groups that share some characteristics that create bonds between them, will assess that they are not treated fairly. Collective response to relative deprivation can become a challenge to the fabric of a country that has multiple collectivities, such as ethnic or racial groups.

This book is about identifying clearly that there is relative deprivation. It is also about wanting to spur us to move forward in dealing with that deprivation.

It was Francis Bacon who argued for an understanding of the world free from theologically distorted realities. We would concur that there should be a drive to develop the most appropriate and accurate assessments of the well-being and development of different peoples as is possible.

. . .

ABORIGINAL CONDITIONS *TODAY*

While many Canadians are aware that the First Nations peoples face certain hardships, they are not aware of the extent of the problems nor how persistent these differences are over time. There was a disturbing indication of this in the results of a poll conducted shortly after The Royal Commission on Aboriginal Peoples Report, which was released in the mid-1990s. In that survey nearly half of the Canadians polled thought that Indian reserves had similar standards of living and well-being as non-Aboriginal communities (Insight Canada, 1996). This is a problem for everyone. Unless we understand the real situation we can never confront it and make real improvements.

In Table 38.1, we summarize some trends that we have observed over the 1981 to 2001 period, comparing some basic indicators between Registered Indians and the Canadian population.

Registered Indian life expectancy improved from 65.7 years in 1981 to 72.9 years in 2001, an increase of 7.2 years, compared with an increase of

---

TABLE 38.1 COMPARING LEVELS OF DEVELOPMENT: REGISTERED INDIANS IN CANADA AND THE CANADIAN POPULATION

		1981	1991	2001
Life Expectancy at Birth (years)	Registered Indians	65.7	70.6	72.9
	Canadian Population	75.6	77.9	78.7
Proportion Completed High School or Higher[1]	Registered Indians	0.33	0.55	0.57
	Canadian Population	0.60	0.68	0.75
Proportion Completed Grade 9 or Higher[2]	Registered Indians	0.60	0.72	0.83
	Canadian Population	0.80	0.86	0.90
Average Annual Income (2000$)[3]	Registered Indians	6,840	8,243	10,094
	Canadian Population	16,554	20,072	22,489

NOTES:

[1] The proportion completed high school or higher is estimated by the population with a secondary school graduation certificate, some post-secondary or trades education, or some university with or without degree, divided by the population aged 19 years and over.

[2] The proportion completed grade 9 or higher is the population aged 15 years and over that has completed grade 9 or higher, divided by the total population aged 15 years and over.

[3] The average annual income is the average income from all sources for the year before the census enumeration, adjusted by the Statistics Canada Consumer Price Index to year 2000 constant dollars (Statistics Canada 2005b).

SOURCE: Statistics Canada Census Data custom tabulations; Statistics Canada 1984, 1990, 1995, 1998, 2005a; Rowe and Norris 1995; Nault et al. 1993; Norris, Kerr, and Nault 1996; DIAND 1998; Verma, Michalowski and Gauvin 2003; Authors' calculations.

3.1 years for the Canadian population. This means that there has been a narrowing of the gap; however, the Registered Indian population remains nearly 6 years behind the Canadian population.

We find that educational attainment also lags behind the Canadian population. While we can see overall improvement for Registered Indians between 1981 and 2001, improvement in educational attainment has not been continuous. In the 1981 to 1991 period there was a narrowing of the gap with the Canadian population in terms of the proportion with high school or higher, whereas in the 1991 to 2001 period the gap actually increased.

The average annual income of both the Registered Indian population and the Canadian population increased over the 1981 to 2001 period. In terms of dollars, there was much less improvement in the average annual income of Registered Indians between 1981 and 2001. The income gap between Registered Indians and other Canadians grew over the entire period, from $9,714 in 1981 to $12,395 in 2001. It is interesting to note that over the twenty-year period we see a slight improvement in the relative annual income. As a proportion of the Canadian population's average income, the Registered Indian population narrowed the average income gap over the twenty-year period from 0.413 to 0.449, although this proportion decreased slightly from 1981 to 1991, to 0.411.

If we look at labour force participation, we can see the same patterns of disadvantage.

KEY LABOUR MARKET INDICATORS FOR ABORIGINALS AND NON-ABORIGINALS IN CANADA 2001

	Non Aboriginal	Registered Indian
Not in the labour force	28.0%	42.0%
Unemployed	7.6%	22.4%

Based on the 2001 Census Public Use Microdata File

Compared to the non-Aboriginal population, many more Registered Indians have chosen (or been forced) not to seek employment, as reflected in the substantially lower labour force participation rates. As well, of those seeking employment, nearly three times as many Registered Indians are unemployed.

We argued above that there is a relative disadvantage for Aboriginal people compared to the Canadian population, and it would appear to us that the patterns of relative disadvantage extend much further than most people understand. In fact, the disadvantage we note here captures only a portion of the issues. For example, we have seen that there is a serious and on-going problem with potable water (Chapters 8 and 9 in White et al., 2006), higher rates of suicide (Chandler and LaLonde, 2004), and high rates of self-reported health problems (Spence, 2007; Chapter 10).

EDUCATIONAL ATTAINMENT: A DETAILED PERSPECTIVE

We generally agree that the development of human capital is very important in the self-actualization of a person. It allows one to choose when and how to integrate into the economic enterprise of the country, region, or community in which one lives, and it also contributes to the production of citizenship.

There is a long scientific tradition in sociology and economics that has established that educational attainment, that is, the acquisition of human capital, is highly correlated with income, wealth, occupational diversity, and a host of other positive outcomes (see Becker, 1964; Coleman, 1988). This relationship has been demonstrated to hold for Aboriginal people as well (Spence et al., 2007; Spence, 2007; White, Maxim, and Spence, 2004; White, Spence, and Maxim, 2005).

If we look closely at the situation for education we see two trends. The Registered Indian population (measured in 2001) has a high school completion rate roughly equal to the rate of non-Aboriginals in 1981; thus, the former are twenty years behind the latter.

When we look at post-secondary education the story is even less positive. The Aboriginal population are at the same levels as the general population was in the 1950s. In fact, we have shown in our research that the gap has been increasing in the last decade (see Hull, 2005). . . . In a knowledge-based economy such as Canada's, this means that the chances for economic integration and higher well-being are going to be reduced as the century moves forward.

We wanted to raise one final disturbing issue. When we look at how Aboriginals, aged 18–29, compare in terms of educational attainment, when compared to a range of other ethnic groups in Canada in 2001, we can see that all Aboriginal groups have much lower rates of high school completion than the other ethnic groups. This indicates to us that there is an exceptional problem facing Aboriginal populations.

This is not the only exceptional problem that faces Aboriginal people. In a study of economic development projects on reserves, by the Strategic Research and Analysis Directorate of Indian and Northern Affairs Canada (INAC), it was found that, compared to the average, it takes between three and four times as long to get businesses developed on reserves.

Scientists and policy-makers have been faced with the on-going problem of understanding the relative levels of human development and predicting the capacity of a community (or nation or people) to develop given the resources they have at their disposal. Those interested in development have long sought to discover techniques for measuring social and economic progress. Even more challenging is trying to pinpoint the weaknesses in the mix of resources in order to increase the likelihood of success.

Despite the fact that Canadian social policy has, for the last half-century, focused on reducing inequalities through the removal of economic barriers, First Nations and other Aboriginal people face serious issues, as we noted in our brief description of the relative deprivation facing Aboriginal people in Canada. . . .

We are calling on Aboriginal and non-Aboriginal leaders, policy-makers, and researchers to make the tough questions part of our dialogue.

Our book raises some very important and controversial issues. Here are a few of them.

We are not saying "spend more" or "spend less." We have no idea whether $8 billion or $16 billion is what is necessary to solve the problems plaguing Aboriginal conditions. We are saying, "let us figure out what is best." What is the proper way to approach the government transfers and claims settlements to communities? We would say that is not clear right now. . . . [T]ransfers are not, on the surface, creating equality between communities, which is what they are supposed to do. They are supposed to make up for the shortfalls experienced by communities that are suffering some disadvantage. This raises two very complex and controversial questions. Should we be subsidizing the "worst-off" communities or stratifying our transfers to reward those that are making gains?

The second question is even more controversial. Are there some communities that are simply not sustainable? As hard a discussion as this would be, it is certainly not one we can avoid forever. The Kasatchewan story most certainly raised the spectre of this issue. Indeed, the suggestion was made to move the community.[8]

The demand for tools to be able to assist all of us, Aboriginal and non-Aboriginal, to make these choices is heartbreakingly obvious. It is not that people are incapable in some individual way; instead, it may be that history has passed some communities by. If we think of non-Aboriginal communities where a natural resource is the driving force behind the local economy, there are cases in which this resource becomes exhausted. The result is that these communities may slowly disappear in the absence of the necessary capacity for long-term sustainability. In the face of climate change, cultural change, and the corresponding change in ways of life in some Aboriginal communities, there may be communities that simply cannot be sustainable, productive, successful places to build families and live one's life.

This whole discussion requires great care. Some Canadians might say, "Why can't

Aboriginal people simply move to another town or city if their home community is not working?" We are well aware that this is not the solution. Aboriginal people have a strong attachment to the land, they desire to have proximity to their families and clans, and many hold to the traditions and cultures of their past. Their home communities are part of their identity. This makes simply dispersing as individuals, when troubles increase, a difficult, if not impossible, choice. However, our research indicates that nearly half of all reserve band members (recognized citizens of First Nations communities) live off-reserve in non-Aboriginal towns and cities (see Norris et al., 2003).

We do not know which, if any, of the First Nations and Inuit communities might be unsustainable, but we do know that we must have the tools to supplement our understanding so that we can discuss the problem. *This is an issue that must be debated by Aboriginal people themselves. Solutions can never work if they are imposed.* There must be a widespread buy-in to whatever course of action is decided. Intra-Aboriginal debate would be paralleled by dialogue between the Aboriginal people and the Canadian government.

The foundation of such a debate must be empirical evidence, otherwise we rest on nothing but ideologies and pre-conceived ideas, including prejudice.

NOTES

1. This phrase is often abbreviated as "POGG". These principles from the introduction to section 91 of the *Constitution Act, 1867*.
2. The Oka crisis was the result of a land dispute between the Mohawk community of Kanesatake and the town of Oka in Quebec during the summer of 1990. This crisis was sparked by a decision taken by the Municipality of Oka to extend a nine-hole golf course on land that the Mohawks claimed was, and had always been, theirs. The 39 hectares of land in question included a Native cemetery and parts of a pine forest. Several books provide detailed accounts of the Oka crisis (e.g., MacLaine et al. 1991; Alfred 1995).
3. During the 65-year period following confederation (1867–1933), Canada's military was engaged 132 times in law enforcement activities in order to restore civil order (Pariseau 1973; Haslip 2006). However, since 1933, Canada's military has been used only twice to restore civil order: the October crisis of 1970 and the Oka crisis of 1990. It is interesting to note that the Canadian Army mobilized over 2,000 troops to restore order in Oka, yet during that same summer in 1990, Canada sent slightly less than 1,000 soldiers to fight in Iraq. The Oka crisis drew worldwide attention, catapulting native land rights into the spotlight.
4. This Royal Commission was established in 1991 to address many of the Aboriginal issues that had come to light as a result of the Oka crisis and the failed Meech Lake Accord. The Commission culminated in a final report published in 1996. The final report consisted of five volumes and the 4,000 pages represent the most in-depth study ever undertaken of the historical relations between the Canadian government and Aboriginal peoples.
5. After failed negotiations, 400 tactical assault members of the RCMP, backed by helicopters and armoured personnel carriers supplied by the military, were deployed against the Aboriginal occupants and their supporters. In one particularly tense moment, the RCMP fired thousands of rounds during a 45-minute blaze of gunfire (Steele 1997).
6. Wilkes (2004) analyzed media reports and noted that there were roughly 100 Aboriginal occupations or protests between 1968 and 2000. Using the same methodology, but different criteria, Clairmont and Potts (2006) found 616 incidents between 1951 and 2000. Chapter two of the Ipperwash Inquiry provides an excellent primer on Aboriginal occupations (Linden 2007).

7. In some respects, this call for action against poverty was probably an off-shoot of the Kelowna Accord. The Kelowna Accord is the common name given to a working paper entitled "Strengthening Relationships and Closing the Gap" which resulted from 18 months of roundtable consultations cumulating at the First Ministers' Meeting in Kelowna in November, 2005. This working paper established targets to improve the education, employment, and living conditions for Aboriginal peoples through additional governmental funding. This accord was never signed, nor were monies ever budgeted for it, before the minority government of Paul Martin fell. The subsequent minority government of Stephen Harper identified different priorities with respect to Aboriginal affairs. While the Kelowna Accord is clearly a political hot potato, Wikipedia provides a brief, but balanced discussion of it.

8. This has unsuccessfully been tried in the past. See White (2003) for a discussion of the Davis Inlet and Port Harrison relocations.

REFERENCES

Alfred, G. R. 1995. *Heeding the Voices of Our Ancestors: Kahnawake Mohawk Politics and the Rise of Native Nationalism.* Oxford University Press.

Beavon, D. and M. Cook. 2003. "An Application of the United Nations Human Development Index to Registered Indians in Canada, 1996." Pp. 201–221 in *Aboriginal Conditions: Research as a Foundation for Public Policy,* edited by White, J. P., Maxim, P. and D. Beavon. Vancouver: University of British Columbia Press.

Becker, G. 1964. *Human Capital.* New York: The National Bureau of Economic Research.

Burrows, J. "Crown and Aboriginal Occupations of Land: A History & Comparison", background paper prepared for the Ipperwash Inquiry, October, 2005.

Clairmont, D. and Potts, J. "For the Nonce: Policing and Aboriginal Occupations and Protests", background paper prepared for the Ipperwash Inquiry, May, 2006.

Chandler, M. and C. Lalonde. 2004. "Transforming Whose Knowledge? Exchanging Whose Best Practices? On Knowing about Indigenous Knowledge and Aboriginal Suicide." Pp. 111–124 in White, J., Maxim, P. and D. Beavon (eds). *Aboriginal Policy Research: Setting the Agenda for Change.* Vol. 2. Toronto: Thompson Educational Publishing, Inc.

Coleman, J. 1988. "Social Capital in the Creation of Human Capital." *American Journal of Sociology* 94 Supplement.

Department of Indian Affairs and Northern Development. 1993. *Population Projections of Registered Indians, 1996–2121.* Ottawa: DIAND.

Fiscal Realities, "Expanding Commercial Activity on First Nations Land: Getting First Nation Land Development Regulations Right", Strategic Research and Analysis Directorate, Indian and Northern Affairs Canada, 1999.

Griffin, D. (Editor). 1988. *Spirituality and Society: Postmodern Visions.* New York: State University of New York Press.

Gurr, T. R. 1970. *Why Men Rebel.* Princeton: Princeton University Press.

Haslip, S. *The Bisons Now Hunt the Indians: A Critical Consideration of Contemporary Provisions Providing for the Use of Military Force Against Aboriginal Peoples (in Canada).* LL.M., University of Ottawa, Faculty of Law, 2002.

Hull, J. 2005. *Post-secondary Education and Labour Market Outcomes: Canada, 2001.* Ottawa: Department of Indian and Northern Affairs Canada.

Insight Canada Research Inc. 1996. *Perspectives Canada* 5(1).

Linden, S. B. *Report of the Ipperwash Inquiry,* Publications Ontario, 2007.

MacLaine, C. and M. S. Boxendale. 1991. *This Land Is Our Land: The Mohawk Revolt at Oka.* Optimum Publishing International Inc.

Maxim, P. and J. White. 2003. "Toward an Index of Community Capacity: Predicting Community Potential for Successful Program Transfer." Pp. 248–263 in *Aboriginal Conditions: Research as a Foundation for Public Policy,* edited by White, J., Maxim, P., and D. Beavon. Vancouver: University of British Columbia Press.

Maxim, P., White, J., and D. Beavon. 2003. "Dispersion and Polarization of Income among Aboriginal and Non-Aboriginal Canadians." In *Aboriginal Conditions: The Research Foundations for Public Policy.* Vancouver: University of British Columbia Press.

Nault, F., Chen, J., George, M. V., and M. J. Norris. 1993. *Population Projections of Registered Indians, 1991-2016.* Report prepared by the Population Projections Section, Demography Division, Statistics Canada. Ottawa: Indian and Northern Affairs Canada.

Norris, M. J., Cooke, M. and S. Clatworthy. 2003. "Aboriginal Mobility and Migration Patterns and the Policy Implications." Pp. 108–130 in *Aboriginal Conditions: Research as a Foundation for Public Policy,* edited by White, J., Maxim, P., and D. Beavon. Vancouver: University of British Columbia Press.

Norris, M. J., Kerr, D., and F. Nault. 1995. *Projections of the Population with Aboriginal Identity in Canada, 1991-2016.* Report prepared by the Population Projections Section, Demography Division, Statistics Canada, for the Royal Commission on Aboriginal Peoples. Ottawa: Canada Mortgage and Housing Corporation and the Royal Commission on Aboriginal Peoples.

Pariseau, J. J. B. Major. 1973. *Disorders, Strikes and Disasters: Military Aid to the Civil Power in Canada, 1867-1933.* Ottawa: Directorate of History, National Defence Headquarters.

Report of the Royal Commission on Aboriginal Peoples. 1996. Canada Communication Group Publishing, Ottawa, Ontario.

Rowe, G. and M. M. Norris. 1995. *Mortality Predictions of Registered Indians, 1982 to 1996.* Ottawa: Indian and Northern Affairs Canada.

Sallee, D. 2006. "Quality of Life of Aboriginal People in Canada "*IRPP Choices.* Vol 12, no 6. November.

Spence, N. 2007. *New Vistas on the Income Inequality-Health Debate: The Case of Canada's First Nations Reserve Population.* PhD Dissertation, Department of Sociology, The University of Western Ontario, London, Ontario.

Spence, N., White, J., and P. Maxim. (2007). "Modeling Community Determinants of Canada's First Nation's Educational Outcomes." *Canadian Ethnic Studies.* (Forthcoming)

Statistics Canada. 1984. *Life Tables, Canada and Provinces 1980–82.* Catalogue no. 84-532. Ottawa: Statistics Canada.

Statistics Canada. 1990. *Life Tables, Canada and Provinces, 1985–87.* Health Reports Supplement 13. Ottawa: Statistics Canada.

Statistics Canada. 1995. *Life Tables, Canada and Provinces, 1990–92.* Catalogue no. 84-537. Ottawa: Statistics Canada.

Statistics Canada. 1998. *Life Expectancy Abridged Life Tables, at Birth and Age 65, by Sex, for Canada, Provinces, Territories, and Health Regions.* CANISM Table 102-0016. Ottawa: Statistics Canada.

Statistics Canada. 2000. *The Consumer Price Index.* Catalogue no. 62-010-X1B. Ottawa: Statistics Canada.

Statistics Canada. 2005b. *Consumer Price Index, Historical Summary.* Ottawa: Statistics Canada.

Statistics Canada Census Data custom tabulations; Statistics Canada 1984, 1990, 1995, 1998, 2005a.

Steele, S. 1997. "Gustafsen Lake Standoff: 15 Charged", *Maclean's* Magazine, June 2.

Verma, R., Michalowski, M., and R. P. Gauvin. 2003. *Abridged Life Tables for Registered Indians in Canada, 1976–80 to 1996–2000.* Paper presented at the annual meeting of the Population Association of American, May 103, Minneapolis.

Walker, I. and H. Smith (Editors). 2002. *Relative Deprivation: Development, Specification and*

Integration. Cambridge: Cambridge: Cambridge University Press.

White, J. P., Beavon, D., and P. Maxim. 2003. *Aboriginal Conditions: The Research Foundations for Public Policy.* Vancouver: University of British Columbia Press.

White, J. P., Maxim, P., and N. Spence. 2004. *Permission to Develop: Aboriginal Treaties, Case Law and Regulations.* Toronto: Thompson Educational Press.

White, J. P., Maxim, P., and D. Beavon (eds). 2004. *Aboriginal Policy Research: Setting the Agenda for Change.* Vol. 1. Toronto: Thompson Educational Press.

White, J. P., Maxim, P., and D. Beavon (eds). 2004. *Aboriginal Policy Research: Setting the Agenda for Change.* Vol. 2. Toronto: Thompson Educational Press.

White, J., Wingert, S., Beavon, D., and P. Maxim. 2006. *Aboriginal Policy Research: Moving Forward, Making a Difference.* Vol. 3. Toronto: Thompson Educational Publishing.

White, J., Wingert, S., and D. Beavon. 2007. *Aboriginal Policy Research: Moving Forward, Making a Difference.* Vol. 4. Toronto: Thompson Educational Publishing.

White, J. P., Anderson, E., and W. Cornett (eds). 2007. *Aboriginal Policy Research: Aboriginal Policy Research: Moving Forward, Making a Difference.* Vol. 5. Toronto: Thompson Educational Publishing.

White, J., Spence, N., and P. Maxim. 2005. "Social capital and educational attainment among Aboriginal peoples: Canada, Australia and New Zealand." Pp. 66–81 in *Policy Research Initiative Social Capital Project Series, Social Capital in Action: Thematic Studies,* edited by Policy Research Initiative. Ottawa: Policy Research Initiative, Government of Canada.

White, J., Maxim, P., and N. Spence. 2004. "A Educational Attainment of Aboriginal Canadians." In White, J., Maxim, P., and D. Beavon (eds). *Aboriginal Policy Research: Setting the Agenda for Change.* Vol. 1. Toronto: Thompson Educational Press.

Chapter 39

Confronting Culture with Science: Language and Public Policy

JERRY P. WHITE

This selection should be read as an example of how sociologists can aid policy-makers in deciding which social programs to fund. In this case, the question being considered is whether the government should fund programs to help First Nations retain their traditional languages. At the very least, as the author (who is also a co-editor of this text) points out, there are two sub-questions here. First, we need to ask whether the effects of language retention are beneficial. As the author's review of some relevant studies indicates, this turns out not to be a simple "yes or no" question. Second, because policy-makers are supposed to be accountable for the funds they spend, we need to know if money spent on language retention is likely to achieve the desired result. This in turn leads to an assessment of what is causing the erosion of traditional languages. So, for example, if linguistic exogamy (someone who speaks a traditional language marrying someone who does not) is a major cause in that erosion, then should we be spending enormous sums of money on programs likely to fail because these programs have no effect on who marries whom?

Language is not simply a way to communicate, although that certainly plays a core role in its construction, use, and understanding. Languages are fundamental to all human cultures, and, understood as such, we see them play a role in defining the existence of those cultures, differentiating them from others, and acting as an evolutionary universal (Parsons 1964). Few Canadians would have trouble recognizing the importance of language given the decades-long controversy over the use and maintenance of language in Quebec. Language has played a similar role in Europe, from the Mongols of the East to the Belgians or the Welsh of the West. Everywhere language and national identity have been linked. This linkage means that the collectivities of peoples, whether community or country, have real attachments and altered experiences as a result of their language retention or lack of it.

A nation is a collectivity that shares some geography, has a common history, culture, and language, and wishes to be identified as a nation. If we understand nations to have these characteristics, then we also have to see collectivities that are deprived of any of these characteristics as losing their nationhood, losing their identity as a nation. The result of the loss of one's land or one's language can come about gradually or abruptly, but experience tells us that it is always resisted. The resistance to the loss of nation, or even the perception of some threat to one's existence as a nation, is a defining point of our human history in the past century. Whether we look at the Hutu and Tutsi, the Afghan and Russian, the Palestinian and Israeli, the Serb, Albanian, and Croatian, or even the French Canadian and English Canadian, in all cases we find an element of the disagreement that relates to the protection of nation. Part of that core disagreement is language.

Nationalism is a two-edged sword. Nationalism has a positive side, where a people can cohere and in that process achieve great feats through collective effort. The first leader of the People's Republic of China, Mao Tse-tung, credited nationalism with playing a key role in defeating the Japanese aggression and occupation in the Second World War. On the other hand, Ramsay Cook is certainly right when he points to how nationalism creates the basis of war, as people engage in conflict about who belongs where and with whom (Cook 1995). For the member of a First Nation, the maintenance of a language may be a dear project, and the redevelopment/reintroduction of a past language may be seen as life giving: "Native languages embody indigenous people's identity and are the most important element in their culture. They must be revived and protected as symbols and sources of nationhood" (Alfred 1999, 136).

To a policy maker, the issues are undoubtedly different. Can the language continue? Is it continuing and why? Can public spending on language protection or reintroduction bring returns? Is it desired and desirable from the First Nations perspective and from societal viewpoints? Does the maintenance of a language have an effect on the socio-economic well-being of the people? Sound research can provide a foundation for weighing the pros and cons of the real world.

O'Sullivan finds that there is no clear answer to the long-standing debate over integration versus positive self-identity. On the one hand, integrationists argue that maintenance of language separation from the dominant economic groups in society is a cause of lower socio-economic development. On the other hand, as O'Sullivan points out, those opposed to assimilation argue that the maintenance of identity

(language is a key part of that) is the essence of nationhood and creates a cohesion that allows collective growth. She finds that Aboriginal language use is associated with non-participation in the dominant culture and dominant economy. However, it is less profoundly related to success when such involvement in the economy is already initiated and language is reintroduced. She feels that neither the integrationist nor the cohesion position is universally valid or completely explanatory. The data for First Nations communities provide some support for instances where it is positive to reintroduce a language that has become endangered or even nearly lost, while in several scenarios that she examines, it appears that the separation created by maintaining a traditional language can suppress socio-economic development. The conclusion we can draw is that you cannot draw hard and fast conclusions. "I hesitate to conclude that Aboriginal language use is a ghettoizing force," she writes (O'Sullivan 2003).

There are indications that the duality of language functions may be a key. The language, functioning as the means of communication, may tend to disadvantage a group, while languages that function as symbols of the group's sameness and shared culture may be positive. Her development of this view is the greatest contribution of Chapter 6. It gives us an interesting framework for explaining why this issue of maintenance versus abandonment is so complex. If we go back to the model developed in Chapter 1, it would appear that maintenance of traditional language might be a contributor to cohesion (Alfred 1999), and it might probably operate through the increasing levels of social capital that can be generated by sharing a cultural attribute such as language. Regardless, the cohesion would likely increase due to the ties to the older generations, the passage of myths and norms of the group, and increased symbolic and communicative interaction.

So why does O'Sullivan find that there are stronger indications of a negative relationship? It is conceivable that language retention does improve cohesion, but that positive outcome is undermined by the negative relationship between human capital development and the saturation of traditional language. O'Sullivan asks, "Why is language saturation high in very low human capital communities?" This is perhaps the key relationship. We know that human capital attainment is lower in the Aboriginal communities than in the general population (White 2003), and we can see here that language saturation has a relationship with communities at the lower end of the human capital spectrum. Perhaps that is how the model works its way through this issue of language, communicative and symbolic. The decline in human capital in Aboriginal communities that is associated with language retention undermines the positive cohesive properties.

Policy implications are manifest. Polls and anecdotal information indicate that the Canadian public is quite prepared to support spending on problems related to the Aboriginal condition. They do, however, appear to demand accountability, both from the First Nations and the government. The demand is that there be a return on any investment. In a constellation of choices about priorities, what is the measured effect of the spending that is made against the projected aims of that investment? This is difficult in the realm of social policy, but is nonetheless expected by the taxpayer. Is it rational to spend money on language reintroduction? Will that work to bring back a language? Is it wise or even possible to protect endangered Aboriginal languages? Will it actually help the First Nations in some way? The public questions us, but researchers and policy makers have few answers.

Norris and MacCon (2003) bring us the most complete review of how languages are maintained as well as why some are disappearing while others are more robust. It also contributes to the discussion that follows from O'Sullivan over what motivates peoples to maintain languages. Norris and MacCon begin with the understanding that, while loss of a language may not doom a culture, it can handicap the transmission of that culture. That cultural maintenance is very positive is taken for granted in their work. This is truly a Canadian policy attribute. The authors concur with the Royal Commission on Aboriginal Peoples declaration that the transfer of language from old to young is critical in the process of maintaining an Aboriginal language, but they find that "even for some of Canada's more viable Aboriginal languages, there is erosion of language use in the home." They conclude that "most of Canada's Aboriginal languages that are currently considered viable may experience growing problems of continuity with younger generations, accelerating the process of language erosion. In the case of already endangered languages, extinction appears to be only a generation away."

The finding that many of Canada's Aboriginal languages have suffered serious decay or extinction may not be surprising to the First Nations Peoples, but it is important to clearly define and understand. Norris and MacCon show us how the current social trends toward linguistic intermarriage of Aboriginal speakers with non-Aboriginal speakers as well as the large number of single-parent families have had devastating effects on language maintenance. They point out that these social processes will continue to undermine even the more robust of the viable languages over the coming years. The learning and use of Aboriginal languages that are reintroduced (usually as second languages) are not positive in the process of protecting traditional languages, according to the authors. Linguistic endogamy, more limited migration, and measures to encourage family stability will be necessary to increase the potential for languages to survive. These are difficult if not impossible issues to influence. The thought of socially engineering marriage patterns is not desirable in any way. Any actions related to language retention will demand the infusion of funds. It is clear that the calls by First Nations for human capital development within the rubric of the traditional language are going to increase. These are very difficult problems that really cry out for an assessment of existing research, and even more extensive research and analysis, prior to policy development.

The lessons for policy, research, and Aboriginal communities here are somewhat clear. The development of demands for action and the policy development to deal with those demands is best done away from simplistic preconceptions. The problem of language retention should not be avoided in research simply because it raises so many political and social difficulties. Policy-relevant research can have some very dynamic and controversial sides.

O'Sullivan (2003) notes: "It may therefore be the case that the death of Aboriginal languages is certain, and to oppose that death may simply be to postpone the inevitable." She says this at the conclusion of her extensive review of the debates over the advisability and viability of promoting language maintenance. Good policy-relevant research raises even the most controversial problems and confronts orthodoxy.

How can we marshal our resources effectively and achieve some measure of success in dealing with the acknowledged problems across the many issues that face the First Nations? How can we be accountable without abandoning people's heartfelt desire to protect language and nation? Is it possible to create the conditions to protect even the currently viable languages, given the social practices among the peoples themselves that mitigate success?

These questions are not answered in this book; they are simply raised. It is our collective responsibility to pursue them to find better answers than we have today. That may involve trying to understand what the affected people actually want. The Ekos survey (Ekos Research Associates 2001) of First Nations on reserves did not find a significant interest in language retention. The major issues were more pragmatic, including health and education. This does not mean that culture is not important, but with finite fiscal resources Aboriginally defined priorities could be one of many tools with which to make decisions.

REFERENCES

Alfred, Taiaiake. 1999. *Peace, Power Righteousness.* Toronto: Oxford University Press.

Cook, Ramsay. 1995. *Canada, Quebec and the Uses of Nationalism.* Toronto: McClelland and Stewart.

Ekos Research Associates. 2001. *First Nations Survey on Reserve.* Ottawa: Department of Indian Affairs and Northern Development.

O'Sullivan, E. Aboriginal Language Retention and Socio-Economic Development in White et al. *Aboriginal Conditions: Research as a Foundation for Public Policy.* Vancouver: UBC Press 2003. pp. 136–163.

Norris, M. J. and K. MacCon. *Aboriginal language: Transmission and Maintenance in Families.* In White et al. (2003).

Parsons, Talcott. 1964. Evolutionary universals in society. *American Sociological Review* 29(3): 339–40.

White, Jerry P., Paul Maxim and Dan Beavon. *Aboriginal Conditions: Research as a Foundation for Public Policy.* Vancouver: UBC Press 2003.

PART 14

Population Studies and Demography

Chapter 40

Stars and Bars

DANIEL LAZARE

How to eliminate racism in society? Common answers to this question call attention to the need for educational campaigns that emphasize tolerance and an appreciation of diversity, and for laws that make it illegal to discriminate on the basis of race or ethnicity and/or to promote hatred against particular social groups. While we can all agree that these approaches are laudable, what they have in common is an emphasis on the individual and the beliefs that individuals hold. Sociologists concerned with race and ethnicity have long argued that these "individualistic" approaches to racism, however well intentioned, have little impact on the forms of institutionalized racism in society that most dramatically affect people's lives. Indeed, some sociologists have argued that a focus on individuals in studying racism actually diverts attention from institutionalized racism in a society and so helps to maintain it. What is institutionalized racism? Basically, the term refers to the fact that society is organized in ways that function to disadvantage particular social groups. Glassner (2000), for example, reviews sociological works that argue that the criminal justice system in the United States has functioned as a mechanism of internal colonization in regard to Native Americans. In this selection, Daniel Lazare makes a similar—and updated—argument in regard to African-Americans. Basically, he argues that racial and class biases in the U.S. have produced "the largest detention system in the advanced industrial world," one that functions to disenfranchise a racial underclass. If Lazare's argument is correct (and addressing that issue in itself should provoke some lively discussion), then ask yourself if it seems likely that this form of institutionalized racism will be eliminated in the near future.

How can you tell when a democracy is dead? When concentration camps spring up and everyone shivers in fear? Or is it when concentration camps spring up and no one shivers in fear because everyone knows they're not for "people like us" (in Woody Allen's marvelous phrase) but for the others, the troublemakers, the ones you can tell are guilty merely by the color of their skin, the shape of their nose or their social class?

Questions like these are unavoidable in the face of America's homegrown gulag archipelago, a vast network of jails, prisons and "supermax" tombs for the living dead that, without anyone quite noticing, has metastasized into the largest detention system in the advanced industrial world. The proportion of the US population languishing in such facilities now stands at 737 per 100,000, the highest rate on earth and some five to twelve times that of Britain, France and

Source: Lazare, Daniel. August 27, 2007. "Stars and Bars" by reprinted with permission from the issue of The Nation. For subscription information, call 1-800-333-8536. Portions of each week's Nation magazine can be accessed at www.thenation.com

other Western European countries or Japan. With 5 percent of the world's population, the United States has close to a quarter of the world's prisoners, which, curiously enough, is the same as its annual contribution to global warming. With 2.2 million people behind bars and another 5 million on probation or parole, it has approximately 3.2 percent of the adult population under some form of criminal-justice supervision, which is to say one person in thirty-two. For African-Americans, the numbers are even more astonishing. By the mid-1990s, 7 percent of black males were behind bars, while the rate of imprisonment for black males between the ages of 25 and 29 now stands at one in eight. While conservatives have spent the past three or four decades bemoaning the growth of single-parent families, there is a very simple reason some 1.5 million American children are fatherless or (less often) motherless: Their parents are locked up. Because they are confined for the most part in distant rural prisons, moreover, only about one child in five gets to visit them as often as once a month.

What's that you say? Who cares whether a bunch of "rapists, murderers, robbers, and even terrorists and spies," as Republican Senator Mitch McConnell once characterized America's prison population, get to see their kids? In fact, surprisingly few denizens of the American gulag have been sent away for violent crimes. In 2002 just 19 percent of the felony sentences handed down at the state level were for violent offenses, and of those only about 5 percent were for murder. Nonviolent drug offenses involving trafficking or possession (the modern equivalent of rum-running or getting caught with a bottle of bathtub gin) accounted for 31 percent of the total, while purely economic crimes such as burglary and fraud made up an additional 32 percent. If the incarceration rate continues to rise and violent crime continues to drop, we can expect the nonviolent sector of the prison population to expand accordingly. A normal society might lighten up in such circumstances. After all, if violence is under control, isn't it time to

come up with a more humane way of dealing with a dwindling number of miscreants? But America is not a normal country and only grows more punitive.

It has also been extremely reluctant to face up to the cancer in its midst. Several of the leading Democratic candidates, for example, have recently come out against the infamous 100-to-1 ratio that subjects someone carrying ten grams of crack to the same penalty as someone caught with a kilo of powdered cocaine. Senator Joe Biden has actually introduced legislation to eliminate the disparity—without, however, acknowledging his role as a leading drug warrior back in the 1980s, when he sponsored the bill that set it in stone in the first place. At a recent forum at Howard University, Hillary Clinton promised to "deal" with the disparity as well, although it would have been nice if she had done so back in the '90s, when, during the first Clinton Administration, the prison population was soaring by some 50 percent. Although he is not running this time around, Jesse Jackson recently castigated Dems for their hesitancy in addressing "failed, wasteful, and unfair drug policies" that have sent "so many young African-Americans" to jail. Yet Jackson forgot to mention his own drug-war past when, as a leading hard-liner, he specifically called for "stiffer prison sentences" for black drug users and "wartime consequences" for smugglers. "Since the flow of drugs into the US is an act of terrorism, antiterrorist policies must be applied," he declared in a 1989 interview, a textbook example of how the antidrug rhetoric of the late twentieth century helped pave the way for the "global war on terror" of the early twenty-first.

In other words, cowardice and hypocrisy abound. Fortunately, a small number of academics and at least one journalist have begun training an eye on America's growing prison crisis. Since there is more than enough injustice to go around, each has zeroed in on different aspects of the phenomenon—on the political and economic consequences of stigmatizing so many young people for life, on the racial consequences of disproportionately punishing young black males and on the sheer moral horror of needlessly locking away real, live human beings in supermax prisons that are little more than high-tech dungeons. Their findings, to make a long story short, are that the damage cannot be reduced to a simple matter of so many person-years of lost time. To the contrary, the effects promise to multiply for years to come. In *American Furies* Sasha Abramsky, a Sacramento-based journalist and longtime *Nation* contributor, convincingly argues that the best way to understand US prison policies is to think of them as a GI Bill in reverse. Just as the original GI Bill laid the basis for a major social advance by making college available to millions of veterans, mass incarceration is laying the basis for an enormous social regression by stigmatizing and brutalizing millions of young people and "de-skilling" them by removing them from the workforce. America will be feeling the effects for generations.

Bruce Western, a Princeton sociologist, offers the best overview. He notes in his new study, *Punishment and Inequality in America*, that mass imprisonment is actually a novel development. For much of the twentieth century, the US incarceration rate held steady at around 100 per 100,000, which would put it in the same ballpark as Western Europe today. But after a slight dip following the liberal reforms of the 1960s, the curve reversed direction in the mid-'70s and then rose more steeply in the '80s and '90s. Considering that Germany, Sweden, Denmark and Austria succeeded in reducing or holding their incarceration rates steady during this period, the US pattern was highly exceptional. But so are US crime rates. Between 1980 and 1991, US homicides hovered at between 7.9 and 10.2 per 100,000, as much as ten times the European average. (The rate has since fallen to around 5.7.) Combined with the crack wave that also exploded in the 1980s, the result was a deepening sense of panic that peaked in mid-1986 with the death of basketball star Len Bias from a cocaine overdose. Although there was no

evidence that crack had anything to do with Bias's death—police found only powdered cocaine in his car—the incident somehow confirmed crack as the new devil substance, "the most addictive drug known to man," in the words of *Newsweek*, and a threat comparable to the "medieval plagues," in the considered opinion of *U.S. News and World Report* (which would have meant that the country was facing an imminent population loss of up to 33 percent). Within a matter of months, Joe Biden had helped shepherd through to victory the Anti-Drug Abuse Act of 1986, an unusually horrendous piece of legislation that etched in stone the 100-to-1 penalty ratio for crack.

Still, it is always interesting to consider which deaths fill people with horror and which ones don't. The year before Bias's death not only saw 19,000 homicides in the United States but nearly 46,000 highway fatalities too, and yet Congress somehow refrained from criminalizing motor vehicles. Crack's status as the drug du jour of a certain class of inner-city blacks should have been the giveaway. What had Congress in a tizzy was not cocaine consumption so much as *black* cocaine consumption, which is why the subsequent repression was bound to be far harder on African-Americans than on whites. Although there is no evidence that blacks use drugs more than whites and indeed some evidence that they use them less, Western notes that black users are now twice as likely to be arrested for drugs and, once arrested, more likely to go to prison or jail. None of this is necessarily racist, at least not in the crudely explicit way we associate with men in white sheets. The reason the police concentrate their efforts in black inner-city neighborhoods, Western notes, is that users congregate there in large numbers, and buying, selling and using tend to take place in public. (It's harder to make arrests behind the closed doors of some suburban McMansion.) If a judge is more inclined to send a poor black defendant to prison, similarly, it is not necessarily because he or she enjoys punishing someone with dark skin but because the judge, according to Western, may "see poor defendants as having fewer prospects and social supports, thus as having less potential for rehabilitation." If your weeping parents can afford to send you to private rehab, you're excused. If not, it's off to the state pen.

Racial and class biases are thus built into the very structure of the drug war. Western is particularly effective on the economic consequences of such grossly disproportionate policies. The standard account of American economic development since the 1970s, told and retold in countless undergraduate classrooms, is that economic deregulation and growth have done much to narrow the once-yawning wage gap between white and black workers. To quote the *New York Times*: "Unemployment rates among blacks and Hispanic people . . . are at or near record lows. Joblessness among high school dropouts has fallen to about half the rate in 1992. And wages for the lowest paid are rising faster than inflation for the first time in decades." A rising tide lifts all boats, whereas all that labor-market rigidity has done for "Old Europe" is to saddle it with persistently high levels of unemployment, an alienated underclass and riots in the *banlieues*. But as *Punishment and Inequality in America* points out, if US economic policies look good, it is only because the country's enormous prison population is not factored into the equation. If workers behind bars are counted, then it quickly becomes apparent "that young black men have experienced virtually no real economic gains on young whites" and that the real black unemployment rate is up to 20 percent greater than official statistics indicate. Rather than freeing up the markets, Western writes, the United States has "adopted policies that massively and coercively regulated the poor." Where the Danes provide their unemployed with up to 80 percent of their previous salary and the Germans provide them with 60 percent, America has deregulated the rich while throwing a growing portion of its working class in jail.

In *Marked*, Devah Pager, who also teaches sociology at Princeton, uses a simple technique to show how mass incarceration has undone the small amount of racial progress achieved in the 1960s and '70s. Working with two pairs of male college students in Milwaukee, one white and the other black, she drilled them on how to present themselves and answer questions. Then, arming them with phony résumés, she sent them out to apply for entry-level jobs. The résumés were identical in all respects but one. Where one member of each team had nothing indicating a criminal record, the other's résumé showed an eighteen-month sentence for drugs. To help insure that the results were uniform, the résumés were then rotated back and forth among the testers.

The results? The white applicant with a prison record was half as likely to be called back for a second interview as the white applicant without. But the black applicant without a criminal record was no more likely to be called back than the white applicant with a record, while the black applicant with a record was two-thirds less likely to be called back than the black applicant without. The black applicant with a record therefore wound up doubly penalized—as a black man and as an ex-con. With the chances of a call-back reduced to just 5 percent, the overall effect, Pager writes, was "almost total exclusion from this labor market." Considering that there are as many as 12 million ex-felons in the United States, a major portion of them black, the result has been to create a huge pool of the semipermanently unemployed where one might otherwise not exist. This is not to disprove sociologist William Julius Wilson, whose study *The Declining Significance of Race* caused an uproar when it was published in 1978. Wilson may have been right: The significance of race may well have been declining by the late '70s. But thanks to a government policy of mass stigmatization, it has come roaring back.

This is not only bad news for those arrested but bad news for those who have to foot the bill for their incarceration and for dealing with the social problems that labor-market exclusion on this scale helps generate. But there are other costs too. In *Locked Out*, Jeff Manza and

Christopher Uggen, professors of sociology at Northwestern and the University of Minnesota, respectively, point out that only two states, Maine and Vermont, permit felons to vote while incarcerated, that most limit felons' voting rights after they complete their terms and that, even if not legally disenfranchised, some 600,000 jail inmates and pretrial detainees are effectively prevented from voting as well. All told, this means that 6 million Americans were unable to vote on election day in 2004. This is not peanuts. Nationwide, one black man in seven has been disenfranchised as a consequence, while in Florida, the state with the most sweeping disenfranchisement laws, the number of those prevented from voting now exceeds 1.1 million.

From a right-wing perspective, this is nothing short of brilliant. After all, what could be better than disenfranchising an unfriendly racial group while persuading the rest of the nation that the group deserves it because its ranks are filled with violent criminals? Since felons and ex-felons tend to be poor and members of oppressed racial minorities, they tend to vote Democratic. Even though the poor are less likely to vote than those higher up on the socioeconomic ladder, Manza and Uggen say there is little doubt that, had the disenfranchisement laws not existed in Florida in November 2000, the extra votes would have provided Al Gore with a margin of victory so comfortable that not even the Republican state legislature could have taken it away. If the ranks of prison inmates and hence of disenfranchised ex-inmates had not multiplied since the '70s, much of the wind would also have been taken out of the sails of the great GOP offensive. Americans have not gone right, in other words. Rather, by taking control of the criminal-justice issue, the right wing has winnowed down the electorate so as to artificially boost the power of the conservative minority.

But how did the right gain control of this all-important issue in the first place? This is the problem that Marie Gottschalk, a professor of political science at the University of Pennsylvania, wrestles with in *The Prison and the*

Gallows, an eccentric but compelling study of mass incarceration's ideological origins. While taking aim at the usual right-wing villains, *The Prison and the Gallows* also goes after various liberals and radicals who, inadvertently or not, also contributed to the construction of "the carceral state." Bill Clinton, for example, not only embraced the drug war and capital punishment— he interrupted his 1992 presidential campaign to fly back to Arkansas and sign the death warrant for a mentally disabled prisoner named Rickey Ray Rector—but also endorsed what Gottschalk calls "a virulently punitive victims' rights movement," going so far as to call for a constitutional amendment in 1996 as "the only way to give victims equal and due consideration."

This was important because the victims' rights movement represented an effort to inject a dose of vengeance into the judicial process and thereby blur the distinction between the private interest of the victim and the public's interest in maintaining order and justice. In Europe, reformers were also concerned with victims' rights. But "extending a hand to victims was seen from the start as primarily an extension of the welfare state," Gottschalk observes, whereas in America, where welfare is a dirty word, it was seen as a way of steering criminal justice in a more punitive direction. . . .

Sasha Abramsky is less interested in the ideological currents that helped pave the way for mass incarceration, although in *American Furies* he does spotlight the fascinating role played by a Berkeley-educated sociologist named Robert Martinson, who, after several years investigating the cornucopia of rehabilitation programs offered at the time by the New York State prison system, summed up his findings in a sensational 1974 article titled "What Works?" His answer: nothing. Martinson's frustration is understandable to anyone who has ever suffered through an encounter group. Yet his conclusions, published in the neoconservative journal *Public Interest*, were grossly one-sided: While many programs do not work, some clearly have a positive effect.

In short order, Martinson's article became the bible of the vengeance-and-punishment set, which seized on it as proof that rehabilitation was a lost cause and that the only purpose of prison was to penalize wrongdoers. Once this ideological impediment was removed, the criminal-justice system slid downhill with remarkable speed. If punishment was good, then more punishment was better. In short order, Massachusetts Governor William Weld was declaring that life in prison should be "akin to a walk through hell," while right-wing Senator Phil Gramm was promising "to string barbed wire on every military base in America" to contain all the criminals he wanted to round up. In Maricopa County, Arizona, which includes Phoenix, a colorful local character named Joe Arpaio got himself re-elected sheriff time and again by parading his inmates about on chain gangs, dressing the men among them in fluorescent pink underwear and serving prisoners food that, as he cheerfully admits, costs less than what he gives to his cats and dogs. "Voters like it everywhere," Abramsky quotes Arpaio as saying of such policies. "I'm on thousands of talk shows. I never get a negative. I get letters from all over the world—and I answer every one. They say, 'Come up here and be our sheriff.'" What makes this all the more repellent is that the people subjected to such humiliation and abuse are rarely killers or rapists but alcoholics, vagrants and other small fry doing time for such misdemeanors as possession and shoplifting.

Amazing how much damage a single article can do, eh? Yet when a conscience-stricken Martinson published a *mea culpa* in the *Hofstra Law Review* five years later ("contrary to my previous position, some treatment programs *do* have an appreciable effect on recidivism"), the media yawned. No big shots interviewed him on TV, and no politicians called to solicit his views. No one wanted to hear that rehabilitation programs work, only that they don't. Beset by personal troubles, professional setbacks and perhaps the realization of how grievously he had allowed himself to be misused, Martinson committed suicide by throwing himself out of a ninth-floor Manhattan apartment in 1980. *American Furies* provides us with a vivid account of the horrors that have followed—the low-level pot dealers and shoplifters sentenced to life in prison in California, Oklahoma, Alabama and other states where various "three strikes" or other habitual-offender laws pertain; the supermax prisoners condemned to spend twenty-three hours a day in barren concrete cells the size of walk-in closets; the epidemics of suicide and self-mutilation; and the stubbornly high levels of violence between and among prisoners and guards—which law-and-order advocates seize upon as reason to build yet more supermax facilities. US prison policy is like a computer program that is designed to spit out the same answers no matter what data are fed into it: Arrest more people, put more of them in prison, build more cells to accommodate them.

Where will it end? As Martinson's story shows, American mass incarceration is not what social scientists call "evidence based." It is not a policy designed to achieve certain practical, utilitarian ends that can then be weighed and evaluated from time to time to determine if it is performing as intended. Rather, it is a moral policy whose purpose is to satisfy certain passions that have grown more and more brutal over the years. The important thing about moralism of this sort is that it is its own justification. For true believers, it is something that everyone should endorse regardless of the consequences. As right-wing political scientist James Q. Wilson once remarked, "Drug use is wrong because it is immoral," a comment that not only sums up the tautological nature of US drug policies but also shows how they are structured to render irrelevant questions about wasted dollars and blighted lives. Moralism of this sort is neither rational nor democratic, and the fact that it has triumphed so completely is an indication of how deeply the United States has sunk into authoritarianism since the 1980s. With the prison population continuing to rise at a 2.7 percent annual clip, there is no reason to think there will be a turnaround soon. Indeed, Gottschalk writes that mass incarceration is so taken for granted nowadays that "it seems almost unimaginable that the country will veer off in a new direction and begin to empty and board up its prisons." Still, she ends on a quasi-optimistic note by quoting Norwegian sociologist Thomas Mathiesen to the effect that "major repressive systems have succeeded in looking extremely stable almost until the day they have collapsed." Indeed, repression is itself often a sign of instability bubbling up from below. This is not much to pin one's hopes on, but it will have to do.

Chapter 41

Population Change and Public Policy in Canada

RODERIC BEAUJOT AND DON KERR

Why study population? The answer, as Rod Beaujot and Don Kerr make clear, is that when populations grow, or when some groups expand and others shrink in relation to one another, the repercussions in the political or social arena can be considerable. In this selection, the authors present a number of different examples that show how this can occur. As you consider each example, ask, just as Ellen Gee asked in Chapter 23, if there are factors besides population that might also explain the patterns being discussed.

The release of the 2001 census has increased our awareness of important changes occurring in the Canadian population. The first release on population size showed that the rate of growth had slowed down, to the point that some were concerned that the population would soon decline. Over half the population growth since the previous census was due to immigration, a finding that highlighted the influence of international migration in Canada's changing population.

THE REASON FOR STUDYING POPULATION

One of the most important features of any society is the number of people and the relative size of the various subgroups. When populations grow or shrink and when subgroups change in relative size, various repercussions may follow.

Consider English–French relations in Canada. For a long time, the French constituted about a third of the population. In response to heavy English immigration, French-Canadian society emphasized the importance of births for maintaining the relative power of the French element in the country. A Catholic priest called for 'la revanche du becreau'—that is, for maintaining a high French birth rate as a means of securing the status of the French in the country. When Quebec fertility fell in the 1960s and the French-speaking population of Canada dropped to nearly a quarter of the total, the long-term relationship between the country's two charter groups was threatened.

Particularly problematic for Quebec was the eagerness of various immigrant groups to associate themselves with the English minority of the province. In the early 1970s, it was even feared that French would no longer be the working language in the province of Quebec. Various measures have been taken in response to this demographic change, such as the Official Languages Act, the policy on multiculturalism, the granting to Quebec the right to have a voice in the selection of immigrants, and the Quebec Charter of the French Language (Bill 101). The constitutional crises of the 1990s, particularly as they pertain to the concept of Quebec as a distinct society, show that Canada is still looking for ways to accommodate its changing demographics.

Aging is another crucial feature of the changing relative size of various subgroups of the population. Although aging is a long-term phenomenon that has been taking place for more than a century, different stages have different consequences. At first, population aging took place because there were fewer children. For instance, between 1966 and 1981 the population grew by 22 per cent but the number of people under the age of 15 declined by 17 per cent. These early stages of aging were relatively easy to accommodate. Although changes in the sizes of different age groups caused difficulties in the school system, in a broad sense, adults were freer because they had fewer children to care for. These changes both enlarged the proportion of the population that was at an employable age and freed women from family responsibilities, thereby encouraging them to join the labour force. These trends permitted an expansion of the social programs that depend on revenues from the taxation of employed persons (particularly health, education, social security, and pension programs).

However, at later stages of aging, it is no longer the relative size of the population of labour-force age that is growing, but rather the numbers of seniors. Even in the period from 1986 to 2001, whereas the population grew by 19 per cent, the number of people aged 65 and over grew by 45 per cent. In 1986, the population aged 65 and over constituted 10.7 per cent of the total, compared to 13.0 per cent in 2001. By 2036 when the baby boomers are all retired, it [the over-65 group] will probably make up a quarter of the population. In effect, our social programs were set up when the demographic and economic circumstances were very different. When the population of labour-force age is growing and real incomes are increasing, it is not hard to enrich our social programs, including those, such as health and pensions, that benefit the elderly. Some observers have come to question whether we will be able to afford all our social programs. Others call for different forms of accommodation, such as greater individual responsibility for personal health, greater repayment for the economic benefits of government-subsidized education, a longer work life, lower pension benefits, and even the promotion of higher birth rates and increased immigration.

Another phenomenon that can be studied from the point of view of population change is health. The comparison of the relative health of various sectors of the population permits an analysis of the differences across groups, and this points to the dynamics of well-being. For instance, men have a lower life expectancy, but women's advantage has shrunk from seven to five years. Besides the purely biological factors in this difference, there are important differences between men and women in the risk factors, including smoking, drinking, and driving. Although the gender differences in smoking for young people have largely disappeared, the mortality of older persons is still affected by past differences in their behaviour. Similarly, the higher life expectancy of married persons can partly be attributed to the 'protective role of marriage.' That is, married people benefit from having someone to help them when they are ill, and married men, in particular, benefit from having better diets than single men and not engaging in such risky activities (Trovato, 1998).

POPULATION AND POLICY

All societies attempt to shape the decisions made by individuals in such a way as to promote common benefit. Behaviour that promotes reproduction will sometimes be encouraged and sometimes discouraged. Behaviour that will prolong a person's life in the society will be encouraged, and the society will often take some responsibility for the health and safety of its citizens. And with respect to immigration, the society as a whole will establish structures, policies, and rules through which entry (and sometimes exit) are controlled in order to produce a social benefit.

There are a number of questions that interest the society as a whole. How many new members are to be added and by what means (through births or immigration)? How are the costs of these additions to be paid, and who receives the benefits? How should the costs and benefits of children be absorbed by the families into which they are born, the extended family, the community, and society as a whole? How are the costs and benefits of immigration to be distributed between, on the one hand, the immigrants themselves and their sponsoring families and, on the other hand, the receiving country, province, city, and community? To what extent are health and safety the responsibility of the individual or the surrounding society? How does society accommodate an aging population in terms of pensions, health care, and regenerating the labour force while ensuring that the young are not disadvantaged? These are among the policy questions that all societies must address.

Public policy on the changing demographics can take two forms: it can attempt to influence the course of demographic events, or it can ensure that society makes the adjustments necessary to accommodate the population change. That is, one can consider how policy may change the population, or one can consider that population changes themselves have implications for public policy. Some policies are aimed directly at influencing population processes, while others have unintended effects on population. Demographic trends also need to be considered in the analysis of such policy issues as support services for the aged, health, education, the labour force, and social security. Especially in a welfare state, that is, where the state takes some responsibility for the welfare of individuals, detailed knowledge about the population is important for those who make policy.

Such policy considerations underline the importance of gathering accurate information. Censuses were first taken to enable rulers to tax their citizens and to determine the number of men available for military service. With the advent of the welfare state, it is particularly important for governments to have accurate and up-to-date information on the population whose welfare they are trying to enhance. It is crucial to know how various groups would benefit or suffer from a given policy.

REFERENCE

Trovato, Frank, ed. 2002. *Population and Society: Essential Readings.* Toronto: Oxford University Press. This collection contains 25 well-chosen articles on the ways in which population and society are related. The readings include a wide array of research and theorizing in population studies.

Chapter 42

The Human Juggernaut

PAUL R. EHRLICH, ANNE H. EHRLICH, AND GRETCHEN C. DAILY

Is the world's population growing at a rate where we will consume our own planet? Can we take steps to ensure that humanity has a future? The authors of "The Human Juggernaut" pose these questions for us to consider. Like Malthus before them and the neo-Malthusians of today, Ehrlich, Ehrlich, and Daily argue that the stork brings more babies than the plough can feed. High fertility and poor environmental practices are leading to a disaster, particularly in the less-developed world. You will have to weigh their arguments against what you understand about demographic transition theory, and technological developments today. You might also consider whether Marx's commentaries are relevant. Is it that the problem is distribution, not production? Is the issue poverty, not overpopulation?

The human enterprise has become a true juggernaut: an inexorable force that consumes and crushes everything in its path. It is now in the process of crushing its own life-support systems, especially those that underpin agricultural production. This represents not just a future threat. Hundreds of millions of people have perished of starvation and hunger-related disease in this century. While their misery can be attributed largely to maldistribution of food, recent trends suggest that the world may soon be faced with absolute shortages.

Serious flaws in our economic accounting system promote a popular illusion of security, concealing the irreversible and potentially devastating loss of critical natural capital. Brightening humanity's future will require radical social and economic change in each of the factors generating human impact: population size, per-capita consumption, and the damage caused by the technologies employed to provide that consumption. Each of these factors has tremendous momentum built into it, making change inherently slow and difficult. Their relative importance varies widely by region. Altogether, the developed nations, despite their smaller populations, at present account for the overwhelming majority of global environmental disruption. The United States, with the third largest population and the highest per-capita impacts in the world, bears the largest share of responsibility.

A child born today in sub-Saharan Africa faces a bleak set of statistics. The odds are one in 10 that he or she will not live more than a year; the odds are one in 20 that the child's mother will die giving birth.

The child born today in sub-Saharan Africa can expect to live for only 50 years—25 years less than children in the industrialized countries.

The newborn African child enters a world in which one person in five does not receive enough food to lead a healthy, productive life. . . .

By the time the child born today is 22, if present population growth continues, sub-Saharan Africa's population will have doubled. When the child is 45, it will have quadrupled. And all this in a region where many people are already poorer than they were 30 years ago.

—Robert McNamara, 1990

When we were conducting an ecotour in East Africa in 1983, a young Tanzanian farmer accompanied our group to act as an interpreter with villagers in northwestern Tanzania, where not everyone spoke Swahili. When we crossed the border into Rwanda, a small, fast-growing, already crowded nation of about 5 million people, the first thing we saw was a river running brick red with eroded soil. The landscape changed completely from a gently rolling plain to rugged, mountainous terrain. Most striking was the density of the farming population, with all of the steep hillsides coated virtually to the top by a checkerboard of small farm plots. Some tiny fields were left fallow but plowed and exposed to the frequent rains; others were producing crops, often planted in wobbly rows marching straight up the hillside. Only a few were planted in horizontal rows following the mountain's contours or with crude terraces to hold water and soil. In the scattered plantings of eucalyptus, each tree was heavily pruned by people lopping off branches for use as firewood.

The Tanzanian farmer, who had had six years or so of schooling, was soberly looking at this scene, and we asked what he thought. "Erosion," was all he said, shaking his head sadly. To anyone with an ecological education, Rwanda was in a precarious state. In 1991, James Gasana, Rwanda's Minister of Agriculture, Livestock, and Forests, wrote about his nation's agricultural problems:

> Population pressure has made us intensify our agriculture and by doing that we have experienced significant soil losses. So we have a high level of population relative to food output. . . . Our problem is that we have no more new

areas that we can colonize. And we have to stop land being lost. We estimate that our arable lands are diminishing each year by about 8000 hectares. . . . We can produce enough food for 5 million people—but we have 7.3 million people. . . . I am afraid that if the rate of population growth continues, we might have serious difficulties.

Rwanda's population increased to about 7.5 million before ethnic hatreds, exacerbated by severe land shortages (some farm families of eight had to scrape a living from plots of less than a third of an acre) and other population-related pressures, caused a ferocious civil war that killed a million people. That holocaust destroyed some of the remaining fragments of natural forest (which is essential to the flow of water for agricultural and household use and is inhabited by one of the last populations of mountain gorillas). As if the poor people of Rwanda did not have enough trouble, the nation had also become a center of AIDS infection.

The situation in Rwanda is not unique. In 1995 we visited the island of Anjouan in the Comoros, northwest of Madagascar. It seemed in worse shape than Rwanda had a dozen years before. Anjouan also is farmed right to the mountaintops. Half of its people are under fifteen years old, the average family size is about seven children, unemployment is roughly 80 percent, and the three of us were continually begged by kids showing signs of malnutrition. The government appears to have no interest in either the environment or family planning. Authorities in nearby Mayotte (still part of France) maintain heavy patrols to ward off economic refugees from the Comoros and Madagascar.

Madagascar also presented us with a dismal picture of population-related environmental catastrophe, with continued deforestation and land degradation threatening the pitiful remnants of its unique flora and fauna. There is all too little recognition in the Malagasy government that survival of the island's lemurs, vangas (a group of birds as fascinating as Darwin's finches), baobab trees, and other natural treasures is crucial to attracting tourists, scientists, and international attention. For example, we visited a Malagasy offshore island famed for its abundant lemurs—its sole tourist attraction. The island, Nosy Komba, had been deforested in response to a rice shortage a few years earlier. The lemurs are now living in a small grove of trees supported by banana handouts from the locals and tourists. They are unlikely to persist in the absence of a suitable habitat and eating an unsuitable diet. When all of Madagascar's natural wealth is gone, it will be just one more desperately poor nation without the resources to support its burgeoning population.

Many of the obvious precursors of total disaster we found in Rwanda, Anjouan, and Madagascar are brewing elsewhere in Africa and in other parts of the less developed world. Whether humanity can come to grips with these and avert further tragedies will foretell a lot about the future of civilization. So we begin our examination of population problems in poor nations (and how to deal with them) where conditions are worst—in sub-Saharan Africa.

Sub-Saharan Africa's problems are rooted in the slave trade, colonialism, neocolonialism, and indigenous post-colonial governmental failure; it has been a long history of exploitation and inequity. Current conditions as well, caused and controlled in no small part by the behavior of today's overpopulated and overconsuming rich nations, are a leading factor in humanity's home continent being tormented by poverty, political disasters, and warfare. It is the shame of those nations that so few of their citizens know or care about what is happening to the hard-working, long-suffering people of Africa.

Sub-Saharan Africa contains great biological and mineral wealth, and its people today make only a small contribution (compared to East Asians, Europeans, and North Americans) to the destruction of Earth's life-support systems. Nevertheless, the region is mired in misery; over the past decades, per-capita GNP has fallen some 15 to 20 percent. In many African countries, political turmoil has accompanied and worsened the effects of droughts and other misfortunes. Other less developed nations match African ones in some measures of misery: several Middle Eastern nations have comparably high birth rates (but lower death rates and higher incomes); Bangladesh and some other Asian nations are equally poor and hungry (but have lower birth and death rates). But none has the full panoply of burdens that citizens of most countries in sub-Saharan Africa bear, and nowhere else have conditions been growing steadily worse for more than a quarter century.

The highest population growth rates in the world prevail in sub-Saharan Africa. The region's 1994 population of about 570 million is projected to expand to over 1.3 billion by 2025. The average number of children borne per woman (the total fertility rate, or TFR) in sub-Saharan Africa was 5.9 (most ranging between five and seven, depending on the nation) in 1994. The populations of sub-Saharan countries were thus expanding by 2 to 3.5 percent per year, rates that if sustained would double their populations in twenty to thirty-four years.

Many African populations would be growing even faster if they did not also still have relatively high death rates. In some of the poorest countries, ten to fifteen babies out of a hundred newborns die before their first birthdays (as contrasted with six in Asia, five in Latin America, and fewer than one in Europe or North America). Nearly as many more African children die before reaching age five.

African population growth rates actually rose between 1970 and 1990, because of both falling death rates and rising fertility resulting from social changes and improvements in health.

The persistence of such high fertility in African societies has been attributed to cultures that put a high premium on fecundity and on the social structure, which includes extended family arrangements. Since the extended family shares responsibility for the children, burdens of childbearing are felt less severely by individual parents. In polygynous African societies, multiple wives and children are important status symbols. Unfortunately, being able to care for them seems not so valued, as was apparent during our visit to Anjouan. There we had the pleasure of meeting Hassan M., a bright young man with a graduate degree from a first-rate American university, who was lucky to have temporary part-time jobs.

Together we came across a group of very excited but sadly malnourished children near a river. Hassan asked what they were so happy about and was told, "We just caught a [small] fish that we can sell for a kilo of rice. Our mother will be so proud—it's the first time we'll eat rice in two weeks." Hassan later remarked to us, "There is no equivalent of child-support payments here. Guys my age are already running from their first wife and children to the next, assuming no responsibility for their welfare. The kids in these huts live on coconuts, and people go hungry here without the media attention of Somalia. One of the first things that has to change to bring down the birth rate is the attitudes of men."

Social pressures on women to have large families are enormous. When Yoruba women in Ghana were asked why they wanted children, they responded that marriage had no meaning if there were no children. Being an unmarried woman is a terrible fate. "For the Akamba there is no 'proper woman,' unless she is a woman who is married. . . . Indeed, one could even say that in Kikambu language there is no word for an unmarried woman." In fact, childless women are without status; in some parts of sub-Saharan Africa, they are stigmatized, pitied, and sometimes even accused of witchcraft. Furthermore, husbands and the extended family make the childbearing decisions for women. The premium on fecundity is also grounded in traditional economic roles of women and children and in the fragility of the environment. These factors help explain why Ghana, despite a quarter century of family planning activity, still has a TFR of six.

Meanwhile, increases in food production have lagged behind population growth since 1967. A widespread, persistent drought in the Sahel (the southern fringe of the Sahara) was responsible for much of the shortfall during the 1970s. But other factors were at work, including erosion and depletion of soils, desertification in arid areas, and the expansion of cultivation onto less productive land. As per-capita food production has steadily fallen in sub-Saharan Africa, per-capita GNP has dropped since the mid-1970s, deepening poverty and forestalling progress in development, including modernization of the agricultural sector.

If the gap between population growth and food production in Africa continues to widen, as it did during the 1980s, the annual food deficit around 1990 of about 10 million metric tons (mmt) of grain, some 10 percent of food needs, could mushroom beyond 200 mmt in 2020. In that case, Africans would have to import up to half the grain needed to feed a population that by then will be more than twice as large. The question then arises as to whether anything like that much grain would be available on the world market, even if Africans could pay for it. According to agricultural economist Lester Brown, China alone might by then need to import all the grain available on the international market.

PART 15

Education

Chapter 43
Teaching Challenges in Higher Education

ANTON L. ALLAHAR

Normally, academic books are not widely read outside the narrow circle of scholars specializing in the topic being discussed. *Ivory Tower Blues: A University System in Crisis* (2007) by James Côté and Anton Allahar (both professors of sociology at the University of Western Ontario) is an exception. This book has proven popular with university professors, high school teachers, and students, as well as with the general public. It has also been the subject of newspaper articles in the *National Post* and the *Toronto Star* and discussed on talk shows such as *Cross Country Checkup* on CBC Radio One and *The Agenda* on TVO. What explains the book's wide popularity? It's certainly not because the authors are selling a "feel good" message. Quite the contrary, they argue that universities in Canada and the United States have become quite dysfunctional institutions for both students and faculty, and things are getting worse. The paper reprinted here is a piece that Professor Allahar wrote for a talk, and it summarizes the themes that the book develops at greater length. For more information about the book, and the reaction it has provoked, see the website that the authors maintain at http://www.ivorytowerblues.com.

INTRODUCTION

One of the most flattering things that has ever been said to me as a teacher goes back a few months to a chance encounter with a student at Loblaws. In a brief and pleasant exchange she volunteered the following: "You know, what I really enjoy about attending your classes is that I find that every one of them is like a guest lecture." Then she thanked me and went about her shopping.

What I took from this is that most classes can become routine and somewhat boring as the semester progresses. The guest lecture brings a fresh face that breaks up the monotony of the accustomed face and voice of the teacher. It is engaging because it promises something new and unfamiliar, something that departs from the predictable. Good teaching must always hold out this promise for if the attention of the listener cannot be retained, the message is likely to be lost.

This is how I felt about guest lectures when I was a student. And the student's comment suggested to me that, at least for this individual, I had not yet entered my dotage as a teacher/professor. I had not become distant or removed from the class in a way that years of doing the same thing may lead one to lose the spark and the ability to communicate excitement to one's students.

On the other hand, the least flattering thing that has ever been said to me as a teacher is: "those who can, do (publish); those who can't, teach." This was said to me by a colleague on

Source: Allahar, A. "Teaching Challenges in Higher Education." London, ON: University of Western Ontario.

the very first day I joined the department of sociology at UWO in 1984. The idea here is one with which we are all too familiar: good teachers are written off as scholars and good scholars are written off as teachers. We also know that a great deal of collegial jealousy is often shown to those who are recognized as outstanding teachers. They are said to pander to the students and to be performers who lack substance!

I want briefly to link these comments to a broader challenge we as teachers have at the university. It begins with what UWO President Paul Davenport recently dubbed the crucial need to "attract and retain highly qualified professors." The challenge I have in mind, however, relates to the unacknowledged standoff between professors and teachers, and the not-too-subtle tendency to view them separately as first-class and second-class citizens of the academic community. Effective teaching requires different social skills, techniques and personality characteristics than does effective research and publication. But for very unclear reasons the former has traditionally been valued less than the latter. It seems to be due to the erroneous idea that not only is teaching "easy" while research is "difficult," but teachers are somehow not as bright as researchers.

As people with PhDs, we were all taught how to conduct research aimed at writing a dissertation that made an original contribution to knowledge. In other words, we were prepared to become what is commonly understood to be university professors. At the same time, in our years as PhD students there was precious little that prepared us for becoming university teachers. Yet upon graduation we sought jobs as professors and were automatically thrust into classrooms where innocent minds awaited our sage instruction. Of course, some professors become good teachers, but that is the luck of the draw. The majority, regrettably, are mediocre to terrible teachers. And it is from the ranks of that majority that the defensive charges of "pandering to students" and "performing" arise.

So how do young or new professors make the leap from researcher to teacher? And how do we get the university to recognize and reward both equally? For it is my conviction that professors who are not effective teachers are as incomplete as professors who are not productive researchers. It is a mutually reinforcing and symbiotic relationship and the value of each cannot be ranked hierarchically. In contemporary times, however, where research and publication are recognized as the sole criteria for government and private sector funding, it is not surprising that the present invidious ranking should emerge; and along with that ranking is the challenge to raise the profile and importance of effective university teaching.

EDUCATION INFLATION

This said, what I want to highlight in the following pages is one challenge or obstacle to effective university teaching: *education inflation*, which is a combination of *credential inflation* and *grade inflation*. Before unpacking this concept, however, I want to acknowledge that my comments are best directed to those who work in the humanities, arts and social sciences, where teaching has increasingly become something of a political undertaking. For given the subjective dimension or component of knowledge in these disciplines, those in the so-called exact sciences have come to be seen as producers of more practical knowledge and hence are viewed as more socially useful or relevant. The biases also carry over to rankings *among* teachers. Thus, those who teach math are seen generally to be *brighter* than those who teach English; in popular parlance one often hears of "a Math whiz" but never "an English whiz"!

Because of the nature of knowledge in the humanities, arts and social sciences, by far, one of the greatest challenges of the job that teachers in these faculties face is grading and returning exams and essays. It is challenging because evaluation there involves a greater margin of subjectivity than, say, in the so-called exact sciences.

Let me hasten to add, however, that the pursuit of knowledge in the humanities, arts and social sciences is no less rigorous than in the exact sciences. Rather, it speaks to their very different subject matter. The geologist who studies rocks is far more able to make firm statements about the composition of her subject matter than the psychologist who studies the motives underlying the behaviour of individuals.

To continue with teaching and grading, when student performances are uniformly good, there is no problem. However, when they are not, there are two problems: (a) the professor has to justify to him- or herself the poor performance of the student(s), and (b) the professor has to justify to the student(s) in question their poor performance(s). Owing to the politicization of higher education, the latter can become problematic. As will be argued, such politics are closely related to credential inflation or the requirement of more and more certification and diplomas (which raises student anxiety), grade inflation (which raises student expectations).

When the *evaluation* of the professor does not match the *expectation* of the student, i.e., when the student does not do as well as she thought she ought to have done, the possibility for conflict is created. How do I deal with this? I talk straight with the students. My first concern is to determine if the student thinks that my exam was *fair*. Sometimes this requires some discussion and clarification of the nature of university instruction and expectations. My next reaction is to let the student know that in my 27 years as a professor at three different universities, I have never once gone to a class unprepared and all I ask is that they return the courtesy. I then ask the student whether she or he thinks that she or he was prepared for the exam. This also requires more discussion and clarification. The point is that, student life being what it is, often most students routinely come to class unprepared (don't do the reading etc.), and many are also unprepared to write their exams.

The reasons for the evaluation/expectation differential are many, but the most common and contentious relates to the fact that people often like to externalize blame for poor performance. It is rare that they look first to the self. Thus, when the exams and papers are graded, I return them and publicly acknowledge the sound performances. While not those who did less well, I do underscore the fact that those who performed well had the exact information as the others. I also let them know that when even one of my students does not perform up to my expectations, I take it very personally and in a discussion first will attempt to determine if the fault lies with me.

AGE AND MATURITY

Today's university students are increasingly young and less mature. However, particularly for the first-year students, and especially given the Ontario double cohort, instructors must take age and maturity into account. Many of their students will be experimenting with new things for the first time: living away from home and parental supervision, sex and sexual relationships, alcohol and drugs, management of their own time and finances, etc. It is a confusing time for them and we must be sensitive to that while trying also to familiarize ourselves with their world. For example, unlike previous generations, which came from what I call literary tradition—we used to read for information and entertainment—this generation is part of an audio-visual tradition. It "clicks on" for information and entertainment. As a result they tend to be less patient with abstract, philosophical ideas. But not wishing to homogenize all students, for analytical purposes do permit me to separate them into three broad groups: (a) the bright and highly motivated ones, who will do very well even without good teachers; (b) the mediocre ones who see university as an entitlement, who are not prepared to exert themselves, and who feel that university education is a right that comes with no responsibilities; and (c) those who don't really want to be in your class, but who are there because of parental insistence and wider societal pressures.

The second and third groups comprise the majority. They did well enough in high school to have gained admission to university, often without a great deal of effort (grade inflation) and come to university expecting more of the same. Add to this the fact that in relating to today's students the instructor must take into account the atmosphere conditioned by the revolution in political correctness that has *empowered* them. As part of this atmosphere there is also what has been called the **cult of self esteem** and the feel-good idea that learning must be seen as fun and enjoyable, or else it is sending the wrong message.

The sentiment is well captured in an opinion piece which *The Economist* dubs "the cloying culture of self-esteem." That culture, it is felt, treats students as fragile entities to be coddled and protected from criticism, from low grades that smack of failure, or from anything else that may cause them discomfort. It is almost as if a "therapeutic philosophy is spreading throughout the educational system" and demanding that high school and university students be treated as if they were in kindergarten (*The Economist*, April 14, 2001: 1; 6). In this climate educational excellence takes a back seat to the therapeutic functions of higher education and education inflation, which has two principal aspects. The first is a society-wide obsession with credential inflation, which in turn leads to the second, grade inflation.

EDUCATION INFLATION AND STUDENT ANXIETY

One of the common descriptions of inflation usually given to a non-specialist in economics is: too much money chasing too few goods. Whenever there is a great deal of money in circulation and the production of goods does not keep pace with demand, an inflationary situation is created and prices rise to levels that have little relation to their actual costs of production. And if this describes economic inflation I claim it is also applicable to education inflation. For in today's highly competitive market economies, where academic credentials are widely used as shortcuts to guide employers in hiring decisions, more credentials mean a better chance at good employment. So, as student demand increases, colleges and universities increase their range of offerings, and the paper chase called credentialism is the result.

Today, the pursuit and accumulation of educational credentials (degrees, diplomas, certificates) are almost ends in themselves, and produce great anxiety among students who feel driven to get more and more. As we know too, increases in the numbers of credentialed persons have served to inflate the qualifications required for any given position. A good case in point is the teaching profession where fifty years ago high school teachers were high school graduates. Today a high school teacher must have at least a BA and a B.Ed., if not an M.Ed. But to the extent that credentials are tickets to privilege, they have also led to calls for democratization and mass education. At the post-secondary level this has meant that all who satisfy the criteria (grade points) are entitled to admission.

But the logic and accompanying process of democratization has its own contradiction. As inflation erodes the value of each diploma there is the fear that soon the Honours BA will go the way of the General BA, and in time the MA will be viewed as the entry-level qualification for most white-collar jobs. To stem the impending crisis, many schools have adopted decidedly undemocratic policies and made moves to restrict access to their programs.

Consider the MBA, for example. In the 1970s and 1980s MBAs monopolized the high-paying jobs in business and finance, and boasted opulent lifestyles. This led economically minded universities and colleges everywhere and almost overnight to offer all variety of certificates, diplomas and degrees in business. Predictably, as the numbers of graduates became inflated, their value declined, and today's dime-a-dozen MBAs (and other business graduates) are faced with serious unemployment and underemployment. To restore the MBA to its elevated position in the credentials hierarchy, many business schools moved to reimpose a traditional form of *social closure* that benefits the privileged: privatization and tuition deregulation. This has created a system of first-class and second-class MBAs, along with a host of other lower-placed business graduates with undergraduate degrees and diplomas. Ironically, therefore, the democratization of business education that sparked the credential inflation in business degrees has had the unintended consequence of reinforcing unequal access to the MBA.

This brings me to the other dimension of education inflation: grade inflation. Because students from the elite classes can afford a better quality of educational preparation for the university experience, the ideal of democratization clashes with the wider class-stratified nature of the society. This, in turn, has fed the movement of *political correctness* where not just class, but race, sex and other privileges are routinely called into question by non-privileged students. As a consequence, the majority of students have grown increasingly assertive and politically manipulative. Thus, one conservative commentator charges that: "thanks to student evaluations . . . students have learned the not-so-subtle art of blackmail" (Wilson 1998:16), which they use against professionally inexperienced TAs and insecure junior professors. And in those cases where students "do not receive the grade they need to pass, they often hold the professor and then the administration responsible" (Karabell 1998:11). This is a major source of grade inflation which has also witnessed the virtual removal of failure as a motivator for students: ". . . we all have a sense that grading isn't what it used to be" and today "the fear of failing has all but disappeared" (Wilson 1998:1).

So whereas greater democratization of educational access is positive, it has also produced credential and grade inflation, thereby aggravating the general crisis facing the system and those who teach in it. Because high grades are tickets to graduate and professional schools, grants, jobs, etc., today's students feel very driven and experience tremendous pressure from family, friends, professors and potential employers to succeed. So compared to the 1960s, the behaviour of today's politically empowered students is far more individualistic and self-serving to the point where the University of Western Ontario's official motto is: **Major in yourself.**

THE CYNICAL TWIST

In certain faculties students now demand a say in setting the curriculum, or in determining the content, form and weighting of tests and examinations, and are not averse to challenging professors' grading decisions. And while greater transparency is to be welcomed, it is not clear that the political actions in question are geared to producing a better teaching and learning environment. For one of the reactions to the empowered and politically correct student has been an apathetic posturing on the part of some professors. As noted by Kamber and Biggs: "lenient grading . . . requires less work, thought and courage than rigorous grading" (2002: 13; 14). These authors also link apathy with declining educational standards: "Most institutions have accepted grading practices that persistently blur the distinction between good and outstanding performance, while they award passing grades for showing up and turning in work—even when that work is poor" (Ibid:2). And: "Years of grade inflation in secondary and post secondary schools may have established an expectation that class attendance and a good-faith effort should be adequate to generate a good grade" (Gaultney and Cann 2001:84). This state of affairs led Jeffrey Young to write cynically in *The Chronicle of Higher Education*: "There's an emerging compact between faculty members and students which goes something like, 'If you don't bother me too much I won't bother you too much—I'll trade you a B if you trade me some peace of mind'" (2002:37). So whereas a "C used to be the grade for an average performance, nowadays, it's a slap in the face" (Wilson 1998:14).

As a consequence of the foregoing an entire, parallel educational industry has grown up alongside the university and college system to accommodate the concerns of professional schools and private sector employers. I am referring here to the institutionalization of the Scholastic Aptitude Tests (SATs) in the United States, whereby universities and colleges basically say to the high schools, "We don't trust the credentials you have conferred on students and before admitting them to our institution, we reserve the right to test and certify them ourselves." As the *National Center for Policy Analysis* reported in 1998, College Board officials in the US found that "more college-bound students have A averages than a decade ago—but they score lower on their SAT exams" (National Center For Policy Analysis, "Clear Evidence of High School Grade Inflation," 2/27/2003:2). The same report goes on to point out that: "The College Board said that test takers with A averages grew from 28 percent of the total to 38 percent in the last 10 years—but their scores fell an average of 12 points on the verbal portion of the SAT and three points on math" (Ibid:2).

And as if this were not enough, the universities appear not to trust their own standards either, so those students who have earned honours bachelors' degrees are not automatically admitted to graduate programs until they have taken and passed Graduate Record Entrance (GRE) examinations. And there is more, for beyond their undergraduate degrees, I know of no professional schools that do not require students to pass special examinations before gaining admission. Thus, in Canada and the United States (among other countries), admissions to law schools requires that one passes the LSAT, medical schools have the MCAT, business schools the GMAT, dental schools the DAT, pharmacy schools the PCAT, and so on. Commenting on the situation in the United States, Richard Kamber and Mary Biggs write:

> With four of five students graduating with GPA's of B-minus or better, with a college degree ensuring neither knowledge of subject matter nor basic skills, employers and graduate schools have had to rely on other measures to sift applicants. Standardized test scores and institutional "reputation" have become more important than the judgements of teachers and scholars. The discouragement of excellence, the concealment of failure, the torpedoing of our own credibility: harsh accusations, hard to believe, and yet these are the consequences of grade conflation (Kamber and Biggs 2002:8).

To address the needs of students who are desirous of entering professional school, a whole host of private, parallel, instructional organizations such as Kaplan, Oxford Seminar Series, and Sylvan Learning Centers, now advertise their services on campuses and on the Internet. Charging very high fees, they are specifically designed for preparing students, who already have one or more accredited university degrees, to take the admission tests. But much like the other school and university curricula that they are meant to replace, they too teach to the tests so that students don't come away any more informed. Instead the latter can only claim to have done well or poorly on the test in question.

CONCLUSION

Clearly any solution to this crisis will have to begin with a re-assessment of the entire education industry. Democratization and the inclusive curriculum are important gains and must be protected. However, they must not become political footballs for powerful interest groups (politicians, administrators, professors and students) with narrow, selfish agendas. Academic standards must not fall prey to political correctness, for thus defined, politics have no place in the classroom, nor do professors who pass the buck and students who spend it. The university must not become a place where "politicians" reside and where genuine scholarship is discouraged.

REFERENCES

Gaultney, Jane and Arnei Cann. 2001. "Grade Expectations" (pp. 84–87). *Teaching of Psychology* (28)2.

Kamber, Richard and Mary Biggs. 2002. "Grade Conflation: A Question of Credibility." *The Chronicle of Higher Education.* April 12.

Karabell, Zachary. 1998. *What's College For?* New York: Basic Books.

Wilson, Bradford. 1998. "The Phenomenon of Grade Inflation in Higher Education." *Association of American Educators.* October 24.

Young, Jeffrey. 2002. "Homework? What Homework? (pp. 35–37). *The Chronicle of Higher Education.* December 6.

Index

28.30.25